Created and Directed by Hans Höfer

Indonesia

Executive Editor: Scott Rutherford

Editorial Director: Brian Bell

Houghton Mifflin

APA PUBLICATIONS

Höfer

Indonesia is a world unto itself. East to west, its thousands of islands are home to 200 million people. Its cultural diversity and physical dimensions defy simple classifications. This was the challenge faced by Apa Publications when, in the early 1980s, we first set out to produce *Insight Guide: Indonesia*. In fact, it was in Indonesia that publisher **Hans Höfer** conceived of the Insight Guide formula and came out with the first book of the series, *Insight Guide: Bali*.

Indonesia is a rich and invigorating source for travel, and thus a natural for Insight Guides. Indeed, Apa Publications has published three Insight Guides about Indonesia, including titles on Bali and Java. In addition, there are distinctive Pocket Guides to Jakarta, Yogyakarta, and Bali, and most recently, a Compact Guide to Bali. Seems that there just aren't enough words to describe the wonders of Indonesia.

Insight Guide: Indonesia was first published in 1983. While there are those who might suggest that, in some parts of Indonesia, time seems to have stopped, sooner or later a travel book, even the best, needs an overhaul to keep up with the times. The chore of disassembling and revamping *Insight Guide: Indonesia,* an Apa bestseller, fell to Apa's executive editor in Singapore, **Scott Rutherford**. Home was Hawaii before Rutherford moved to Tokyo for four years, where he worked on publishing and television projects before continuing on to Singapore. With a dubious degree in philosophy and a background as a writer and editor, and as a National Geographic photographer, he found Indonesia's eclectic offerings to his liking.

Rutherford

Given the vastness of Indonesia, Rutherford called upon a number of people to assist in this revamp. **John Haseman** spent two decades in Asia as a U.S. defense attache. His postings included Indonesia, Burma, Vietnam and Thailand. Now a travel writer, Haseman speaks fluent Bahasa Indonesian, along with Thai and Burmese. **Joseph Yogerst** has been a regular contributor to Insight Guides over the years, in addition to numerous other publications. After living in Asia for many years, Yogerst now calls southern California his home. **Julia Clerk**, a writer also based in southern California, wrote the food essay and contributed to the essential and time-consuming Travel Tips updating.

Looking at the Bali and Lombok material was **Debe Campbell**, a longtime resident of Indonesia, first in Jakarta and now Bali. Campbell has been a regular Apa contributor, and speaks fluent Bahasa Indonesian. The sections on Jakarta, Yogyakarta, and Bandung were tended to by **Genevieve Spicer**, based in Jakarta, where she's involved in writing and media projects. Prior to Indonesia, Spicer spent several years in Tokyo working for Japanese television. Using her expertise in Islamic studies with a degree from Jakarta's Institute of Islamic Studies, **Dra. Asriati** contributed to the essay on Islam.

Spicer

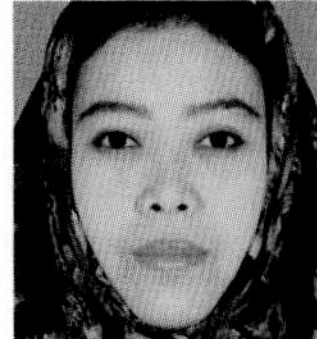
Dra. Asriati

Sumatra is no small place, and updating information on this immense island fell to **Dave Heckman**, who has lived in Sumatra for many years, roaming its outback in his work as a conservationist.

The original edition of *Insight Guide: Indonesia* was put together by **Eric Oey**, a former marketing manager at Apa and the project editor for the first Insight Guide to Indonesia. Residing in Singapore, Oey holds a doctorate in linguistics and Malay philology from the University of California, Berkeley.

Satyawati

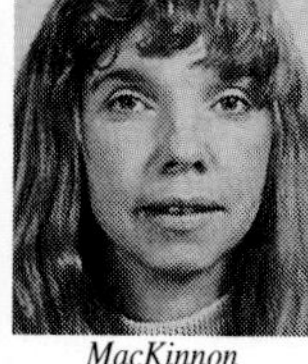
MacKinnon

Oey enlisted a number of specialists for the original Insight Guide. The section on history benefits from the expertise of two leading Indonesian academics, **Satyawati Suleiman** and **Dr. Onghokham**. Sayawati was a senior researcher with the Archaeological Publishing Department in Jakarta, and has published several books on Indonesian history. Onghokham, whose special interest is the social history of Java, has lectured at the University of Indonesia in the Department of History. **Kathy MacKinnon**, a zoologist, gained her doctorate from Oxford, after which she worked with the World Wildlife Fund's Indonesia program for several years. **Peter Hutton**, who wrote *Insight Guide: Java,* served as a major resource for the Java material. Hutton spent two decades as an advertising executive in Southeast Asia.

The original chapters on Bali and Lombok are the work of **Made Wijaya** and **Prof. Willard Hanna**. Wijaya, an Australian by birth who spent over a decade in Bali, also contributed to *Insight Guide: Bali.* Hanna has been writing about Asia since 1930. The articles covering Nusa Tenggara, Kalimantan, Maluku and Irian Jaya were the efforts of **Dr Kal Müller**, a widely-published photojournalist and doctor of anthropology. Müller also contributed to *Insight Guide: Mexico.*

Paramita

Michel Vatin and **Frederic Lontcho** co-authored the original section on Sumatra. Sulawesi and the feature on Indonesian textiles were written by **Paramita Abdurachman**, one of Indonesia's leading writers in the field of Indonesian culture and history. The performing arts in Indonesia are covered by essays on *gamelan* music, and dance and drama, by **Michael Tenzer**, **Bernard Suryabrata** and **Soedarsono**. Tenzer received his doctorate in music from the University of California, Berkeley, and studied *gamelan* in Bali for two years. Suryabrata, a professor of enthnomusicology at the School of Folk Art in the National University, Jakarta, has the special distinction of having studied under Jaap Kunst – the best-known name in the field of *gamelan.* Soedarsono, an expert on the history of Southeast Asian performing arts, shared his knowledge on dance and drama.

Others who have assisted or contributed to *Insight Guide: Indonesia* include **Trina Dingler Ebert**, **Julia Gajcak**, **Manfred Kalcher**, **Andrew Ashmore**, **Jeremy Allan**, **Patricia Chin**, **Liz Mortlock**, **Iwan Tirta**, **William Collins** and **Dewi Anwar**.

CONTENTS

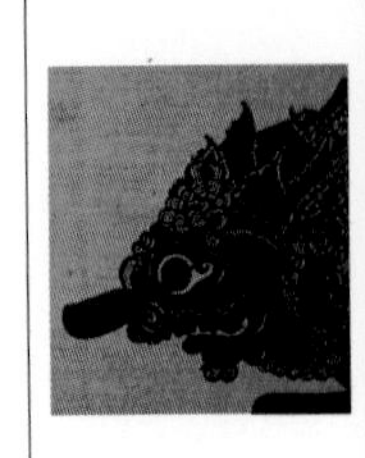

Preceding pages: a duck herder in Central Java; a guard at Medan palace.

Java

The Outer Islands

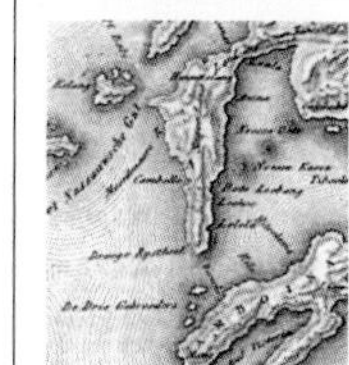

Maps

Getting Acquainted

Planning the Trip

Practical Tips

Attractions

Places

Language

Further Reading

Right: rally race through Sumatran palm oil plantation.

TEAM MITSUBISHI RALLIART

HYATT
HYATT

INTRODUCTION

The Republic of Indonesia, or *Republik Indonesia,* can claim to be one of the few nations on earth to span such a broad spectrum of world history and human civilization – from its ancient Hindu-Javanese temples to its modern luxury resorts, and from the stone-age lifestyle in Irian Jaya to the modern metropolis that is Jakarta.

Indonesia's motto, *Bhinneka Tunggal Ika,* or Unity in Diversity, is no mere slogan or nationalistic propaganda. Indonesia's population of slightly over 200,000,000 people (it has doubled since 1960) is derived from 300 different ethnic and cultural groups, who speak over 250 distinct languages. The common unifying element, other than the idea of Indonesia as country, is the national language of Bahasa Indonesian, quite similar to Malay.

Almost 90 percent of the people are of the Moslem faith, and ten percent, Christianity. There are also a few percent who claim Hindu and Buddhist beliefs. Most of the time, at least in the rural areas, these beliefs are augmented by local, centuries-old traditions and rituals. Forty percent of the population is under 15 years of age, and can expect to live far past 60 years.

The fourth most populous nation in the world, Indonesia straddles two geographically-defined racial groups, the Asians to the west and the Melanesians in the east. Most Indonesians are Asians, particularly in the western part of the archipelago. Over the centuries, mostly through commerce and trade, Indians, Arabs and Europeans have mingled with the indigenous people. The largest nonindigenous part of Indonesia's population is of Chinese origin, controlling nearly three-quarters of the nation's wealth, while making up only 2 to 3 percent of the population. This has not gone unnoticed by the other ethnic groups.

Indonesia's people are unevenly distributed across the archipelago. Java and Bali account for nearly two-thirds of the population. Approximately 40 percent of Indonesians are Javanese – nearly 100 million people living on Java, an area the size of California. Of the remainder, just over 15 percent are Sundanese, and 12 percent Malay. The government has been relocating landless people from densely-populated Java to the more remote provinces. The program's success is yet not clear, but in some places it has caused friction between the locals and transplanted Javanese.

Indonesia probably derives its name from *indos nesos,* meaning "Indian islands" in an ancient trading language of the area. The archipelago spreads out 5,100 kilometers (3,200 mi) – or one-eighth of the earth's circumference – across the southern hemisphere, west to east and just below the equator. Straddling both the Indian and Pacific oceans, Indonesia encompasses the major islands of Sumatra, Java, Nusa Tenggara (Lesser Sundas), Maluku (Moluccas), Sulawesi (Celebes), Kalimantan (part of Borneo) and Irian Jaya (western New Guinea). Rounding out the archipelago's 55,000 kilometers

Preceding pages: wayang kulit puppets; a few of the archipelago's volcanoes; planting rice, Lombok; Welcome Statue and Jalan Thamrin, Jakarta. Left, morning rounds.

(34,000 mi) of coastline are over 13,000 additional islands. Given its position atop clashing tectonic plates, Indonesia is volcanic and prone to earthquakes. There are over 200 active volcanoes in the archipelago, and 80 of those have a recent history of activity.

Indonesia's largest cities in population are Jakarta, Surabaya, Bandung, Medan and Semarang. Politically, Indonesia is divided into 24 *propinsi,* or provinces. There are also two *daerah istimewa,* or special autonomous districts: Aceh, on Sumatra, and Yogyakarta, on Java. The *daerah khusus ibukata* is the metropolitan district of Jakarta, on Java.

Given its size and population, Indonesia's importance in world affairs has been somewhat less than one might expect. This could change, as the country attempts to shift from being a supplier of raw materials to one of manufactured commodities. Important to the country's economy are exports of oil, timber, rubber, coffee, and palm-oil products. The trade in spices – nutmeg and cloves – that opened up the archipelago to colonial interests centuries ago is no longer a factor in Indonesia's economy. One income earner that the government is nurturing, however, is tourism.

Anthropologists, artists, musicians, writers and statesmen have visited the archipelago for decades. Since the late 1960s, the islands have also attracted a steadily growing number of tourists – between 1983 and 1995, the number of foreign visitors increased by 400 percent (to more than 4 million a year), and tourism revenue grew 800 percent, to almost US$5 billion annually. The government, well aware of the importance of tourism as a foreign exchange earner, actively supports tourism.

All of this, fortunately, does not mean that Indonesia is being overrun with tourists. Far from it. It is quite true, of course, that a disproportionate number of visitors to Indonesia end up on Bali. And once there, most of them cluster in the southern part, which is probably for the better, as it leaves the remainder of Bali unfettered. Indonesia is trying to encourage travelers to visit other parts of the archipelago. And, indeed, unlike many other tropical destinations, Indonesia is a huge country, in both population and land area, with significant cultural and geological diversity. Foreigners constitute an almost insignificant presence in most parts of the archipelago, and whether in Jakarta or Dili, the traveler need not feel like part of a noisy, arrogant group of tourists. Indonesia allows the traveler to feel unique, both as a visitor seeing a place or a people for the first time, and as a guest warmly welcomed by the Indonesians.

Notes: In most cases, we use Indonesian geographical terms in this book, rather than English. For example, Lake Toba is Danau Toba, Biak Island is Pulau Biak, and Mount Bromo is Gunung Bromo.

There are two ways to spell President Soeharto's name: Suharto, and Soeharto. The latter is older and more traditional, and it is how he himself has chosen to spell it, as have most Indonesian media. We do the same. Likewise with the former president, Soekarno.

Right: Koran studies clarify the Moslem's worldview.

Excavations in northern Thailand have revealed that a metal-producing culture may have existed there much earlier than in either China or India. The theory is not without considerable controversy, and a definitive answer may never be forthcoming. Nevertheless, its discovery has overturned the notion of Southeast Asia as a prehistoric backwater. Some scholars speculate that this region was, in fact, one of the great prehistoric cradles of human development.

Such speculation, however, is still premature in the case of Indonesia, where relatively few neolithic sites have been excavated and dated with precision.

Java Man: Indonesian archaeological findings have contributed more than their share of controversy in the past. In 1890, a Dutch military physician discovered a fossilized primate jawbone in central Java with distinctively human characteristics. The jawbone was found with fossils of mammalian species that were thought to have died out several hundred thousand years ago; the jaw was, at first, discounted as belonging to an extinct species of apes. But in the following year, two more humanoid fossils were uncovered in similar circumstances, thought then to be the world's first evidence of Darwin's long-sought "missing link."

Unfortunately, Darwin's evolutionary theories were still in hot dispute at the time, and the discovery, dubbed Java Man, was vehemently denounced by religious groups. It was not until more than two decades later, with the discovery of similar fossils outside Beijing in 1921, that the theory was eventually vindicated.

Java Man and Peking Man are now recognized as members of the species *Homo erectus,* a direct ancestor of people who inhabited the Old World from about 1.7 million until 250,000 years ago. The body skeleton of *Homo erectus* was essentially modern, but the skull was thick, long and low, possessing a massive face with strongly protruding brow ridges. Many fossils of this type have been discovered in central Java, some more than a million years old. Replicas are on display at the Geological Museum in Bandung, and at the Sangiran museum, outside Surakarta.

Research has show that *Homo erectus* probably could not speak, but could utter sounds by which to communicate. They were omnivores and food gatherers who lived in caves as well as in open campsites. They also produced an extensive stone tool kit that included flaked choppers, axes and handadzes. Thousands of stone tools dating from between 500,000 and 250,000 years ago have been collected from the end of the Baksoka River, near Pacitan, in south-central Java. Similar tools have also been found in Flores and Timor, which raises the possibility that *Homo erectus* may have spread to the eastern islands. Unfortunately, these tools cannot be accurately dated.

Preceding pages: royal insignia are items of status and power. Left, the serene beauty of a bodhisattva at Candi Sari (9th century). Right, reconstructed skull of Java Man.

Modern people: The classification of more recent humanoid fossils is still very much in doubt, particularly for the transitional species between *Homo erectus* and modern humans. Central to the problem of classification is the question of whether modern people evolved in a single place (thought by some to be sub-Saharan Africa) and then spread to other areas, or whether parallel evolutions occurred in various places and at different rates. Fossil records can be interpreted to support both views. In the Indonesian sphere, the controversy is centered around the dating and classification of the so-called Solo Man fossils, discovered between 1931 and 1933 next to the Solo River, at Ngandong, in central Java. Some scholars classify Solo Man as an intermediate species dating from perhaps 250,000 years ago, of distinct Southeast-Asian evolutionary descent from *Homo erectus*.

Others insist that Solo Man was simply an advanced *Homo erectus* species who survived in isolation and then hit an evolutionary dead-end. Fossil records of modern humans (*Homo sapiens*) dating from as early as 60,000 years ago have been found on the Chinese mainland, and this compares favourably with the appearance of *Homo sapiens* in other parts of the world, although two imprecisely-dated African fossils are said to be more than 90,000 years old. Modern people also inhabited Indonesia, New Guinea and Australia by about 40,000 years ago, perhaps earlier.

All Southeast Asian *Homo sapiens* fossils prior to about 5,000 BC have been identified as members of the Australoid group of people who survive today in isolated pockets of Southeast Asia and the Philippines as negritos. It is therefore thought that Australoid peoples were the original inhabitants of the entire region, and then were later absorbed by subsequent Mongolian migration, or else driven to the uplands or pushed eastward.

Beginning about 20,000 years ago, there is evidence of human burials and partial cremations; several cave paintings (mainly hand stencils, but also human and animal figures) found in southwestern Sulawesi and New Guinea may be 10,000 or more years old.

The neolithic centuries are characterized here, as elsewhere, by the advent of village settlements, domesticated animals, polished stone tools, pottery and food cultivation. The neolithic age's first appearance is everywhere being pushed back in time by new archaeological findings, but worldwide it appears to have begun soon after the end of the last ice age, around 10,000 BC. In northern Thailand, one recently-discovered neolithic site has been reliably placed in the 7th millennium BC. For Indonesia, however, there is no evidence prior to the 3rd millennium BC, and most sites are of a more recent date. In southwestern Sulawesi and eastern Timor, plain pottery pots and open bowls dating from about 3,000 BC have been found, together with shell bracelets, discs, beads, adzes, and the bones of pig and dog species that may have been domesticated.

Isolated neolithic finds of incised and cord-marked pottery have been made in Sulawesi, Flores, Timor, Irian and Java, but well-dated neolithic sequences are notably lacking, particularly in western Indonesia.

The first agriculturalists in Indonesia probably grew taro before the introduction of rice. In fact, rice came to much of Indonesia only in recent centuries, and taro is still a staple crop on many eastern islands, together with bananas, yams, breadfruit, coconuts and sugar cane. Bark-cloth clothing was produced with stone-pounding tools, and pottery was shaped with the aid of a wooden paddle and a stone anvil tapper.

Neolithic Indonesians were undoubtedly seafarers, like their Polynesian cousins who were spreading across the Pacific at this time. Nautical terms bear significant similarity throughout the Austronesian family of languages, and stylized boat motifs are depicted on pottery and in early bronze reliefs, as well as on the houses and sacred textiles of primitive tribes. Today, the outrigger is found throughout Indonesia and Oceania. At the end of the neolithic period, megaliths were constructed on many islands. These were variously places of worship or tombs. The most striking of these are the carved stone statues of men riding and wrestling animals, found on the Pasemah plateau in southern Sumatra. No definite date can be given for these and other megaliths, although it has been suggested that they are less than 2,000 years old. (Stone-slab tomb megaliths are still made on Nias and Sumba.)

Dong Son bronze culture: It was once thought that Southeast Asia's Bronze Age began with the Chinese-influenced Dong Son bronze culture of northern Vietnam, in the first millennium BC. However, the discovery of 5,000-year-old copper and bronze tools at Ban Chiang and Non Nok Tha, in northern Thailand, has raised the possibility of similar developments elsewhere in the region. Nevertheless, all early Indonesian bronzes known to date are clearly of the Dong Son type and probably date from between 500 BC and 500 AD.

The finest Dong Son ceremonial bronze drums and axes are distinctively decorated with engraved geometric, animal and human motifs. This decorative style was highly influential in many fields of Indonesian art, and seems to have spread together with the

Left, central Javanese neolithic stone tools. Above, Dong Son bronze-age ceremonial drum.

bronze casting technique, as ancient stone moulds have been found at various sites in Indonesia. The sophisticated lost-wax technique of bronze casting was employed, and bronzes of this type have been recovered as far east as New Guinea.

Who were the Indonesian producers of Dong Son bronzes? It is difficult to say for sure, but it seems that small kingdoms based upon wet-rice agriculture and foreign trade were flourishing already in the archipelago during this period. Articles of Indian manufacture have been found at several prehistoric sites in Indonesia, and a panel from a bronze drum found on Sangeang Island, near Sumbawa, depicts figures in ancient Chinese dress. Early Han texts mention the clove-producing islands of eastern Indonesia, and it is certain that by the second century BC, trade was widespread in the archipelago.

Rise of sophistication: Beginning in the second century AD, a number of sophisticated civilizations emerged in Southeast Asia – civilizations whose cosmology, literature, architecture and political organization were all closely patterned upon those of India. These kingdoms are known for the wonderful monuments which they created: Borobudur, Prambanan, Angkor, Pagan and others, many of which were "rediscovered" in the 19th century.

Yet their creators remain largely an enigma. Who built these Indian monuments and how is it that Southeast Asians came to have such a profound knowledge of Indian culture in ancient times? Part of our bewilderment is undoubtedly the long-standing misconception of Southeast Asia as a cultural backwater, when, in fact, it was a thriving trade and cultural center in prehistoric times.

While the reality of the Indianization process was far more complex than will probably ever be known, the most plausible theory is that Southeast Asian rulers Indianized their own kingdoms, either by employing Indian Brahmans or by sending their own people to India to acquire the necessary knowledge.

The motivation for doing this is clear: Sanskrit writing and texts, along with sophisticated Indian ritual and architectural techniques, afforded a ruler greater organizational control, wealth and social status. It also enabled him to participate in an expanding Indian trading network.

Indianized kingdoms: Knowledge of the early Indonesian kingdoms of the classical or Hindu period is very shadowy, gleaned solely from old stone inscriptions and vague references in ancient Chinese, Indian and classical texts. However, the first specific references to Indonesian rulers and kingdoms are found in written Chinese sources.

Written in the south Indian *pallawa* script, the stone inscriptions were issued by Indonesian rulers in two different areas of the archipelago: Kutei on the eastern coast of Kalimantan, and Tarumanegara on the Citarum River, in West Java near Bogor. Both rulers were Hindus whose power seems to have derived from a combination of wet-rice agriculture and maritime trade.

There is also the interesting figure of Fa Hsien, a Chinese Buddhist monk who journeyed to India in the early fifth century to obtain Buddhist scriptures, later to be shipwrecked on Java on his way home to China. In his memoirs, Fa Hsien noted that there were many Brahmans and heretics on Java, but that the Buddhist Dharma there was not worth mentioning. His comments highlighted Indianized Indonesia – while some early kingdoms were mainly Hindu, others were primarily Buddhist. The distinction would become increasingly blurred.

Another fact of life for the Hinduized states of Indonesia was that their power depended greatly on control of the maritime trade. It appears that Tarumanegara in West Java first controlled the trade for two centuries or more, but that at the end of the seventh century, a new Buddhist kingdom at Palembang took over the vital Malacca and Sunda Straits. This kingdom was Srivijaya, and it ruled throughout the next 600 years.

Srivijaya and *p'o-ssu* trade: The kingdom of Srivijaya left behind no magnificent temples or monuments, as it was a maritime kingdom that relied for existence not on agriculture, but on control of the trade. Most of its citizens were sailors who lived on boats (as do many of the coastal Malay *orang laut,* or sea people, today). Knowledge of Srivijaya is consequently sketchy, and the kingdom was not even identified until 1918.

It has been speculated that Srivijaya rose to prominence as a result of a substitution of Sumatran aromatics for expensive Middle Eastern frankincense and myrrh – the so-called *p'o-ssu.* But Srivijaya was also located in a strategic position and is said to have had the largest ships in the world at the time, and they appear to have achieved regular direct sailings to India and China by the late eighth century.

Although Srivijaya controlled all coastal ports on either side of the Malacca and Sunda straits, none of these areas was suitable for wet-rice agriculture. The nearest such area was in central Java, and from the early eighth century onward, great Indianized kingdoms established themselves here. They first supplied Srivijaya with rice, and then later began to compete with it for a share of the maritime trade.

Sailendras and Sanjayas: From the beginning, there was tension in central Java between competing Buddhist and Hindu ruling families. The first central Javanese temples and inscriptions, dating from the eighth century, were the work of a Hindu ruler, Sanjaya. Soon thereafter, however, a Buddhist line of kings known as the Sailendras (Lords of the Mountain) seem to have come from the northern coast of Java to impose their rule over Sanjaya and his descendants.

The Sailendras maintained close relations with Srivijaya (both rulers were Buddhists) and controlled Java for about a century. During this relatively short period, they constructed the magnificent Buddhist monuments of Borobudur, Mendut, Kalasan, Sewu and many others in the shadow of Mount Merapi. In ancient times, this area must have

Left, from the mid 5th century, inscription and footprints of Purnavarman – Hindu ruler of Tarumanegara in West Java. Right, Candi Plaosan, a Buddhist sanctuary built in the 9th century.

supported a vast population, which participated in the erection of these monuments.

Meanwhile, the Sanjayan line of kings ruled continuously over outlying areas of the realm as vassals of the Sailendras, building many Hindu temples in remote areas of Java, such as the Dieng Plateau and Mount Ungaran, south of Semarang. Around 850, a prince of the Sanjaya dynasty, Rakai Pikatan, married a Sailendran princess and seized control of central Java. The Sailendras fled to Srivijaya, blocking all Javanese shipping throughout the South China Sea for more than a century.

Mysterious move: Rakai Pikatan commemorated his victory by erecting the splendid

temple complex at Prambanan, which can be considered a Hindu counterpart of Buddhist Borobudur.

A succession of Hindu kings ruled in central Java, but then suddenly the capital was transferred to east Java around 930. A number of factors might account for this move. As noted earlier, the Sailendran kings, once installed at Srivijaya, were successful in shutting off the vital overseas trade from Java's north coast, and may even have been threatening a return to central Java. An eruption of Mount Merapi at about this time may also have closed the roads to the north coastal ports and covered much of central Java in volcanic ash. Then, too, there is the possibility of epidemics or of mass migrations to the more fertile lands of east Java.

An eastern Javanese empire prospered in the tenth century and actually attacked and occupied Srivijaya for two years. Srivijaya retaliated a quarter of a century later with a huge seaborne force that destroyed the Javanese capital, killed the ruler, King Dharmawangsa, and splintered the realm into numerous petty fiefdoms. It took nearly 20 years for the next great king, Airlangga, to fully restore the empire.

Airlangga was King Dharmawangsa's nephew and he succeeded to the throne in 1019 after the Srivijayan forces had departed. With the help of loyal followers and advisors, he reconquered the realm and restored its prosperity.

He is best known, however, as a patron of the arts and as an ascete. Under his rule the Indian classics were translated from Sanskrit into Javanese. To appease the ambitions of his two sons, he divided his empire into two equal halves, Kediri and Janggala (or Daha and Koripan). Kediri became the more powerful of the two, and it is remembered today as the source of numerous works of old Javanese literature, mainly adaptations of the Indian epics in a Javanese poetic form known as the *kekawin.*

Singhasari and Majapahit: In subsequent centuries, Java prospered as never before. The rulers of successive east Javan empires were able to combine the benefits of a strong agricultural economy with income from a lucrative overseas trade. In the process, the Javanese became the master shipbuilders and mariners of Southeast Asia. During the 14th century, at the height of the Majapahit empire, they controlled the sea lanes throughout the Indonesian archipelago, as well as to faraway India and China.

The Singhasari dynasty was founded by Ken Arok in 1222. During his rule of Janggala, Ken Arok revolted against his sovereign, the ruler of Kediri, and set up his new capital at

Singhasari, near present-day Malang. Kertanagara was the last king of the Singhasari line to succeed Ken Arok. He was an extraordinary figure, a scholar as well as a statesman, who belonged to the Tantric Bhairawa sect of Buddhism. In 1275 and again in 1291, he sent successful naval expeditions against Srivijaya, and wrested control of the important maritime trade.

Far left, the image of Durga in the main chamber of the Hindu temple at Prambanan. Left, King Airlangga as Visnu on garuda. Above, a sculpture of Ken Dedes, the wife of Ken Arok, representing her as a goddess.

In fact, Kertanagara became so powerful that Kublai Khan, the Mongol emperor of China, sent ambassadors to him to demand tribute. Kertanagara refused and disfigured the Khan's ambassador, a gesture that so enraged the great Khan that in 1293 he sent a powerful fleet to Java for revenge. The fleet landed, only to discover that Kertanagara had already died at the hands of Jayakatwang, one of his vassals. The Chinese remained on Javanese soil for about a year, just long enough to defeat the murderous Jayakatwang. Battles raged for many months, eventually producing victory for Kertanagara's son-in-law, Wijaya, and his Chinese allies. In the end, Wijaya entrapped the Mongol generals and chased the foreign troops back to their ships. The Chinese fleet returned to China, and its commanders no doubt were severely punished by the Khan for their failure.

Wijaya married four of Kertanagara's daughters and established a new capital in 1294 on the bank of the Brantas River, between Kediri and the sea (near present-day Trowulan). This was an area known for its *pahit* (bitter) maja fruits, and the new kingdom became known as Majapahit.

Aerial photographs reveal that the city had an extensive system of canals and barges that were probably used to transport rice and other trade goods down the river from Majapahit to the seaports.

Majapahit was the first empire to truly embrace the entire Indonesian archipelago. Later Javanese rulers, ancient and modern, have always looked upon this kingdom as their spiritual and political forerunner. Majapahit reached its zenith in the middle of the 14th century under the rule of Wijaya's grandson, Hayam Wuruk, and his brilliant prime minister.

Majapahit's decline set in almost immediately after Hayam Wuruk's death in 1389. However, a smoldering struggle for supremacy erupted into civil war between 1403 and 1406, and although the country was reunited in 1429, Majapahit had lost control of the western Java Sea and the straits, to a new Islamic power located at Malacca.

Toward the end of the 15th century, Majapahit and Kediri were conquered by the new Islamic state of Demak, on Java's north coast, and it is said that the entire Hindu-Javanese aristocracy then fled in exile to nearby Bali.

B O E R O
Boero
Michiels Eiland
het Nassauwsche Gat
Cambello
Drooge Rysthoek
De Drie Gebroeders
Amblauw
A M B O I N A
Kasteel Victoria
Hoek van Noessaniwel
Duiven Eiland
in een Graad

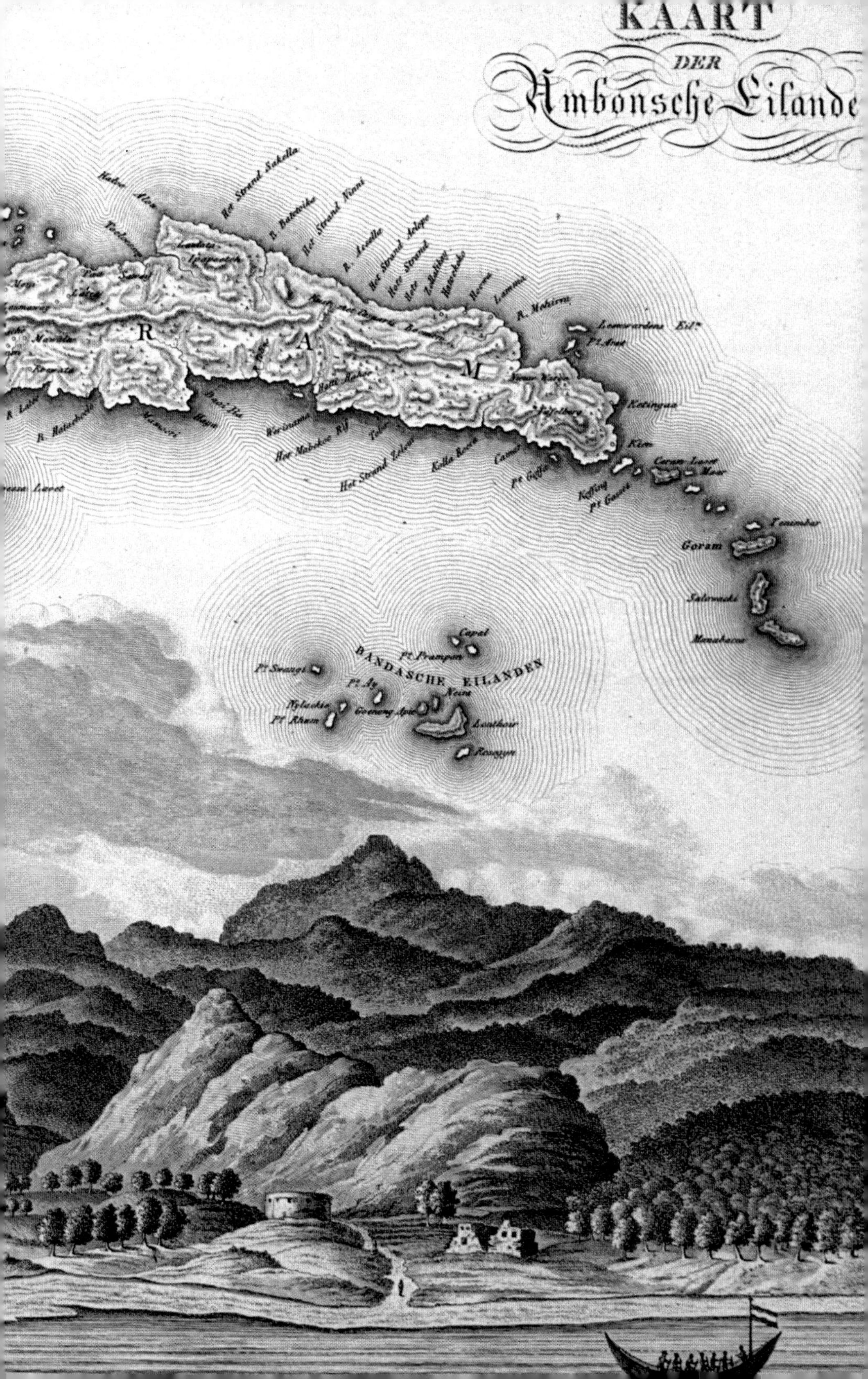

KAART DER Ambonsche Eilanden

R A M

BANDASCHE EILANDEN

Goram

Manabasso

Capal

Pt. Swangi

Pt. Ay

Neira

Lonthoir

Rosegyn

Pt. Rhun

Goenong Api

Het Strand Sakella

Het Strand Nines

Pt. Arant

Ketingan

Kim

Ceram Laout

Tenmbar

Kelfing

Het Mahakee Rif

Het Strand Zelaa

Kelta Rock

Pt. Geffie

سورة الفاتحة
بسم الله الرحمن الرحيم
الحمد لله رب العالمين الرحمن
الرحيم مالك يوم الدين
اياك نعبد واياك نستعين
اهدنا الصراط المستقيم صراط
الذين انعمت عليهم غير المغضوب
عليهم ولا الضالين

Islam arrived in the Indonesian archipelago, not through a series of holy wars or armed rebellions, but rather atop the crest of a peaceful economic expansion along the trade routes of the East.

Although Muslim traders had visited the region for centuries, it was not until the important Indian trading center of Gujarat fell into Muslim hands, in the 13th century, that Indonesian rulers began to convert to the new faith. The trading ports of Samudra, Perlak and Pasai on the northeastern coast of Sumatra became the first Islamic domains in Indonesia. Marco Polo mentions that Perlak was already Muslim at the time of his visit in 1292, and the tombstone of the first Islamic ruler of Samudra, Sultan Malik al Saleh, bears the date 1297.

Trade and Islam: Conversion to Islam was not accomplished on the basis of faith alone; there were compelling worldly benefits to be obtained. Islamic traders were becoming a dominant force on the international scene. They had controlled the overland trade from China and India to Europe, via Persia and the Levant, for some time. With the major textile producing ports of India in their hands, they began to dominate the maritime trade routes through South and East Asia, as well. Conversion thus ensured that Indonesian rulers could participate in the growing international Islamic trade network. And equally important, Islam provided these rulers with protection against the encroachments of two aggressive regional powers – the Thais to the north, and the Javanese.

To understand the Islamization of Indonesia, an understanding of the basic political and economic structure of the region at that time is necessary. There were essentially three important types of kingdoms. First, there were the coastal states around the Straits of Malacca that produced little food and few trade goods of their own, but that relied on trade and control of the seas for their existence. Then there were the vast inland states on Java and Bali that produced surpluses of rice in irrigated paddies and possessed large populations. Finally, there were the tiny kingdoms on the eastern Maluku islands producing valuable cloves, nutmeg and mace – precious for trade – but little food.

All these kingdoms imported luxury goods from abroad: textiles and porcelain, precious metals, medicines, and gems. The coastal and spice-producing states also needed to import rice. And the trade was not only interisland, but involved foreigners as well, principally Indians and Chinese, but also Arabs, Siamese, and Burmese.

Preceding pages: Ambon was the eastern extent of Islamization. Left, a page from a Koran in Aceh, Sumatra – for more than four centuries a powerful Muslim sultanate. Right, tombstone of Sultan Malik al Saleh – the first Islamic monarch.

Islam received its greatest boost when, in 1436, the shrewd ruler of the port of Malacca suddenly converted to the Muslim faith upon returning from an extended stay in China. Up until now, Malacca had been a vassal of China and ruled by descendants of the prestigious Hindu line of Palembang (Srivijaya), and peninsula kings who had been attacked and evicted by the Javanese and the Thais during the 14th century. China had proved a valuable patron of Malacca since its founding in 1402, but by 1436, China's influence in the region was on the wane, and the Thais were once again demanding tribute.

By embracing Islam, the ruler of Malacca gained protection against Thai advances. And as a port ruled by a dynasty with a long tradition of catering to overseas traders, Malacca was then in an excellent position to capitalize upon the commercial successes of the Islamic world. By 1500, Malacca was to become the greatest emporium in the East, a city comparable in size to the largest European cities of the day.

During the 15th century, all of the trading ports of the western archipelago were brought within Malacca's orbit, including the important ports along the north coast of Java. Traditionally, these ports owed their allegiance to the great inland Hindu-Javanese kingdoms, acting in effect as import-export and shipping agents, exchanging Javanese-grown rice for spices, silks, gold, textiles, medicines, gems and other items in a complex series of value-added transactions. After about 1400, however, the power of the inland Javanese rulers was rapidly declining, and the rulers of the coastal cities were seeking ways to assert their independence and retain profits of the trade. Gradually, through intermarriage between leading Islamic traders and local aristocrats, relations were cemented with the Malacca Muslims.

Islam on Java: If Islamization at first occurred peacefully in the coastal kingdoms of Java, a turning point was reached sometime in the early 16th century, when the newly-founded Islamic kingdom of Demak (on the northcentral coast) attacked and conquered the last great Hindu-Buddhist kingdom on Java. They drove the Hindu rulers to the east and annexed the agriculturally-rich Javanese hinterlands. Demak then consolidated its control over the entire north coast by subduing Tuban, Gresik, Madura, Surabaya, Cirebon, Banten, and Jayakarta – emerging as the master of Java by the 16th century.

The traditional account of the Islamization of Java is quite different, but equally interesting. According to Javanese chronicles, nine Islamic saints (*wali sanga*) propagated Islam through the Javanese shadow plays (*wayang kulit*) and gamelan music. They introduced the *kalimat shahadat,* or Islamic confession of faith and the reading of Koranic prayers, to performances of the *Ramayana* and *Mahabarata* epics. No better explanation could be given for the origins of Islamic syncretism in Java.

In this period, Islam was the faith of traders and urban dwellers, and firmly entrenched in the maritime centers of the region. Many of these towns were quite substantial; on the Malay Peninsula, Malacca is estimated to have had a population of at least 100,000 in the 16th century – as large as Paris, Venice and Naples, but dwarfed by Beijing and Edo Tokyo, which then had roughly one million inhabitants each. Other cities in Indonesia were comparably large. Such statistics indicate that the urban population of Indonesia in the 16th century at least equaled the agrarian population. Thus, the typical Indonesian of that period was not a peasant, but a town dweller engaged as an artisan, sailor, worker or goods trader.

Indonesia cities were also physically different from cities in Europe, the Middle East, India, or China. For the most part built without walls, Indonesian cities were located at river mouths or on wide plains, and relied upon surrounding villages for their defense. An official envoy from the Sultanate of Aceh to the Ottoman empire explained that Acehnese defenses consisted not of walls, but of "stout hearts in fighting the enemy and a large number of elephants." Indonesian cities tended also to be very green. Coconut, banana and other fruit trees were everywhere, and most of the widely-spaced wooden or bamboo houses had vegetable gardens.

The royal compound was the center for defense, and it might have walls and a moat. With perhaps no more than five million people in the entire archipelago, land had no intrinsic value except what people made of it. In 1613, when the English wanted some land to build a fortress in Makassar, they had to recompense the residents not for the space, but for the coconut trees.

Portuguese meddling: During the 16th century, Islam continued to spread throughout the Indonesian archipelago, but the whole system of Islamic economic and political alliances was swiftly overturned in the dramatic conquest of Malacca by a small band of Portuguese, in 1511. Although the Portuguese were never able to control more than a portion of the total trade in the region, the capture of Malacca itself had far-reaching consequences.

Never again was an Islamic state able to exert the sort of regional influence once exercised by Malacca. Instead, a number of competing Islamic centers vied with each other – and, too, with the Europeans – for the area's trade, with the end result that the Dutch were later able to divide and conquer almost all of them.

The Islamic kingdom of Aceh, at the northern tip of Sumatra, was best situated to benefit from the fall of Malacca. Islamic traders

Left, print of the historic mosque at Banten – one of the towns subdued by the Islamic kingdom of Demak. Above, Portuguese ships at Ternate.

resorted increasingly to Aceh's harbor, and a succession of aggressive Acehnese rules slowly built an empire by conquering lesser ports all along the eastern coast of Sumatra. Although repeated attacks on Portuguese Malacca and Islamic Johor to the north on the Malay Peninsula were unsuccessful, Aceh nevertheless established itself as the major sea power in the Indonesian archipelago. The Acehnese remained powerful and fiercely independent long after that golden age, resisting the Dutch into this century. Today, Aceh is one of the most devoutly Muslim regions in Indonesia.

Shifts of power: During the second half of the 16th century, Java's center of power abruptly shifted from the north coast to an area of central Java, near Borobudur. The new kingdom was called Mataram, the name of both of the area and the classical Javanese kingdoms once located here. Mataram first conquered Demak; the eastern half of Java and other northern coastal ports were subdued by about 1625.

Although the Mataram dynasty was Muslim, it patterned itself after the great Hindu-Buddhist empires of previous centuries. Court chroniclers traced the lineage of the Mataram line to the deva-rajas of Majapahit, rather than to the Islamic rulers of Demak. In fact, the fall of Majapahit to Demak was described in these chronicles as the "disappearance of the Light of the Universe," a rather odd viewpoint for a Muslim writer who describes the demise of an infidel kingdom at the hands of an Islamic saint. Clearly, identification with the prestigious Majapahit royal house was of greater importance than religious solidarity with the coastal powers. And, indeed, the Islam of the central Javanese courts became an extremely eccentric one, a potpourri of ancient mystical and paganistic practices, European pomp and Islamic circumstance.

Islam came to the remaining islands of eastern Indonesia only sporadically. The trading port of Makassar, now the city of Ujung Pandang, in Sulawesi, became an important Islamic center, expanding rapidly towards the end of the 16th century. It captured a substantial share of the eastern spice trade for several decades, until it was finally forced to submit to the Dutch in 1667. Makassar was very cosmopolitan, with kings and nobles who spoke Arabic and Portuguese, and who were the patrons of scholars.

Portuguese reports speak of the Islamic conversion of Makassar in the following way. Undecided whether to adopt Islam or Christianity, the Makassarese sent their emissaries to Aceh and to Portuguese Malacca, requesting that religious teachers be sent. The Acehnese, according to the account, simply arrived first.

In the Spice Islands of Maluku – Ternate, Tidore, Hitu, Ambon and Banda – most of the local rulers converted to Islam fairly early (sometime in the 15th century) and maintained close ties with, first, Malacca, then Makassar. However, in the 16th and 17th centuries, these kingdoms were conquered by a succession of European powers; those who survived converted to Christianity.

On other islands, Jesuit missionaries arrived even before the Muslims, and together with late-arriving Dutch Calvinists, established many Christian strongholds. However, in terms of numbers, if not geography, Islam continues to be the dominant force throughout the archipelago, with over 80 percent of Indonesians declaring themselves disciples of Mohammed.

Left, Muslim traders had a crucial role in the expansion of Islam. Right, a 19th-century rendering of the mosque of Banten.

1 Marché à Bantam. 2 Douane. 3. Chinois, habitans de Java, etc. avec toutes sortes de marchandises.
10. Tour où l'on fait sentinelle. 11. Château

1 Marckt tot Bantam. 2. Tol huys. 3. Chineesen, Iavanen etc. met aller leij Koopmanschappe
Vol Kraemen. 9 Mosquée 10 Wacht tooren. 11.

a Leide Chez Pierre vander Aa.

r Pois. 5. Epiceries. 6 Fruits. 7 Meubles. 8. Rue de la Cour pleine de boutiques. 9 Mosquée.
a Ville. 13 Le Port.

Hun gewicht. 5. Specerijen. 6. Fruijten. 7. Huijs raeden. 8 de Hof straet
l. 12. de Stad. 13. de Haven.

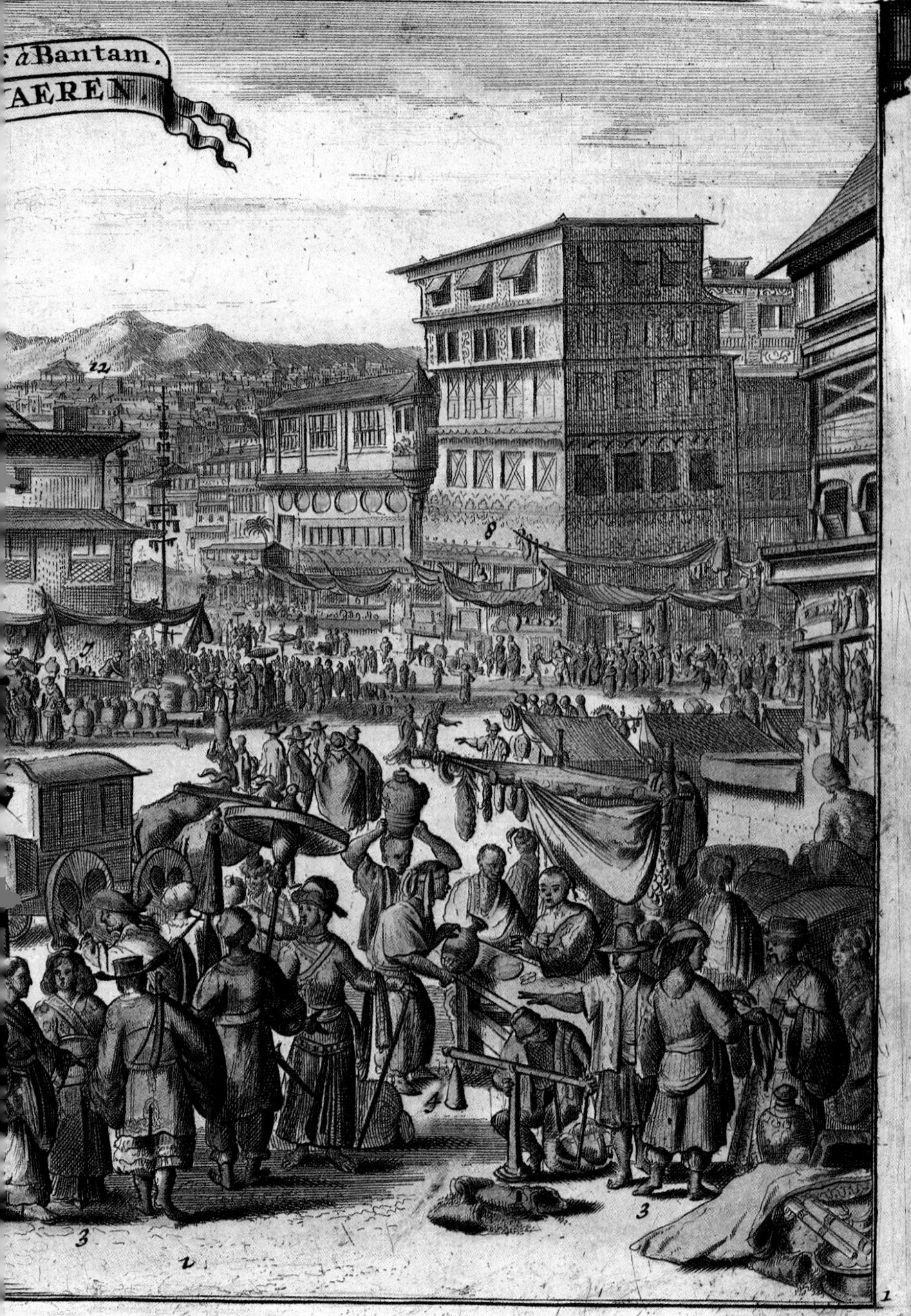

THE DUTCH COLONIAL YEARS

The saga of the Dutch in Indonesia began in 1596, when four small Dutch vessels, led by the incompetent and arrogant Cornelis de Houtman, dropped anchor in Banten, then the largest pepper port in the archipelago. Repeatedly blown off course and racked by disease and dissension, the de Houtman expedition was a disaster. In Banten, the sea-weary Dutch crew went on a drinking binge and had to be chased back to their ships by order of an angry prince, who then refused to do business. Hopping from port to port along the north coast of Java, de Houtman wisely confined his sailors to their ships and managed to purchase some spices. Arriving in Bali, the entire crew jumped ship, and it was some months before de Houtman could muster a quorum for the return voyage.

Arriving back in Holland two years later, with only three lightly-laden ships and a third of the original crew, de Houtman's voyage was nonetheless hailed a success. So dear were spices in Europe that the sale of the meager cargo sufficed to cover all expenses, even producing a modest profit. This touched off a veritable fever of speculation in Dutch commercial circles, and in the following year, five consortiums dispatched a total of 22 ships to the Indies.

Dutch East India Company: Since the 15th century, ports of the two Dutch coastal provinces in northern Europe, Holland and Zeeland, had served as entrepots for goods shipped to Germany and the Baltic states. Many Dutch merchants grew wealthy on this trade, and following the outbreak of war with Spain in 1568, they began to expand their shipping fleets rapidly, so that by the 1590s, they were trading directly with the Levant and Brazil.

Thus, when a Dutchman published his itinerary to the East Indies in 1596, it occasioned the immediate dispatch of de Houtman and later expeditions. Indeed, so keen was the interest in direct trade with the Indies that all Dutch traders soon came to recognize the need for cooperation, in order to minimize competition and maximize profits. In 1602, they formed the United Dutch East Indies Company (known by its Dutch initials, VOC), one of the world's first joint-stock corporations. It was empowered to negotiate treaties, raise armies, build fortresses and wage war in Asia on behalf of Holland.

In its early years, the VOC met with only limited success. Several trading posts were opened, and Ambon was taken from the

Preceding pages: Bantam in its heydays in a Dutch engraving. Left, Sultan Hamengkubwono VIII of Yogyakarta with the Dutch Resident. Right, Jan Pieterszoon Coen, architect of the Dutch empire in the Far East.

Portuguese in 1605. But Spanish and English, not to mention Muslim, competition kept spice prices high in Indonesia and low in Europe. Then, in 1614, a young accountant, Jan Pieterszoon Coen, convinced the directors that only a more forceful policy would make the company profitable. Coen was given command of VOC operations, and promptly embarked on a series of military adventures that were to set the pattern of Dutch behavior in the region.

Coen's first step was to establish a permanent headquarters at Jayakarta, on the northwestern coast of Java, close to the pepper-producing parts of Sumatra and the strategic

Sunda Straits. In 1618, he sought and received permission from Prince Wijayakrama of Jayakarta to expand the existing Dutch post, and proceeded to build a stone barricade mounted with cannons. The prince protested that fortifications were not part of their agreement; Coen responded by bombarding and destroying the palace. A siege of the fledgling Dutch fortress began, in which the powerful Bantenese and a recently-arrived English fleet joined the Jayakartans. Meanwhile, Coen escaped to Ambon, leaving a handful of his men in defense of the fort and its valuable contents.

Five months later, Coen returned to discover his men still in possession of their post. Although outnumbered 30 to 1, they had rather unwittingly played one foe against another by agreeing to any and all demands, but never actually surrendering their position due to the mutual suspicion and timidity of the three opposing parties. Coen set his adversaries to flight in a series of dramatic attacks, undertaken with a small force of 1,000 men that included several score of Japanese mercenaries. The town of Jayakarta was razed to the ground and construction of a new Dutch town begun, including canals, drawbridges, docks, warehouses, barracks, a central square, a city hall and a church – all protected by a high stone wall and a moat. In short, another Amsterdam.

Coen subsequently learned that during the darkest days of the siege, many of the Dutch defenders had behaved in a most unseemly manner: drinking, singing and fornicating. Worst of all, they had broken open the company storehouse and divided the contents among themselves. Those involved were immediately executed and memories of the infamous siege soon faded – save one. The defenders had dubbed their fortress Batavia, and the new name stuck.

His next step was to secure control of the five tiny nutmeg- and mace-producing Banda Islands. Coen brought an expeditionary force there and, with the infamous Japanese samurai, rounded up and killed most of the 15,000 inhabitants within a few weeks. Three of the islands were transformed into spice plantations, managed by Dutch colonists and worked by slaves.

In the years that followed, the Dutch gradually tightened their grip on the spice trade. From Ambon, they attempted to negotiate a monopoly in cloves with the rulers of Ternate and Tidore. But the smuggling of cloves and clove trees continued. Traders obtained these and other goods at the new Islamic port of Makassar, in southern Sulawesi. The Dutch repeatedly blockaded Makassar and imposed treaties barring the Makassarese from trading with other nations, but were unable for many years to enforce them. Finally, in 1669, following three years of bitter and bloody fighting, the Makassarese surrendered to superior Dutch forces.

Dutch control: The Dutch achieved effective control of the eastern archipelago and its lucrative spice trade by the end of the 17th century. In the western half of the archipelago, however, they became increasingly embroiled in fruitless intrigues and wars, particularly on Java. This came about largely because the Dutch presence at Batavia disturbed a delicate balance of power on Java.

Batavia came under Javanese attack as early as 1628. Sultan Agung, third and greatest ruler of the Mataram kingdom, was then aggressively expanding his domain and had recently concluded a successful five-year siege of Surabaya. He now controlled all of central and eastern Java, and he next intended to take western Java by pushing out the Dutch and then conquering Banten.

He nearly succeeded. A large Javanese expeditionary force momentarily breached Batavia's defenses, but was then driven back outside the walls in a last-ditch effort led by Coen. The Javanese were not prepared for such resistance and withdrew for lack of provisions. A year later, Sultan Agung sent an even larger force, estimated at 10,000 men and provisioned with huge stockpiles of rice for what threatened to be a protracted siege. Coen, however, learned of the location of the rice stockpiles and captured or destroyed them before the Javanese even arrived. Poorly-led, starving and sick, the Javanese troops died by the thousands outside the walls of Batavia. Never again did Mataram pose a threat to the city.

Relations between the Dutch and the Javanese improved during the despotic reign of Amangkurat I (1646–1677). They had common enemies – the *pesisir* trading kingdoms of the northern Java coast. It was ironic, then, that the Dutch conquest of Makassar later resulted, indirectly, in their ally's demise.

The Makassar wars of 1666–1669 and

their aftermath created a diaspora of Makassarese and Buginese refugees. Many of them fled to eastern Java, where they united under the leadership of a Madurese prince, Trunajaya. Aided and abetted by the Mataram crown prince, Trunajaya successfully stormed through central Java and plundered the Mataram capital in 1677. Amangkurat I died while on the retreat, fleeing from the enemy forces.

Once in control of Java, Trunajaya renounced his alliance with the young Mataram prince and declared himself king. The crown prince pleaded for Dutch support, promising to reimburse all military expenses and to award the Dutch valuable trade concessions. The Dutch swallowed the bait and mounted a costly campaign to capture Trunajaya. This ended in 1680 with the restoration of the crown prince, now styling himself Amangkurat II, to the throne.

But the new king was in no position to fulfill his end of the bargain with the Dutch; his treasury had been looted and his kingdom was in ruin. All he had to offer was territory, and although he ceded much of western Java to the VOC, they would still suffer a heavy financial loss.

In 1799, Dutch financiers received stunning news: the VOC was bankrupt. During the 18th century, the spice trade had become less profitable, while the military involvement in Java had grown increasingly costly. It was a great war in Java (1740–1755), however, that dealt the death blow to delicate Dutch finances. And once again, through a complex chain of events, it was the Dutch themselves who inadvertently precipitated the conflict. The details of the struggle are too convoluted to dissect here, but it began in 1740 with the massacre of the Chinese residents of Batavia, and ended 15 years later, after many bloody battles, broken alliances and shifts of fortune had exhausted almost everyone on the island. Indeed, Java was never the same again, for Mataram had been cleft in two, with rival rulers occupying neighboring capitals in Yogyakarta and Surakarta. Nor did the VOC ever recover from this drain on its resources, even though it emerged as the preeminent power on Java.

In the traumatic aftermath of the VOC bankruptcy, there was great indecision in Holland as to the course that should be steered in the Indies. In 1800, the Dutch government assumed control of all former VOC possessions, now renamed Netherlands India, but for many years no one could figure out how to make them profitable.

<u>Above</u>, one of many battles between the Dutch army and Indonesian forces.

Raffles renaissance: A brief period of English rule under Thomas Stamford Raffles (1811-1816) soon followed. Raffles was in many ways an extraordinary man: a brilliant scholar, naturalist, linguist, diplomat and strategist, "discoverer" of Borobudur and author of the monumental *History of Java.* In 1811, he planned and led the successful English invasion of Java and was then placed in charge of its government at the age of 32.

Raffles's active mind and free-trade philosophy led him to make reforms almost daily, but the result was bureaucratic anarchy. Essentially, he wanted to replace the old mercantile system (from which the colonial government derived its income through a monopoly on trade) with one in which income was derived from taxes and trade was unrestrained. This enormous task had barely begun when the order came from London, following Napoleon's defeat at Waterloo, to restore the Indies to the Dutch.

Nevertheless, many of his land-tax ideas were eventually levied by the Dutch, and they made possible the horrible exploitation of Java in later years. And his invasion of Yogyakarta in 1812 led ultimately to the cataclysmic Java War of 1825–1830.

Carnage to cultivation: So numerous were the abuses leading to the Java War, and so great were the atrocities committed by the Dutch, that the Javanese leader Pangeran Diponegoro (1785–1855) has been proclaimed a great hero even by Dutch historians. He was indeed a charismatic figure: crown prince, Muslim mystic and man of the people. His guerrilla rebellion against the Dutch and his own rulers might have succeeded but for a Dutch trick: luring him out of hiding with the promise of negotiation, Diponegoro was captured and exiled to Sulawesi. The cost of the conflict in human terms was staggering: 200,000 Javanese and 8,000 Europeans lost their lives, many from starvation and cholera rather than from death on the battlefield.

By then, the Dutch were in desperate economic straits. All efforts at reform ended in disaster with the government debt reaching devastating amounts. New ideas were sought, and in 1829, Johannes van den Bosch submitted a proposal to the crown for what he called a *Cultuurstelsel* or cultivation system of fiscal administration in the colonies. His notion was to levy a tax of 20 percent (later raised to 33 percent) on all land in Java, but to demand payment not in rice but in labor or use of the land. This would permit the Dutch to grow crops that they could sell in Europe.

Van den Bosch soon assumed control of Netherlands India, and in the estimation of many, his system was an immediate, unqualified success. In the very first year, 1831, it produced a substantial profit. And within a decade, millions of guilders were flowing annually into Dutch coffers from the sale of coffee, tea, sugar, indigo, quinine, copra, palm oil and rubber. With the windfall profits received from the sale of Indonesian products during the rest of the 19th century, the Dutch not only retired their debt, but built new waterways, dikes, roads and a national railway system.

In reality, of course, the pernicious effects of the cultivation system were apparent from the beginning. While, in theory, the system called for peasants to surrender only a portion of their land and labor, in practice certain lands were worked exclusively for the Dutch by forced labor. The island of Java, one of the richest pieces of real estate on earth, was transformed into a huge Dutch plantation, imposing unimaginable hardships and injustices upon the Javanese. Privately-owned plantations largely replaced government ones after 1870, but, in fact, some government coffee plantations continued to employ forced labor well into this century.

Far left, Prince Diponegoro and right, a Javanese soldier. Above, on the site of Jayakarta, the new town of Batavia had many of the features of Amsterdam.

Outside of Java, military campaigns throughout the 1800s extended Dutch control over areas still ruled by native kings. The most bitter battles were fought against the powerful Islamic kingdom of Aceh, during a war that began in 1873 and lasted more than 30 years. Both sides sustained horrendous losses. In the earlier Padri War between the Dutch and the Minangkabau of west Sumatra (1821–1838), the fighting was almost as bloody. In the east, Flores and Sulawesi were repeatedly raided and finally occupied by the early 1900s. The success of an Englishman, James Brooke, in establishing a private empire in Sarawak (northwestern Borneo) in the 1840s caused the Dutch to pay more attention to the southern and eastern coasts.

But the most shocking incidents occurred on Lombok and Bali, where on three occasions (1894, 1906 and 1908) Balinese rulers and their courtiers, armed only with ceremonial weapons, stormed headlong into Dutch gunfire after ritualistically purifying themselves for a *puputan* (royal suicide) and thus avoiding the humiliation of defeat.

In some ways, these tragic suicides symbolized the abrupt changes wrought by the Dutch: they had achieved the unification of the entire archipelago of Indonesia at the expense of its indigenous kingdoms, sultans and tens of thousands of people.

At the beginning of the 20th century, signs of change were everywhere in the Indies. Dutch military expeditions and private enterprises were making inroads into the hinterlands of Sumatra and the eastern islands. Steam shipping and the Suez Canal (opened in 1869) had brought Europe closer, and the European presence in Java was growing steadily. Gracious new shops, clubs, hotels and homes added an air of cosmopolitan elegance to the towns, while newspapers, factories, gas lighting, trains, tramways, electricity and automobiles imparted a distinct feeling of modernity. Indeed, thousands of newly-arrived Dutch immigrants were moved to remark on the quite tolerable conditions that greeted them in the colonies – that is to say, it was just like home, or even better.

In the Indies, nationalism was slow in developing but inevitable. A small but growing number of Indonesians were receiving Dutch education. By the turn of the century, there came the remarkable figure of Raden Ajeng Kartini (1879–1904), the daughter of an enlightened Javanese aristocrat and whose ardent yearnings for emancipation were articulated in a series of letters written in Dutch, and later published in English as *Letters of a Javanese Princess*, with a foreword by Eleanor Roosevelt.

The irony is, from a Dutch point of view, that 19th-century European idealism provided much of the intellectual basis of Indonesian nationalism. As early as 1908, Indonesians attending Dutch schools began to form a number of regional student organizations dedicated to the betterment of their fellows. Although small, aristocratic and idealistic, such organizations nonetheless spawned an elite group of leaders and provided forums in which a new national consciousness was to take shape.

National awakening: In 1928, at the second all-Indies student conference, the important concept of a single Indonesian nation (one people, one language, one nation) was proclaimed in the so-called *sumpah pemuda* (youth pledge). The nationalism and idealism of those students later spread in the print media and through the non-government schools. By the 1930s, as many as 130,000 pupils were enrolled in these non-government Dutch and Malay schools – twice the number attending government schools.

The colonial authorities watched the formation of the Dutch-educated urban elite with some concern. Two political movements of the day provided much greater cause for alarm, however. The first and most important of these was the pan-Islamic movement, with roots in the steady and growing stream of pilgrims visiting Mecca, from the mid-19th century onwards, and in the religious teachings of the *ulama* (Arabic scholars). What began in Java in 1909 as a small Islamic traders association (*Sarekat Dagang Islamiyah*) soon turned into a national confederation of Islamic labor unions (*Sarekat Islam*), with two million members in 1919. Rallies were held, sometimes attracting as many as 50,000 people, and many peasants came to see in the Islamic movement some

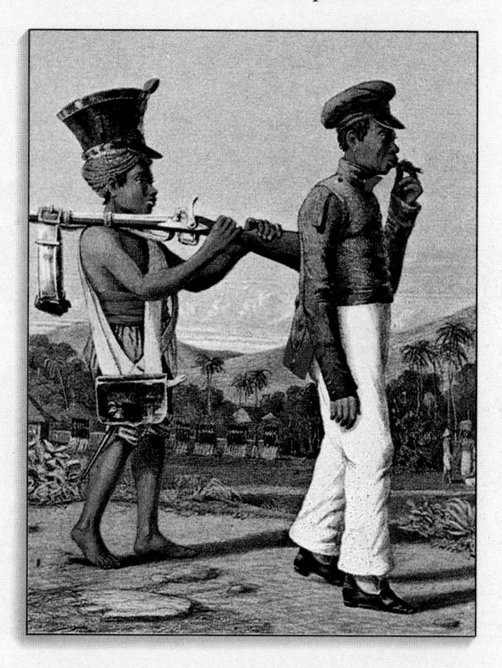

<u>Preceding pages</u>: Soekarno reads the declaration of independence. <u>Left</u>, early oil exploration in Sumatra – where Indonesia's vital oil revenue originated. <u>Right</u>, 19th-century print captures some of the adjuncts of colonialism.

hope of relief from oppressive colonial and economic conditions.

The Indonesian communist movement was also founded around 1910 by small groups of Dutch and Indonesian radicals. It soon moved to embrace both Islam and international communism. Many of its leaders gained control of local Islamic workers' unions and frequently spoke at Islamic rallies, but after the Russian Revolution of 1917, they also maintained ties with the Comintern and increasingly espoused Marxist-Leninist doctrine.

The period from 1910 to 1930 was a turbulent one. Strikes frequently erupted into violence, and while, at first, the colonial government took a liberal view of these rebellious activities, many Indonesian leaders were eventually arrested and moderate Muslim leaders soon disassociated themselves from political activities. The rank-and-file deserted their unions, and while the communists fought on for several years in a series of poorly-organized rebellions in Java and Sumatra up through 1927, they too were crushed.

Leadership of the anti-colonial movement then reverted to the student elite. In 1927, a recently-graduated engineer by the name of Soekarno, together with his Bandung Study Club, founded the first major political party with Indonesian independence as its goal. Within two years, his *Partai Nasional Indonesia* (PNI) had over 10,000 members. Shortly thereafter, Soekarno was arrested for "openly treasonous statements against the state." Although publicly tried and imprisoned, he was later released. A general crackdown ensued, and after 1933, Soekarno and all other student leaders were exiled to distant islands, where they remained for almost ten years. As they were sent off, ringing in their ears was the statement by the Dutch governor-general that the Dutch had "been here for 350 years with stick and sword and will remain here for another 350 years with stick and sword." The flower of secular nationalism, it would seem, had been effectively nipped in the bud.

Japanese occupation: There was a king of 12th-century Java, Jayabaya, who had prophesied that despotic white men would one day rule, but that following the arrival of yellow men from the north (who would remain just as long as it takes the maize to ripen), Java would be freed forever of foreign oppressors and would enter a millennial golden age. When the Japanese invasion came, it is not surprising that many Indonesians interpreted this as a liberation from Dutch rule.

The immediate effect of the Japanese invasion of Java in 1942 was to show that Dutch military might was essentially a bluff. The Japanese encountered little resistance, and within just a few weeks, they rounded up all the Europeans and placed them in concentration camps. Initially, there was jubilation, but it immediately became apparent that, like the Dutch, the Japanese had come to exploit the Indies, not to free them.

Throughout the occupation, all imports were cut off and Japanese rice requisitions steadily increased, creating famines and sparking peasant uprisings that were ruthlessly stomped out by the Japanese.

The occupying Japanese found it necessary to rely on Indonesians and to promote a sense of Indonesian nationhood in order to extract their desired war materials. Indonesians were placed in many key positions previously held by Dutch nationals. The use of the Dutch language was banned and replaced by Indonesian. And nationalist leaders were freed and encouraged to cooperate with the Japanese, which most of them did.

When it eventually became apparent, in late 1944, that Japan was losing the war, the Japanese began to promise independence in an attempt to maintain faltering Indonesian support. Nationalist slogans were encouraged, the nationalist anthem (*Indonesia Raya*) was played, the Indonesian red-and-white flew next to the Japanese red-and-white. Indonesian leaders were brought together for discussions, and close to 200,000 young people were hurriedly mobilized into paramilitary groups.

Postwar revolution: In 1945, on the same day that the second atomic bomb was dropped onto Japan, three Indonesian leaders were flown to Saigon to meet with the Japanese military commander for Southeast Asia. The commander promised them independence for all the former Dutch possessions in Asia and appointed Soekarno chairman of the preparatory committee, with Mohammed Hatta as vice-chairman. They arrived back in Jakarta, and the next day, Japan surrendered unconditionally to the Allies. Following two days of debate, Soekarno and Hatta proclaimed *merdeka,* independence, on August 17th. The long process of constructing a government was begun.

The following months were chaotic. News of the Japanese surrender spread like wildfire and millions of Indonesians enthusiastically echoed the call for merdeka. The Dutch eventually returned to the islands, but Holland was in a shambles and world opinion was against them.

The nationalist leaders, too, were hesitant

Left, opposition to the Dutch found a voice in groups such as these medical students. Above, the movement for independence spawned marches and gatherings.

and divided, awed by the swift course of events and undecided whether to press for full victory or negotiate a compromise. The ensuing struggle was a strange combination of bitter fighting, punctuated by diplomacy.

In the end, heroic sacrifices on the battlefield by tens of thousands of Indonesian youths placed the Dutch in an untenable position. Three Dutch "police actions" gave the returning colonial forces control of the cities, but each time the ragtag Indonesian army, under the inspired leadership of the youthful commander-in-chief, Gen. Sudirman, valiantly fought back.

Finally, in 1949, the United States ceased the transfer of Marshall Plan funds to the Netherlands and the UN Security Council ordered the Dutch to withdraw their forces from Indonesia and negotiate a settlement. This done, Dutch influence rapidly crumbled, and on 17 August 1950 – the fifth anniversary of the merdeka proclamation – all previous governments and agreements were unilaterally swept away by the new government of the Republic of Indonesia.

The final chapters of Indonesian independence were written still later. The Dutch held on to the western half of New Guinea after granting independence to the rest of Indonesia, on the grounds that their New Guinea colony was not a part of the Netherlands East Indies. A nasty guerrilla war in the jungles, as well as United Nations pressure, eventually resulted in the transfer of the huge western half of the island to Indonesia, where it became the country's 26th province, Irian Jaya. And in 1975, after the Portuguese administration hastily abandoned its colony of East Timor, Indonesian military forces assisted pro-Indonesian elements in the former colony to gain control. The area became Indonesia's 27th province.

Euphoria swept through the cities and towns of Indonesia following the withdrawal of Dutch forces. Mass rallies and processions were held; flag-waving crowds thronged the streets shouting the magical words – *Merdeka, merdeka. Freedom, freedom.* Independence had come at last, and Indonesians were in control of their destiny.

Headaches of a new nation: Meanwhile, in Jakarta, the slow and arduous process of constructing a peacetime government began. While the unifying power of the revolution had done much to forge a coherent state, the fact of Indonesia's complex ethnic, religious and ideological diversities remained. Moreover, massive economic and social problems faced the new nation – a legacy of colonialism and war. Factories and plantations were shut down, capital and skilled personnel were scarce, rice production was insufficient to meet demand, people were overwhelmingly poor and illiterate, and the population was growing at spiraling rates.

The inability of any single political group to dominated effectively clearly called for a system of government in which a variety of interests could be represented. Largely due to the high profile of Dutch-educated intellectuals among the nationalists, a western-style parliamentary system was adopted.

From the beginning, however, the existence of more than 30 rival parties paralyzed the system. A string of weak coalition cabinets rose and fell at the rate of almost one a year, and attempts at cooperation were increasingly stymied, not only by a growing ideological polarization, but also by religious and regional loyalties. Parties became more preoccupied with ensuring their own survival than with the nation's pressing economic and social needs, frustrating those who wished to see freedom produce more tangible results. Most impatient of all were Soekarno, whose powers as president had been limited by the provisional constitution of 1950, and the army leadership, who felt entitled to a greater political say.

Left, despite Dutch intentions to return to Indonesia after the Japanese defeat, independence came in 1950. Above, Soekarno (left) with his first cabinet, of which Hatta (to right of Soekarno) was vice-president.

A series of separatist communist uprisings in Sumatra, North Sulawesi and West Java, in the late 1950s, gave Soekarno his cue. He declared martial law and gave the army a free hand to crush the rebels. By 1959, with the rebellions under control, Soekarno resurrected the "revolutionary" constitution of 1945 and declared the "Guided Democracy".

"Guided" democracy: Under the new political system, power was focused in the hands of the president and the army leadership, at the expense of political parties, whom Soekarno now regarded as counter-revolutionary. Militant nationalism became Soekarno's new recipe for national integration, and blame for all sorts of economic and political problems was placed squarely at the feet of foreign imperialism and colonialism. In the international arena, Soekarno achieved a significant impact by convening the 1955 Asia-Africa Conference in Bandung. Attended by Third World leaders such as Chou Enlai, Nehru and Nasser, the conference led to the formation of the Non-Aligned Movement and placed Indonesia in the forefront among emergent Third World nations.

In the early 1960s, Soekarno's anti-colonial sentiments became more militant. A long and successful campaign to wrest control of western New Guinea from the Dutch was followed closely by military confrontation with newly-independent Malaysia in 1963. Soekarno's audacity and contempt for America ("To hell with your aid!" he told the Americans) earned him the reputation of *enfant terrible* among the Asian leaders.

But perhaps Soekarno's nationalistic elan was, in some ways, just what Indonesia needed. Many Indonesians saw him as a father figure who offered a strong vision.

Yet Soekarno's reliance on his charisma and his lack of attention to day-to-day administration created a vacuum in which the government and the nation floundered. While Soekarno attempted to offset the growing influence of the military by courting the Partai Kommunist Indonesia – the PKI, most active of the civilian parties – the nation's economy crashed. Foreign investment fled, deficits left the government bankrupt, and inflation skyrocketed to 700 percent. By 1965, the social, cultural and political ferment was intense.

Military coup: The political tinderbox was ignited in the early hours of 1 October 1965 when, with the apparent encouragement of the PKI, a group of radical army officers kidnapped and brutally executed six leading generals. However, the rebel officers soon lost the initiative to Gen. Soeharto, then commander of the Army Strategic Reserve. In a few hours, Soeharto assumed command of the army and crushed the attempted coup.

The nation was shocked by news of the generals' execution, and the communists were accused of attempting to overthrow the government. A state of anarchy ensued, in which moderate Muslim and army elements sought to settle the score. Thousands upon thousands were killed as long-simmering frustrations erupted into mob violence, first in northern Sumatra, then later in Java, Bali and Lombok. The blood-letting continued for months, and the period from 1965 to 1966 is remembered today as the darkest in the republic's history.

Meanwhile, a political struggle broke out in Jakarta between the army – supported by students, intellectuals, Muslims and other middle-class groups – and Soekarno, with his considerable populist/nationalist following. Finally, on 11 March 1966, Soekarno was persuaded to sign a document bestowing wide powers on Gen. Soeharto.

Although Soeharto was not formally installed as Indonesia's second president until 1968, immediate reforms quickly began. Martial law was declared and order was restored. The communist party and all Marxist-Leninist teachings were outlawed. The civil administration was radically restructured and restaffed. A major realignment in foreign policy restored relations with the United States and the West, while severing ties with China and the Soviet Union.

Economic changes: Building its political legitimacy upon promises to revive the moribund Indonesian economy, the new Soeharto administration wasted no time in addressing the fundamental problems of inflation and stagnation. American-trained economists guided the rapid reintegration of Indonesia into the world economy, liberalized foreign investment laws, and imposed monetary controls. Western aid was sought – and received – to replenish the nation's exhausted foreign exchange reserves. These measures formed the cornerstones of Soeharto's economic "new order" and served dramatically to curb inflation, and to set the nation on a course of rapid economic growth by the early 1970s.

Indonesia's first five-year plan, *Replita I,* was designed to encourage growth by attracting foreign investment. Most of the plan's targets were achieved, as investors moved in to take advantage of Indonesia's vast natural reserves of copper, tin, timber and oil. As the political stability of the region seemed more assured, a second wave of investors, largely Japanese and local Chinese, set up a wide variety of urban-based manufacturing industries. By 1975, textiles alone accounted for nearly US$ 1 billion of investments.

Black bonanza: By far the greatest benefits, however, came from oil. The story began in northern Sumatra in 1883, when a Dutch planter took shelter from a storm in a local's shed and noticed a torch burning brightly. Inquiring, he was led to a nearby spring where a black viscous substance lay thick across the water. The discovery soon led to

the formation of Royal Dutch Shell Company, and eventually to the establishment of Indonesia as the world's fifth-largest and Asia's sole OPEC producer.

Since the mid 1980s, the government, mindful that natural resources deplete without replacement, has stressed the development of the non-petroleum sector, such as manufacturing and service industries. (By the mid 1990s, the Indonesian economy had shifted emphasis, so that the non-petroleum sector produces more than half of the gross domestic product. While oil and gas deposits in Sumatra, Kalimantan, and elsewhere are still an important sector of the economy, the country is no longer dependent for its economic advancement upon petroleum.)

Left, Soekarno reads a statement to the press handing over power, while his successor Soeharto looks on. Above, Soekarno and Soeharto.

Stability and social change: Despite the problems of separatism and demagoguery that defined the first 20 years of independence, the past thirty years have been characterized by political stability. The tenor of the Soeharto regime and its supporters is well defined by the slogan, "Development yes, politics no!" (Never mind that many profitable Indonesian companies are dominated by members of Soeharto's family.) The big winner was the government's political group Golkar, which consists of representatives chosen from various professional religious, ethnic and military constituencies.

Yet politics refused to go away entirely. A proposed secular-marriage law brought an angry response from Indonesia's Muslim majority in 1973 and had to be dropped. And pressure has mounted for the government to provide for a greater distribution of the wealth and benefits of economic growth, to curb the level of foreign debt, to contain inflation and to eradicate corruption. Frustration, particularly over economic matters, has erupted from time to time. Among the influential middle class, however, opposition has been muted by prosperity. Most Indonesians, both urban and rural, consider themselves better off after thirty years of Soeharto's policies, and, in fact, they are.

Growing population: Significant advances have been made in population control and agriculture. By the mid 1990s, Indonesia's population stood at almost 200 million. Java and Bali are the most seriously-overcrowded islands, representing only seven percent of Indonesia's total land area while housing 60 percent of its people.

The government first attempted to ease the pressure with the resettlement of Javanese and Balinese villagers to the sparsely-populated islands of Sumatra, Kalimantan and Sulawesi. However, this proved slow and costly, and since 1970, it has been complemented by an intensive family-planning campaign that has managed to reduce the birth rate to just over one percent annually.

Many workers have been absorbed into the budding manufacturing sector, but it is a constant struggle to keep up with a labor force that grows by 2.5 million a year – equal to nearby Singapore's population.

Directly linked is the challenge of food production. As the population expands, so agriculture absorbs a progressively smaller percentage of the total labor force. In 1960, the figure was over 75 percent, while today only about half of the Javanese people are engaged in food production. This has created a massive unemployment problem, in which millions of landless laborers have moved into the cities to seek work, where most struggle as manual laborers.

Rice is Indonesia's stable food and crucial in feeding the large population. The introduction of new high-yield rice strains, multiple cropping, better irrigation, and chemical fertilizers and pesticides resulted in a spectacular 50 percent increase in rice production between 1974 and 1984, when the country became self-sufficient in this commodity. However, a drought in the early 1990s caused a decline in rice production and forced Indonesia to import rice again. Production continues to fall, due largely to the decrease in paddy area brought about by increased urbanization and industrialization.

For the past decade or so, the government has followed a steady course of economic and financial deregulation and privatization in an effort to diversify the economy and attract non-petroleum foreign investment. There is little doubt that the oil-and-gas sector has served Indonesia well, but the government does not want to be held hostage to depleting supplies and fluctuating prices.

Indonesia's economy is stable, but there are still some crucial areas that need to be addressed. Graft remains rampant and red tape stifling. But no area needs more urgent attention than the country's infrastructure problems. An estimated US$50 billion needs to be invested to alleviate crippling bottlenecks in telecommunications, transport, electricity and water supply. The government has turned to the private sector for help, from both domestic and foreign investors.

What's next?: In 1995, two events clarified contemporary Indonesia. It was, most importantly, Indonesia's 50th anniversary as a declared republic, no small matter given the scattered geographical spread and ethnic diversity of the archipelago. At the same time as the celebrations, Indonesia saw the inaugural flight of its home-developed and home-built N-250 70-seat commuter airplane. So confident were the designers that the plane's first-ever flight was televised live. Questions arose, of course. Why did Indonesia need to build such a craft when there were plenty of alternatives, and plenty of pressing economic needs on a more basic level? National pride, quite simply, a symbol of national progress.

As a republic, Indonesia has had only two leaders. President Soeharto, now in his mid 70s, is expected to run for a seventh term in 1998. Or he may not. The rumors multiply. A successor, nonetheless, has yet to appear. And while the government has been opening doors and encouraging foreign investors, the economy is still controlled by a select group of people, some of them well-connected, if not related, to Soeharto.

Indonesia is a nation that appears, even to the most casual observer, nearly on the brink of becoming a substantial economic and political power in Southeast Asia. It's not yet there, given its problems with infrastructure and bureaucratic bottlenecks. Moreover, the government retains tight controls on the press and politics; too, there are continuing problems in East Timor and Irian Jaya. But the odds are looking good for the Indonesians.

Left, President Soeharto. Right, oceanic oil.

GEOLOGY AND NATURE

The Indonesian archipelago is by far the world's largest – more than 16,000 islands strewn across 5,120 kilometers (3,200 mi) of tropical seas, just south of the equator. When superimposed on a map of North America, Indonesia stretches from Seattle to Bermuda. On a map of Europe, it extends from Ireland east to the Caspian Sea, and beyond.

Of course, four-fifths of the area is occupied by ocean, and many of the islands are tiny, no more than rocky outcrops populated, perhaps, by a few seabirds. But 3,000 islands are large enough to be inhabited, and New Guinea and Borneo rank as the second- and third-largest islands in the world (after Greenland). Of the other major islands, Sumatra is slightly larger than Sweden, Sulawesi is roughly the size of Great Britain, and Java is as large as California. With a total land area of 2 million square kilometers (780,000 sq mi), Indonesia is the world's fourteenth-largest nation.

Befitting its reputation as the celebrated Spice Islands of the East, this archipelago also constitutes one of the most diverse and biologically fascinating areas. Unique geologic and climatic conditions have created spectacularly varied tropical habitats – from the exceptionally fertile rice lands of Java and Bali to the luxuriant rain forests of Sumatra, Kalimantan, Sulawesi and Maluku, to the savannah grasslands of Nusa Tenggara and the jungle-laced, snowcapped peaks of Irian Jaya.

The geological history of the region is complex. All of the islands are relatively young; the earliest island dates only from the end of the Miocene, 15 million years ago – just yesterday on the geological time scale. Since then, the archipelago has been the scene of violent tectonic activity, as islands were torn from jostling super-continents or pushed up by colliding tectonic plates, and then enlarged in earth-wrenching volcanic explosions. The process continues today – Australia is drifting slowly northward, as the immense Pacific plate presses south and west to meet it and the Asian mainland. The islands of Indonesia lie along the lines of impact, a fact that is reflected in their geography and in the region's seismic instability.

In fact, these islands were often connected to each other and to the mainland during the Ice Ages, when sea levels receded as much as 200 meters and the entire Sunda shelf was exposed as a huge subcontinent. Today, these islands are fringed with broad plains, expanding as alluvial deposits collect.

Preceding pages: mystery in the rain forest. Left, Anak Krakatau during an eruption. Right, Sulawesi's varied geography provides a habitat for many endemic species.

Volcanoes, and then more: Not only do volcanoes dominate the landscape of many islands with majestic smoking cones, they also fundamentally alter the islands' size and soils by spewing forth millions of tons of ash and debris at irregular intervals. Eventually, much of this gets washed down to form gently-sloping alluvial plains. Where the ejecta is acidic, the land is infertile and practically useless. But where it is basic, as on Java and Bali and in a few scattered localities on other islands, it has produced spectacularly-fertile tropical soils.

Of the hundreds of volcanoes in Indonesia, over 70 remain active, and hardly a year passes without a major eruption. On a densely-populated island like Java, this inevitably brings death and destruction. When tiny Mount Krakatau, off Java's west coast, erupted in 1883 with a force equivalent to that of several hydrogen bombs, it created tidal waves that killed more than 35,000 people on Java. The eruption, 18 times larger than that of Mount St. Helens in America's Pacific Northwest, was heard as far away as Sri Lanka and Sydney, and the great quantities of debris hurled into the atmosphere caused vivid sunsets all over the world for three years afterwards.

But the Krakatau explosion was dwarfed by the cataclysmic 1815 eruption of Mount Tambora, on Sumbawa, the largest in recorded history. Around 90,000 people were killed and over 80 cubic kilometers of ejected material blocked the sun for many months, producing a "year without summer" in 1816.

Arboreal canopies: The archipelago's vegetation varies greatly according to rainfall, soil and altitude. On the wetter islands, the luxuriance of the rain forests is amazing. The main canopy of interlocking tree crowns may be 40 meters (130 ft) above ground, with individual trees as high as 70 meters (230 ft). Beneath this grows a tangle of palms, epiphytic ferns, rattans and bamboos, covered by innumerable lichens and mosses.

One would imagine that to support such growth, the soils would have to be very rich, but this is generally not so. The rain forests of Sumatra, Kalimantan, Sulawesi and Irian Jaya typically thrive on very poor and thin soils that have been heavily leached of minerals by incessant rains. The rain forest flourishes due to a ecosystem that essentially holds most of its minerals and nutrients in the form of living tissues. As these die and fall to the ground, they immediately decompose and are absorbed in a self-fertilizing system largely independent of the soil.

Lowland rain forests display the greatest diversity. Stands of a single tree are rare; rather, the lowland forest is composed of a fantastic mosaic of different species. In Kalimantan alone, for example, 3,000 different tree species are known.

In remote and diverse Irian Jaya, more than 2,500 species of wild orchids are found in the rain forest, including the world's largest, the tiger orchid with its three-meter-long spray of yellow-orange blooms.

Alpine forests, mangrove swamps: At high altitudes, temperatures drop and cloud cover increases, resulting in slower growth, fewer species and a less-complex ecology. Rain forests give way to more specialized montane forests dominated by chestnuts, laurels and oaks. Higher up, one finds rhododendrons and stunted moss forests – dwarf trees draped in lichens. Higher still, there are alpine meadows with giant edelweiss and other plants more reminiscent of Switzerland than the tropics. This unexpected habitat can be seen at Mount Gede National Park, only 100 kilometers (60 mi) south of hot, humid Jakarta. On Indonesia's highest peaks – the Lorentz mountains of Irian Jaya that rise to over 5,000 meters (16,000 ft) – are the only ice fields in the eastern tropics.

In the vast tidal zones of eastern Sumatra, Kalimantan and southern Irian, specialized mangrove trees with looping roots and air-breathing nodules flourish. These trap silt washed down by rivers and creep slowly forward behind a wall of growing coral, forming new land. Mangrove swamps are inhabited by fish that skip out of the water and by the amazing proboscis monkey.

Moving east from central Java across Bali and Nusa Tenggara, the climate becomes drier and lowland jungles are replaced by deciduous monsoon forests and open savannah grasslands. Depending upon how dry the climate is, these forests are partly or wholly deciduous, with fewer species but many broadleaf trees like teak, which shed their leaves during the dry season. This renders them highly vulnerable to forest fires, and indeed, most of the natural forests on Sumbawa, Komodo, Flores and Timor have been either cut or burned off in recent centuries by people. The exposed land has then been devoured by voracious *alang-alang* (elephant grasses); today, there are only useless grasslands and scrub where once stood valuable hardwood forests.

Not only are Java and Bali among the few islands where volcanic ejecta is basic and not acidic – so that frequent volcanic eruptions have, in fact, continually improved the soils by adding mineral-rich nutrients – but they are also areas that achieve something of a golden mean in climate, with plentiful rainfall and sunshine during alternating dry and wet seasons, each lasting half of the year.

Due to the dramatic population imbalance between Java and Bali compared to the rest of Indonesia, as well as Java's importance as a political center within the archipelago, many observers tend to distinguish between an inner Indonesia (Java and Bali, including Madura and West Lombok) and an outer Indonesia (all other islands).

Whereas inner Indonesia has been characterized for centuries by high population densities and labor-intensive irrigated agricul-

Left, Mahameru is the highest mountain in Java. Above, mangroves along the Cihandeuleum River, at Ujung Kulon in West Java.

ture, outer Indonesia is the home, traditionally, of rain forests, thinly-spread farming communities and riverine trading networks.

Today, the outer islands are also the source of almost all valuable exports: rubber and palm oil from Sumatra; petroleum, copper, and bauxite from Sumatra, Bangka, Billiton and Irian Jaya; timber from Kalimantan.

For some time, Java has suffered from problems of erosion, soil exhaustion and pollution. Now, as the nation's export resources are increasingly being called upon to support a burgeoning population, there are the beginnings of massive deforestation, leading to erosion and the replacement of rain forest by useless grassland.

These problems have been recognized by the Indonesian government, which is taking steps to encourage selective cutting and reforestation; six percent of the nation's land has been set aside as nature reserves and national parks. These are not just for the protection of a few wild animals; they safeguard a genetic treasure trove containing many species that may be valuable to people, as well as providing watershed population and recreational facilities. Although human impact on the environment has been severe in the more heavily-populated areas of Sumatra, Java, Bali and Nusa Tenggara, much of Indonesia remains pristine wilderness.

Of particular interest to tourists is the extensive system of national parks, nature reserves and protected forests, now numbering over 300 comprising some 120,000 square kilometers (46,000 sq mi). Sixteen of these are national parks, being developed for recreational use, and many of the smaller natural reserves and protected forests are also accessible and worth visiting.

The national parks vary greatly in size, habitats, wildlife and visitor facilities. Some are quite remote and require weeks to visit, while others are quite accessiblé. Several parks also have special marine areas with excellent snorkeling and scuba diving, where one can observe fabulous coral reef marine life, or swim with grim-faced whales.

Flora and fauna: The plant life of Indonesia originates almost exclusively from the Asian mainland, and it is abundant, exotic and incredibly diverse – almost 40,000 different species belonging to 3,000 different families, with 10 percent of all plant species in the world. Most of these are natives of the varied equatorial rain forest, with its thousands of varieties of wild orchids, ferns, fruits, spice trees, and the world's largest parasitic bloom.

The animals of Indonesia are just as diverse, having come from two quite different sources at opposite ends of the archipelago. From the west came the Asian mammals, and from the east came the pouched marsupial species and plumage birds so typical of Australia. In total, more than 500 mammals are found in Indonesia, from the tigers, orangutans and elephants of Sumatra to the freshwater dolphins of Kalimantan, to the tree kangaroos and wallabies of Irian.

Fifteen hundred species of birds are known, many of them rare Australasian plumage species, like the cockatoo, flightless cassowary, numerous parrots and more than 40 species of birds-of-paradise. In addition, countless reptiles, amphibians and invertebrates populate the seas and coasts, including giant turtles and the huge, carnivorous monitor lizards of Komodo.

The boundaries of the Asian and Australasian faunal regions are far from clear; the islands of Sulawesi, Maluku and Nusa Tenggara lying between them are, in fact, transitional and therefore of great interest to zoologists. Here are found both Asian and Australasian species, as well as endemic species found nowhere else in the world. Today, this area is known as Wallacea, in honor of the great 19th-century naturalist, Sir Alfred Russell Wallace, who was the first to recognize the geographical separation in faunal types that occurs here.

Of all the islands of Wallacea, Sulawesi is the most biologically interesting. Most of the island's mammals, including deer, civets and tarsiers, are of obvious Asian origin; however, the two types of cuscus found here are marsupial and typically Australasian.

But Sulawesi has many curious animals uniquely its own – including the *anoa* dwarf buffalo; the babirusa, a "deer" pig with curved tushes growing from the top of its snout; the giant palm civet; and the heavy-set black macaque, which, despite its resemblance to a miniature gorilla, is actually a monkey and a close cousin of the pig-tailed macaques of neighboring Borneo. Sulawesi has a rich avifauna, too, made up of both Asian and Australasian species: hornbills, kingfishers, babblers, cockatoos and the amazing maleo bird, which buries its eggs in warm sandy areas, leaving its young to hatch themselves.

All national parks and nature reserves come under the jurisdiction of the Directorate-General of Forest Protection and Natural Conservation (PHPA), based in Bogor. Although a few reserves, like Pangandaran in southcentral Java, can be entered by paying a small entrance fee, most require a permit from PHPA headquarters in Bogor, or at other regional offices.

Left, early Dutch painting depicts Sumatran volcano. Above, the black-capped lory. Right, a magnificent lesser bird-of-paradise.

For one traveling the length of Indonesia, the complexity and diversity of peoples, languages, customs and cultures found in the Indonesian archipelago are truly astounding, and thoroughly embracing. Living here are over 100 distinct ethnic groups, each with its own cultural identity, who together speak a total of more than 300 mutually-unintelligible languages.

Anyone traveling widely in Indonesia soon recognizes the enormous physical differences of people from one end of the archipelago to the other – differences in pigmentation, hair type, stature and physiognomy. To explain this range of racial types, scholars once postulated a theory of wave migrations to the archipelago. According to this theory, various Indonesian groups arrived from the Asian mainland in a series of discrete but massive migratory waves, each separated by a period of several centuries. The wave theory, however, has lost considerable currency in recent years.

Migratory theories: The first wave of migrants, it was thought, were the primitive dark-skinned, wiry-haired negritos – people of pygmy stature who today inhabit remote forest enclaves on the Malay peninsula, in the Andaman Islands north of Sumatra and on several of the Philippine islands. It has commonly been suggested that the negritos somehow migrated the length of the Eurasian continent, from Africa, eons ago.

The second wave, too, were thought to have arrived from Africa or perhaps India. These peoples were dubbed the Australoids, and are the Melanesian inhabitants of New Guinea, including Irian Jaya, and Australia. They traditionally lived in semi-settled villages in remote areas, where they hunted and gathered, but they also raised crops and animals, and produced a variety of handicrafts, including pottery and vegetable-fiber cloths.

The third wave, proto-Malays, were thought to have migrated from China by way of Indochina. They are light-skinned people, with almond-shaped eyes, who somehow acquired a mixture of certain Australoid features, such as curly hair and brown skin. Most of these groups still inhabit highland or remote inland regions, although they are by no means primitive.

The last wave, the deutero-Malays, were described as pure Mongoloids, hence related to and much resembling the Chinese. These peoples today inhabit the plains and coastal region of all the major islands, and many developed large hierarchical kingdoms, attaining a level of pre-modern civilization comparable to that found anywhere in the world. As these Mongoloids arrived, they are said to have forced all earlier groups to move on to marginal mountain areas and dense upriver jungles, or to the dry eastern islands – monopolizing the best agricultural lands and the most strategic river estuaries for themselves.

One virtue of this wave theory is that it does, at least, attempt to connect the great variety of physical traits to the similarly broad range of cultural types found in Indonesia. Yet, in fact, race and culture do not correlate as easily as previously believed. The basic problem is that no one knows

Preceding pages: Sultan of Yogyakarta and his wife. Left, Dayak woman with child and family wealth. Right, tea plantation, Java.

exactly what is meant by "race". As ideal types, it is fine, but in practice, of course, sharp racial boundaries do not exist, and distinguishing features have a way of dissolving into meaningless abstractions. It is now clear that in Indonesia, as elsewhere, physical appearance doesn't correlate in any systematic way with language or culture.

In fact, the real picture is more complex than this. First of all, the existence of *Homo erectus* (Java Man) fossils in Indonesia – million-year-old remains of one of our earliest ancestors – suggests that the so-called negrito and Australoid people, with their sun-screening skin pigmentation, actually evolved partially or wholly in the tropical rain forests of Southeast Asia, just as the light-skinned Mongoloid types evolved in the cold temperate regions of east and central Asia. Of course, during the last Ice Ages, when land bridges linked the major islands of the Sunda shelf to the mainland, these peoples circulated freely and even crossed the oceans, populating Australia by about 50,000 years ago. There can be no doubt that Mongoloid-type peoples did migrate to the region much later, but the question is how.

The wave theory of coordinated, coherent mass movements seems unlikely for a number of reasons. In a fragmented region like the Indonesian archipelago, village and tribal groups have always been constantly on the move, at least in historic times, dissolving and absorbing each other as they go. It is more realistic, therefore, to imagine a situation in which small groups of Mongoloid hunters, gatherers and cultivators percolated into the region slowly, absorbing and replacing the original Australoid inhabitants over a period of many millennia.

Linguistic babel: Indonesians speak such a variety of different languages that the exact number would largely depend upon an arbitrary definition of what constitutes a distinct language, as opposed to a dialect. Most estimates place the total above 300, only a handful of which have been adequately studied. Languages such as Javanese, Balinese, and Bahasa Indonesian (the national language, which derives from a literary dialect of Malay) are closely related, belonging to the Malayo-Polynesian branch of the Austronesian language family, but they are as different from one another as are French and Spanish.

Linguists have long postulated that great linguistic diversity means an area has been settled and stable for a very long time. In fact, one of the purposes of lexico-statistical studies (the comparison of related languages to determine the percentage of words they share) is to locate the ancestral homeland of a language family – assumed to lie in the region of greatest diversity. Within the scattered Austronesian family, this ancestral homeland appears to be located in western Melanesia, an area between the north coast of New Guinea and the Solomon Islands.

For this reason, some scholars have begun to speculate that the Mongoloid inhabitants of Indonesia migrated not via mainland Southeast Asia, as had previously been thought, but rather from southern China via Taiwan, Hainan and the Philippines to Melanesia. From here, so the theory goes, there occurred a diaspora of Austronesian speakers, some of whom sailed east to populate the Pacific islands, others of whom traveled west to Indonesia and even across the Indian Ocean to Madagascar. No definite time frame is given for these migrations, but they are thought to have begun around 7,000 years ago, and to have greatly accelerated about 5,000 years ago.

Cultural distinctions: When it comes to defining and classifying ethnic groups, there are basically two schools of thought. One holds that each group, tribe or people should be treated as a unique case, and that a complex, holistic view of the group's culture should be sought. Only when enough Indonesian cultures are adequately documented, according to this view, can any meaningful comparisons be made.

Left, Balinese and Javanese faces. Above, a Minang haji and a Batak.

There is much to recommend such a cautious approach. Of course, the problem is that ethnographic information is by its very nature never complete. What we know about a culture is largely determined by the questions we ask. An opposing view, therefore, says that we should begin by establishing certain general guidelines for classifying Indonesian ethnic groups, then work to refine and revise them.

One important distinction focuses on the two main agricultural patterns found in Indonesia: *ladang* and *sawah*. Ladang agriculture, also referred to by the Old English word swidden and by the descriptive phrase slash-and-burn, is practiced in forested terrains, generally outside of Java and Bali. The ladang farmer utilizes fire as a tool, along with axe and bush knife, to clear a forest plot. By carefully timing the burn to immediately precede the onset of rains, the farmer simultaneously fertilizes and weeds the land.

Depending upon local soil conditions and preferences, the main staple crop planted might be a grain like rice or corn, a tuber such as yams or taro, or a starch-producing palm like sago. Rice is the preferred crop in the western islands; tubers and sago palms predominate in the eastern and southeastern islands. In addition to the staple, farmers also plant a great variety of other food crops, in effect recreating the symbiotic system of a tropical forest found in nature, while also providing a more varied diet for themselves. After several years, however, the land in these areas, never rich to begin with (most nutrients are provided by ash from the burn), is depleted and new plots must be cleared.

For obvious reasons, the swidden, or ladang, method can support only a small population. In Kalimantan, for instance, home of the Iban and Dayak tribes, the average density is less than 10 persons per square kilometer. The size and complexity of social organization within such ladang communities is also limited. Nuclear families are generally autonomous, labor is exchanged with fellow villagers or kinsmen on a carefully-calculated basis, and warfare, headhunting and slave raiding traditionally kept villages isolated from one another.

While these semi-nomadic swidden farmers now comprise less than a tenth of Indonesia's total population, they are scattered throughout more than two-thirds of the nation's land area.

Most Indonesians, by contrast, inhabit the narrow plains and coastal regions of the major islands, where the principal farming method employed is sawah, or wet-rice paddy cultivation. In fact, two-thirds of Indonesia's population (over 100 million people) lives on Java and Bali, which between them comprise less than ten percent of Indonesia's land. Here, the average rural population densities can soar as high as 2,000 people per square kilometer (5,000/sq mi) – by far the world's highest.

Sawah cultivation is a labor-intensive form of agriculture that can be successfully practiced only under the special conditions of rich soil and adequate water, but one that seems capable of producing seemingly limitless quantities of food. The farmers who plant wet-rice paddies actually reshape their environment over a period of many generations, clearing the land, terracing, leveling and diking the plots, and constructing elaborate irrigation systems. This permits multiple cropping and extremely high yields, for the productivity of sawah plots responds dramatically to added care in all phases of the crop cycle.

As a result, this system has both required and rewarded a high degree of social cooperation. Particularly in Java and Bali, populous villages have long been linked with towns – economically and culturally – through a single, hierarchically-defined framework that has coordinated labor to maintain the fragile irrigation works. The food surpluses produced by these peasant villages have, in turn, permitted an urban opulence and refinement.

As might be expected, the sawah societies of Java and Bali are strikingly different from the ladang communities of the outer islands. The Javanese, for example, put great emphasis on cooperation and social attitudes. Village deliberations are concluded not by majority or autocratic rule, but by a consensus of elders or esteemed individuals. *Rukun,* or harmony, is the primary goal, achieved through knowing one's place within society and acting out the assigned role. To be *sopan santun* (well-mannered) is the rigid social norm, and realized in a masterful display of elaborate etiquette developed into something more than just a convenient social style; instead, they became a richly elaborated theater of status rituals and insignia.

The distinction made here between wet-rice and swidden communities is, of course, simplistic. Not only are many other means of food procurement practiced in Indonesia – hunting, trapping, fishing and foraging, to name but a few – but, in fact, each area and each people seem to have developed their own way of doing things.

In several fertile highland plateaus of Sumatra – home of the Batak, Minangkabau and Besemah peoples, who were traditionally swiddeners – wet rice has been grown now for several centuries. Yet the villages often maintain what appear to be archaic forms of ladang community organization.

Time, balance and harmony: A favorite expression in Indonesia is *jam karet,* which translates, literally, as rubber time. Rarely must a social event or a meeting start at the appointed hour; time can be stretched to suit the occasion.

The notion of balance and harmony is also important in personal contacts. Great respect and deference are shown to superiors and elders, and there are distinct speech levels that are used according to the status of the person. These fine social divisions may hark back to the Hindu caste system as yet another example of Indonesia's heritage. To lose face, to be made ashamed (*malu*) is something to be avoided, and many Indonesians will suggest that something can be done when they know perfectly well it cannot. But in this way, they do not give offence, and the listener knows as well as the speaker that the answer has, in fact, been a polite and graceful, No. *Halus,* or refined behavior, is also infinitely preferred to *kasar,* or coarse deeds.

Childhood's end: Cheeky, mischievous, wide-eyed and laughing, Indonesia's children are visible everywhere. They are also extraordinarily self-possessed little bodies. Never ignored, always loved, and yet firmly controlled by an invisible discipline (and they are never chastised in public, for they rarely misbehave), they are part of the family and community group from birth. They are not just a cipher, but are an active and contributing member of family and community. It is not unusual for a little girl of five to care for younger brothers and sisters while the parents work in the fields, an assumption of responsibility that often astounds foreigners. There is no child beating, no cruelty.

Left, men from Timor and Irian Jaya. Right, Dayak woman.

Children, loved as they are, represent one of Indonesia's major problems. Java, for example, is grossly overpopulated. Family planning units get close to their targets, but the targets are modest and often not enough. There are too few teachers, and too few schools. The gap between the haves and the have-nots is enormous, and increasing.

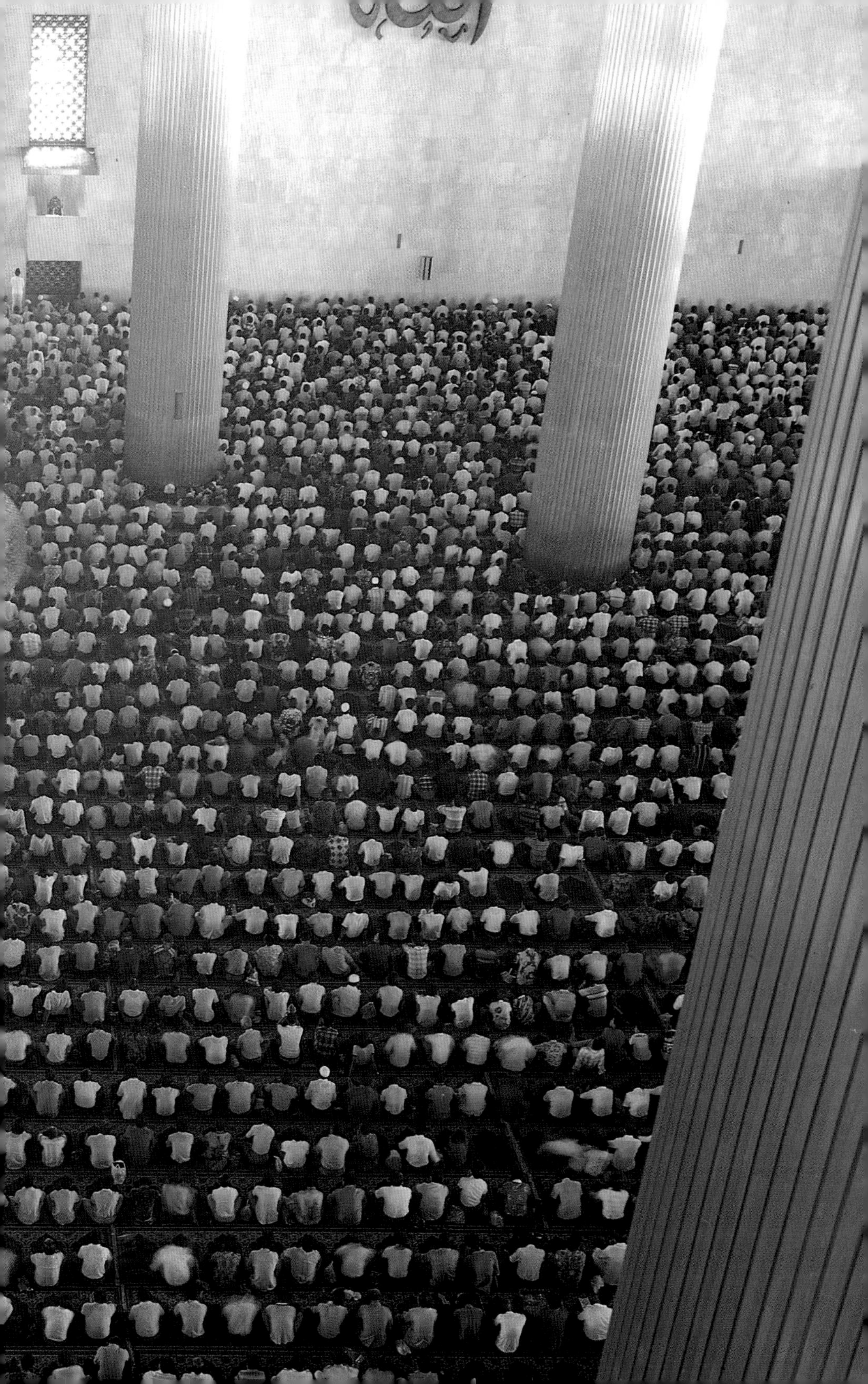

ISLAM

In classical Arabic, *islam* means to surrender. As defined in the Koran, it means to surrender to the will and law of God. It is this voluntary acceptance of the Koran's word that defines the Muslim.

Based upon the teachings of Muhammad, usually referred to as the Prophet, Islam is one of the world's most important religions. Over a billion believers extend from the Arab lands of the Middle East – where Islam originated and blossomed – and North Africa, west to southern Spain, and east through Turkey, Iran, Afghanistan, Pakistan, India and eventually into Southeast Asia, especially Indonesia, Malaysia and the Philippines. (Moreover, it is the second-largest religion in Europe.)

In Indonesia, Islam was a pivotal fulcrum for the region's history. Expanding trade contacts and commerce peacefully spread Islam throughout the region. By the late 13th century, Islam had gained a foothold in Sumatra, and within a couple of centuries, it was embedded throughout Southeast Asia, anchored by a powerful Islamic commercial and political center in Malacca, on the Malay Peninsula. And when the colonial powers began to dominate the region, it would be Islam, both as a nationalist and religious force, that would oppose colonialism.

The history of Islam's development in Indonesia is one of cultural accommodation, essential from the first contact of Islam with the Indonesian archipelago. The Indonesian islands are an affiliation of many ethnic and cultural groups, traditions, languages and religions. For that reason, throughout Indonesia's history, there has often been a general inclination towards a convergence of basic social, cultural and political needs. In many ways, the traditional tolerance of Islam (disregarding the fanatic stereotype that dominates Western media) has permitted a give and take. Although Indonesia is the world's largest Islamic country, there is a history of religious tolerance, and freedom of religion is guaranteed by the constitution.

Preceding pages: listening to the imam inside the Istiqlal Mosque, Jakarta. Left, in traditional Islam, study of the Koran is part of daily life.

Islam proposes how Muslims should live together with other Muslims, and with non-Muslims without disturbing their beliefs.

Nearly 90 percent of the population is Muslim, with most of the remainder being Christian (primarily Protestant). There is a small, but powerful, minority of Buddhists. As was the case with Buddhism, Hinduism was at one time a significant power in the archipelago, but now one finds it limited to Bali and western Lombok.

Islam is practiced most traditionally in western Sumatra, especially in Aceh, and in western Java, southeastern Kalimantan and in parts of Nusa Tenggara. Outside of these areas, Muslim is the professed religion, but the strict Islamic rituals of fasting and prayers, for example, are less strictly followed. On Java, perhaps one third to one half follow strict practices. In many rural areas, the practice of Islam (as have Christianity and other beliefs) has been affected by more traditional animistic practices.

Travelers to Muslim countries in Southeast Asia, such as Indonesia or Malaysia, can't help but sense the depth of the Islamic faith in the daily lives of believers. Belief and practice of the religion necessarily define the nature and quality of life itself, and of the community. The rituals of the religion are intertwined with the basic needs and acts of daily life.

Koran and Sunna: Islamic beliefs and practices are based upon two important touchstones for the Muslim: the Koran and the Sunna. The Koran is considered to be the word of God as spoken to Muhammad (c. 570–632) during the last 22 years of his life, through the angel Gabriel. And as it is the word of God, the Koran and its 114 chapters is irrefutable and faultless. The Sunna, less well-known to outsiders, reflects the traditional norms regarding assorted concerns and issues, based upon what Muhammad himself did or said regarding those concerns and issues. Although secondary to the Koran, it is a fundamental and essential component for most Muslims.

Little known amongst non-Muslims is that Islam accepts most Biblical miracles and prophets, in both the Old Testament and

New Testament. Abraham, Moses, and Jesus, for example, are important prophets for the Muslim. Adam was the first prophet, later forgiven by God for his sins. But they were early prophets; Muhammad came later as the last and final prophet, and thus revealed a more perfect word of God. The Koran itself is considered Muhammad's eclipsing miracle, as perfect as possible on earth. More fundamentally in Islam, all religions are essentially representations of the same divine truth, except that, again, Islam is closest to that truth.

Islam is a monotheistic belief. God is omnipotent and singular. (One does find, however, permutations of this fundamental idea in some parts of Indonesia, where local and often polytheistic beliefs, and in some places, from Hinduism and Buddhism, have been melded with Islam. This modifying of practice and doctrine is not restricted to Islam, however; one finds assimilations and modifications amongst Buddhist, Hindu and Christian believers within the archipelago.) Like Christianity, there is a heaven and a hell, one for the good and one for the bad.

The world's creation was an act of mercy by God, for if God had not done so, there would be nothingness. Everything on earth has its designated function and form, defined and suited to making a harmonious world. Nature is here to be exploited by humanity, and as for human beings themselves, our purpose is simple: be in the service of God. But, unlike Christianity, which is more individualistic, humanity's responsibility includes establishing social systems that are pure and free from vice and corruption. God also judges societies and nations, which are, in fact, subject to the same transgressions and weaknesses as people. World history reflects the results of God's judgments regarding nations and societies; those that are good, persist. Those that are not, such as colonialism, eventually are superceded by other states and cultures. (Indeed, that colonialism was replaced by an independent state, and one that is mostly Muslim, reinforces this view.)

The basis of an Islamic society is the sustenance of the community of the faithful, guided by the Sharia, or Islamic law. This law defines a community's moral goals; in fact, in many Muslim countries, Islam defines all the law, both moral and legal.

According to the Koran, people are proud, if not egotistical, and easily susceptible to selfishness and greed. (Satan is a significant factor in earthly affairs.) Belief in the Koran will assist people to rise above these inadequacies by establishing an inner ethical bearing called *taqwa.* Through this quality, good and evil, and right and wrong, are recognizable. In the end, a person is judged by taqwa, not by monumental earthly deeds or accomplishments.

It has been the duty of prophets – from Adam to Muhammad, all of whom are mortals – to show not only individuals the way to taqwa, but entire societies. The history of religion up to Muhammad might be considered as evolutionary, with an incremental growth towards perfection.

Islamic cornerstones: There are five "pillars," or duties, that are fundamental cornerstones of Islamic belief and society: profession of faith, prayer, alms giving or voluntary charity, fasting, and pilgrimage.

Prayers, for example, are best done communally in a mosque, although if unable to do so, a Muslim can say them alone. Even in a metropolis like Jakarta, every neighborhood has a mosque, however humble and however adjacent to the glass-and-steel skyscrapers, from which the *muezzin* calls the faithful to daily prayers, nowadays through loudspeakers, given the noise of urban Indonesia.

Fasting during the month of Ramadan – which is based upon the lunar, not solar, calendar – is seen as both a celebration and as a test of one's faith; from dawn to dusk during Ramadan, one must not drink or eat anything, smoke or engage in sexual intercourse, much less do sinful actions or harbor sinful thoughts.

A pilgrimage to Mecca at least once in life is often a life-long goal and apex of one's endeavors. Even the lowest-paid Muslim saves over the years to make the pilgrimage. Such a pilgrimage offers the Muslim the ultimate opportunity to affirm one's faith: "There is no God but Allah and Muhammad is his Prophet."

Another five pillars: The five "pillars" of Islam – prayer, pilgrimage, charity, fasting, faith – should *not* be confused with *Pancasila,* a social tool conceived by Soekarno in 1945 to reflect – and encourage – unity in the people of the archipelago. Whether or not the Islamic pillars served as a model for Soekarno, Pancasila too can be translated as five pillars or principles: a belief in a singular and omnipotent God, a civilized and fair humanitarianism, a democracy guided by wisdom and representation, social justice for all Indonesians, and, finally, a united Indonesia.

A device intended to unify an extremely diverse people separated by vast distances, Soekarno's Pancasila was outlined so as to ensure that Indonesian identity was *not* defined in reference to Islam.

Left, young boys gather to study the Koran with an elder. Above, a lake-side mosque.

Indonesia is by far the world's largest Muslim nation, with about three-quarters of the population believers. The remainder profess Christianity, Hinduism and Buddhism. In fact, however, Indonesians have an almost infinite variety in what they do and believe in spiritual matters – religious beliefs and practices are strongly affected by local traditions passed from generation to generation. These locally-defined beliefs form the fabric of each society, known as the *adat*, or custom, of an ethnic group or community.

So great is the identification of most Indonesians with their respective adat that these are commonly said to constitute ethnic identity. To a Malay, for example, conversion to Islam is regarded as *masuk Melayu* – becoming a Malay. Likewise, a Balinese who converts to Islam or Christianity is said to be no longer Balinese. And among the Javanese, children not yet familiar with the social values and mystical sensibilities of their elders are considered *durung Jawa* – not yet complete and full Javanese.

The adat and religion of any given Indonesian group tend to be remarkably eclectic. The classic example is that of the average Javanese – a self-declared Muslim who firmly believes in the existence of Indian deities and in the indigenous folk heroes portrayed in the ever-popular *wayang kulit* shadow play, as well as in a host of deities, ghosts, spirits, demons and genies said to inhabit the worldly environment. Typically, in addition to fulfilling the requirements of the Islamic faith, the Javanese will burn incense and leave small offerings to local spirits; hold frequent communal feasts (*selamatan*) to celebrate special occasions and to mitigate the disruptions of unsettling events; seek and heed the advice of a local *dukun* or mystic in times of distress; and trust to the magical potency of an inherited *keris* dagger and a variety of other talismans.

Central to the adat observances of most Indonesians is the ritual communal feast, in which ceremonial foods are offered up to the spirits and blessed, then publicly consumed, in order to ensure the well-being of the participants and strengthen the solidarity of the group.

The most common example of such a feast is the Javanese selamatan ("safe guarding"), in which special foods are eaten (for example, a *tumpeng*, or inverted cone of colored rice accompanied by various meat dishes), incense is burned, Islamic prayers are intoned and formal announcements or requests are made by the host. A selamatan may be given at any time and for almost any reason – most commonly to celebrate birth, marriage, circumcision, death or an anniversary, or to initiate a new project or a new building,

or to dispel bad luck or invite good fortune.

In Bali, festive activities center about the village temple, where every 210 days a communal birthday feast (*odalan*) is held on the anniversary of its consecration. For several days beforehand, the entire village is engaged in preparing elaborate decorations, altars and offerings.

On the day of the festival, delicately-carved sandalwood idols are brought out of their special compartment, wrapped in sacred weavings and then infused with the protective spirits of the village, who are then escorted to the seashore or the riverbank in a colorful procession. Symbolic ablutions are performed and everyone is blessed and then the procession returns to the temple, where the spirits receive their offerings and possess mediums who tell if the celebrations and offerings have been satisfactory, answer questions and give advice.

The villagers feast, and various entertainment is staged throughout the night – a chance for young dancers, puppeteers and gamelan musicians to star. Finally, as dawn breaks over the horizon, the *pemangku* leads the village in a ritual adoration of the rising sun, and then everyone goes home to bed.

These and other types of feasts frequently have to do with enhancing the fertility and prosperity of the participants by strengthening, purifying or augmenting something known to many Indonesian peoples as *semangat* – the life forces, or vital principles thought to inhabit and animate not only humans but plants, animals, sacred objects and also entire villages or nations. These forces bring bad as well as good consequences, and it is generally believed that by boosting their own life-giving semangat, people are able to achieve and maintain a fragile balance.

The semangat of human beings is thought to be concentrated in the head and hair, and in the past, the Toraja of Sulawesi, the Dayak of Kalimantan and the Dani of Irian Jaya sought to promote their own semangat at the expense of an adversary through head-hunting raids. Skull trophies were once regarded as powerful talismans that would enhance the prosperity of a community, and also ward off sickness, war, famine or ill fortune.

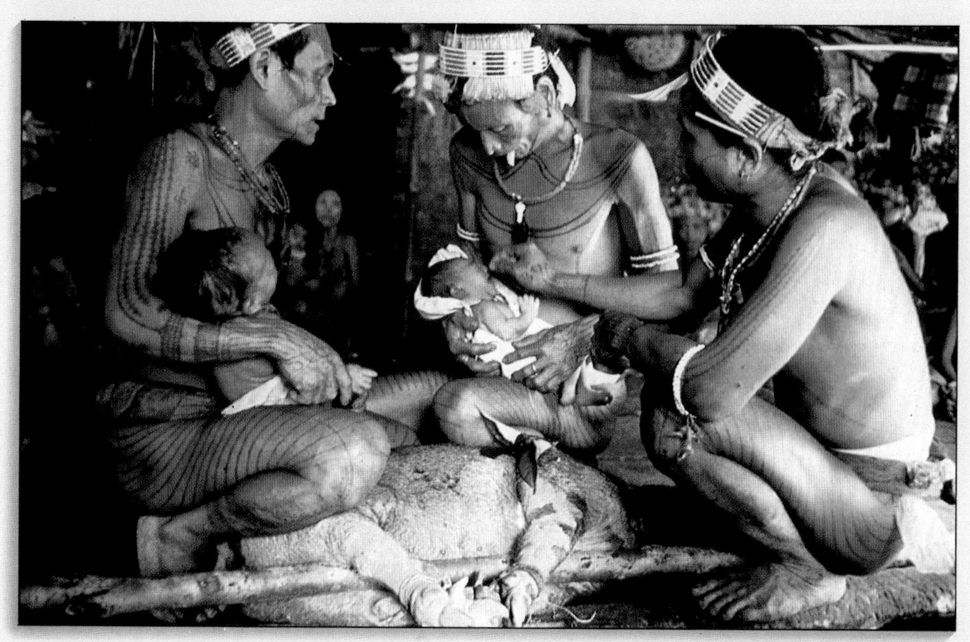

Left, the final day of the Sekaten feast. Above, a purification birth rite takes place over a pig carcass; pigs are a touchstone of Irian life.

A ceremonial first haircut often serves to initiate an infant into human society. The exchange of snippets of hair or the ceremonial knotting of the hair of a bride and groom together is an integral part of many Indonesian marriage rites, while human hair curiously features in the costumes of many supernatural characters. Likewise, hair clippings are disposed of carefully (as are nail trimmings), lest they fall unknowingly into the hands of an enemy sorcerer.

Blood, too, is thought to be infused with semangat, which can be especially easily transmitted or conferred. On many islands, the pillars of a new house are anointed with the sacrificial blood of animals to render them strong and durable. And it used to be widely reported that, in many parts of the archipelago, victors in battle drank the blood of their slain enemies, or smeared it over themselves, to augment their own semangat with that of the fallen.

Many Indonesians believe that this soul substance is also found in plants. The most common example is that of the powerful but sensitive semangat associated with the rice plant. There are many versions of the legend accounting for the origins of domesticated plants, but most describe a beautiful woman who is given the choice of death or sexual submission to her stepfather, her twin brother or a gruesome ogre. She chooses death, and from her buried remains grow rice, palm trees, fruits and edible tubers. In some areas, she is known as Dewi Sri and is described variously as the wife of Vishnu or the daughter of Batara Guru, the protectress or embodiment of the sacred rice spirit. In Bali, special temples are dedicated to Dewi Sri and her image; the triangular *cili* delicately cut from palm fronds or formed of colored rice-dough adorns temples during festivals.

Throughout the cultivation cycle, ritual precautions are taken to ensure the well-being of the rice soul. If harmed or even startled, she might leave and the crop could fail. When the grain is being harvested, special care is taken to treat the grain-laden plants with respect. Short, curved blades are often used, concealed in the palm of the hand so that the rice spirit cannot "see" that she is about to be violated. Soothing incantations or apologies are often muttered as the rice is cut. Traditionally, music was played, dances performed and poetry was recited in some communities while the harvest was in progress. Grains that are to become next year's seed are often wrapped in swaddling and treated as newborn infants. Representative stalks of rice are sometimes "married" and hung up in the granary until the next rice-planting cycle begins in a few months.

All ancient and curious objects, mountains and bodies of water are likewise thought to be imbued with a special semangat. Bezoar stones, mineral deposits found in animals and in the nodes of certain bamboos, are used for magic and healing, while more generally, any object that is designated a *pusaka* or sacred heirloom is credited with harboring a vital spiritual essence that requires special veneration and care. Antique keris daggers, lances, spear heads, cannons, gems, jewelry, textiles, ceramics, manuscripts, gravestones and masks can all become pusaka and may contain a soul of their own or that of a previous owner. Such objects are often in the custody of a king, priest, chief or an elder, a link between the living and the powerful ancestral spirits.

Much of a community's private and public ritual life often centers around the management of its human souls, both living and dead. In this, there are invariably certain individuals in the communities who possess specialized knowledge or skills in such matters. Special attention is always devoted to funerary rites, in which the dead are ritually venerated and can be transformed into protective clan or village deities.

It is commonly believed that the soul of a person may become detached during life, and that this can result in diminished strength or illness. Even under normal conditions, it is thought that the soul wanders during sleep. Sorcery can entice unwitting souls away.

A distinction is made virtually everywhere between good and bad spirits, resulting respectively from good and bad deaths. A bad death, generally premature or violent, releases a vengeful ghost or *hantu* that may bring considerable misfortune on a household or community. The soul of a woman who dies at childbirth is pictured as a bird with long talons that jealously stabs and rents the stomachs of pregnant women. This so-called *pontianak* can also assume the shape of a beautiful maiden, who waits at night beneath a banyan tree to seduce and emasculate passing men. Elaborate rituals must then be performed by a shaman to mollify the evil hantu and banish it from the area.

Good deaths must also, of course, be attended by a lengthy sequence of elaborate funerary rites. When a person dies, it is universally thought that the soul is at first resentful and potentially harmful. Some rites are therefore specifically designed to confuse the soul and to dissuade it from returning to seek the company of the bereaved. It is a widespread custom in Sumatra, Kalimantan, Southern Sulawesi and Halmahera, for instance, to send the corpse out of the house through a gap in the wall or floor of the house, which is then sealed.

Almost everywhere such events are open to all, provided those in attendance respect local customs and mores concerning conservative dress and decorous behavior. Nobody who has witnessed a Balinese funeral procession and cremation, a Toraja funeral sacrifice, or a Javanese marriage ceremony will never forget the dignity, color, and sounds of such events.

Far left, Christian of Flores at Easter. Left, a Balinese trance ritual. Above, Hindu cremation of a Balinese raja.

Dance and Drama

There is such a variety of dance and dramatic traditions throughout the archipelago that it is impossible to speak of a single, unified tradition. Each Indonesian ethnic and linguistic group possesses its own unique performing arts. Nevertheless, there has been a good deal of borrowing amongst the groups, and most have several things in common.

Dance, storytelling and theater are ubiquitous in Indonesia, elements of a cultural life that is all-encompassing and fulfilling a wide variety of sacred and secular needs. Dancers, shamans, actors, puppeteers, priests, storytellers, poets and musicians are members of the community performing vital roles in informing, entertaining, counseling and instructing their fellows in the well-worn ways of tradition.

Dance and ritual life are inseparable among so-called primitive tribes in Indonesia, most of whom have their shaman dances performed by priests or priestesses for purposes of exorcism and spirit propitiation. The Batak *datuk* (magician) of highland Sumatra, for example, holds a magic staff as he threads with tiny steps over a magic design he has drawn on the ground. At the climax of this dance, he hops and skips, thrusting the sharp end of his staff into an egg on the ground.

Most tribes also have their ritual group dances, performed to mark rites of passage – births, funerals, weddings, puberty – and agricultural events, as well as to exorcise sickness or evil spirits, and, of course, to prepare for battle or celebrate victory.

Sometimes ritual dances are performed by a select group, but often all males or females in the community join in. Female movements are generally slow and deliberate, with tiny steps and graceful hand movements; men lift their knees high and use their hands as "weapons," often in imitation of martial arts movements (*pencak silat*). Accompaniment is provided by chanting, pounding the rice mortar *(lesung)*, and sometimes by bamboo chimes or flutes.

Preceding pages: a wayang orang performance at the Mangkunegaran Court in Solo. Left, Serimpi dancers at Dalem Pujokusuman. Right, the zaiwo (men's dance) of Sumba.

Group dances often involved the entrancement and possession of participants, best known of which is the Balinese *barong*, immortalized in the Margaret Mead film of the 1950s, Trance and Dance in Bali. The barong dance-drama, now performed for hundreds of tourists each day (and worth seeing) is a contest between the opposing forces of good and evil in the universe, represented by a good beast called the barong and the evil witch Rangda. A group of men armed with swords (*keris*) attempts to kill Rangda, but

she possesses them and turns their swords back on themselves. They are saved only thanks to the intervention of the benevolent barong. By the end of the play, some of the dancers are so deeply entranced that they must be exorcised by sacrificing a chicken over them and burning incense.

Another Balinese family of dances, the dramatic *sanghyang* trance dances, also involve the putative possession of dancers by gods and animal spirits. The most famous of these is the *sanghyang dedari* or heavenly nymph dance, in which two young girls dressed in white enter a circle of 40 to 50 chanting men, the *kecak* chorus. When they are finally possessed by goddesses, the girls are clothed in glittering costumes and borne aloft on the shoulders of the men, touring the village to drive out evil influences.

On Islamic Java, the trance dance has developed into something of a commercial spectacle. It is variously known as *kuda kepang, kuda lumping, recog* and *jatilan,* and it consists of one or more riders on hobby horses made of leather or plaited bamboo, accompanied by musicians, masked clowns and perhaps also a masked lion, tiger or crocodile similar to the barong.

Such hobbyhorse troupes were once commonly seen at weekly markets and in crowded city squares during festival days, but they are now rare. The riders would begin in an orderly fashion, trotting in a circle, then one of them would become entranced and start behaving like a horse, charging back and forth wildly, neighing and eating grass or straw. The others might follow his lead, and sometimes there might be a confrontation between the masked animal and the horsemen. Eventually the riders would be brought out of trance by their leader, and money would be collected from the assembled crowd.

Court dances of Java: Before the turn of the century, all traditional rulers of the coastal and inland kingdoms maintained palace dance-and-theatrical troupes. But following the Dutch conquests, most court traditions lapsed into obscurity. Only in central Java are courtly performances and royal patronage of dancers, actors and musicians still found, and appreciated.

Java has by far the oldest known dance and theater traditions in Indonesia. Stone inscriptions dating from the eighth and ninth centuries speak of dances and theatrical performances. And the walls of the great central Javanese temples of this period – Borobudur, Prambanan and others – are adorned with numerous reliefs depicting dancers and entertainers, from lowly market minstrels and roadside revelers to sensuous court concubines and prancing princesses.

Most of the dances in central Java today are attributed to rulers of one of several Islamic dynasties, particularly those of the 16th to 18th centuries. Undoubtedly, the vocabulary of movements and music employed are much older. Throughout the 19th century, rulers frequently were credited for dances choreographed for special occasions. Often it was the palace dance master who actually concocted the piece, but a few rulers were also accomplished dancers and musicians in their own right.

The most famous of all Javanese court dances is the Bedoyo Ketawang, performed in the Surakarta palace on the anniversary of the Susuhunan's coronation. This is a sacred and private ritual dance said to have been instituted by Sultan Agung in the early 1600s, the greatest of the Mataram kings. It celebrates a reunion between the descendant of the dynasty's founder, Senopati, and the powerful goddess of the south sea, Kyai Loro Kidul.

Nine female palace guards perform the stately Bedoyo Ketawang attired in royal wedding dress, and so sacred is it that they may rehearse only once every five weeks on a given day. Until recently, no outsiders were permitted to witness the performance, for it is claimed that Loro Kidul herself attends and afterwards "weds" the king.

The reliefs at Borobudur, depicting popular dances and musical entertainment, suggest that dance once figured prominently in Javanese life. However, outside of the courts, one will find that very little dancing remains in this area today.

Balinese dance: There are clear indications that dance and drama have played a central role in Balinese life since time immemorial. Following the demise of Balinese kingdoms at the beginning of this century, the focus for all Balinese dance and drama shifted from the courts to the villages.

In Balinese dance, considerable Indian influence is evident. Balinese dance costumes, with their glittering headdresses and elaborate jewelry, are clearly of Hindu-Javanese origin and, as in Java, Balinese dancers adopt the basic Indian stance.

The other important Javanese court dance, Serimpi, was traditionally performed only by princesses or daughters of the ruling family. It portrays one or two dueling pairs of Amazons who move in unison, fighting with dainty daggers and tiny bows and arrows. Following the establishment of outside dance schools in the early 1900s, it became the standard taught to all young women.

Left, the dance being performed by these men from Mollo, Timor, serves as one preparation for battle. Above, Bali's I Nyoman Mario, the legendary dancer from the 1930s, seen here performing the kebyar.

But unlike the Javanese, who developed slow, controlled, continuous movements performed with eyes downcast and limbs close to the body, the Balinese dancer is charged with energy, eyes agape, darting this way and that, high-stepping, arms up, moving with quick, cat-like bursts that would startle a Javanese. The Balinese distinguish between dances that are sacred (*wali*), ceremonial (*bebali*) and simply for watching (*bali-balihan*). The last category of dances appears to have developed exclusively among

THE RAMAYANA

One of the two main stories informing Javanese theatre and dance is the *Ramayana*. (The other one is the *Mahabharata*.) It's a moral tale, full of instructions and examples on how to lead the good life. It praises the rectitude, wisdom and perseverance of the noble *satriya* or warrior class, and stresses faithfulness, integrity and filial and fraternal devotion.

The *Ramayana* acknowledges that the trek along the path of virtue demands humility, self-sacrifice, deprivation and compassion. It is a cautionary tale – less a battle between good and evil (in which evil must always lose) than a recognition of the perpetual ebb and flow of the spirits of darkness and light.

In its homeland, India, the *Ramayana* has been known for 3,000 years. With the spread of Indian religions and culture through Southeast Asia, the *Ramayana* became part of the mythology of Burma, Thailand, Laos, Cambodia, the Malay Peninsula, and especially of Java and Bali. The epic is long and complex.

The characters: In the *Ramayana*, the chief characters are Rama, his wife Sita, his brother Laksmana, the monkey general Hanuman, the demon king Rawana, and Rawana's brother, Wibisana. Rama is semi-divine (an incarnation of Visnu), and a consummate archer.

Rama is of noble birth, for he moves in a refined (*halus*) manner. Even in battle, he is graceful and delicate, using his mind as much as muscles. Rawana, Rama's implacable foe, thrusts and struts upon the stage, every step filled with menace. His head turns sharply with each movement. His face (whether a grease-painted human one, a mask, or a puppet head) is an impassioned, furious red in keeping with his aggressive, hostile nature.

The Story: Rama, Laksmana and their half-brother, Barata, are the sons of the king of Ayodya. An accomplished bowman, Rama wins the hand of beautiful Sita in an archery contest, but through the intervention of Barata's mother, Rama is prevented from succeeding his father as king. Rama, Sita and Laksmana go into exile, refusing Barata's entreaties to return. In the forest they meet a sister of Rawana, king of the demons (*raksasas*); she falls in love with Rama, is spurned, and then turns to Laksmana, who promptly cuts off her nose and ears.

Rawana, determined to avenge this indignity, sends off a servant in the form of a golden deer. Rama stalks the animal and kills it. Its dying cries sound like Rama calling for help, and Laksmana, taunted by Sita, goes in search of his brother. In his absence Rawana appears as a holy beggar and confronts Sita, who refuses his appeals to desert Rama. Rawana assumes his natural terrifying form, abducts Sita, and flies off with her. The gallant bird Jatayu attempts to rescue her, but is mortally wounded. Before dying, he tells Rama and Laksmana what has happened to Sita.

Searching for Sita, the brothers meet Hanuman, a general in the kingdom of the apes, who takes them to meet Sugriwa, his king. Sugriwa, who has been usurped by his brother, seeks Rama's aid in regaining his throne. Rama kills the errant brother, and the grateful monkey king places his army at Rama's disposal. Rama and Laksmana set off with Hanuman and the white ape army, and learn that Rawana has carried Sita across the sea to the island of Langka, Rawana's homeland. Hanuman undertakes a daring reconnaissance of Langka and finds Sita in a garden of Rawana's palace. He gives her a token from Rama, and Sita in turn gives Hanuman one of her rings, but Hanuman is discovered by Rawana's guards, captured after a desperate fight, and is sentenced to be burnt at the stake. With the pyre blazing, he wrenches free, his tail a mass of flames, and sets fire to the palace before fleeing from Langka.

Hanuman carries Sita's ring to Rama, and the ape armies gather on the shore opposite Langka and build a giant causeway across the sea. On the island, a tumultuous battle ensues. One of Rama's magic arrows eventually fells Rawana, and the victors return home with Sita to a boisterous welcome. Rama receives the throne from his half-brother Barata. ■

the nobility, but they are now performed by villagers as part of a ceremonial repertoire.

The *legong keraton* was originally a court dance developed for royal amusement, but it is now seen frequently at village temple ceremonies throughout Bali. Traditionally, legong was performed by two very young girls, introduced by a court attendant (*condong*) who sweeps the stage clean and presents the dancers with fans. Sheathed in glittering gold costumes, with headdresses crowned by frangipani blossoms, the two dancers then enact one of a dozen or so possible stories. Today, more than two women may perform the dance, and they need not be very young.

The *baris,* or warrior dances, on the other hand, seem to have developed out of old ritual battle dances. A good baris performance is a true test of wits for dancers and musicians, for they must respond to each other's signals to produce the quivering bursts of synchronized energy that are the essence of the dance.

New dances are being created all the time. The powerful *kecak* dance was adopted from the Sanghyang Dedari at the beginning of this century, and is now performed by as many as a hundred chanting and swaying men, dressed only in loincloths. The kecak is by far Bali's most popular tourist spectacle.

In the 1930s, the legendary dancer and choreographer, I Nyoman Mario, introduced a dance known as the *kebyar,* based upon a type of gamelan music that appeared in northern Bali around 1915. It is performed by a virtuoso soloist, using the upper parts of his body while sitting to interpret the capricious moods of this scintillating music. Mario's other creations include *oleg tambulillingan,* which depicts two bumblebees making love in a garden of flowers.

Balinese and Javanese theater: In Java, all theater seems to have its roots in the *wayang* puppet theaters, among which the flat leather shadow puppet play, the *wayang kulit,* is preeminent. This is evident from the fact that all Javanese theater, whether performed by actors or by puppets, is referred to as wayang. Performed by actors on a stage, *wayang topeng* (mask drama) and *wayang orang* (dance-drama) are the best known, with many of the tales, ichnography and characters' movements borrowed from the shadow play.

Of these, the wayang topeng is undoubtedly the oldest, evident in east Java in the 14th century. It enacts tales from the Panji cycle of epics concerning the founding of the 13th-century Singhasari dynasty. Whereas

Left, Sita, Rama's wife. Above, scene from Ramayana at the Dalem Pujokusuman.

on Bali, mask plays are still popular, on Java they lost favor at the Islamic Javanese courts sometime after the 16th century, and now survive only in northern coastal villages.

Javanese wayang orang or *wayang wong* (literally, human wayang) dance-dramas are said to have been created in the 18th century by one or another of central Java's rulers. This has become a partisan matter, in which Surakartans claim their Prince Mangkunegara I as the originator of the genre, and Yogyakartans insist that it was their Hamengkubuwono I created it.

Neither ruler truly invented the wayang orang, for dance-dramas existed in Java from a much earlier time. But both rulers were

extremely active in creating new pieces, and a strong rivalry developed that intensified during the 19th century, when Javanese rulers became more and more concerned with matters of cultural prestige, and, fortunately, possessed the time and the means to devote to cultural pursuits

Wayang orang became a part of the state ritual in these kingdoms, performed in an open pavilion to commemorate the founding of the dynasty and the coronation of the king, as well as at lavish royal weddings. The great age of wayang orang was during the 1920s and 1930s, when productions lasted days and would often employ 300 to 400 actors.

There are now three commercial wayang wong companies in Java that hold nightly performances for the public: Sri Wedari in Surakarta, Ngesti Pandhawa in Semarang and Bharata in Jakarta.

Modern trends: Traditional Indonesian dance and drama is today in great danger of being swamped by modern entertainment. Even in the central Javanese palaces, the financial burden of maintaining dance and musical troupes is becoming too great, and Indonesians on the whole seem less inclined to support the old palace arts.

The government has done its best to remedy the situation by establishing performing arts academies (ASTI) in various cities, and tourism is providing commercial demand for traditional dances, albeit in non-traditional settings like hotel poolsides.

On Bali, every village has its own dance troupe, and these now have an impetus to improve and expand their repertoire for a steady schedule of tourist performances. Dancers of the barong in the village of Batubulan, for example, perform every morning for bus loads of foreigners, then at night they often dance again in elaborate *topeng* or *arja* dramas before enthralled villagers.

A new generation of Indonesian choreographers, educated at the performing arts academies and familiar with western classical and modern dance, is now at work. Since the 1950s, teachers such as Bagong Kussudiardjo in Yogya, Wayan Dibia in Bali and Sulawesian Wiwiek Siepala in Jakarta have been adapting traditional dance work. One result has been the *sendratari* (literally, art-drama-dance), which is essentially a traditional dance-drama minus the dialogue, but one that incorporates some modern movements and costumes.

The first sendratari, an adapted version of the Javanese wayang orang, was staged in the early 1960s, supposedly at the urging of a Cook's Tour operator. Today, this Ramayana ballet spectacular, with a cast of over 200, is performed over four nights, around every full moon during the dry season months (May to October), on a large stage erected in front of the elegant 9th-century Prambanan temple complex.

Left, students from ASTI perform a fan dance combining tradition with a modern idiom. Right, this legong dancer is from Bali.

MUSIC OF MOONLIGHT: GAMELAN

> Gamelan music is comparable to only two things: moonlight and flowing water. It is pure and mysterious like moonlight and ever-changing like flowing water.

Since 1893, when Claude Debussy first heard a Javanese ensemble perform at the Paris International Exhibition, the haunting and hypnotic tones of the *gamelan* have fascinated the West. This music has been sensitively studied by scholars such as Jaap Kunst and Colin Mcphee, and is now indisputably recognized as one of the world's most sophisticated musical arts. In Indonesia, gamelan music has always been the sound of everything civilized.

The term gamelan derives from *gamel*, an old Javanese word for handle or hammer, as most of the instruments in the orchestra are percussive. The interlocking rhythmic and melodic patterns found in gamelan music are said to originate in the rhythms of the *lesung* – the stone or wooden mortars used for husking rice. Others ascribe these patterns to the rhythmic chanting of frogs in the rice fields after dusk, or the wonderful cacophony of roosters crowing at dawn.

No one knows exactly when the first gamelan orchestra came into being. Metallophones (bronze, brass or iron percussion instruments) date back to prehistoric times, and the manufacture of bronze gongs and drums is associated with the Dong Son bronze culture that is thought to have reached Indonesia, from Indochina, in about the third century BC. Since then, large bronze gongs have formed the heartbeat of this distinctive music, with a deep and penetrating sound that can be heard for miles on a quiet night.

Gamelan ensembles most commonly perform as accompaniments to dance and theaters. *Karawitan* is the Indonesian term coined in the 1950s by Ki Sindusawarno, the first director of the music conservatory in Surakarta, for the entire range of Javanese and Balinese performing arts that incorporate gamelan music.

Preceding pages: crowding around the gamelan orchestra at a wayang kulit performance. Left and right, royal gamelan at Surakarta.

In Java, karawitan and related arts reached heights of refinement in the Islamic courts of the 18th and 19th centuries. Renowned instrument sets supposedly date from the Majapahit era centuries earlier in East Java, and there are references to the instruments from 1,000 years ago. The aristocratic refinement of the gamelan in Java has resulted in slow, stately and mystical music, designed to be heard in the large audience hall of the aristocratic home, and to convey a sense of awesome power and emotional control.

From five to 40 instruments make up a gamelan orchestra, and most of them are never played other than as part of an ensemble. In fact, the two instruments that do see regular solo use, the *rebab* (a two-stringed bowed lute, probably of Middle Eastern origin) and the *suling* (bamboo flute), are non-percussive and thought to have been later additions to the orchestra.

The basic principle underlying all gamelan music is that of stratification. It is essentially a technique of orchestration in which the density of notes played on each instrument is determined by its register; higher instruments play more notes than lower ones. In

THE FAHNESTOCK EXPEDITION

In 1986, the U.S. Library of Congress in Washington, D.C., received a letter from Mrs Margaret Fahnestock.

Was the library interested, she asked, in some old recordings that had been gathering dust in her attic for forty years? The recordings of music, she explained, had been made amongst the South Pacific islands prior to World War II by her late husband, Sheridan Fahnestock, and his brother, Bruce.

The answer was yes, and the Library accepted the music on behalf of the Endangered Music Project, a branch of the Library that had been preserving traditional, and untainted, music from the rain forests of South America and the Caribbean by archiving recordings.

Several days later, the collection arrived at the Library of Congress. Recorded on a stack of 16-inch discs that stood waist-high was music from Java, Bali, and other islands in the Pacific. The recordings' acetate coatings were severely deteriorated, and it took all the skill of the Project's engineers, using the latest technology, to restore the recordings. Soon after, the Library announced to the public that it had uncovered a collection of traditional Indonesian music that had not been influenced by Western culture, rock-and-roll, or global tourism.

Who were the Fahnestock brothers? Born in Washington, D.C., they were sons of a successful inventor. When he was just 21, Sheridan Fahnestock organized one of the longest and most fruitful scientific expeditions ever to sail to the South Seas. His brother, Bruce, joined him as entomologist and chronicler. Their mother, 50 and now a widow, also came along.

Dual expeditions: They set sail in the *Director,* a schooner they'd bought second-hand. The first voyage lasted three years, collecting scientific samples for the American Museum of Natural History. Out of money, they sold *Director* in the Philippines, continuing on to Beijing and arriving just as the Japanese invaded China.

Returning to America, they organized another South Sea expedition in 1940. More than anything else on their first expedition, the brothers had been captivated by the music of the Pacific, especially that of Indonesia.

A rich widow gave them a beautiful 137-foot, three-masted schooner, which they named *Director II,* along with elaborate recording equipment. With President Franklin Roosevelt's official blessings, they set sail with their mother and 15 scientists.

When *Director II* left New York, it carried two Presto disc-cutters – at the time, state-of-the-art recording devices. Along with their 16-inch discs of aluminium coated with cellulose acetate, the Fahnestocks brought along three kilometers of insulated microphone cable, enabling them to record on shore while the equipment remained safely aboard the boat, with two skilled technicians at the controls.

Once in the South Pacific, they recorded music from Tahiti, Samoa, Fiji and the Dutch East Indies, now Indonesia.

With the threat of war, Roosevelt asked them to gather intelligence on local defence facilities around Java, undercover, while the brothers continued to record the music of the islands. It was during this time that they made their finest recordings – in eastern Java, Bali and Madura. In late 1941, they completed their recordings, and Bruce returned to America with the discs. Sheridan took *Director II* to Australia, where it hit a shoal on the Great Barrier Reef and sank. Both brothers returned to the South Pacific as soldiers. Bruce was killed in New Guinea.

Most sophisticated and euphonious of the Fahnestock recordings are those from Bali, reproducing the gamelan orchestras of the Balinese temples. The fact that these recordings may sound primitive by modern digital standards serves, paradoxically, to make them even more compelling to today's ears. It's a haunting experience listening to the music.

A selection of the music from Indonesia has been released by Rykodisc, on CD and cassette, as *Music for the Gods – The Fahnestock South Sea Expedition, Indonesia,* the second installment in the U.S. Library of Congress Endangered Music Project. ■

addition, instruments are grouped according to their function. Gongs, for example, maintain the basic structure of the music, while mid-register metallophones carry the theme and other instruments provide ornamentation. The *kendhang* – wooden drums with skins stretched over both ends – lead the orchestra by controlling the tempo of the piece. Many Indonesian musicians metaphorically compare the structure of gamelan music to a tree. The roots, sturdy and supportive, are the low registers; the trunk is the melody; and the branches, leaves and blossoms represent the delicate complexity of the ornamentation.

In central Java, the main *balungan* (skeleton) of a piece is played on the various *saron* (small- to medium-size metallophones, with six or seven bronze keys lying over a wooden trough resonator), and on the *slentem* (metallophones with bamboo resonators). Faster variations on the balungan are played simultaneously on the elaborating instruments: the *bonang* (a set of small, horizontally-suspended gongs), *gender* (similar to the slentem), *gambang* (a wooden xylophone), and *celempung* (a zither with metal strings). Together with the sulting, the rebab and the vocalists, they create the complex, rich and sensual sound that is unique to gamelan music.

Vocal parts in an ensemble became popular in Java only in the 19th century, but it is now common to have soloists as well as a chorus. Female (*pesinden*) singers seem to be more popular, but the sound of voices is regarded merely as another element in the overall texture of the orchestra, and the singing is not necessarily given prominence over the instrumental parts. Lyrics are only rarely understood, as they are normally composed in a archaic or literary language. Too, they become lost as they are woven into the overall fabric of the music. For Westerners, it often requires concentration to appreciate.

Above, a full gamelan orchestra.

A common misconception of gamelan compositions is that they are improvised, perhaps because scores are rarely used. Most compositions (*gendhing*) are as rigidly determined as they are lucidly performed. There are literally thousands of pieces, and every region of Java has its favorites. Each gendhing has its own name and theme (*balungan*), usually corresponding to the specific *wayang* character, dance or ritual for which the gendhing is played.

Balinese gamelan: In Bali, the gamelan exhibits overwhelming variety. Dozens of completely different types of ensembles exist, some of which are found all over the island, others of which are restricted to isolated areas. But on the whole, Balinese musical performances are noted for their capriciousness, stridency, and rhythmic vitality – particularly in contrast to the slow and measured gamelan performances of Java.

One of the most frequently encountered ensembles in Bali is the gamelan *gong kebyar*. Kebyar refers to a particularly flashy style of music that originated in the north of the island around 1915, but the ensembles that play it have since expanded their repertoire to include other styles. In the gong kebyar, four difference gongs mark the musical phrase. They are, in order of descending size: the gong, *kempur, kempli* and *kemong*.

The melodic theme is carried by two pairs of large metallophones: the *jegogan* and *calung*. A ten-piece *gangsa* (high-pitched metallophones) section ornaments the theme, and the *reong* (Bali's version of the Javanese bonang) is played by four musicians producing a rippling stream of visceral, syncopated figurations. A pair of kendhang drums leads the group, interlocking with each other to produce spectacular rhythms. The drummer of the lower-pitched kendhang is generally also the leader, teacher, and composer for the ensemble. A set of shimmering cymbals (*cengceng*) and several bamboo flutes (*suling*) complete the orchestra.

Learning the art: Gamelan musicians were traditionally trained by other musicians in their spare time, without any reference to written scores. In the central Javanese palaces, some musicians began to receive special training for their courtly duties at the beginning of this century. Since independence, however, several government music academies have been founded, and students now learn in a more formal setting.

At the village level, it is often difficult to distinguish amateurs from professionals. Many village artists are quite expert in the music of their region, and yet no special status is assigned to them, nor is any sizeable payment given for their services. Some gamelan musicians are itinerant, making the rounds of traditional performances, be they theatrical or ceremonial or both, including the ever-popular shadow play or *wayang kulit* circuit. There are many famous artists who lead this precarious life, but the financial rewards are minimal.

The big orchestras are still royal heirlooms, and the musical style of a royal house is considered to be a part of the orchestra. In Java, instrument sets are invariably a family possession, even in the villages, and are often highly decorative. Good examples of Javanese court gamelans can be seen in the Sasono Budaya Museum, in Yogya, and the Mangkunegaran Palace, in Solo. Once a year during the Sekatan festival celebrating the Prophet Mohammed's birthday, the court gamelans of Yogya and Solo are played in the mosque to an audience of thousands – in clear conflict of fundamental Islamic beliefs, but testimony to the enduring eclecticism in the Javanese.

Balinese gamelans are normally owned and maintained cooperatively by village music clubs (*sekaha*). The Balinese religious calendar prescribes a hectic schedule of performances for temple festivals, and the provincial government has taken an active role in preserving lesser-known musical styles that may be in danger of extinction. Islandwide, inter-village musical competitions provide an impetus for composers and performances to constantly expand the expressive essense of the music.

Left, the gamelan Kyahi Bermoro of Yogyakarta. Right, gamelan music is an integral part of Javanese culture.

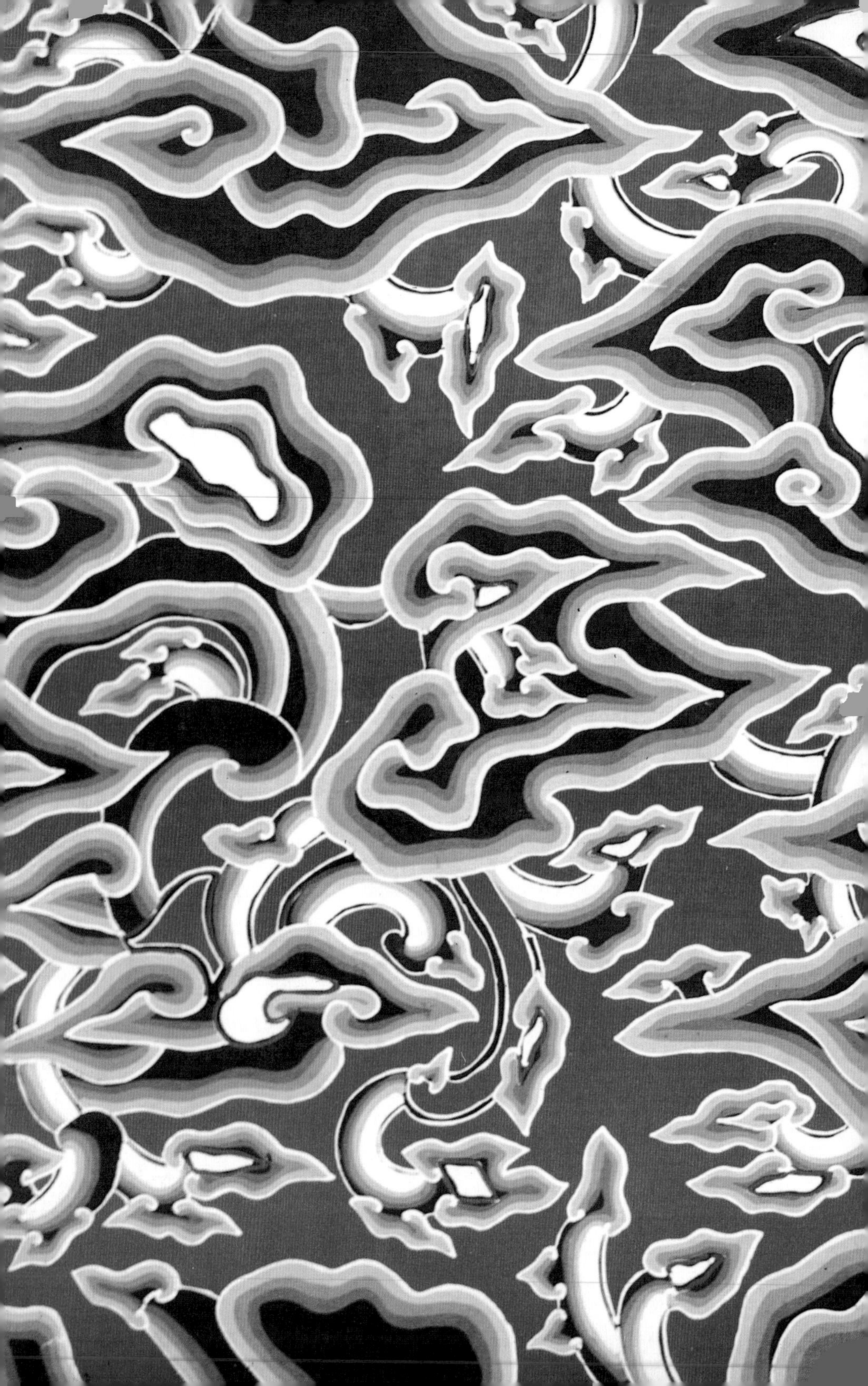

TEXTILES

Textile connoisseurs are quick to point out that Indonesia possesses the greatest diversity of traditional textiles in the world – the colorful bark cloths of Kalimantan, Irian Jaya, and Sulawesi; the plain weaves and exquisite *songket* silks of Sumatra; the beautiful *batik* of Java and the renowned *ikat* of the eastern islands. For Indonesians, textiles reconfirm and maintain many old and hallowed sartorial associations, and also symbolize wealth, status and religious beliefs.

Each of Indonesia's more than 350 ethnic and linguistic groups appears to have had, at one time or another, its own distinctive textile tradition. Some of these may date back 2,000 years or more, and are preserved today in remote upriver or mountainous areas. Many have also been influenced by foreign (especially Indian) textiles. As early as the 14th century, Indian fabrics were imported on a large scale, and during the 16th and 17th centuries, Indian *patola* cloths were particularly influential. Colonial rule also left its mark in textile use, and in the use of motifs derived from coins and porcelain.

Migrants as well as traders have played a role in the diffusion of textile techniques and motifs. For example, the northern coasts of Ceram and Irian Jaya were home to traditional weaving communities that may have originated in the Banggai islands, off the east coast of Sulawesi.

Symbolism: The spinning, dyeing and weaving of yarn were traditionally regarded as symbolic of the process of creation, and of human birth in particular. Weaving was generally an exclusively female activity. Men were permitted to participate only in the dyeing of certain colors of the thread, analogous with their role in human conception. Dyeing required the utmost privacy, with partitions often set up around the work area. Trespassers drank the dye so it wouldn't spoil. Pregnant, menstruating or sick women were excluded from the work.

Preceding pages: the Chinese cloud-and-rock motif is common along the north coast. Left, women wearing Sumban hinggi (ikat fabric). Right, "soul cloth" of the highland Batak tribes, of northcentral Sumatra.

The mounting of the threads upon the loom was done on an auspicious day, for at other times the threads would break. In some coastal villages, this meant a full moon and a high tide. If a death occurred in the village, the weaving would stop at once; otherwise, the spirit of the departed would exact vengeance, bringing sickness upon the weaver and causing the threads to lose their strength.

Finished products were sanctified by metaphysical and psychological associations, and so were regarded as powerful objects that

could protect the weaver; they were also often necessary for life-cycle rituals.

An entire language of textiles developed. For example, the brown-and-white *ragidup* (pattern of life) cloths of the Bataks were presented to a woman seven-months pregnant with her first child, as a "soul cloth" (*ulos ni tondi*). Her in-laws would drape it around her shoulders, and then the pattern would be "read" by a knowledgeable elder.

The best-known ritual textiles are the so-called ship cloths, once found in several areas of southern Sumatra and with a central motif that resembled a ship (or sometimes a bird). Human figures are generally depicted on the ships, often together with a variety of plants, animals and valuable objects. Up until the 19th century, a ship cloth was essential for the performance of all important southern Sumatran life-cycle rituals: birth, circumcision, marriage and death.

The sacred *maa* cloths of the Torájans of southern Sulawesi are carefully kept in special baskets, and are still considered necessary for all major rituals. Some maa are considered effective for the population of fertility spirits, and opening a powerful cloth is said to bring immediate rainfall.

Certain cloths, colors and motifs were set aside for the exclusive use of kings and nobles, and specific courtly duties were designated by particular fabrics. On many islands, textiles were required in dowries, and small squares of cloth were used for centuries as currency on the island of Buton.

Prehistoric development: Textiles from all periods of Indonesia's history are still being produced. The bark cloths found among upland tribes in Kalimantan, Sulawesi, and Irian Jaya display an extremely high degree of artistry, even though they harken back to a prehistoric development.

The Torajans boiled and fermented the inner bark of pandanus, mulberry or other trees before beating – with special wooden and stone mallets – the resultant pulp into extremely soft and pliable sheets. This cloth (*fuya*) was then dyed, painted or stamped using natural pigments. Finally, it was cut and sewn into headwraps, blouses, ponchos and bags, and often embroidered.

Clues as to the nature of earlier weavings may exist in the simple vegetable-fiber fabrics still found in some areas. Many of these do not even require a loom, and therefore fall somewhere in between the categories of weaving and basketry. Up until recently, certain tribes in Kalimantan, Flores, Sulawesi and Timor produced warrior tunics from bast (bark) fibers by twining them, a simple process in which two weft fibers are alternately wrapped above and below a passive warp.

Garments made of plaited grasses, pandanus or sago leaves, bamboo, palm and other plant fibers are not unknown today. And more sophisticated weavings produced from wild banana and pineapple fibers are still found in northeastern Sulawesi, and on the nearby islands of Sangihe and Talaud. The local name of these fabrics is *hote,* though they are also known as *koffo* or Manila hemp cloths. Most are decorated with geometric patterns (diamonds, scrolls, stars) formed by dyeing short lengths of fiber and incorporating them into the weft.

Since cotton requires cultivation, spinning and finally the use of a loom, it's generally thought of as a later development in a society, though it is, in fact, indigenous to the region and is grown and woven by many so-called primitive peoples. The technique closely associated with the advent of cotton in Indonesia is warp ikat. This is a traditional method of design in which the warp threads of a cloth are tie-dyed prior to being woven. Spinning the threads and preparing the dyes, tying the warp threads and then repeatedly immersing and drying them to achieve the desired color requires tremendous skill and patience, but in the hands of a master weaver, the result can be intricate, detailed motifs executed in deep, rich colors.

A fine cloth produced with natural dyes used to take eight to 10 years to complete. Natural-dye recipes are extremely complex, some of them requiring sophisticated carriers and mordants. Traditionally, it appears that indigo, *mengkudu* root (a red dye) and *soga* (a brown dye from roots and barks) were the main dyes; Turkey red and cochineal were popularized by Islamic traders.

All warp ikat are distinguished by the grouping of motifs into horizontal or longitudinal bands, a logical outcome of the warp-dyeing process. The most famous of these is the *hinggi* or mantle from the east coast of Sumba. These cloths are known for their rich colors, fine details, and bold, horizontal fields of stylized human and animal figures. They are normally produced in pairs, one to wrap around the body and one to drape over the shoulders, and have served as valuable trade items for centuries. They were exported extensively by the Dutch in the 19th century.

The tendency today is to produce large fields rather than several detailed bands, but the mass production of hinggi using quick chemical dyes has resulted in a lot of inferior work. So-called Sumba blankets are now produced in Bali and Java for the tourist trade, while the older, traditional pieces are scarce and astronomically priced.

People on the small arid islands of Roti and Sawu (between Sumba and Timor) also produce highly distinctive warp ikats recognizable by their narrow longitudinal bands, symmetrically patterned with rows of delicate flowers, stars or diamonds in white and red against a background of indigo. Roses and tulips are commonly depicted, copied from Dutch fabrics and porcelain.

Rotinese ikat is similar to those of Sawu in coloring and detail, but instead of longitudinal bands, it has adopted the compositional

Far left, Timor cloth with characteristically bright colors. Left, Limar cloth – ikat and songket. Above, tying off the thread in the ikat process prior to dying.

BATIK

Batik textiles are such an integral part of Javanese culture that it is difficult to imagine a time when the Javanese did not possess them. Yet the batik process, as we know it, may not be very old. Scholars debate whether or not the wax-resist dyeing process was brought to Java from India, where it has been known for centuries. Although names for various batik motifs have been traced to Javanese literary works dating from the 12th century, in fact, the terms *batik* and *tulis* (as applied to textile design) do not appear in Javanese court records until the Islamic period, when Indian traders were already active in the archipelago.

No one disputes, however, that Javanese batik is by far the finest in the world. There developed in Java, possibly in the 17th or 18th century, a tool known as the *canting*, a pen used to apply molten wax to cloth and capable of executing very detailed designs. A complex technology of wax and resin compounding, dye preparation and fixing, and a whole repertoire of elaborate motifs developed.

Starting with patience: Batik is produced on Sumatra, Sulawesi and Bali, but none can really compare with that of Java. The reason is quite simple: fine batik requires extraordinary patience. Beginning with a white silk or cotton cloth, the first step in handmade batik is to sketch a design. Areas that are not to be colored in the first dyeing must then be covered with wax. This can take hundreds of hours of painstaking labor. The cloth is then immersed in a prepared dye solution and dried. (When natural dyes were used, repeated immersions and dryings were required, and a single dyeing would take months.)

Next, the cloth must be re-waxed in preparation for the second dyeing. Sometimes this is accomplished by boiling out all the wax and re-waxing the entire cloth, but sometimes it involves scraping certain areas and adding wax to others. The dyeing and re-waxing process is then repeated as many times as is necessary to produce the number of colors required.

Dragons and clouds: At one time, the designs catalogued numbered over 1,000, and the regional styles numbered more than 20, primarily in central Java (Yogya and Solo) and along the northern coast. In central Java, batik-making was the preserve of aristocratic women, whereas on the north coast, it was an industry pursued by Chinese, Arab and even by Dutch artisans.

The differences in coloring and design were considerable. In central Java, certain motifs were set aside exclusively for the court and members of the aristocracy. These included *kawung* (large ovals arranged in fours like leaves of a clover), *ceplok* (an eight-pointed flower motif deriving from the Indian *patola*), *sawit* or *garuda* wings (of a mythical Hindu bird), and the *parang rusak barong*, or broken sword motif, that consists of diagonal rows of interlocking scrolls.

Two primary colors were used, indigo and *soga*, a brown dye obtained from the bark of a tree. These came in many shades, and elaborate dye recipes called for the addition of substances like palm sugar, bananas, fermented cassava and chicken meat.

On the north coast, yellows, mauves, ochres, greens and pale blues were more popular, showing Chinese, European, and Islamic influence. In Cirebon, a Chinese clouds motif that symbolizes mystical energy was incorporated in all of the courtly batik designs. In one of the most famous motifs, the *mega mendung* or menacing rain clouds, they appear in bright contrasting shades of red, blue, pink or green, like some supernatural storm. Chinese dragons and phoenixes appeared together with Hindu *naga* and elephants and European lions, and some central Javanese motifs were executed in uncharacteristically bright colors. The most popular designs were of European origin, however: bouquets of flowers with hovering hummingbirds, or elegant, long-legged storks and herons.

It is fair to say that at the turn of the century, everyone in Java wore batik. The advent of *batik cap* (batik produced with the use of a stamp, the *cap*) revitalized the industry during the 1890s, as even the peasants were then able to afford this cruder, mass-produced product. Batik was also widely exported from Java to other islands.

scheme of the Indian patola cloth – a field of many eight-pointed stars or flowers framed with striped borders and bands of triangles (*tumpal*) at either end.

Two types of simple back-strap looms are used for warp ikat. With both, the warp tension is maintained by means of a strap placed around the weaver's back as she sits on the ground. String heddles are employed to create individual sheds and a bamboo comb is sometimes introduced to maintain the warp spacing.

Weft and double ikat are found in only a few scattered areas, and it is thought that the technique was introduced from India. The distinguishing feature of Indonesian weft ikat, fashioned by tie-dyeing the weft threads of a cloth before weaving, is that it is generally produced in silk.

Weft ikat occurs primarily in the Islamic coastal trading areas: Palembang, Riau, Gresik and Ujung Pandang, but also on the island of Bali. The Palembang and Bangka weft ikat are extremely sophisticated, done on silk in rich tones of red, blue and yellow, often with supplementary gold threads in the weft. Indian, Javanese and Chinese motifs are all employed, sometimes simultaneously, reflecting the cosmopolitan milieu of these trading ports. Today, inferior examples are still produced near Palembang, and are worn on holidays and at weddings as part of a formal, ritual costume.

Tenganan Pegeringsingan, in eastern Bali, is one of only three places in the world (the others being in India and Japan) to traditionally produce the fabulously difficult double ikat – fabrics decorated by tie-dyeing both warp and weft before weaving. These *geringsing* cloths are dyed with indigo and mengkudu red, producing a reddish-purple design on a cream background. Loosely woven, some apparently imitate the Indian patola (also a double ikat). Others are clearly indigenous in design, such as the *geringsing wayang kebo,* with its symmetrical groupings of wayang figures around a central four-pointed star.

Above, a woman "wears" the weaving loom in order to work.

Considered by the Balinese to be the most sacred of all textiles, geringsing cloths are used in many important ceremonies throughout the island, including tooth filings and cremations. Within the village of Tenganan, wearers of these cloths were once said to be protected from evil influences and illness (geringsing means "without sickness"). The fact that Tenganan is one of the few Bali Aga (original, or non-Hindu) villages on the island is intriguing. Either the geringsing cloth is of very ancient, pre-Hindu origin or the production of the cloth was surrounded by certain taboos or restrictions that only the Bali Aga disregarded.

It appears that a textile revolution took place in Indonesia after the 14th century, when Islamic (and later European) traders began to flood the archipelago with Indian textiles. Not that Indian textiles were new – they had probably been imported for centuries for the nobility. Rather, it was the scale of the trade and its impact on local textile usage that was unprecedented.

The use of cotton and silk was traditionally the preserve of the Indonesian aristocracy, but a democratization of textiles occurred as

a result of the spice trade. Traders discovered that they could obtain valuable Indonesian spices in exchange for Indian cottons and silks. Indonesians, meanwhile, discovered that they could have fine textiles in exchange for easily-gathered cloves, nutmeg, peppers and aromatic woods.

Perhaps the most important innovation of this period was the cotton plain weave, now found throughout Indonesia and worn by the majority as the all-purpose *sarung* or body wrap. Noted by its simple striped or checked design, it was a significant advance over the cruder bark cloths and plaited vegetable-fiber fabrics that commoners previously wore.

These plain weaves today go under a variety of names, and are produced in or around the great coastal trading centers founded during the Islamic period – on the north coast of Java, the north and east coasts of Sumatra, and in south Sulawesi. The plain weave is found inland also, for instance, in central Java, where the striped *lurik* is a part of the traditional Javanese costume, and also in the Minangkabau regions of central Sumatra.

The Indian textile revolution extended also to fabrics that were considered rare and valuable, or even magical. The Indian patola, a double-ikat silk fabric produced in Gujarat, became the single most influential and widely imitated textile in Indonesia. It was incorporated into the ritual life of many people and became part of the costumes of kings on many islands, including Java.

The bright, shimmering colors of the patola must have appeared quite unusual compared to the more somber reds, browns and blues of the native ikat. As less of the cloth was imported after 1800, many weavers in Indonesia set about producing replicas in silk and cotton. Today, the characteristic eight-pointed flower, or *jilamprang,* design is seen everywhere in the archipelago.

Another textile inspired by the flowering of trade with the Islamic world is the songket – weavings produced with gold-and-silver-covered thread imported from India. The most famous songket are those of Palembang, with glittering gold threads woven into bright red silk to form a fine geometrical pattern that often covers the entire cloth. Unlike the plain weave, in which the warp and weft threads alternate in a regular fashion, the songket is produced by "floating" the metallic weft over and under a number of warp threads at a time.

The Minangkabau of western Sumatra are also known for their silver-threaded songket, produced against a background of wine-red silk. And in Bali, a whole range of songket are produced, from simple sarungs with small geometric gold or silver patterns, to wildly exuberant festive costumes combining gold and silver designs in silks of purple, green, yellow and blue. Some of the traditional Balinese animal and wayang figures are also executed in songket.

Left, Lembata woman spinning cotton. Right, the most sacred textile in Bali – geringsingan cloth.

Indonesian food is perhaps less well-known than its Asian counterparts in China, Japan or Thailand, but that doesn't mean it isn't worthy of international acclaim. In fact, Indonesian cuisine is so varied that travelers can be assured of finding at least one dish that becomes a lifelong favorite.

The country's strategic and historic location astride the Asian and Pacific trade routes has resulted in a mixture of influences evident in many aspects of Indonesian life – and particularly in the archipelago's cuisine.

Chinese influence is most obvious in stir-fried food produced in huge steaming *wok*. Marinated meat on skewers, known locally as *sate,* owes its heritage to Middle Eastern kebabs. And the nation's popular curries could only have originated in India. But in today's Indonesia, all of these various culinary traditions have been blended and localized to form regional cuisines on nearly every major island.

The national staple: Rice is the staple food on most of the islands, and nearly every menu offers dishes prefixed with the word *nasi,* which means they are prepared or served with rice. Perhaps the most famous is *nasi goreng:* fried rice with an assortment of vegetables and chicken, prawns or meat – or even a combination of the three. If the word *istimewa* ("special") appears, it means the dish comes with a fried egg on top.

Another staple is *mie,* or noodles. In *mie goreng* (fried noodles), the noodles are fried in coconut oil with meat, vegetables and perhaps fried egg, with hot chili shrimp paste and lime on the side. Both mie goreng and nasi goreng are popular breakfast dishes.

One of the best ways to sample a wide variety of Indonesian food is to order *nasi campur.* But be warned: this sampler dish is a plateful of steamed rice, fried white bait fish, fresh and preserved vegetables, fried egg, roasted peanuts, shredded coconut, fiery chili *sambal* sauce, oversized crispy *krupuk* (fried rice and prawn crackers), and a selection of beef, chicken and mutton sate.

Another good introduction to local cuisine is a traditional *nasi padang* restaurant, where an array of tasty local dishes will be offered at the table, including *ayam* (chicken), *lembu* (beef), *kambing* (goat), *sayur* (vegetables), *ikan goreng* (fried fish), various curries and maybe an assortment of entrails, plus a huge helping of steamed rice. Diners are charged only for what is eaten, so depending on budget, try a variety of dishes, or do as most locals and choose only a few main dishes and fill up on the rice. As a general rule, the vegetable dishes are cheapest and the beef the most expensive. (To avoid complications, it's a good idea to find out the price of each dish before beginning the meal.)

Colonial culinary influence: Much of the Dutch influence has long since faded away, but a more elaborate form of the nasi padang known as *rijstaffel* traces its roots back to colonial times. Rijstaffel (literally, "rice table") is a series of meat and vegetable courses, served with rice and spicy condiments, presented at the table with much ceremony by a string of sarung-clad waitresses.

Expect about five to six courses in the typical rijstaffel meal, a far cry from Dutch colonial days when the serving might include as many as 350 separate dishes. Due to the elaborate nature of this meal, it's primarily offered at tourist restaurants and hotels.

Other popular dishes found throughout the archipelago include *ayam goreng* (fried chicken), *cap cai* (an Indonesian version of chop suey), and *rendang* (meat chunks served in a rich and spicy sauce). Off the beaten track, it's a good idea to check what type of meat has been used in the rendang to avoid unwanted contact with animal innards. *Soto ayam* is a popular chicken soup, thickened with *santen* (coconut cream). *Sop* is somewhere between a soup and stew, a thick broth laden with vegetables or meat, or both.

Left, Javanese desserts and fruits. Above, broiled sate, Balinese style.

Soybeans are a rich source of protein for Indonesians, and there are many popular soybean-based dishes, including *tahu* (soybean cake) and *tempe* (fermented soybeans), often served in individual portions wrapped in banana leaves.

Regional cuisines: Regional specialties are as varied as the country's geography and people. Even on some of the larger islands, there are distinct culinary differences from region to region. Java is a good example. Perhaps the best known dish from Jakarta and West Java is *gado-gado*, a vegetable-and-tofu salad laced with a rich sweet peanut sauce and served with plenty of *krupuk* crackers. In general, in central Java, the food will turn sweeter and more spicy. In Surabaya and East Java, the food is saltier than elsewhere on the island, but still plenty spicy.

The traditional foundations of Balinese cuisine are duck and pork dishes, as well as sweet and sticky rice treats like *lonton* and *ketan*. But the recent influx of tourists means that just about any type of food – from elsewhere in Indonesia and the rest of the world – is readily available in Bali.

South Sulawesi is known for its seafood dishes that run the gamut from shrimp, lobster and crab, to carp, eel and sea slugs. The Irianese are said to offer the best *ikan bakar* (baked fish) in the whole country. Some of

the Dayak tribes of Kalimantan consider roast lizard a mouthwatering delicacy. The grass that cows belch up after their first digestion process is a popular dish in northern Sumatra, while mice and dogs are common fare in Minahasa kitchens.

As a general rule, the more rural the area, the higher one's chances of having meals prepared with meat and animal parts that may not agree with palate (or conscience).

Traditional Indonesian eating houses are known as *warung* and are makeshift foodstalls set up on the pavements of busy streets and in market places. Not the most romantic setting, but most favorites can be found at ridiculously low prices. The standards of hygiene are low and refrigeration virtually nonexistent, so cast-iron stomachs are a prerequisite for sampling street fare.

If you don't want to miss the cultural experience of visiting a warung, make a relatively "safe" meal by ordering thick, deliciously sweet coffee (*kopi*) or some fresh fruit that is peeled. Or try some of the warung designed for tourists.

Coffee, tea or Bintang? Indonesians often drink hot Chinese tea (*teh pahit*) with their meals, but iced tea (*teh es*), local coffee (kopi), and fruit juices and bottled sodas are usually available.

Local alcoholic beverages include Bintang beer (whose roots lie in the popular Dutch Heineken brand), *tuak* (palm wine), *brem* (rice wine), *badek* (rice liquor) and *arak,* the apex of potent rice spirits.

The rainbow of fresh tropical fruit available in Indonesia often astounds visitors. There are more than 40 varieties of bananas (*pisang*), pomelos (*jeruk Bali*), and pineapples (*nanas*), plus an array of lesser-known delicacies. Durians might best be described as large green "hand grenades" that smell rather strange but taste like caramel peach. Rambutans are bright red and have a strange hairy, if not spiky, exterior, but the flavor is very similar to lychee. And the skin of the *salak* (which is said to taste like an apple) closely resembles that of a snake.

Bananas, because of their supply, make a popular dessert baked, deep-fried of boiled. But rice also serves as a common dessert base. Look for *ketan* (rice pudding) and *babur santen* (rice porridge cooked in coconut milk, with a palm sugar sweetener).

Perhaps the most popular dessert is *es campur,* the Indonesian equivalent of the ice cream sundae. Es campur doesn't have a universally-accepted set of ingredients, but shaved ice is usually the base. A number of things can be poured over the ice, including fruit syrup and coconut milk, cubes of brightly-colored gelatin, tapioca or steamed rice cakes and various other sweet things.

It should also be mentioned that Western food and other specialty cuisines are readily available at the more popular tourist destinations and in major cities.

Left, ever-popular durian. Right, a girl from Ambon in dance costume holds dish of fruit.

INDONESIA

While the airplane increasingly makes exploring Indonesia reasonably certain and tidy, Indonesia is one of those lands that, if the imagination is permitted to roam and ramble, begs to be explored and traveled on the ground and over the water. It is a country of islands, large and small, an archipelago wrapping itself around one-eighth of the world's circumference. It simply begs to be traveled by boat, perhaps best by yacht, if available.

Jakarta is, of course, Indonesia's capital city and unquestionably the only true metropolis of the country. Nestled on Java's north coast, Jakarta is not especially beautiful nor walkable, although at night, its electrified skyline is actually quite elegant. But Jakarta is the city of hope for many people, the one place that best exemplifies a united Indonesia.

Java is home to over half of the nation's population, easy to understand considering its superbly fertile soil. Volcanoes have made it so, and volcanoes continue to make it so. On Java, one also finds some of Indonesia's most elegant aesthetic endeavors – music, dance and drama, textiles, architecture.

Sumatra is where spice traders and Islam first anchored after passage from India, and later from Europe. Unlike Java, Sumatra's soil is not especially good for farming, although volcanoes thrive. But there are verdant jungles and wondrous gatherings of wildlife, and perhaps Indonesia's most independent people.

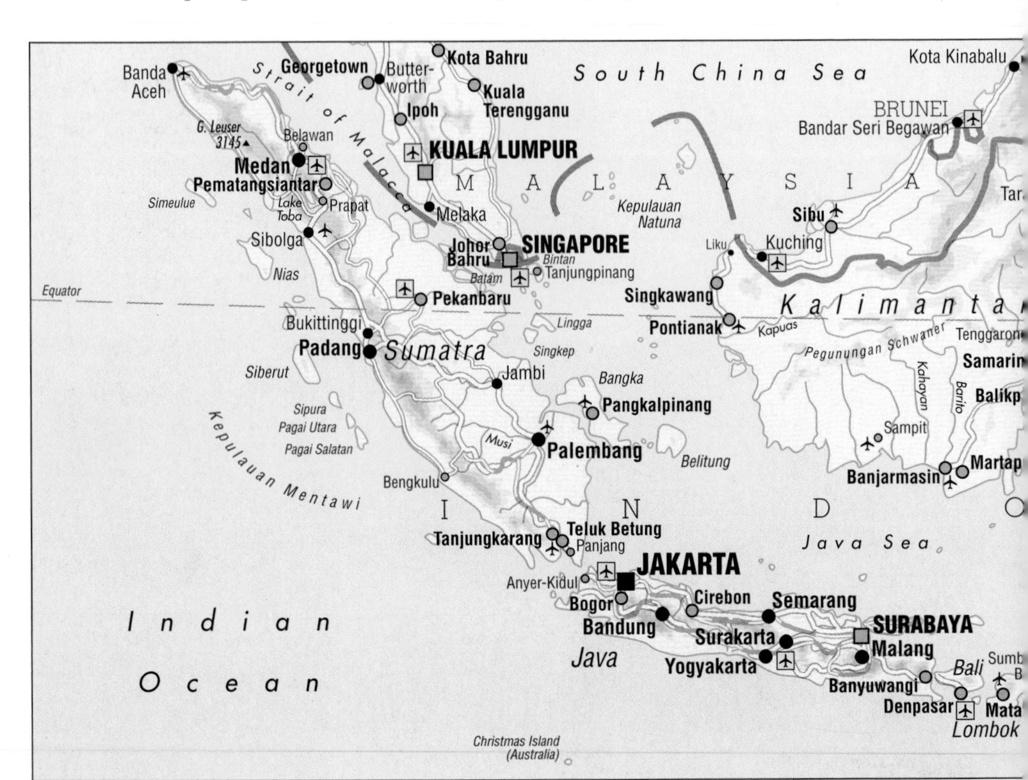

On the other side of Java is Bali, which needs little introduction, as most visitors to Indonesia seem to be heading directly there. Beyond Bali is Lombok, and then Nusa Tenggara, or what the colonial Europeans called the Lesser Sundas. From here eastward, the archipelago islands are small in comparison to Java and Sumatra, at least until one reaches New Guinea, the western half of which is Irian Jaya, a land of unknown peoples and mountain valleys until early this century. Due north of Java is Kalimantan, Indonesia's portion of the island of Borneo. Kalimantan was once synonymous with remoteness and inaccessibility and headhunters; now it suggests timber wealth and oil frontiers.

East are Sulawesi and Maluku, those magical Spice Islands. At one time, in all the world, only here did nutmeg and cloves and mace grow, making these islands the obsession of European nations. It took a world war to knock lose the colonial grip, leaving in its place *Republik Indonesia.*

Note: In most cases, we use Indonesian geographical terms in this book, rather than English. For example, Lake Toba is Danau Toba, Biak Island is Pulau Biak, and Mount Bromo is Gunung Bromo.

Preceding pages: mountain landscape; seeking shelter from monsoon rains; Cirebon boats; rural village, or kampung.

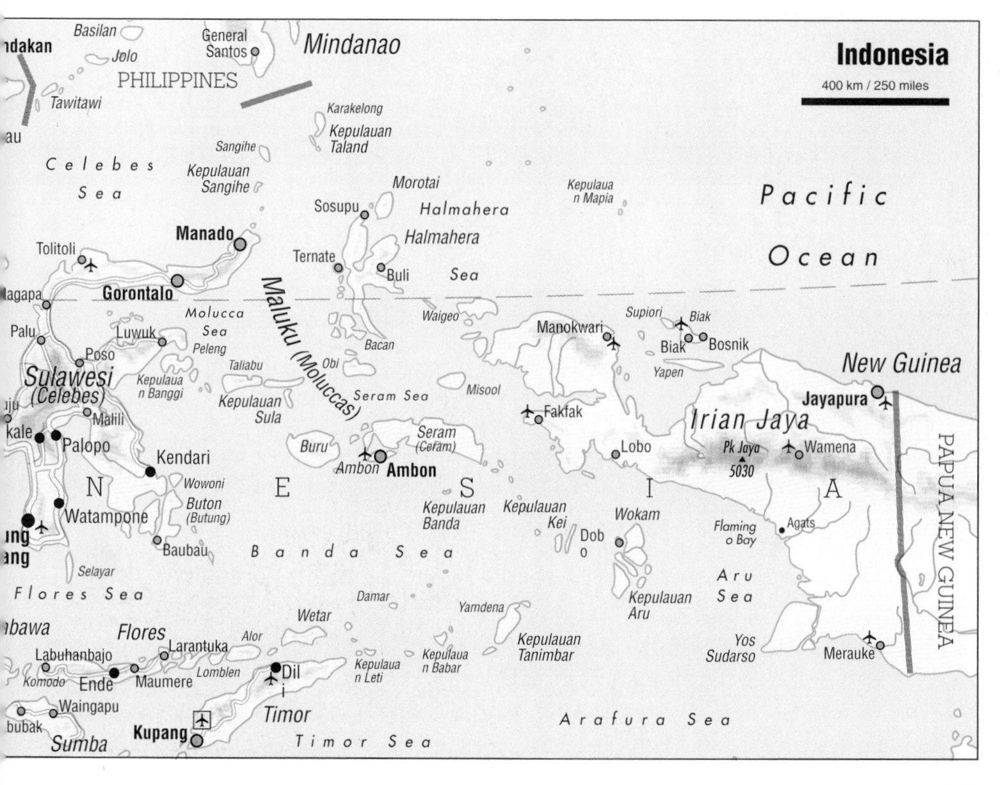

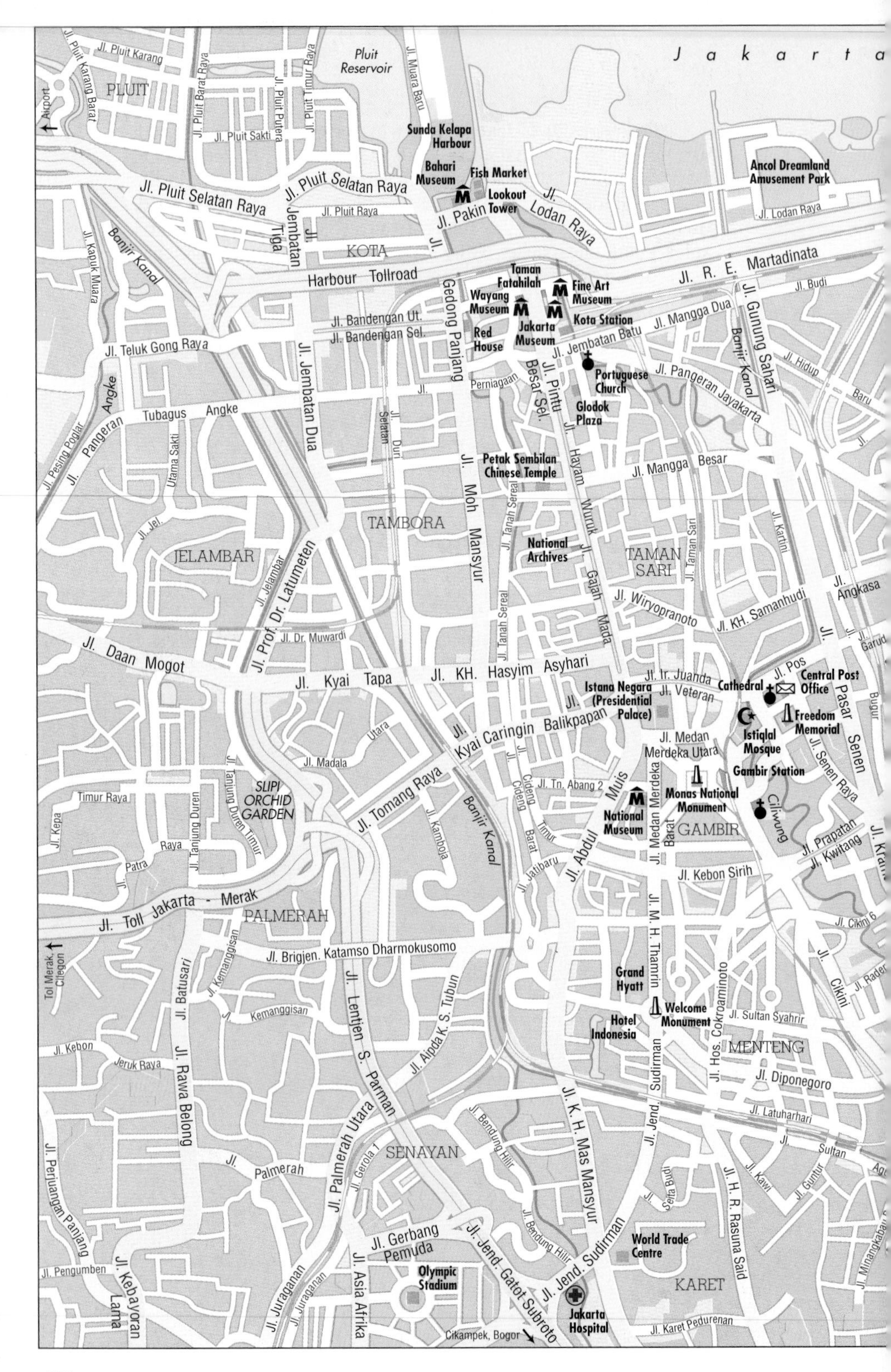
Jakarta
Pluit Reservoir
PLUIT
Airport
Jl. Pluit Karang
Jl. Pluit Karang Barat
Jl. Pluit Barat Raya
Jl. Pluit Putera
Jl. Pluit Timur Raya
Jl. Pluit Sakti
Jl. Muara Baru
Sunda Kelapa Harbour
Bahari Museum
Fish Market
Lookout Tower
Ancol Dreamland Amusement Park
Jl. Pluit Selatan Raya
Jl. Pluit Raya
Jl. Jembatan Tiga
Jl. Pakin
Jl. Lodan Raya
KOTA
Harbour Tollroad
Jl. R. E. Martadinata
Jl. Kapuk Muara
Banjir Kanal
Taman Fatahilah
Fine Art Museum
Wayang Museum
Jakarta Museum
Kota Station
Red House
Jl. Bandengan Ut.
Jl. Bandengan Sel.
Gedong Panjang
Jl. Jembatan Batu
Jl. Mangga Dua
Jl. Gunung Sahari
Jl. Budi
Jl. Teluk Gong Raya
Portuguese Church
Jl. Pangeran Jayakarta
Jl. Hidup Baru
Jl. Pintu Besar Sel.
Perniagaan
Glodok Plaza
Jl. Pangeran Tubagus Angke
Jl. Pesing Poglar
Utama Sakti
Jl. Jembatan Dua
Jl. Selatan
Jl. Duri
Petak Sembilan Chinese Temple
Jl. Mangga Besar
Jl. Hayam Wuruk
Jl. Moh Mansyur
TAMBORA
JELAMBAR
Jl. Jel.
Jl. Jelambar
Jl. Prof. Dr. Latumeten
Jl. Tanah Sereal
National Archives
TAMAN SARI
Jl. Taman Sari
Jl. Kartini
Jl. Gajah Mada
Jl. Wiryopranoto
Jl. KH. Samanhudi
Jl. Angkasa
Jl. Garud
Jl. Dr. Muwardi
Jl. Daan Mogot
Jl. Kyai Tapa
Jl. KH. Hasyim Asyhari
Jl. Ir. Juanda
Jl. Veteran
Istana Negara (Presidential Palace)
Cathedral
Jl. Pos
Central Post Office
Freedom Memorial
Jl. Pasar Senen
Bugur
Istiqlal Mosque
Jl. Kyai Caringin
Jl. Balikpapan
Jl. Madala
Utara
Jl. Medan Merdeka Utara
Gambir Station
Jl. Senen Raya
Timur Raya
SLIPI ORCHID GARDEN
Jl. Tanjung Duren
Jl. Tanjung Duren Timur
Jl. Tomang Raya
Jl. Kamboja
Banjir Kanal
Jl. Cideng Barat
Jl. Tn. Abang 2
Timur
Jl. Abdul Muis
Monas National Monument
National Museum
Jl. Medan Merdeka Barat
GAMBIR
Ciliwung
Jl. Prapatan
Jl. Kwitang
Jl. Kepa
Raya
Patra
Jl. Jatibaru
Jl. Kebon Sirih
Jl. Toll Jakarta - Merak
PALMERAH
Jl. Cikini 6
Tol Merak, Cilegon
Jl. Brigjen. Katamso Dharmokusomo
Jl. Kemanggisan
Jl. Batusari
Jl. Lentjen S. Parman
Jl. Aipda K. S. Tubun
Jl. M. H. Thamrin
Grand Hyatt
Welcome Monument
Hotel Indonesia
Jl. Hos. Cokroaminoto
Jl. Sultan Syahrir
Jl. Cikini
Jl. Raden
MENTENG
Jl. Kebon Jeruk Raya
Jl. Rawa Belong
Jl. Jend. Sudirman
Jl. Diponegoro
Jl. Latuharhari
Jl. Sultan Agung
Jl. Peruangan Panjang
Jl. Palmerah
Jl. Palmerah Utara
Jl. Gerola 1
SENAYAN
Jl. Bendung Hilir
Jl. K. H. Mas Mansyur
Jl. Setia Budi
Jl. H. R. Rasuna Said
Jl. Kawi
Jl. Guntur
Jl. Minangkabau
Jl. Gerbang Pemuda
Jl. Jend. Gatot Subroto
World Trade Centre
Jl. Pengumben
Jl. Kebayoran Lama
Jl. Juraganan
Jl. Asia Afrika
Olympic Stadium
KARET
Jakarta Hospital
Cikampek, Bogor
Jl. Karet Pedurenan

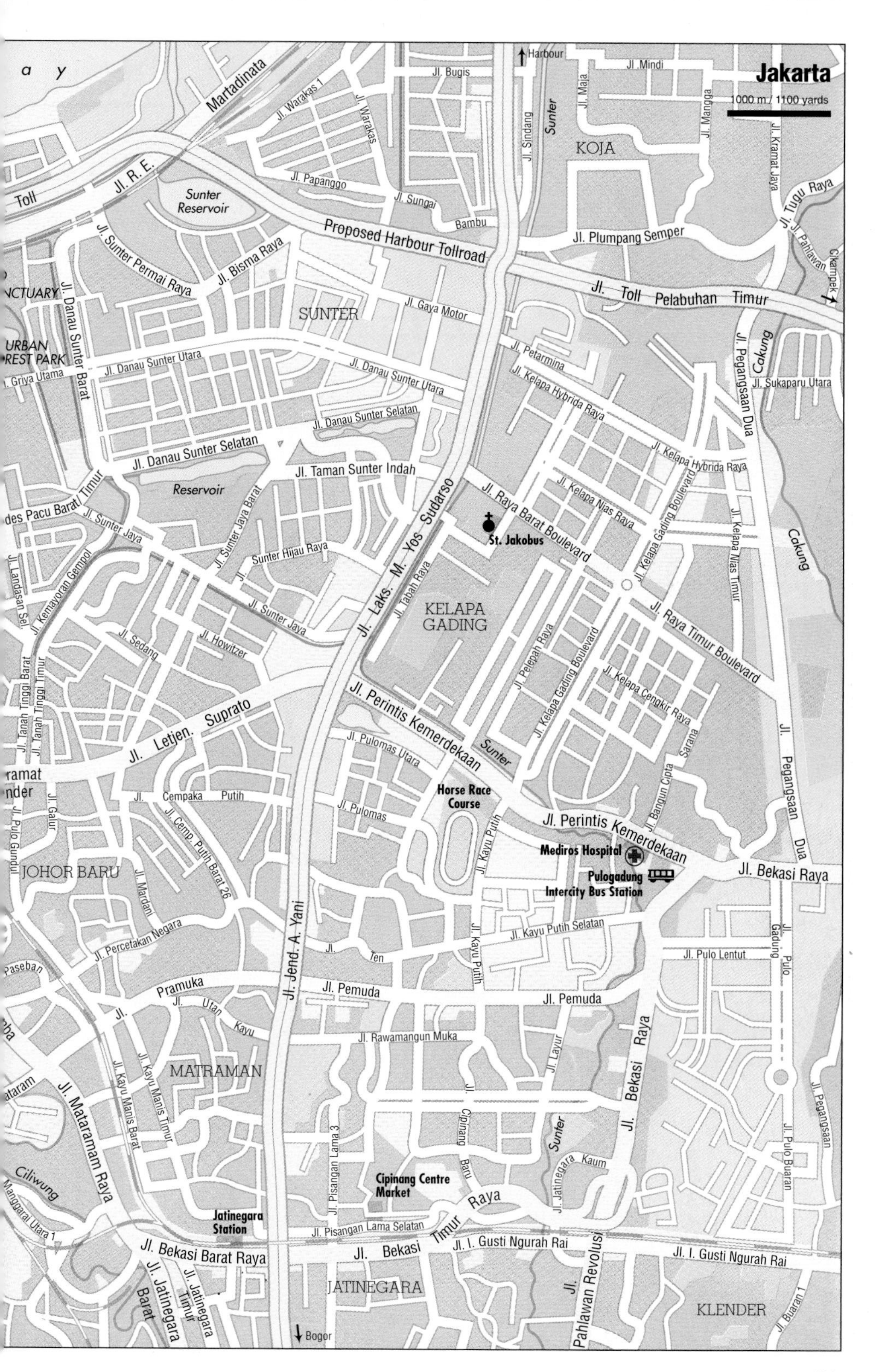
Jakarta
1000 m / 1100 yards
Harbour
Jl. Mindi
Jl. Bugis
Martadinata
Jl. Warakas 1
Jl. Warakas
Jl. Sindang
Sunter
Jl. Maja
KOJA
Jl. Mangga
Jl. Kramat Jaya
Toll
Jl. R. E.
Sunter Reservoir
Jl. Papanggo
Jl. Sungai
Bambu
Proposed Harbour Tollroad
Jl. Plumpang Semper
Jl. Tugu Raya
Jl. Pahlawan
Cikampek
Jl. Sunter Permai Raya
Jl. Bisma Raya
Jl. Toll Pelabuhan Timur
Jl. Danau Sunter Barat
Jl. Gaya Motor
SUNTER
Jl. Danau Sunter Utara
Jl. Petarmina
Jl. Pegangsaan Dua
Cakung
Jl. Sukaparu Utara
Jl. Kelapa Hybrida Raya
Jl. Danau Sunter Selatan
Jl. Taman Sunter Indah
Reservoir
Jl. Laks. M. Yos Sudarso
Jl. Raya Barat Boulevard
St. Jakobus
Jl. Kelapa Nias Raya
Jl. Kelapa Gading Boulevard
Jl. Kelapa Nias Timur
Jl. Sunter Jaya Barat
Jl. Sunter Jaya
Jl. Sunter Hijau Raya
Jl. Landasan Sel.
Jl. Kemayoran Gempol
Jl. Tabah Raya
KELAPA GADING
Jl. Raya Timur Boulevard
Jl. Sedang
Jl. Howitzer
Jl. Pelepah Raya
Jl. Kelapa Cengkir Raya
Jl. Tanah Tinggi Barat
Jl. Tanah Tinggi Timur
Jl. Letjen. Suprato
Jl. Perintis Kemerdekaan
Sunter
Sarana
Jl. Pulomas Utara
Horse Race Course
Jl. Bangun Cipta
Jl. Cempaka Putih
Jl. Cemp. Putih Barat 26
Jl. Pulomas
Jl. Kayu Putih
Mediros Hospital
Pulogadung Intercity Bus Station
Jl. Bekasi Raya
Jl. Pulo Gundul
Jl. Galur
JOHOR BARU
Jl. Mardani
Jl. Percetakan Negara
Jl. Kayu Putih Selatan
Jl. Ten
Jl. Pulo Lentut
Jl. Pulo Gadung
Paseban
Jl. Pramuka
Jl. Utan Kayu
Jl. Jend. A. Yani
Jl. Pemuda
Jl. Rawamangun Muka
Jl. Layur
Jl. Bekasi Raya
MATRAMAN
Jl. Kayu Manis Barat
Jl. Kayu Manis Timur
Jl. Mataraman Raya
Jl. Cipinang Baru
Jl. Pegangsaan
Jl. Pulo Buaran
Ciliwung
Manggarai Utara 1
Jl. Pisangan Lama 3
Cipinang Centre Market
Sunter
Jl. Jatinegara Kaum
Jatinegara Station
Jl. Pisangan Lama Selatan
Raya
Jl. Bekasi Timur
Jl. I. Gusti Ngurah Rai
Jl. Bekasi Barat Raya
Jl. Jatinegara Barat
Jl. Jatinegara Timur
JATINEGARA
Jl. Pahlawan Revolusi
KLENDER
Jl. Buaran 1
Bogor

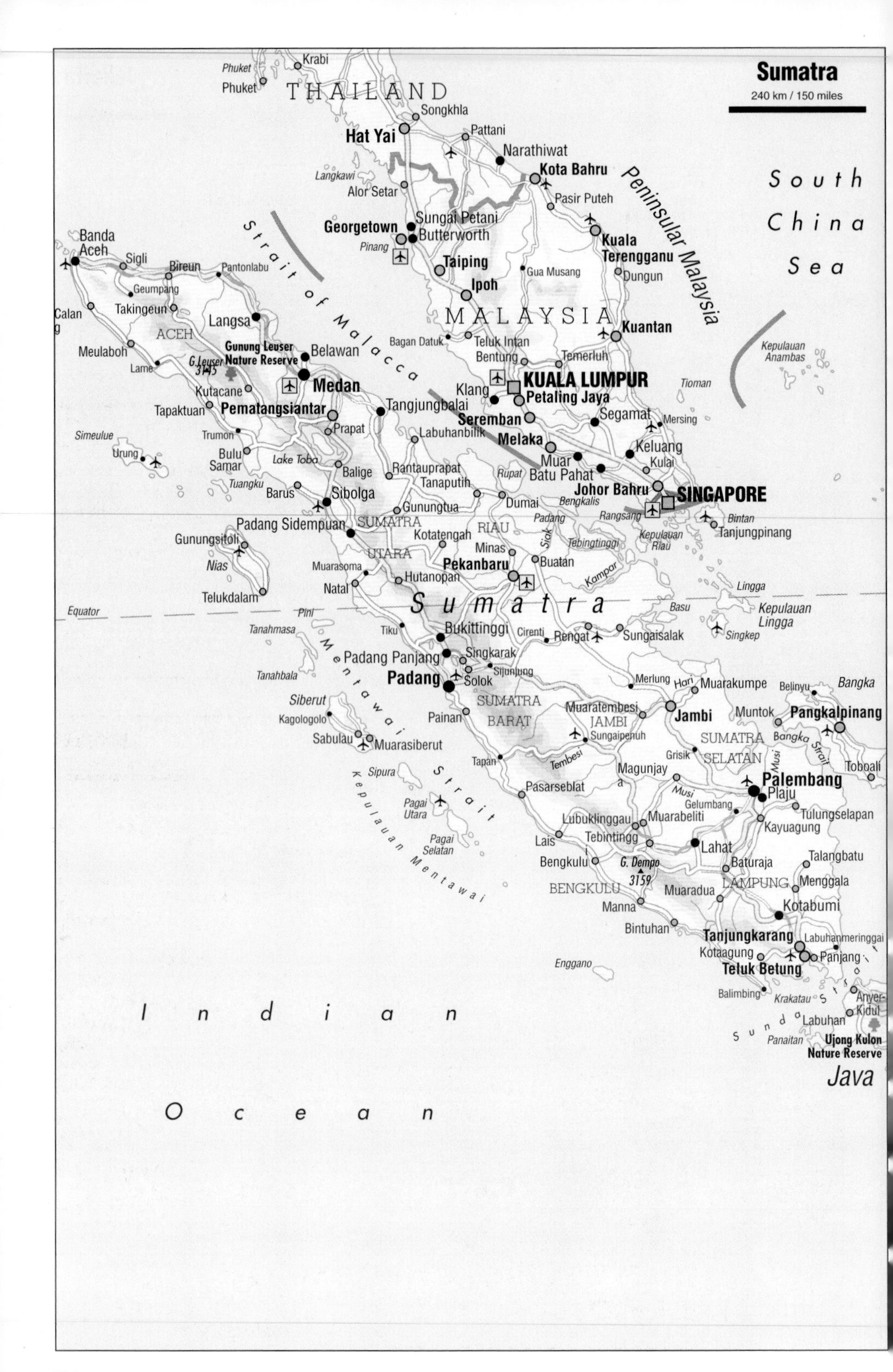
Sumatra
240 km / 150 miles
South China Sea
THAILAND
MALAYSIA
Peninsular Malaysia
Strait of Malacca
Sumatra
Indian Ocean
Mentawai Strait
Kepulauan Mentawai
Java
Krabi
Phuket
Songkhla
Hat Yai
Pattani
Narathiwat
Kota Bahru
Langkawi
Alor Setar
Pasir Puteh
Sungai Petani
Georgetown
Butterworth
Pinang
Taiping
Kuala Terengganu
Gua Musang
Dungun
Ipoh
Kuantan
Bagan Datuk
Teluk Intan
Bentung
Temerluh
KUALA LUMPUR
Petaling Jaya
Klang
Seremban
Melaka
Segamat
Mersing
Tioman
Kepulauan Anambas
Muar
Batu Pahat
Keluang
Kulai
Johor Bahru
SINGAPORE
Banda Aceh
Sigli
Bireun
Pantonlabu
Geumpang
Takingeun
Calan
Langsa
ACEH
Meulaboh
Gunung Leuser Nature Reserve
G. Leuser 3145
Belawan
Lame
Medan
Kutacane
Tapaktuan
Pematangsiantar
Tangjungbalai
Prapat
Labuhanbilik
Simeulue
Trumon
Urung
Bulu Samar
Lake Toba
Balige
Rantauprapat
Tanaputih
Rupat
Tuangku
Barus
Sibolga
Gunungtua
Dumai
Bengkalis
Padang Sidempuan
SUMATRA UTARA
RIAU
Padang
Rangsang
Bintan
Tanjungpinang
Gunungsitoli
Kotatengah
Siak
Tebingtinggi
Kepulauan Riau
Nias
Minas
Muarasoma
Pekanbaru
Buatan
Hutanopan
Kampar
Natal
Lingga
Telukdalam
Equator
Pini
Basu
Kepulauan Lingga
Tanahmasa
Tiku
Bukittinggi
Cirenti
Rengat
Sungaisalak
Singkep
Padang Panjang
Singkarak
Tanahbala
Sijunjung
Padang
Solok
Merlung
Hari
Muarakumpe
Belinyu
Bangka
Siberut
SUMATRA BARAT
Muaratembesi
Jambi
Muntok
Pangkalpinang
Kagologolo
Painan
JAMBI
Sabulau
Muarasiberut
Sungaipenuh
SUMATRA SELATAN
Bangka Strait
Tapan
Tembesi
Grisik
Musi
Toboali
Sipura
Magunjay
Palembang
Plaju
Pasarseblat
Musi
Gelumbang
Pagai Utara
Tulungselapan
Lubuklinggau
Muarabeliti
Kayuagung
Lais
Tebintingg
Lahat
Pagai Selatan
Bengkulu
G. Dempo 3159
Baturaja
Talangbatu
BENGKULU
Muaradua
LAMPUNG
Menggala
Manna
Kotabumi
Bintuhan
Tanjungkarang
Labuhanmeringgai
Kotaagung
Panjang
Enggano
Teluk Betung
Balimbing
Krakatau
Anyer-Kidul
Labuhan
Sunda Strait
Panaitan
Ujong Kulon Nature Reserve

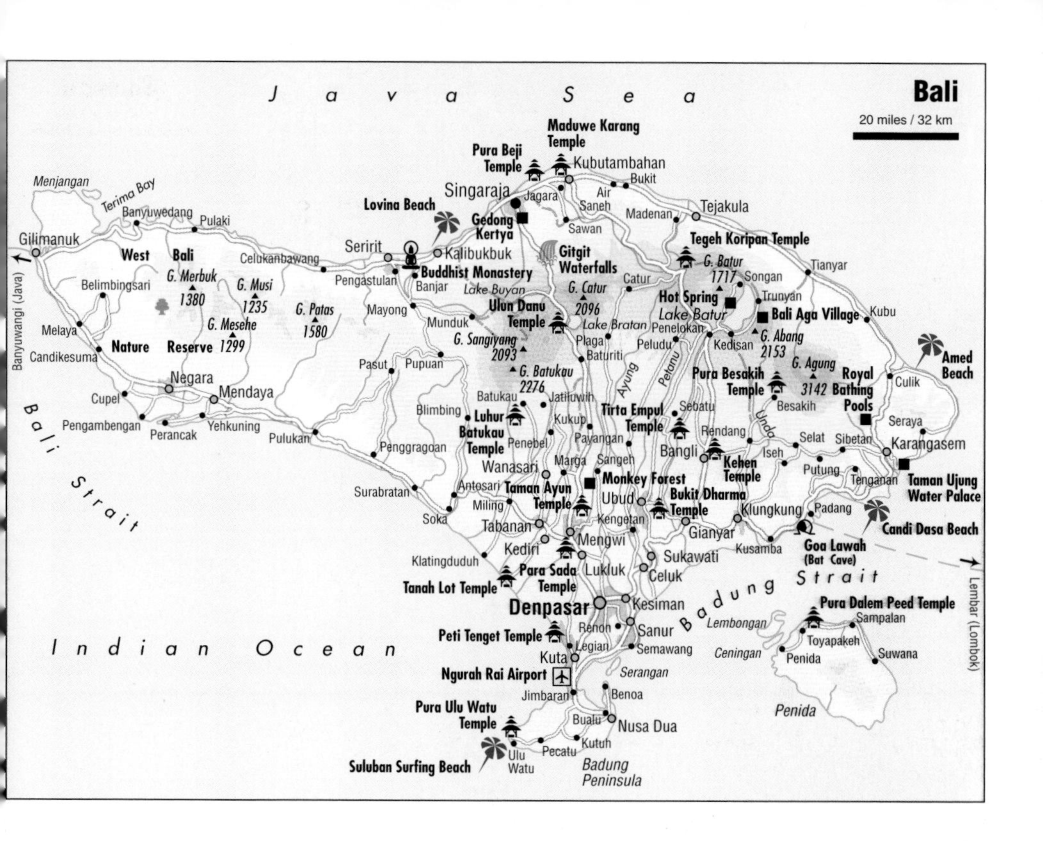
Bali
20 miles / 32 km
Java Sea
Indian Ocean
Bali Strait
Badung Strait
Banyuwangi (Java)
Lembar (Lombok)
Menjangan
Terima Bay
Banyuwedang
Pulaki
Gilimanuk
West Bali Nature Reserve
G. Merbuk 1380
G. Musi 1235
G. Patas 1580
G. Mesehe 1299
Belimbingsari
Melaya
Candikesuma
Negara
Mendaya
Cupel
Pengambengan
Perancak
Yehkuning
Pulukan
Celukanbawang
Seririt
Pengastulan
Banjar
Kalibukbuk
Buddhist Monastery
Lovina Beach
Singaraja
Jagara
Gedong Kertya
Pura Beji Temple
Maduwe Karang Temple
Kubutambahan
Bukit
Air Saneh
Sawan
Madenan
Tejakula
Gitgit Waterfalls
Lake Buyan
Mayong
Munduk
Ulun Danu Temple
G. Catur 2096
Catur
G. Sangiyang 2093
G. Batukau 2276
Lake Bratan
Plaga
Baturiti
Pasut
Pupuan
Batukau
Jatiluwih
Blimbing
Luhur Batukau Temple
Penebel
Kukup
Payangan
Penggragoan
Wanasari
Marga
Sangeh
Surabratan
Antosari
Miling
Taman Ayun Temple
Monkey Forest
Ubud
Soka
Tabanan
Kengetan
Kediri
Mengwi
Klatingduduh
Para Sada Temple
Lukluk
Tanah Lot Temple
Denpasar
Kesiman
Renon
Sanur
Legian
Semawang
Peti Tenget Temple
Kuta
Ngurah Rai Airport
Serangan
Jimbaran
Benoa
Pura Ulu Watu Temple
Bualu
Nusa Dua
Kutuh
Suluban Surfing Beach
Ulu Watu
Pecatu
Badung Peninsula
Ayung
Petanu
Tirta Empul Temple
Sebatu
Tegeh Koripan Temple
G. Batur 1717
Songan
Hot Spring
Lake Batur
Trunyan
Penelokan
Peludu
Kedisan
Bali Aga Village
G. Abang 2153
Tianyar
Kubu
Amed Beach
Culik
Pura Besakih Temple
Besakih
G. Agung 3142
Royal Bathing Pools
Seraya
Rendang
Bangli
Kehen Temple
Unda
Selat
Sibetan
Karangasem
Iseh
Putung
Tenganan
Taman Ujung Water Palace
Bukit Dharma Temple
Gianyar
Klungkung
Padang
Candi Dasa Beach
Sukawati
Celuk
Kusamba
Goa Lawah (Bat Cave)
Pura Dalem Peed Temple
Sampalan
Lembongan
Ceningan
Toyapakeh
Penida
Suwana

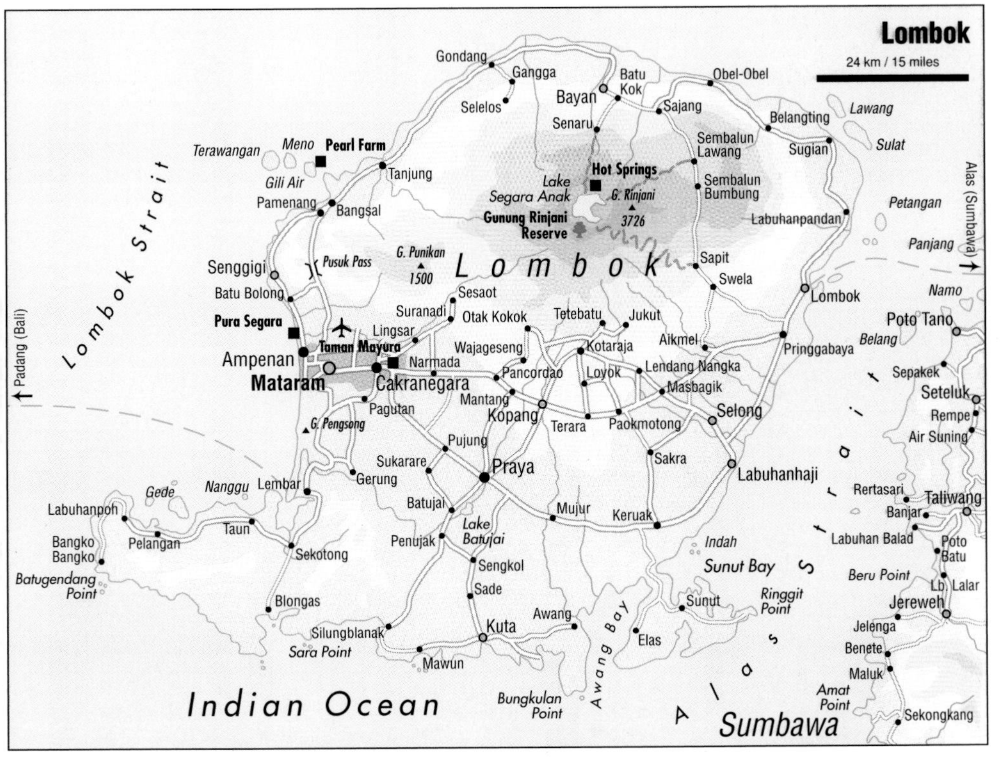
Lombok
24 km / 15 miles
Lombok Strait
Alas Strait
Indian Ocean
Padang (Bali)
Alas (Sumbawa)
Gondang
Gangga
Selelos
Batu Kok
Bayan
Senaru
Sajang
Obel-Obel
Belangting
Lawang
Sulat
Sembalun Lawang
Sugian
Terawangan
Meno
Pearl Farm
Gili Air
Tanjung
Pamenang
Bangsal
Lake Segara Anak
Hot Springs
G. Rinjani 3726
Gunung Rinjani Reserve
Sembalun Bumbung
Labuhanpandan
Petangan
Panjang
Senggigi
Pusuk Pass
G. Punikan 1500
Sapit
Swela
Lombok
Namo
Batu Bolong
Sesaot
Suranadi
Otak Kokok
Tetebatu
Jukut
Pura Segara
Lingsar
Taman Mayura
Wajageseng
Kotaraja
Aikmel
Pringgabaya
Belang
Poto Tano
Ampenan
Narmada
Loyok
Lendang Nangka
Sepakek
Mataram
Cakranegara
Pancordao
Masbagik
Seteluk
Pagutan
Mantang
Kopang
Terara
Paokmotong
Selong
Rempe
Air Suning
G. Pengsong
Pujung
Sukarare
Praya
Sakra
Labuhanhaji
Gede
Nanggu
Lembar
Gerung
Batujai
Rertasari
Taliwang
Labuhanpoh
Taun
Mujur
Keruak
Banjar
Bangko Bangko
Pelangan
Sekotong
Penujak
Lake Batujai
Indah
Labuhan Balad
Poto Batu
Batugendang Point
Sengkol
Sunut Bay
Beru Point
Lb. Lalar
Sade
Sunut
Ringgit Point
Jereweh
Blongas
Awang
Awang Bay
Elas
Jelenga
Silungblanak
Kuta
Benete
Sara Point
Mawun
Maluk
Bungkulan Point
Amat Point
Sumbawa
Sekongkang

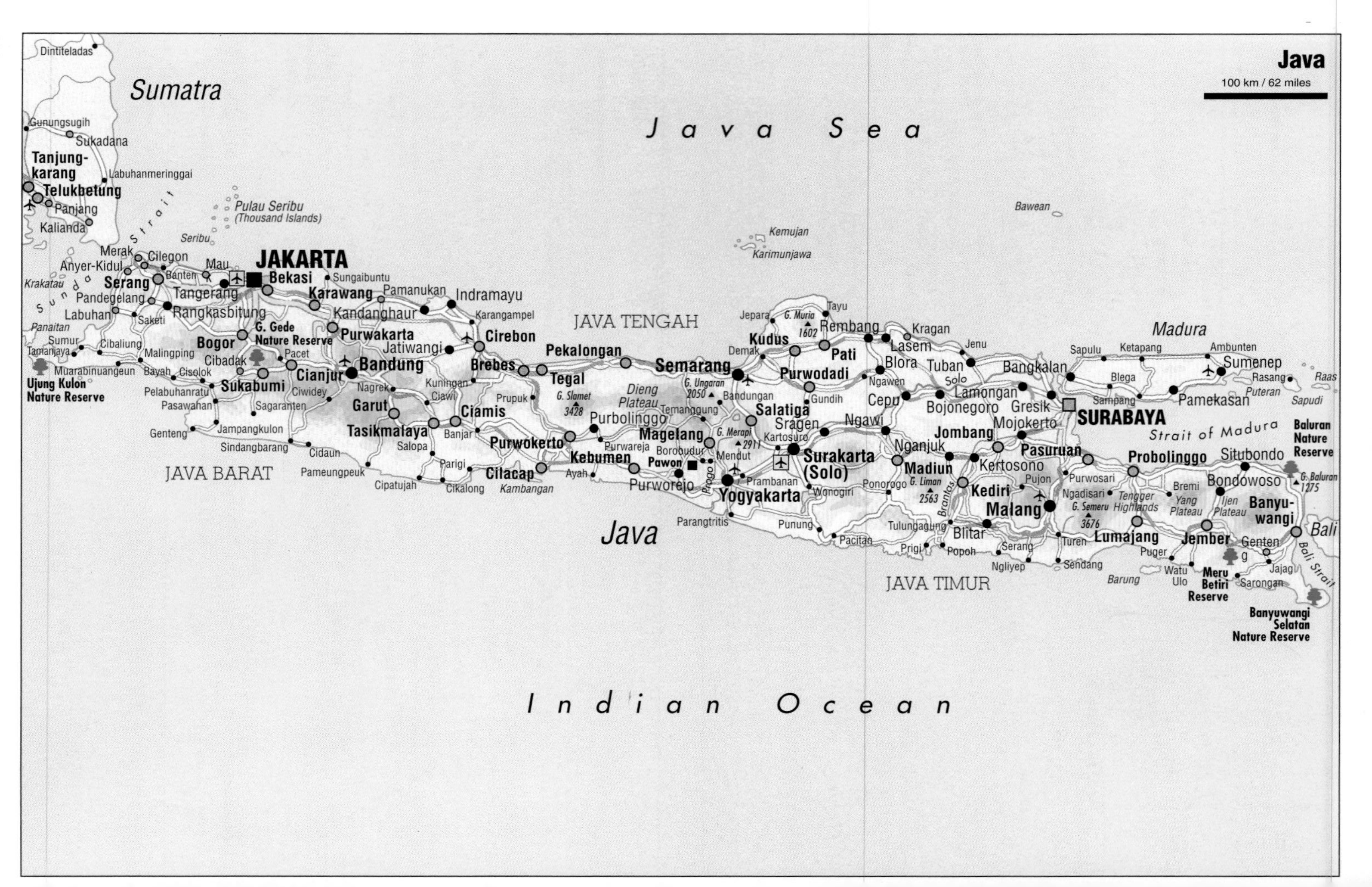
Java
100 km / 62 miles
Java Sea
Indian Ocean
Java
Sumatra
Dintiteladas
Gunungsugih
Sukadana
Tanjung-
karang
Labuhanmeringgai
Telukbetung
Panjang
Kalianda
Sunda Strait
Pulau Seribu
(Thousand Islands)
Seribu
Krakatau
Merak
Cilegon
Anyer-Kidul
Banten
Mau
JAKARTA
Bekasi
Sungaibuntu
Serang
Tangerang
Karawang
Pamanukan
Indramayu
Pandeglang
Rangkasbitung
Kandanghaur
Karangampel
Labuhan
Saketi
Panaitan
Sumur
Tamanjaya
Cibaliung
Malingping
Bogor
G. Gede
Nature Reserve
Purwakarta
Jatiwangi
Cirebon
Cibadak
Pacet
Bandung
Ujung Kulon
Nature Reserve
Muarabinuangeun
Bayah
Cisolok
Sukabumi
Cianjur
Pelabuhanratu
Pasawahan
Ciwidey
Nagrek
Kuningan
Ciawi
Brebes
Tegal
Pekalongan
Semarang
Garut
Sagaranten
Tasikmalaya
Ciamis
Prupuk
Genteng
Jampangkulon
Sindangbarang
Cidaun
Pameungpeuk
Cipatujah
Salopa
Banjar
Parigi
Cikalong
Purwokerto
Cilacap
Kambangan
JAVA BARAT
JAVA TENGAH
G. Slamet
3428
Dieng
Plateau
Purbolinggo
Purwareja
Kebumen
Ayah
Temanggung
Magelang
Borobudur
Pawon
Purworejo
Progo
Mendut
G. Ungaran
2050
Bandungan
Demak
Jepara
G. Muria
1602
Tayu
Kudus
Rembang
Pati
Lasem
Kragan
Purwodadi
Gundih
Salatiga
Sragen
G. Merapi
2911
Kartosuro
Prambanan
Yogyakarta
Surakarta
(Solo)
Wonogiri
Parangtritis
Punung
Pacitan
Blora
Ngawen
Cepu
Ngawi
Tuban
Jenu
Solo
Bojonegoro
Lamongan
Nganjuk
Madiun
Ponorogo
G. Liman
2563
Jombang
Kertosono
Mojokerto
Gresik
Bangkalan
Kediri
Brantas
Tulungagung
Blitar
Prigi
Popoh
Serang
Ngliyep
Malang
Pujon
Pasuruan
SURABAYA
Sampang
Blega
Sapulu
Ketapang
Madura
Ambunten
Sumenep
Rasang
Pamekasan
Puteran
Sapudi
Raas
Bawean
Kemujan
Karimunjawa
Strait of Madura
Probolinggo
Purwosari
Ngadisari
Tengger
Highlands
G. Semeru
3676
Turen
Sendang
Lumajang
Bremi
Yang
Plateau
Situbondo
Bondowoso
Ijen
Plateau
Jember
Puger
Barung
Watu
Ulo
Meru
Betiri
Reserve
Banyu-
wangi
Genteng
Jajag
Sarongan
Baluran
Nature
Reserve
G. Baluran
1275
Bali
Bali Strait
Banyuwangi
Selatan
Nature Reserve
JAVA TIMUR

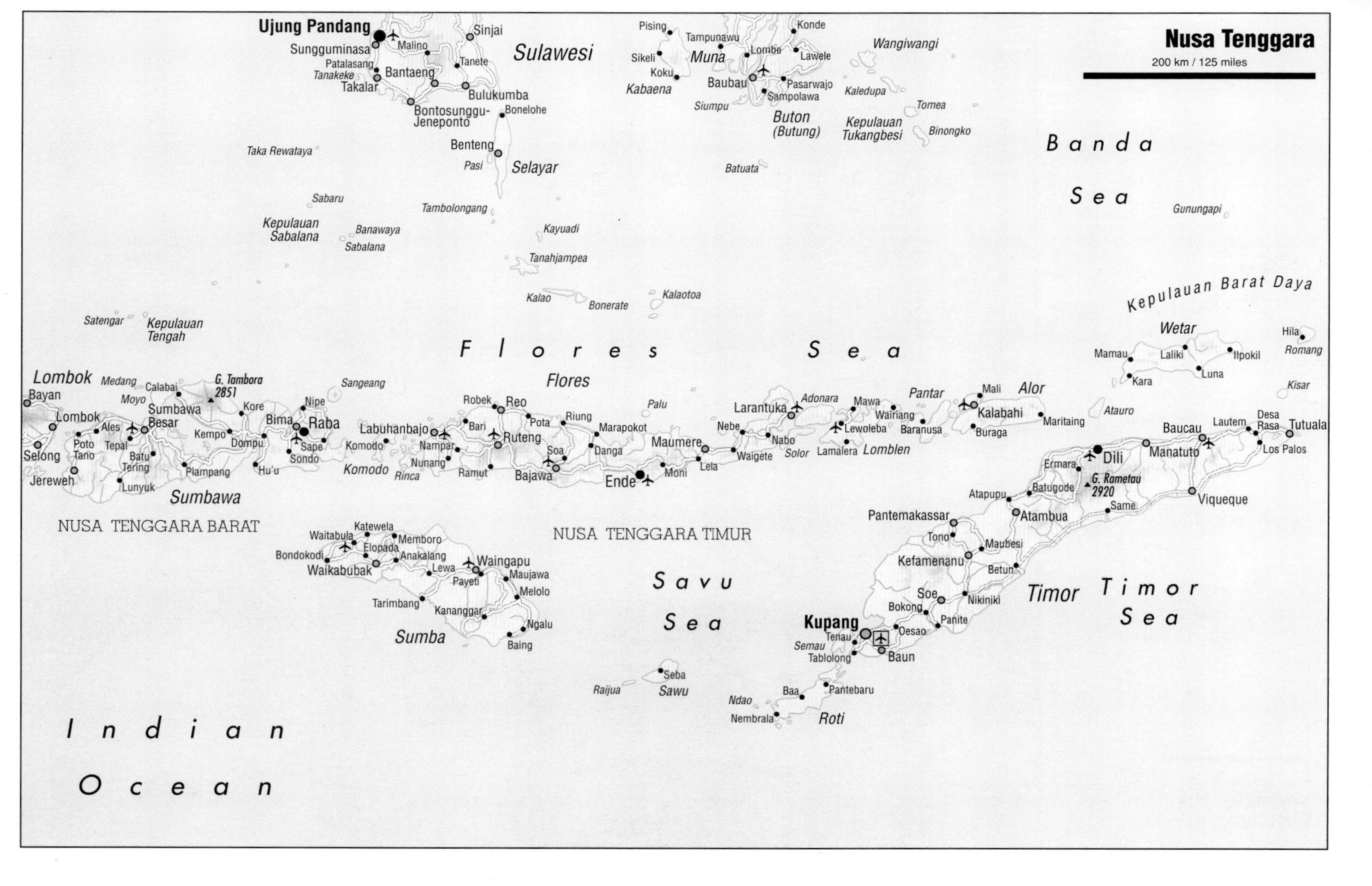

Nusa Tenggara
200 km / 125 miles
Banda Sea
Flores Sea
Savu Sea
Timor Sea
Indian Ocean
NUSA TENGGARA BARAT
NUSA TENGGARA TIMUR
Sulawesi
Ujung Pandang
Sungguminasa
Patalasang
Tanakeke
Takalar
Malino
Bantaeng
Sinjai
Tanete
Bulukumba
Bontosunggu-Jeneponto
Bonelohe
Benteng
Pasi
Selayar
Pising
Tampunawu
Sikeli
Muna
Koku
Kabaena
Lombe
Konde
Lawele
Baubau
Pasarwajo
Sampolawa
Siumpu
Buton (Butung)
Batuata
Wangiwangi
Kaledupa
Tomea
Binongko
Kepulauan Tukangbesi
Taka Rewataya
Sabaru
Kepulauan Sabalana
Banawaya
Sabalana
Tambolongang
Kayuadi
Tanahjampea
Kalao
Bonerate
Kalaotoa
Satengar
Kepulauan Tengah
Lombok
Bayan
Lombok
Selong
Jereweh
Poto Tano
Ales
Tepal
Batu Tering
Lunyuk
Medang
Moyo
Calabai
Sumbawa Besar
G. Tambora 2851
Kempo
Kore
Dompu
Plampang
Sumbawa
Hu'u
Bima
Nipe
Raba
Sape
Sondo
Sangeang
Komodo
Labuhanbajo
Nampar
Nunang
Rinca
Robek
Reo
Bari
Ruteng
Ramut
Pota
Riung
Soa
Bajawa
Flores
Marapokot
Danga
Ende
Palu
Maumere
Moni
Lela
Nebe
Waigete
Larantuka
Adonara
Nabo
Solor
Lewoleba
Lamalera
Lomblen
Mawa
Wairiang
Baranusa
Pantar
Mali
Kalabahi
Buraga
Alor
Maritaing
Atauro
Kepulauan Barat Daya
Wetar
Mamau
Laliki
Kara
Luna
Ilpokil
Hila
Romang
Kisar
Gunungapi
Dili
Manatuto
Baucau
Lautem
Desa Rasa
Tutuala
Los Palos
Viqueque
Ermara
G. Rametau 2920
Batugode
Atapupu
Atambua
Same
Pantemakassar
Tono
Maubesi
Kefamenanu
Betun
Soe
Nikiniki
Bokong
Panite
Timor
Kupang
Tenau
Semau
Tablolong
Oesao
Baun
Baa
Pantebaru
Ndao
Nembrala
Roti
Seba
Sawu
Raijua
Waitabula
Katewela
Memboro
Elopada
Bondokodi
Anakalang
Waikabubak
Lewa
Waingapu
Payeti
Maujawa
Melolo
Tarimbang
Kananggar
Ngalu
Baing
Sumba

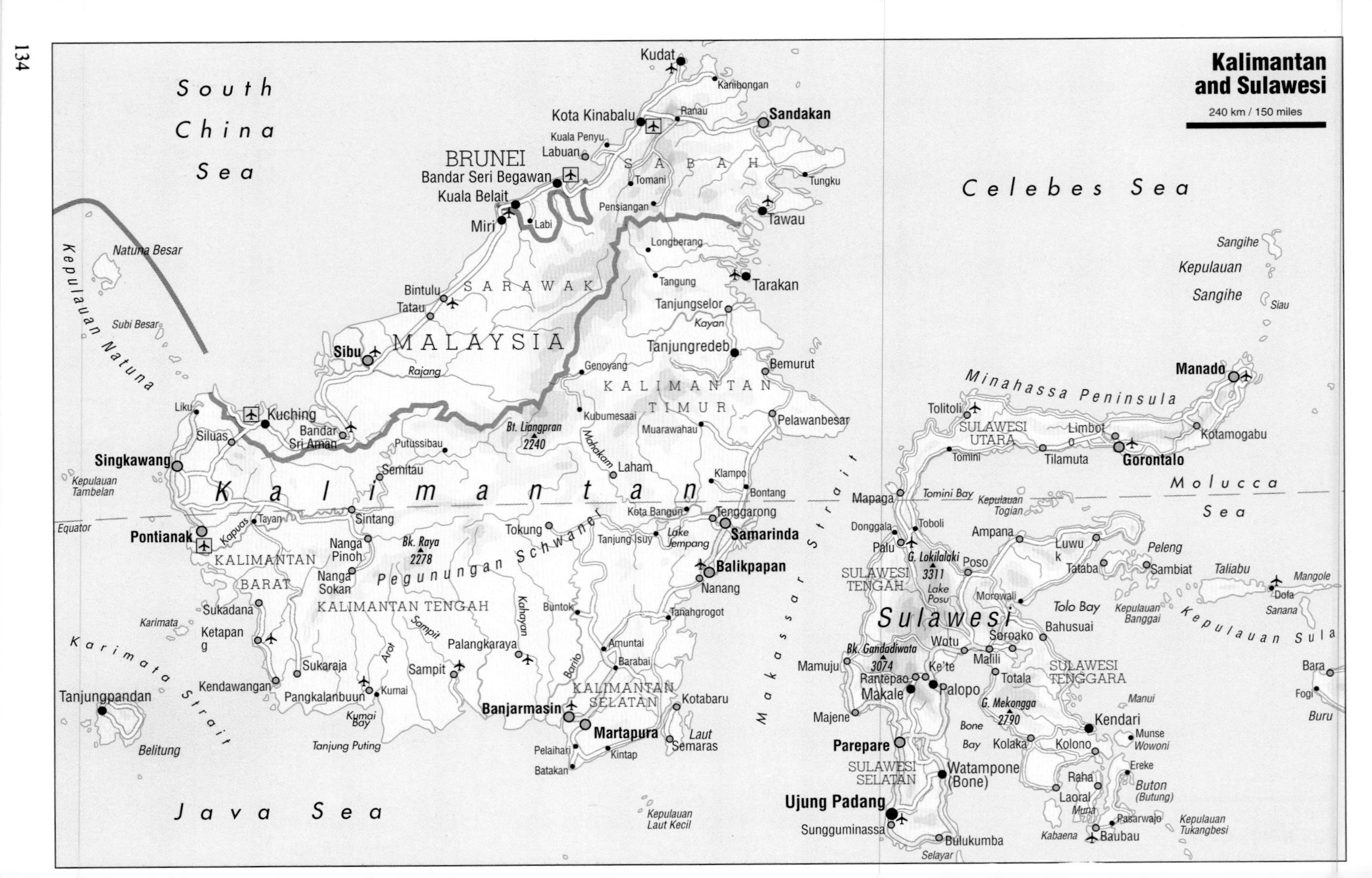
Kalimantan and Sulawesi
240 km / 150 miles
South China Sea
Celebes Sea
Java Sea
Molucca Sea
Kepulauan Natuna
Natuna Besar
Subi Besar
Kepulauan Tambelan
Equator
Karimata
Karimata Strait
Belitung
Tanjungpandan
BRUNEI
Bandar Seri Begawan
Kuala Belait
Miri
Labi
Labuan
Kuala Penyu
Kota Kinabalu
Ranau
Kudat
Kanibongan
Sandakan
SABAH
Tomani
Tungku
Pensiangan
Tawau
Tarakan
Longberang
Tangung
Tanjungselor
Kayan
Tanjungredeb
Bemurut
Pelawanbesar
SARAWAK
MALAYSIA
Bintulu
Tatau
Sibu
Rajang
Liku
Kuching
Siluas
Bandar Sri Aman
Singkawang
Putussibau
Semitau
Bt. Liangpran 2240
Genoyang
Kubumesaai
KALIMANTAN TIMUR
Muarawahau
Mahakam
Laham
Klampo
Bontang
Kota Bangun
Tenggarong
Samarinda
Tanjung Isuy
Lake Jempang
Balikpapan
Nanang
Tanahgrogot
Kalimantan
Pontianak
Kapuas
Tayan
Sintang
Tokung
Nanga Pinoh
Bk. Raya 2278
Nanga Sokan
Pegunungan Schwaner
KALIMANTAN BARAT
KALIMANTAN TENGAH
Sukadana
Ketapan g
Sukaraja
Kendawangan
Pangkalanbuun
Kumai
Kumai Bay
Tanjung Puting
Arot
Sampit
Sampit
Palangkaraya
Kahayan
Buntok
Barito
Amuntai
Barabai
KALIMANTAN SELATAN
Kotabaru
Banjarmasin
Martapura
Laut Semaras
Pelaihari
Kintap
Batakan
Kepulauan Laut Kecil
Makasar Strait
Sangihe
Kepulauan Sangihe
Siau
Manado
Minahassa Peninsula
Tolitoli
SULAWESI UTARA
Limbot o
Kotamogabu
Tomini
Tilamuta
Gorontalo
Mapaga
Tomini Bay
Kepulauan Togian
Donggala
Toboli
Palu
Ampana
Luwu k
G. Lokilalaki 3311
Poso
Tataba
Peleng
Sambiat
Taliabu
Mangole
Dofa
Sanana
SULAWESI TENGAH
Lake Posu
Morowali
Tolo Bay
Kepulauan Banggai
Kepulauan Sula
Sulawesi
Bahusuai
Soroako
Wotu
Bk. Gandadiwata 3074
Mamuju
Malili
Rantepao
Ke'te
Totala
SULAWESI TENGGARA
Bara
Fogi
Buru
Makale
Palopo
G. Mekongga 2790
Manui
Majene
Bone Bay
Kendari
Munse
Wowoni
Parepare
Kolaka
Kolono
Ereke
SULAWESI SELATAN
Watampone (Bone)
Raha
Buton (Butung)
Laoral
Muna
Ujung Padang
Pasarwajo
Kepulauan Tukangbesi
Sungguminassa
Bulukumba
Kabaena
Baubau
Selayar

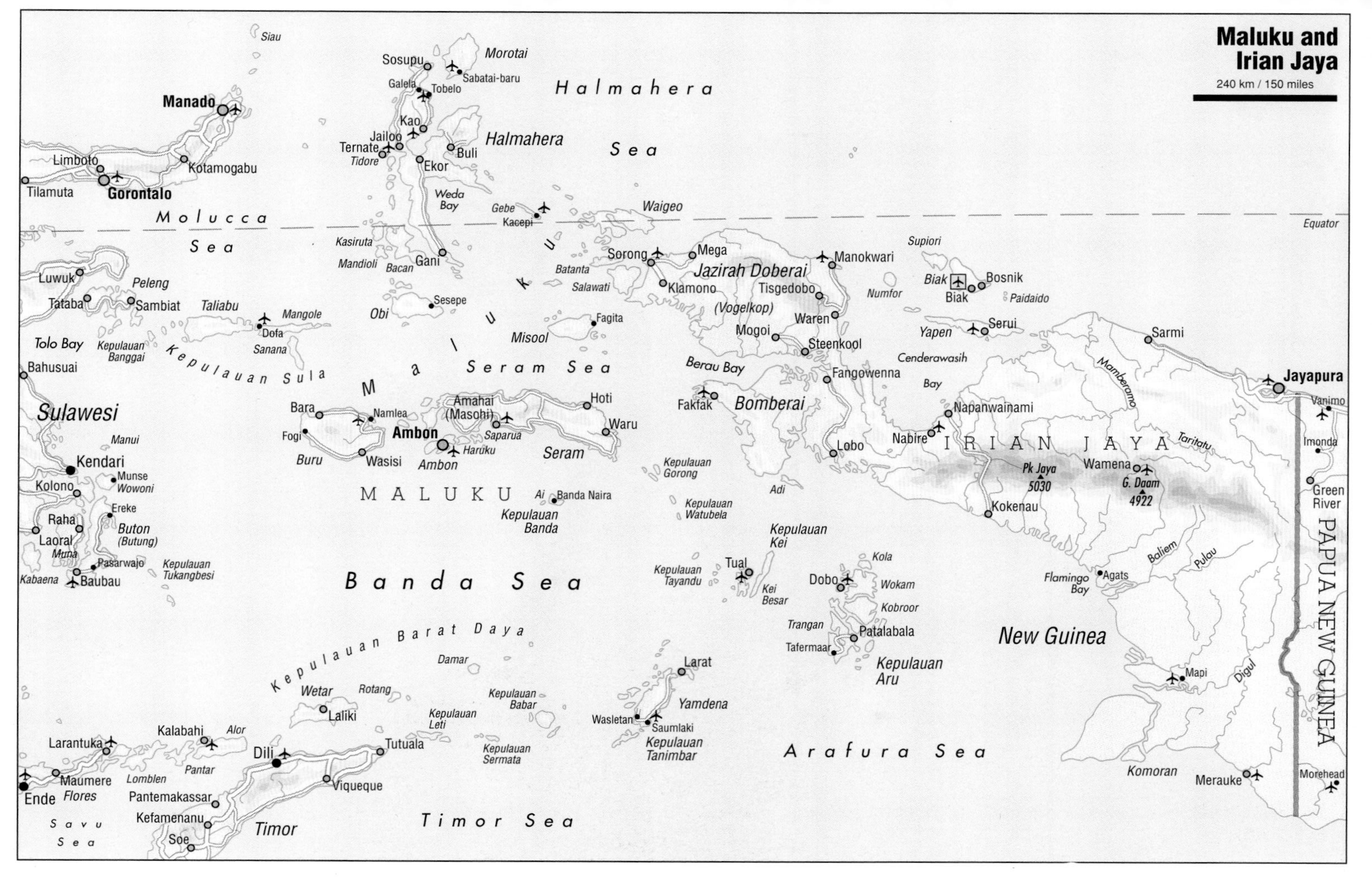

Maluku and Irian Jaya
240 km / 150 miles
Siau
Manado
Limboto
Kotamogabu
Tilamuta
Gorontalo
Molucca Sea
Sosupu
Morotai
Galela
Tobelo
Sabatai-baru
Kao
Jailolo
Ternate
Tidore
Buli
Ekor
Halmahera
Halmahera Sea
Weda Bay
Gebe
Kacepi
Waigeo
Equator
Kasiruta
Mandioli
Bacan
Gani
Luwuk
Tataba
Peleng
Sambiat
Taliabu
Mangole
Dofa
Sanana
Tolo Bay
Kepulauan Banggai
Kepulauan Sula
Bahusuai
Sulawesi
Obi
Sesepe
Maluku
Misool
Fagita
Batanta
Salawati
Sorong
Mega
Klamono
Jazirah Doberai
Tisgedobo
(Vogelkop)
Mogoi
Waren
Steenkool
Manokwari
Supiori
Numfor
Biak
Bosnik
Paidaido
Yapen
Serui
Cenderawasih Bay
Sarmi
Mamberamo
Jayapura
Vanimo
Imonda
Green River
Seram Sea
Berau Bay
Fakfak
Bomberai
Fangowenna
Lobo
Napanwainami
Nabire
IRIAN JAYA
Taritatu
Pk Jaya 5030
Wamena
G. Daam 4922
Kokenau
Bara
Namlea
Fogi
Buru
Wasisi
Ambon
Haruku
Amahai
(Masohi)
Saparua
Seram
Hoti
Waru
Manui
Kendari
Munse
Wowoni
Kolono
Ereke
Raha
Buton
(Butung)
Laoral
Muna
Pasarwajo
Kabaena
Baubau
Kepulauan Tukangbesi
MALUKU
Ai
Banda Naira
Kepulauan Banda
Kepulauan Gorong
Kepulauan Watubela
Adi
Kepulauan Kei
Tual
Kepulauan Tayandu
Kei Besar
Kola
Dobo
Wokam
Kobroor
Trangan
Patalabala
Tafermaar
Kepulauan Aru
Flamingo Bay
Agats
Baliem
Pulau
New Guinea
PAPUA NEW GUINEA
Banda Sea
Kepulauan Barat Daya
Damar
Wetar
Rotang
Laliki
Kepulauan Babar
Kepulauan Leti
Larat
Yamdena
Wasletan
Saumlaki
Kepulauan Tanimbar
Kepulauan Sermata
Mapi
Digul
Arafura Sea
Komoran
Merauke
Morehead
Larantuka
Kalabahi
Alor
Dili
Tutuala
Maumere
Flores
Ende
Lomblen
Pantar
Pantemakassar
Viqueque
Kefamenanu
Soe
Timor
Timor Sea
Savu Sea

SUMATRA

Over 1,000 years ago, Sumatra was the site of Southeast Asia's greatest trading empire – the kingdom of Srivijaya, which had its capital in the vicinity of present-day Palembang. Sumatra became an important gateway between India, the Middle East and Europe, and Southeast Asia, especially when the spice trade developed with the Old World colonial powers.

The island of Sumatra – third-largest in the archipelago and fifth-largest in the world (roughly the size of Sweden) – is Indonesia's most important territory. In just about every way – strategically, economically and politically – Sumatra has always formed a pivotal backbone for the nation.

Second among Indonesia's islands in population with 30 million people, but first in exports (principally oil, natural gas, rubber, tin and palm oil, but also tobacco, tea, coffee and timber), Sumatra stands at the crossroads of Asia, heir to an ancient and illustrious past and home to a broad spectrum of dynamic and fiercely-independent peoples. Sumatra is also the third most popular tourist destination in Indonesia, after Bali and Java.

Sumatra is formed by a longitudinal range of mountains – a double fold in the earth's crust with a central trough split by numerous towering volcanoes. There are about 90 volcanoes in the range, 15 of them active. But unlike in Java and Bali, they frequently eject material of an acidic nature, which does nothing to improve the fertility of the surrounding soils. This thousand-mile-long chain of active volcanos makes for a volatile geological environment. Eruptions and earthquakes are frequent and often destructive.

Oil was discovered in this area in the late 1880s, leading to the formation of the Royal Dutch Shell Company. Additional oil fields were subsequently found all along the eastern coast, and Sumatra now produces about three-quarters of Indonesia's petroleum output. This has created an economic boom in the large coastal cities like Medan, Pekanbaru, Jambi and Palembang. In other coastal areas, shipping, trading and fishing are traditional mainstays of the local economy.

Sumatra continues to suggest the exotic, whether it be the independent people of Aceh and the tribal clans of the Batak, or the Sumatran tiger and not-yet-extinct volcanoes. Overshadowed in travelers' minds by adjacent Java, Sumatra is, in fact, less crowded and no less interesting, geographically or culturally. Moreover, it is but a couple of hours by boat from Singapore, that glittering city of Oz, just across the Strait of Malacca.

Preceding pages: a smile brighter than the sun on a hat seller, Sumatra. Left, being towed on Danau Toba.

MEDAN AND ACEH

As early as the 7th century, Sumatra's southeastern coast was the site of Southeast Asia's greatest trading empire – the Buddhist kingdom of Srivijaya, which had its capital somewhere in the vicinity of present-day Palembang. Srivijaya had no agricultural lands to speak of, but existed solely by controlling the flow of ships and goods through the narrow Sunda and Malacca straits – then, as now, strategic gateways linking the Pacific and Indian oceans.

Srivijaya maintained its control over the straits for about seven centuries, though not without competition and several severe setbacks. Their final defeat at the hands of Majapahit forces from East Java, in 1377, set the stage for Islam's rapid advance into the archipelago. From the fall of Srivijaya until the late 19th century, Sumatra's coasts were ruled by various river-based Islamic trading kingdoms.

Islam obtained its first foothold on Sumatra at the end of the 13th century, with the conversion of several small trading ports on the island's northeastern shore. The name of one of them – Samudra – has come to refer to the island as a whole. From the late 16th century onward, this northern coastal area became the home of Indonesia's most powerful modern kingdom – the Sultanate of Aceh.

Ethnic homeland: The majority of Sumatrans do not live along the coasts, but rather in the long range of undulating foothills, plateaus, river basins and highland lakes along the island's spine, where they make a living as subsistence cultivators. This is the homeland of two major ethnic groups – the Minangkabau and the Batak – and a number of minor ones (the Gayo, Alas, Kubu, Kerinci, Rejang, Lampung and others). The highlands were once covered in dense rain forest and inhabited by many exotic Asian mammals (elephants, tigers, rhinos, gibbons, orangutans), but the land is increasingly being cleared and planted with food crops.

Sumatra today is divided into eight provinces: Aceh, North Sumatra, West Sumatra, Riau, Jambi, Bengkulu, South Sumatra and Lampung. These administrative units often include a number of smaller islands lying some distance offshore. Riau Province, for instance, includes not only the Riau Archipelago south of Singapore, but also the oil-rich Anambas and Natuna islands in the middle of the South China Sea. Likewise, the province of South Sumatra includes the tin islands of Bangka and Belitung (Billiton), which, between them, produce about 20 percent of the world's tin.

Northern metropolis: From the booming industrial metropolis of Medan to the forested Alas River Valley (haunt of primitive tribes), to the fiercely independent Islamic stronghold of Aceh, Sumatra's northernmost segment is easily its most diverse. Most visitors enter this region via **Medan**, a sprawling and crowded city of about 2.5 million, and with one of the strongest economic growth rates and highest per capita incomes in all of Indonesia. Once the

Left, lucid colors over Danau Toba. Right, Medan crowds at road rally.

marshy suburb of a small court center, Medan developed into a commercial city after the Dutch overran the Deli Sultanate in 1872. Fourteen years later, it became the regional capital.

Modern Medan has retained many architectural gems from its colonial days, of which rococo, art-deco and art nouveau styles were especially popular. The largest concentration of these commercial buildings is found along Jalan Jendral A. Yani and around **Merdeka Square**: General Post Office, former White Societet (now Bank Negara), Hotel de Boer (now Hotel Dharma Bhakti), Grand Hotel Medan (now the Granada Medan), and the estate offices of Harrison & Crossfield's (now P.T. London Sumatra Indonesia).

Chinese shops line Jalan A. Yani. Here also is the mansion of millionaire Tjong A Fie. Despite enormous wealth acquired from modest beginnings as a horse trader, he died of malnutrition in a concentration camp during the Japanese occupation; his mausoleum stands in the Pulau Bryan cemetery.

The central market district is just adjacent to the downtown area, and an ever increasing flow of buses, trucks, cars, motorcycles and pedicabs converges about the main markets of Pasar Kampung Keling, Pasar Ramas, Pasar Hong Kong, and the Central Market.

At the southern end of Medan's longest street, Jalan Sisingamangaraja, stands the imposing **Mesjid Raya**, built in a rococo style in 1906 to match **Istana Maimun**, the nearby sultan's palace. Constructed by an Italian architect in 1888, it is the largest mosque in the city. The nearby palace is still the residence of the sultan's descendants and may be visited during the day. Inside are memorabilia such as Dutch furniture and lamps, portraits and old weaponry. Cultural performances can be arranged, portraying many of the colorful Malay and tribal dances of the many peoples of northern Sumatra.

Across the Deli River, on the west side of Medan, is the old European plantation town. Its wide avenues, flanked by huge colonial villas, are

Left, fruit market at Brastagi. Right, Medan Grand Mosque.

planted with flowering trees. The art-deco **Immanuel Protestant Church**, erected in 1921, is on Jalan Diponegoro, while on Jalan Hang Tuah is **Vihara Gunung Timur**, Indonesia's largest Chinese temple. It's said to be such a powerful place that photographs taken within will remain unexposed. Nevertheless, cameras are not permitted. Both Buddhists and Taoists worship here, while **Vihara Borobudur**, next to the Danau Toba Hotel, is used solely by devotees of the Buddha. A Hindu temple, **Sri Mariaman,** off Jalan Arifin, is the spiritual center for Medan's sizeable Indian community.

Elsewhere in Medan, the **Taman Margasatwa Zoo** has a varied collection of native Sumatran wildlife. **Medan Fair** has permanent cultural and agricultural exhibits, and an amusement park. And the **Bukit Kubu Museum** surveys Sumatra's tribal lifestyles.

Down the Deli River is **Belawan**, Indonesia's third-largest port. The harbor is currently in the throes of a major expansion program intended to help relieve bottlenecks in exporting. Well off the main road, 100 kilometers (60 miles) west of Medan and past the orchard city of **Binjai** (famous for its rambutans and durians), is **Bohorok**, a World Wildlife Fund rehabilitation center for orangutans. Wardens help domesticated apes adapt to the jungle before releasing them in the wild.

Resistant, resilient Acehnese: At the northwest tip of Sumatra, **Aceh Province** has traditionally been the archipelago's first point of contact with external influences. Hinduism and Buddhism were brought by Indian traders in the 7th and 8th centuries, and Islam through Arab and Indian Muslims in the 13th century.

Like the ancient Buddhist kingdom of Srivijaya at the other end of Sumatra, Aceh was strategically located to take advantage of sea trade passing through the nearby straits. During the Golden Age under Sultan Iskandar Muda (ruled 1604 to 1637), Aceh expanded to include all the major ports of eastern Sumatra and several on the Malay pe-

River adventure, Aceh.

ninsula. Though the Acehnese were unable to hold onto these conquered areas for long, they maintained a strong fleet and an active trading economy for many centuries, and later proved to be a major thorn for Dutch invaders.

The Dutch declared war on Aceh in 1873. It took more than 10,000 troops – the largest military force the Dutch ever mustered in the East Indies – and thousands of casualties to finally defeat the sultan and overrun his fortress at Banda Aceh. A subsequent Islamic jihad, or holy war, to oust the Dutch ended in defeat in 1878. Guerrilla activities then spread inland to Gayo tribal territories, where the rebel-controlled pepper trade financed the purchase and smuggling of arms from the British. The Dutch resorted to a counterinsurgency force of native troops armed with rifles and *klewang* sabres, used to slice off their enemies' heads.

These *mareechausee* troops made steady progress, enabling the Dutch to build a railroad along the coast from Medan to Banda Aceh, via Langsa, Sigli and Bireuen. Colonial officials entrenched themselves in these towns and used them as bases of control. Despite a setback in 1896, when Teuku Omar, a local chief highly trusted by the Dutch, joined the guerrillas (he is revered today as an Acehnese hero), relative peace came to Aceh after about 1903. But the Dutch maintained strong garrisons here up until the Japanese invasion of 1942. The province has been granted the status of *Daerah Istimewa* (Special Autonomous District). Today, Aceh's economy relies largely on trade and vast reserves of natural gas and oil at Lhokseumawe.

The Acehnese are still fiercely independent; a strong Islamic movement and some extremist separatist activity are often thorns in the side of the central government. Until recently, an armed guerrilla movement was still active in some rural areas.

The grand tour: Although the coastal road to Aceh is better and shorter, it is also flat and excessively busy. The route suggested here follows the Alas Valley

Dutch officers survey the field of battle during the Aceh wars.

through the spectacular Mount Leuser Nature Reserve. Starting from Medan, the first stop is **Brastagi**, a hill resort and market town 70 kilometers (40 mi) to the south. The Dutch built guest houses, villas and an imposing hotel, the Bukit Kubu, in a park at the entrance to the town. Brastagi has a cool climate, ideal for growing French beans, carrots, tomatoes, passion fruit, flowers and oranges. Nearby Karo Batak villages, with their massive wooden clan houses, may also be visited from here.

The next town, **Kabanjahe**, stands at a crossroads between Aceh Province and the Danau Toba region. Southern Aceh, including portions of the Batak plateau, has rich swamp-free volcanic soils, and so rubber palms, oil palms, tea and tobacco all flourish. In the surrounding area are the traditional Karo Batak villages of **Barus Jahe** and **Lingga**, massive and square high-roofed buildings with carved and painted roof caps. A lucky visitor might have a chance to witness a Karo Batak wedding or rice harvest festival. Nearby are two impressive waterfalls: **Sikulap** and **Sipisopiso**.

Gayo and Alas country starts at **Kutacane**. The Batak were vassals of these mountain tribes when the Acehnese sultan first conquered the region in the 17th century and then imposed Islam, making the Gayos and the Alas his own vassals. Some Gayos, called *orang lingga,* retain their animistic beliefs and practices high in the mountains, far from the main roads. They believe natural harmony is achieved by sacrificing buffaloes and fowl, and offering fruit and vegetables to the spirits of trees, rocks, mountains, and lakes.

Kutacane, set amid rice paddies and coconut trees and surrounded by high jungle-covered mountains, is a small market town with a traditional shop-lined main street and bus station.

North, a narrow road winds up the Alas River Valley through a jungle corridor in **Mount Leuser Nature Reserve**. Surrounding sputtering 3,460-meter (11,370 ft) **Gunung (Mount) Leuser**, Sumatra's second-highest peak, this reserve reaches all the way to the

Sipisopiso Waterfall.

west coast and is probably one of the most accessible in Indonesia.

Just north of the park boundary is **Blangkejeren**, with numerous century-old Gayo and Alas houses. Long and low, they shelter as many as 60 people from several families with a common male ancestor; unmarried men, pubescent boys and travelers stay in a communal house.

A Japanese-built track constructed by slave labor during World War II connects Blangkejeren to **Takeguen**, the Gayo capital. Takingeun is built on the banks of 25-kilometer-long (15 mi) **Danau Laut Tawar**. The water is clean, cool and refreshing, but local people do not swim. Fearing they may be pulled into the underwater realm of a seductive fairy, they opt instead for the public baths and hot springs at **Kampong Balik**. A paved road follows the west side of the lake, affording spectacular views of alternating lake-side rice paddies and pine-clad mountain slopes.

The east coast town of **Bireuen** is the chief marketplace for Gayo coffee, cinnamon, cloves and tobacco. Like many towns and villages north of Banda Aceh, Bireuen is an Acehnese settlement. Traditional Acehnese villages are surrounded by rice fields or coconut groves. The rectangular houses are built on stilts of solid *bangka* wood and covered with *nipah* palms; a hole carved in the roof lets smoke escape. Extended families build their houses within the same compound and every village has a mosque and a *balairong* (communal house), used during the day as a meeting place and at night as a dormitory.

While the Acehnese social system is patriarchal, residence is matrilocal. When a man gets married, he lives with his wife's family – a practice that contradicts conventional Muslim practices (though not native *adat* tradition).

Civil war and rail ruins: At the estuaries of the Krong Baru and Krong Tuka rivers, **Sigli** was known as Padri when it was the principle port from which Acehnese *haji* (pilgrims) departed to Mecca. The tragic Padri War started here in 1804; the Dutch took the town

Left, father and son. Right, Acehnese wedding dress.

and completely destroyed it in the process. Remains of the *padri kraton* (fortress) can be seen on the outskirts of town, along the road to Banda Aceh. At nearby Kampong Kibet is the grave of Sultan Maarif Syah, the first Islamic sultan of Aceh, who died in 1511.

Sigli was rebuilt and became a major stop along the rail line. Although the track, which runs parallel to the coast road, has not been used in over 20 years, the town's most impressive sight is still the station, a wooden colonial building now deserted except for goats grazing between rails and children at play in the empty coal yard. In the abandoned sheds, locomotives and cars are rusting, while rows of machine tools lay idle.

The climate is mild, and the town has the look of a turn-of-the-century European resort. At one end of the villa-lined sea promenade stands the skeleton of what was once the harbormaster's home. Three cemeteries – Muslim, European and Chinese – with their tombstones set among coconut trees, grace a neck of land across the Krong Baru River.

Banda Aceh, capital of the province, is also built on two rivers, Krong Aceh and Krong Daroy. Although the fortress and palace of the Sultan of Aceh were destroyed along with the great mosque when the Dutch invaded in 1874, vestiges of Aceh's glorious past can still be found. Jalan Teuku Umar is the site of the **Gunungan**, a palace built by Iskandar Muda or his son at the beginning of the 17th century, and of the royal princesses' baths of the same period. On Jalan Kraton are the tombs of a dozen 15th-century and 16th-century sultans of Aceh, while another series of royal tombs on Jalan Mansur Sjah includes that of Iskandar Muda. They in turn surround the **Rumoh Aceh Awe Gentah Museum**, a former aristocrat's house displaying daggers, textiles and jewelry.

Most of the Dutch killed in the Aceh War, including a number of generals and other senior officers, are buried at the Christian cemetery on Jalan Iskandar Muda. With wrought-iron art-nouveau gates, the entrance stands between two marble plates on which are engraved the

Banda Aceh's Grand Mosque.

names of all the soldiers killed in Aceh. Many are works of sepulchral art; impressive is the stele to the *mareechausee*, erected by the East Sumatran Tobacco Planters Association.

The **Mesjid Raya**, or great mosque, though built of wood, was constructed without a single nail. At night, the huge white structure and its black domes are illuminated. The interior is marble and may be visited by non-Muslims, except during prayer times. Behind, and to the west, are the market and the Chinese quarter along Jalan Perdagangan.

The center of Banda Aceh's night life is **Penayung**, a small square on the other side of the Krong Aceh. This is the place to sit, talk with friends, and order drinks or a meal from hawkers.

A nearby village, **Kampung Kuala Aceh**, is a place of pilgrimage. Among mangroves and fish ponds facing the sea lies the grave of Teungku Sheikh Shaj Kuala (1615–1693), a holy man who translated the Koran into Malay, and who wrote religious books. Today, Aceh's university bears his name.

The wind-and-wave-battered beaches of **Lohong**, **Lampuk** and **Lhokinga**, on the west coast about 20 kilometers (12 mi) from Banda Aceh, are not for swimming. They receive the full force of the Indian Ocean and have an extremely strong undertow. At Lampuk, you'll have a hard time even standing knee high in the water. Some 60 kilometers (40 mi) farther down the coast and a short distance inland is the village of **Lamno**. Its inhabitants, said to be descended from Portuguese stranded there three centuries ago after a shipwreck, do indeed have green eyes and faces that are recognizably Iberian.

Banda Aceh is not Indonesia's Land's End. That distinction belongs to **Pulau Weh**, an island reached by plane or ferry. The island's main town, **Sabang**, flourished through the 1970s as a duty-free port linked to Calcutta, Malacca, Penang and Singapore. When the central government withdrew the free-port status, most of the island's economy withdrew as well. The local Chinese temple (Tua Peh Kong Bio) is the north-

Smiles for the stranger.

ernmost in Indonesia. Pulau Weh is renowned for its gin-clear aquamarine waters, ideal for scuba diving.

Batak lands: The Batak, one of the great highland peoples of Sumatra, inhabit a fertile volcanic plateau, south of Medan, roughly oval in shape, that covers much of northern central Sumatra. In the middle of this plateau lies lovely Danau Toba, with lush, green Pulau Samosir near its center. Geologists tell us that this crater lake was created by the world's greatest volcanic explosion many eons ago, and this entire area was once very remote. Danau Toba is the largest and deepest lake to be found in Southeast Asia.

More than 3 million members of six distinct Batak tribes make their homes in the high country, which stretches 500 kilometers (300 mi) north-south and 150 kilometers (90 mi) east-west around Danau Toba. Each of these groups – the Toba, Karo, Pakpak, Simalungun, Angkola and Mandailing Batak – have their own dialects, customs and architectural styles.

The Batak apparently migrated from the Himalayan foothills of upper Burma and Thailand over 1,500 years ago, settling in these mountains because of similarities to their ancestral homelands. Contact with coastal peoples led to the adoption of wet-rice agriculture, the plow and water buffalo, cotton and the spinning wheel, Sanskrit vocabulary and writing, and a pantheistic religion.

Wedged between two fervently Muslim peoples, the Minangkabau and the Acehnese, the Batak somehow remained isolated, animistic and cannibalistic until the middle of the last century, when German and Dutch missionaries converted many of them to a mystical sort of Christianity. Northern Batak are still animists, while southern Batak, especially the Mandailing, are Muslim. But traditional adat and bygone customs are still prominent among most Batak. Cemeteries display stone sculptures of dead ancestors, shamans communicate with spirits, and priests consult astrological tables to make decisions for their clans.

When they were first discovered by

Highland ramble.

the Dutch, the Batak were heralded as primitive cannibals isolated for centuries from the rest of the world. It seems the tribes were engaged in a perpetual state of ritual warfare with their neighbors; headhunting and cannibalism were common. But the Batak were anything but primitive. In fact, they were already sophisticated and settled agriculturalists, possessing elaborate crafts, calendars and cosmological texts written in an Indic alphabet. Buddhist stupas and statues dating from between the 11th and 14th centuries, and perhaps earlier, have been discovered on the southern edges of the plateau, and it seems that the Batak were in close contact with the ancient Hindu empires of Sumatra and Java.

As with the Minang and other highland Indonesian tribes, Batak houses are massive multi-family wooden dwellings raised on stilts, with tall thatched roofs that recall the shape of a boat or a sail. Typically, dwellings are about 18 meters (60 ft) long. Built with rope and wooden pegs, without nails, they are so sturdy they can withstand a century of wear. The roof is higher on the ends than in the middle: although it was originally thatched, corrugated iron is increasingly used, requiring less-frequent replacement, but drowning out conversations when it rains. Mosaics and woodcarvings of mystical patterns and mythical creatures decorate gable ends. Between 10 and 12 families live in separate areas surrounding a central corridor and four fireplaces, where people work, play, cook and visit.

A Batak clan (*marga*) consists of several close-knit communities (*huta*) tracing descent from a single male ancestor. The webs of kinship and clan loyalties are especially strong, and in some cases fiercely defended. Major weddings and funerals can draw kinsfolk in the thousands. Genealogies, going back five centuries, are carefully kept, as they determine status in personal relations and formal ceremonies.

Medan to Danau Toba: The main route from Medan to Danau Toba runs east and south along the coast through the market towns of **Tebingtinggi** and Pematangsiantar. Side roads along the first 50 kilometers (30 mi) offer access to fine beaches such as **Pantai Cermin** and **Sialangbuah**, renowned for its mudskipper amphibians that swim like fish and climb trees.

Pematangsiantar, 130 kilometers (80 mi) from Medan, is the second-largest city in North Sumatra. This cool highland rubber and palm-oil center is notable for its **Simalungun Museum**, on Jalan Sudirman, containing an excellent display of Batak artifacts, including woodcarvings.

Around 170 kilometers (110 mi) from Medan, the road reaches Danau Toba at **Prapat**. A tourist resort (hotels, gold course) with a refreshingly brisk climate and a fine Saturday market, Prapat is nestled up the lake's eastern shore.

A longer, more westerly Medan–Prapat route runs through Brastagi and the **Karo Batak highlands**. Only a short bus trip from Kabanjahe is a spectacular viewpoint near the northern tip of Danau Toba that overlooks the remote Tongging Valley and the Sipisopiso

Tapping for rubber.

Waterfall. From here, the road skirts Toba's eastern shore, passing through the Monday-market village of **Haranggaol**, and continuing to Prapat.

Situated on a high plateau 160 kilometers (100 mi) south of Medan, **Danau Toba** is the focus of the Batak Highlands. The largest lake in Southeast Asia (1,700 sq km, 635 sq mi), Toba was formed by a huge prehistoric volcanic eruption. It's one of the highest (900 m, 2,950 ft) and deepest (450 m, 1,480 ft) lakes on earth. Enclosed by pine-covered mountain slopes and cliffs, the climate is cool but not bracing and sometimes rainy but rarely saturated.

The best place to experience Toba's spell is **Pulau Samosir**, a 1,000-square-kilometer (400 sq mi) island that floats near the center of the lake. Boats depart from Prapat for Samosir daily, taking visitors directly to the dozens of *losmen* scattered in Tomok, Ambarita and on the Tuk Tuk Peninsula.

Most lake-side losmen have both electricity and hot water, and visitors do not lack for comfortable accommodations. There are few vehicles on the island, but local buses run almost all the way around the island, carrying people and goods to and from markets. Samosir is regarded as the original home of the Batak in Sumatra, and the Toba Batak are considered the "purest" Batak tribe. Most tourists restrict their exploration to the central east coast, but there are many villages on the west coast and the remote central plateau of the island.

The main entry point for boats from Prapat is **Tomok**, a 30-minute cruise across amazingly quiet water. The tomb of animistic King Sidabutar is here – carved like a boat, with a fine head, and suspiciously blood-colored. In an enclosure opposite the tomb are ritual statues of a buffalo sacrifice with a *gondang* band, a *raja* and queen, and executioners who have lost their knives. A small museum in the royal house nearby is kept by a dignified old aristocrat. At the end of an avenue of souvenir booths leading from the jetty are dozens of stands selling *ulos kain* (a beautiful woven fabric), two-stringed mandolins,

Ambarita village on Samosir.

ornate woodcarvings, Batak calendars and considerably more.

Tuk Tuk is a tourist village composed largely of small hotels. On the peninsula are a new community hall for Batak dances and a few traditional houses, as well as inexpensive losmen.

With the arrival of Christianity on Samosir in 1848, Toba Batak took enthusiastically to Lutheran hymnals. Sunday church services are fine entertainment, though there are many other opportunities to hear tribal ballads (*ture ture*) in village cafes (*warung*).

Ambarita, an hour's walk from Tuk Tuk, has three megalithic complexes. The first is just up from the jetty and is notable for its 300-year-old stone seats and the tomb of Laga Siallagan, first *raja* of Ambarita. If an enemy were captured in Ambarita, neighboring raja were invited to this hilltop complex for a conference, before moving to the second megalithic cluster – stone chairs where raja and headmen met to decide the fate of the enemy prisoner. The meeting place is now enclosed in a large courtyard in the village proper; sharing its terrace is a mound used for animistic prayers. South of Ambarita is the third complex, which includes a unique breakfast table. The prisoner was beaten to death here, decapitated, chopped up on a flat stone, cooked with buffalo meat for the raja's breakfast, then washed down with blood.

Simanindo, at Samosir's northern tip and a half-day walk from Tuk Tuk, is 16 kilometers (10 mi) from Ambarita. Ferries run to Simanindo from Tigaras on the eastern shore north of Prapat. The village has a huge former king's house, which has been restored and is now a traditional Batak museum. Look for the buffalo horns out front, one for each generation, and the fine sculptures outside. A 10-minute boat ride off Simanindo is little **Pulau Tao**, where a few tiny bungalows offer escape to those who find even Samosir too hectic.

Although **Pangururan**, on Samosir's west coast, can be reached in half a day by the coastal path from Simanindo, a hike across the island's forested central plateau offers unforgettable views. From Tomok, one can climb past the king's tomb to the plateau above in about three hours. Pangururan is another 13 kilometers beyond and can be reached in less than 10 hours. On top, stay the night at one of the villages before pressing on to Roonggurni Huta and the swimming lake.

It may be necessary to ask directions from locals frequently. In the wet season, this climb is extremely muddy and slippery. Because the terrain is steep, it's easier to take a ferry to Pangururan and hike back to Tuk Tuk.

Pangururan is so close to the Sumatran mainland that it is connected by a short stone bridge. Its main attraction is an hour's walk away – the *air panas*, or hot springs, halfway up the hill and commanding a fine view of the lake.

Every Sunday, a round-island cruise lasting most of the day departs from several villages, stopping at many of the islands and villages. Or take a stroll along the island's only road and listen to the glorious hymns at the many churches, a lofty way to spend the morning.

Left, portrait from Medan area. Right, traditional architecture over Danau Toba.

WEST SUMATRA

Just as northern Sumatra is dominated by the Batak and Acehnese peoples, West Sumatra is the land of the Minangkabau. From the hill station of Bukittinggi to the port of Padang, the gentle and sophisticated Minangkabau culture pervades the region and provides a striking contrast with the rougher Batak of the hinterland.

Tradition says that the Minangkabau derive their name from victory (*menang*) in an ancient fight between Sumatran and Javanese water buffalo (*kerbau*) over land ownership. The Sumatrans entered a calf, starved it for 10 days before the fight, and bound an iron spike to its nose. Frantic in pursuit of its mother's milk, the calf impaled and killed its Javanese counterpart. Today, the buffalo is the tribal symbol.

The Minangkabau are related to the Malays of the east Sumatran coast and are thought to be descended from an inland or western branch of the later Srivijayan empire. Their language is similar to Malay. But in many other ways, the Minangkabau are quite different from other Sumatrans.

Anthropologists are fascinated by the Minangkabau, who despite their staunch Islamic devotion, comprise the largest matrilineal society on earth – upholding a social system in which property and responsibilities are distributed through the mother's family, and men are therefore responsible for their sisters' children more than their own. Since their conversion to Islam in the 16th century, however, this system has been gradually eroding, particularly now that more Minangs (more than 4 million) live in large towns and cities all over Indonesia, than in their traditional homeland in the Padang Highlands (where about 3 million remain).

This is partly the result of another distinctive Minang trait: the traditional tendency for women to stay at home and tend the fields, and for the men to roam far and wide as itinerant traders and craftsmen. And because of their high rate of literacy and formidable managerial skills, the Minangkabau have played a vital role in Indonesia's political, economical and intellectual development. Many famous Indonesian leaders and writers have been of Minang descent.

Minangkabau villagers are skillful *padi* farmers and craftsmen, as well as competent merchants. The more traditional Minangkabau still live in multifamily longhouses (*rumah gadang*). Every man and woman maintains lifetime membership in his or her maternal *rumah*. Children grow up in the mother's longhouse. While a man has little influence in his wife's longhouse, he inherits property through his mother and may wield control and even become a clan chief (*pangulu*) through his natal rumah. The pangulu, who inherits his position from a brother or maternal uncle, decides property, ritual, marital and other disputes for his clan.

Through the highlands: Travelers heading south from Danau Toba on the Trans-Sumatran Highway reach Sumatra's west coast at **Sibolga**, a port town and

Left, wedding wear, Palembang. Right, clock tower at Bukittingi.

terminus for boats to Nias, 70 kilometers (45 mi) south of Prapat. Inhabitants of this region are mainly Mandailing Batak farmers. The next major town to the south is **Padang Sidempuan**, noted primarily for its succulent *salak* fruits.

Hidden in the jungle about two hours' drive east of Sidempuan, 15 kilometers (9 mi) from the market town of Gunung Tua, are the 39 isolated **Padanglawas ruins** – 11th- and 12th-century redbrick Hindu temples. At least four temples are well preserved, others are being restored, and fragments of religious statuary and other sacred artifacts are scattered around the area.

At the village of **Bonjol**, the highway crosses the equator. A large globe and sign across the road give ample notice. Here, also, the island of Sumatra is at its widest. The village is also known as the headquarters of 19th-century Padri leader Tunku Imam Bonjol, who led a bloody rebellion against the Dutch.

The Minangkabau Highlands begin just south of here, rising to a high point below Padang at 3,850-meter (12,480 ft) **Gunung Kerinci** – Sumatra's highest peak. Eons of faulting have resulted in the creation of numerous mountain lakes, including deep and beautiful Maninjau, Singkarak and Kerinci.

The delightful hill town of **Bukittinggi**, nestling amid mountain greenery at 920 meters (3,000 ft) above sea level, is the Minangkabau "capital." Government offices, a museum and a small university make it the administrative, cultural and educational center of the region. The climate is cool and sunny; people are relaxed and friendly. Music pulses from taxis and shop fronts as handsome *dokar* – horse carts – ply the hilly streets.

The central landmark in Bukittinggi is the clock tower, with its stylized roof, standing in the town square. Geographically, the town's highest point is the **Rumah Adat Baandjuang Museum**. (*Bukittinggi* means high hill; the museum is its peak.) The 140-year-old building is a classic *rumah adat* (clan house). Exhibits include wedding and dance costumes, headdresses, musical

Leg power.

instruments, various village crafts and historic weaponry.

On another hilltop on the western side of town stands **Fort de Kock**, built by the Dutch in 1825. The fortress itself doesn't contain much of interest, but it provides a good vantage point to look out over farmland to smoldering 2,440-meter (8,000 ft) **Gunung Merapi** and Ngarai Sianok Canyon.

This rocky steep sided gorge, four kilometers long, is sometimes grandiloquently called the Grand Canyon of Indonesia. A narrow path leads from a lookout on the south side of Bukittinggi through the chasm to **Kota Gadang**, a village famed both for its silver and gold filigree and hand-embroidered shawls (based on Flemish lace-making). It has also produced a number of leading intellectuals, including two former Indonesian prime ministers – Haji Agus Salim and Mohamed Natsir.

Giant flowers and stalactites: An easy day-trip 40 kilometers (22 mi) west of Bukittinggi, Danau Maninjau is a crater lake renowned for its serenity and remote beauty. Canoes and motorboats can be rented at the lake shore. About 12 kilometers north of town at **Batang Palapuh** the giant Rafflesia flower blooms in July and August. **Ngalau Kamang**, 15 kilometers away is a cave two kilometers in length and boasts a dazzling array of stalactites and stalagmites. **Payakumbuh**, 40 kilometers (25 mi) east, is the gateway to the cliffs and waterfalls of **Harau Canyon**.

The rural highlands area between Bukittinggi and Batu Sangkar are arguably the most scenic area on Sumatra. The fertile lands grow any number of different fruits and vegetables as well as highland irrigated rice. The unique upturned bow-shaped Minangkabau houses are everywhere, adding an architectural footnote to the natural landscape. And two smoking volcanic peaks tower over everything.

A car can cover the 100 kilometers (60 mi) south from Bukittinggi to Padang in a couple of hours. The route passes through a saddle between two active volcanos, before passing through

Padang dawn.

Padang Panjang, one of the most pristinely beautiful in all of Minang country. There is an arts academy here for Minang traditions, including music and dance. A beautiful campus includes excellent theater facilities for performances. On Padang Panjang's outskirts is another botanical garden and a cultural center, with a library and artifact collection. A short distance south is **Danau Singkarak**, larger than Maninjau and easily accessible by rail or road, and Solok, a mountain town famous for its woodcarvings and high-roofed houses. East of Padang Panjang is **Batusangkar**, once the residence of the Minangkabau kings, which boasts a magnificent and preserved *rumah adat* and a reconstructed traditional royal palace, with accompanying rice barns.

Padang, West Sumatra's provincial capital, is the third-largest city on the island with a population of more than 300,000. Its wide streets, traditional architecture and horse-drawn *dokar* give it the feel of a sleepy backwater – despite the presence of a seaport at Teluk Bayur, 6 kilometers from the center of town. Spicy-hot *nasi padang* is the city's claim to fame – between 10 and 20 dishes eaten cold with rice.

Padang's museum has fine exhibits of Minangkabau artifacts, and Andalas University features an Institute of Minangkabau Studies. Otherwise, there are few "sights" in Padang, other than the brief river crossing and hike up through a Chinese cemetery to Padang Hill, overlooking the ocean.

About 10 hours' south of Padang, the massive **Kerinci-Seblat Nature Reserve** – Indonesia's largest national park – sprawls across a 345-square-kilometers (210 sq mi) stretch of jungle mountains dominated by the volcanic cone of Gunung Kerinci. You can turn off the coast road at Tapan and proceed inland (in a four-wheel-drive vehicle) to **Sungai Penuh**, the main town at the heart of the reserve. The region is also accessible by a narrow paved road that climbs up into the mountains from the inland **Trans-Sumatra Highway**.

Footpaths lead in all directions from

Characteristic landscape of the Padang highlands.

here – to Gunung Tujuh and its beautiful crater lake; to the high-altitude marsh surrounding Danau Bentu; and to the wild rain forests around Gunung Seblat, the last such woodlands in southern Sumatra. Elephants, rhinos, tigers, tapirs, clouded leopards and sun bears still roam the region. There are no orangutans, but there *are* occasional sightings of the mysterious *orang pendek* (a hairy, squat, strong "man") and the mythical *cigau* (half lion, half tiger).

Small island strings: Running parallel to Sumatra's west coast, about 100 kilometers (60 mi) offshore, are a string of ancient islands – the peaks of an undersea non-volcanic ridge separated from Sumatra by a deep trench. These islands – Simeulue, Nias, the Batu and Mentawi groups, and Enggano – have been worlds apart for half a million years; their wildlife and human inhabitants have developed in isolation.

Pulau Nias is the largest, best known and most accessible island. One hundred kilometers (60 mi) and 50 kilometers (30 mi) wide, it is home to one of Southeast Asia's most unique cultures, expressing itself today mainly in an ancient architectural style, stone sculptures and stone-jumping rituals.

While dances are still performed, they are primarily for paying tourists. *Fahombe* is the most memorable performance; acrobatic tribesmen leap feet first over stone columns several meters high and half a meter (20 in) broad. *Tutotolo* is a warrior dance in which young men leap in ritual combat.

Niasan villages are veritable fortresses, with great stone paved central "runways." Stilt houses stand in parallel rows on hillsides, a bamboo barricade protecting them from outside attack.

Northern Nias, raided by Acehnese slave traders for centuries, has few cultural remnants, although the capital, Gunungsitoli, is here. The remote center of the island is culturally rich, however; in its jungle stand the ruins of abandoned villages with huge statues. The south has retained its traditional villages and some folklore and is the best area for casual villagers.

Left, Nias warrior. **Right**, stone jumper of Nias.

Teluk Dalem, in southern Nias, is the port of entry for regular boats from Sibolga and Padang. Visitors can use the town as a home base and travel out to the villages by bus.

There are now scheduled flights to Gunungsitoli from Medan, although transportation from there to the cultural attractions of southern Nias remains rough and difficult. Plan to spend most of a day riding a bus along Nias's atrocious roads.

An impressive 150-year-old royal palace standing 15 meters (50 ft) high is preserved in **Bawomataluwo**, a 15-kilometer (9 mi) drive from Teluk Dalam. Ornamental motifs on posts and panels are finely carved to represent crocodiles, boatmen and princesses. In front of the palace and throughout the village, there are carved stone megaliths – nearly 300 of them.

The 4,500 residents of **Hilismaetano** live in 140 traditional houses, though their Great House was destroyed by war. **Hilimondegaraya's Great House** was dismantled and shipped off in 1922 by a Danish professor, who also took a Nias wife. **Gomo** is the original home of the Nias people; there is a fine village with traditional houses nearby.

Nias has become a port of call for several luxurious cruise ships, whose deluge of passengers has increased expectations of Niasan vendors. Accommodations in southern Nias are slowly improving, but there is, as yet, no international-style hotel.

Surfers have discovered the marvelous waves of **Lagundi Bay**, with the result that numerous homestays and small *losmen* now line the beach there. No doubt it will eventually blossom into something more substantial.

Of the other islands off Sumatra's west coast, **Pulau Siberut**, in the Mentawai chain, is worthy of note. Missionary influence and rapid deforestation by loggers have irrevocably changed the face of the island, but a World Wildlife Fund campaign in underway on behalf of the people and their unique fauna and flora. **Pulau Enggano**, the least-developed of all the west coast

The cheerful...

islands, is interesting from a cultural point of view. Aside from Nias, there are no visitor facilities on the islands; it is necessary to rely on the hospitality of residents and government officials.

Southern Sumatra: The southern half of Sumatra is at once the island's richest and most primitive region. Lampung Province alone accounts for 40 percent of Indonesian government revenues through its oil and rubber resources, yet people-eating tigers can still be seen on the main highways. And while Javanese migrants have resettled and cultivated previously-remote jungles, there are still animistic tribes like the Kubu and Sakai who roam the swampland hunting birds and monkeys.

Four huge provinces – Lampung, South Sumatra, Bengkulu and Jambi – make up the southern half of Sumatra. Nearly all of Jambi and the eastern two-thirds of Lampung are broad alluvial lowlands no more than 30 meters (100 ft) above sea level, and as much as 200 kilometers (125 mi) wide. The whole area is drained by numerous meandering rivers, including the Batang Hari, navigable for nearly 500 kilometers (310 mi) inland, and the Musi, Sumatra's largest. Western Lampung province is mountainous, rising to volcanic peaks of more than 3,000 meters (above 10,000 ft) before dropping sharply to the Indian Ocean at the former British colonial outpost of Bengkulu.

The Trans-Sumatran Highway runs the full length of the island, from Telukbetung to Aceh, and this region now has a fine transportation network.

Jambi, a lush jungle river port on the Batang Hari, about 200 kilometers (125 mi) north of Palembang, is a surprisingly cosmopolitan city; 160,000 Chinese, Japanese, Arabs, Indians, Malaysians, Javanese and other nationalities live here. Occasionally, a tiger wanders in from the surrounding jungle and carries off an unwary victim. As with Palembang, oil supports the economy to a great extent, and there are large exploration camps in western Jambi province.

Road and water connections between

... and the serious.

Jambi and Palembang are slow and rugged, although the highway between the two cities is now paved. Those who opt for an overland (or river) journey, however, will come across some remarkably isolated tribes. In the swamps along the Batang Hari and Musi rivers, and between them along the Rawas and Tembesi, the Kubu people live in bamboo lean-tos with leaf roofs. Despite their waterlogged environment, they avoid contact with water, convinced it will make them sick. They gather bananas and other fruits in bamboo baskets, and hunt wild pigs and apes.

North of Jambi, near the Kuantan and Indragiri rivers, the Orang Mamaq dwell in pile houses above the swamps. Traditionally hunters and fishermen who gather fruit from the jungle to supplement their diets, they have begun cultivating rice in recent times.

Farther north, as far as Pekanbaru, live the nomadic Sakai people. Their name in Malay means subordinate, but they refer to themselves as Orang Batin, the inner people. Like their southern neighbors, the Sakai people support themselves mainly by hunting and fishing – their favorite food is monkey. A strong belief in magic is intrinsic to Sakai culture.

Booming oil towns: South Sumatra's metropolis, **Palembang**, is second in Sumatra only to Medan. A city of 600,000 has grown on the banks of the Musi River, about 200 kilometers (125 mi) from the coast. A major port for well over 1,200 years, Palembang was, up until the 13th century, the major focus of trade in the Indonesian archipelago and a great international bazaar. It was also a spiritual center where thousands of Mahayana Buddhist monks studied and translated texts.

Palembang was nurtured during the Dutch colonial era as a riverine entrepôt, servicing the tin mines found on Pulau Bangka, beyond the mouth of the Musi. Forest products, rubber and coffee plantations in the vicinity contribute to the city's economy today, but oil is the real source of the wealth that has turned Palembang into Indonesia's richest city.

Wedding dress, Palembang.

There is a US$200 million petrochemical complex at **Plaju**, and a massive refinery, with a daily capacity of 75,000 barrels, at **Sungei Gerong**. Pertamina, the state oil monopoly, has shown its gratitude to Palembang by constructing a television station, sports stadium, clock tower and an elegant minaret for the main mosque.

Palembang has houses and shops raised on piles above the Musi, with river merchants plying their trade from boats, not unlike the *khlong* of Bangkok. Jalan Sudirman is the best street for shopping, and Jalan Veteran for dining. The city's red-light district has made its home in Kampung Baru. The region produces fine woven fabrics and has unique dances – including the Gending Srivijaya, dating from the 7th century, and resembling classic Thai forms. The **Rumah Bari Museum**, occupying several buildings, contains important megalithic statuary, Hindu and Buddhist sculptures, primitive ethnic crafts and weaponry, Chinese porcelain, and a display on natural history.

Megaliths and forts: West of Palembang, not far off the rail line to Lubuklinggau, is the town of **Lahat**, gateway to the Pasemah Highlands. Dotting this mountain plateau are carved megaliths, tombs, pillars and other stone ruins thought to date from about 100 AD. These are considered the best examples of prehistoric stone sculpture in Indonesia. Oddly-shaped rocks have been fashioned into figures of armed warriors either riding elephants, wrestling buffaloes or fighting snakes. There are dolmens, sanctuaries, colored paintings and other works of art in the area of volcanic **Gunung Dempo**.

Bengkulu (Bencoolen) was founded in 1685 by the British. Fort York, built in 1690, was destroyed but **Fort Marlborough**, constructed in 1762, has survived splendidly. Built as a castle, there's a gate house that contains old gravestones with English inscriptions.

Sir Stamford Raffles, who later founded Singapore, was lieutenant-governor of Bengkulu from 1818 to 1823. He introduced coffee and sugar cultiva-

East coast refinery.

tion, established schools, and fought a royal decision to hand control of Sumatra over to the Dutch in 1824. His scientific zeal (as first president of the Zoological Society of London) led to the naming of the giant Rafflesia flower in his honor. It can be found in Bengkulu at the **Dendam Taksuda Botanical Gardens**.

Coming from Java: Crossing the Sunda Strait from West Java, the Sumatran port of entry is **Bakauhuni**, the harbor for **Teluk Betung**. The ferry passes within view of Pulau Krakatau, the enormous island volcano that erupted in 1883, killing 30,000 people and dramatically affecting the climate worldwide for a year.

About two-thirds of the residents of central and southern Lampung province are Javanese farmers who migrated here – either voluntarily or assisted by the government – to relieve overcrowded conditions on Java. Although the policy was begun by the Dutch over 50 years ago and has accelerated since 1970, its effectiveness is debatable: the Javanese still tend to overpopulate the rice land upon which they live and work. The south Sumatran railway, which has its terminus at Teluk Betung's twin city of **Tanjungkarang**, wends its way north as far as Palembang, with a western branch to Lubuklinggau. There is little of real visitor interest in this part of Sumatra; archaeological remains are few and far from main routes, and many settlements are Javanese.

But Tanjungkarang is the gateway to **Way Kambas Nature Reserve**. Comprising estuaries, marshes and open grassland along the southeast coast, this park is the best place on the island to see wild elephants. Tigers and wild boars are also plentiful, and bird watching is an avian delight.

Yet it has been an uphill battle to conserve this rich coastal land. Migrant farmers, loggers, Jakarta-based developers and other entrepreneurs have claimed tens of thousands of hectares; three disastrous fires nearly eliminated what once was a substantial forest; and tigers were legally hunted until 1974. Park authorities in Tanjungkarang can

Fort Marlborough at Bengkulu.

arrange for visitors to take a four-hour (one-way) boat trip from **Labuhan Meringgi**, 12 kilometers south of the reserve, to the Way Kambus estuary, navigable for 25 kilometers (16 mi) inland from the coast.

Strategic Riau archipelago: Between the swampy shores of Sumatra and the Malay Peninsula lies a chain of more than three thousand small islands. These and the eastern Sumatran lowlands comprise the province of **Riau**, one of the fastest growing parts of Indonesia in terms of economics, population and in visitor interest.

While most of Riau remains untouched, change has come swiftly to Batam and Bintan, the islands closest to Singapore. Batam is being transformed into the industrial heartland of Riau, and into a weekend retreat from Singapore, with luxury hotels set around golf courses. Bintan has been earmarked for development into a major beach resort similar to Bali's Nusa Dua. **Pekanbaru**, the provincial capital and the largest city in mainland Riau, is a thriving oil-production center. Elsewhere in Riau, fishing and timber are still the mainstays of the local economy.

Riau is considered one of the heartlands of Southeast Asian culture, and it was the center of Malay civilization from the 16th through to the 18th centuries. The islands became part of a vast Malay empire founded by Sultan Parameswara at Malacca in 1402. With the arrival of the Portuguese in the early 16th century, the sultan fled south, establishing new capitals at Johor and Penyengat. Although the region later evolved into separate sultanates, it was essentially one cultural and economic zone until the British and Dutch divided the area in the early 19th century.

Total population of the province is about 2.5 million, but that figure could reach 3 million by the turn of the century as immigration continues from elsewhere in Indonesia. Varied cultures make this a rich ethnographic region. Mainland Riau is inhabited by coastal Malays, while the island's population include Malays, Bugis *orang laut* (sea gypsies), Chinese, Arabs and Indians.

The Bugis are renowned seamen in self-imposed exile from their native Sulawesi homeland, living aboard wooden *pinisi* sailing craft and trading throughout the archipelago on adjacent seas. The *orang laut* are seafaring nomads who are born, live and die on their small boats. Although they have maritime settlements from Burma to the Philippines, they more commonly sail or row their boats through a labyrinth of interisland channels and mangrove swamps, fishing and trading.

Pulau Bintan is the largest of all the Riau islands. For years it remained largely undisturbed, an expanse of jungle, swamp and mountains, with isolated *kampung* that betray little 20th-century influence. But like neighboring Batam, the island is changing fast. Several industrial zones have been mapped out and the entire northern shore is being developed into a mega-resort with dozens of hotels and other tourist facilities. The energetic little city of **Tanjung Pinang** is the largest town on the island. A quick two-hour ferry ride from Singa-

Spicy Padang food.

pore, Tanjung Pinang is strategically situated at the intersection of sea lanes connecting Singapore, Sumatra, Java, Madura and Sulawesi. The harbor is a port of call for all sorts of vessels: Chinese junks, cargo ships, fishing boats, indigenous craft from Sulawesi and Madura, and the Sumatran *nade* – a coastal freighter with large sails, and which is modeled after old Portuguese and Spanish caravels.

Good hotels are available and small boats may be hired to explore other tiny islands in the immediate area. Tanjung Pinang is also a jumping off spot for trips to the smaller Riau islands and the Lingga Archipelago. In addition, there are weekly ferry connections to Jakarta. The small but interesting **Riau Museum** is situated on Jalan B.G. Katamso in the eastern suburbs. The collection includes clothing, weapons, musical instruments and furniture that once belonged to the Riau sultans. You can also catch a speedboat to **Senggarang**, a Chinese kampung on the far side of the Riau River. The village has four shrines including the **Banyan Temple**, a 200-year-old clan house suspended in the arms of a giant banyan tree.

Just across the water from Tanjung Pinang is a small island called **Penyengat**, a cradle of the Malay civilization. This was once the home base of the sultans of Riau, with a lavish court and royal city that encompassed nearly 10,000 citizens. A book called the *Bustanul Katibin,* the first Malay grammar, was published on Penyengat in 1857, laying the foundation for Bahasa Indonesia, the lingua franca of the entire Indonesian archipelago.

More than 2,000 people live on Penyengat today, spread among five kampungs. People go about their daily chores much as they did a hundred years ago when the sultans reigned: mending their fishing nets and fixing boats, harvesting papayas and coconuts, or washing clothes.

Just beyond the main ferry pier is the old **Royal Mosque** built in 1818. Nearby is the **royal graveyard** where many of the sultans are buried. A path leads across the island – past the **Palace of Raja Ali Marhum** – to the southern shore, where there are several ruins of old mansions.

The most impressive of these is the **house of Tungku Bilek**, an elegant two story structure nearly engulfed by jungle vegetation. On a hill overlooking the town is **Bukit Kursi Fort**, built in the late 18th century as a defense against the Dutch.

Trikora Beach on Bintan's east coast is an unspoiled stretch of white sand and coconut palms with beautiful turquoise water. There are hotels and guest houses for those who want to spend the night. Stretching 14 kilometers (9 mi) along the north coast is **Pasir Panjang Beach**, which is being transformed into the Bintan Beach International Resort (BBIR) – a sprawling complex of hotels, golf courses and holiday condos scheduled for development over the next 15 years. The first beach hotel opened in 1994, and a ferry terminal is being built at Tanjung Sebung to handle passengers directly from Singapore.

West of Bintan is the large island of **Batam**, which has been developed into a major industrial satellite of Singapore. The island is popular with weekend visitors from Singapore, who come for the golf courses, beaches, duty-free shopping and delicious seafood. Ferries and hydrofoils ply nearly every hour, from sunrise to sundown, from Singapore to Sekupang or Batu Ampar on Batam. **Nagoya**, the island's largest town, was built by Japanese soldiers during World War II, although it bears little resemblance to its namesake in Japan. The town has numerous hotels, restaurants, discos and karaoke bars to cater to visiting businessmen and construction workers.

Riau province's capital and biggest city is **Pekanbaru**, a busy port on the Sumatran mainland, 160 kilometers (100 mi) up the Siak River from the coast. This friendly Caltex oil town, with a large foreign population, is a good base for exploring nearby jungle abodes of the durian-loving Sumatran rhinoceros, tigers, elephants and birds. Four hours' downriver, at the village of **Siak Sri Indrapura**, is a palace built in 1723.

Colors above Bintan Island.

JAVA

The fertile island of Java, home to one of the human race's earliest ancestors, is a world unto itself. Over 100 million people live here on an island the size of California; the population density is at least double that of any other place of comparable area on the planet.

Beyond sheer weight of numbers, however, the Javanese also possess a rich historical record and a unique cultural heritage. Java's dance and dramatic traditions, *wayang* puppets, *gamelan* music and *batik* textiles are famous the world over, as are its ancient temples and elegant palaces. The island's physical beauty is less widely renowned, but no less captivating. Tropical rain forests, alpine meadows, pristine beaches – Java has a place for almost everyone.

For thousands of years, this has been a land of the rhinoceros, Javan tiger, wild ox, mouse deer and Javan gibbon, flying fox, monitor lizard, saltwater crocodile, python, and peacock, all of which still inhabit the island's few remaining jungle refuges. The naturalist Alfred Russell Wallace was so struck by the flora and fauna that he proclaimed Java "that noble and fertile island – the very Garden of the East."

Java is distinguished by its many volcanoes, and, indeed, volcanoes are such a dominant feature of the landscape that one of the island's cones is nearly always within view. Approximately 30 of these behemoths are still active, and in several parts of the island, they produce cauldrons of bubbling mud (*solfatara*), vented jets of gas (*fumarole*) and hot sulphur springs. Every few years, a subterranean convulsion produces massive eruptions of ash and lava, unleashing poisonous gases, clouds of scorching dust (*ladoe*) and avalanches of boiling mud (*lahar*), which wipe out entire villages, sometimes killing hundreds and rendering thousands homeless.

Yet despite their awesome destructiveness, volcanic eruptions are the ultimate source of Java's legendary fecundity. The volcanic ejecta is rich in soluble plant nutrients (unlike in neighboring Sumatra), fertilizing the soil to an extraordinary degree.

Java is also a cultural potpourri. There is a repertoire of dance, drama and comedy that draws inspiration from the Hindu epics, the exploits of Islamic warriors, and the tales of ancient Javanese folk heroes. There are mosques where white-capped *haji* finger their prayer beads, Chinese temples where stone lions guard the gates, and churches where choirs sing. There are trance rituals whose origins are as misty as humankind's own beginnings, and puppets of leather and wood that mesmerize audiences during all-night performances. And there is Indonesia's gamelan, a music of gongs and chimes as glistening and fluid as quicksilver, yet as textured as the face of Java itself.

Preceding pages: planting rice in flooded paddy fields. Left, the scenic road to Dieng Plateau.

WISMA INDOCEMENT
ARTHALOKA
Bank Dharmala
Marlboro

JAKARTA

For the majority of its residents, Jakarta is a city of promise. This hope for a better life has caused the city's population to more than double in the last two decades – over 15 million people live in the greater metropolitan area.

The city has grown tremendously in recent years, with the addition of skyscrapers, motorways and middle-class suburbs. Capital to the world's fourth most populous nation, Jakarta is a metropolis that sometimes verges on the chaotic, but not quite. Yet.

With the growth, of course, has come an often nauseating pollution and packed traffic, both of which can quench leisurely strolls around the city. Partly as a result, Jakarta doesn't have much of a reputation among travelers. But this is a *big* city and many visitors are not prepared for that. As for getting anywhere, the city operates on *jam karet,* or rubber time, not punctuality.

The busy Thamrin-Sudirman corridor, through the heart of the city, is a wall of glimmering glass and steel, with some of the most interesting high-rise architecture in Southeast Asia. A whole new Central Business District (CBD) is under construction in the Senayan area. The bustling Glodok and Blok M districts throb with neon signs and modern shopping centers. Tanjung Priok is the nation's busiest port, and nearby Ancol and Pluit are being developed into waterfront resort communities. In fact, much of Jakarta is hardly recognizable from a decade ago. Yet there are other parts of the city that seem frozen in time. Little residential districts with market gardens and makeshift *kampung* dwellings impart something of a village atmosphere to many back alleys.

Jakarta's attractions, nonetheless, are abundant. Ask the locals. Those with an interest in Indonesian history and culture will tell about Jakarta's fine museums, colonial architecture, performing arts and rich intellectual life. Adventurous types will probably regale you with tales of traditional temples and busy markets in obscure corners of the city. Bon vivants will more likely speak of a favorite antique shop, an excellent seafood restaurant or an exciting disco. Most residents will also express a sense of being in the thick of things, of living at the epicenter of the nation's commercial, cultural and political life. And everyone will tell you about their friends: funny, fun-loving, irreverent, irrepressible – Jakartans are the city's greatest asset. So give Jakarta a chance.

Queen city of the east: The mouth of the Ciliwung River, where Jakarta is located, has been settled since very ancient times; it developed into a major pepper port during the 15th and 16th centuries. In 1618, the architect of the Dutch empire in the Indies, Jan Pieterszoon Coen, moved his headquarters here. Coen subsequently attacked and razed the town of Jayakarta – the name by which the port was then known – and ordered construction of a new town: **Batavia**. The fortunes of Batavia under the Dutch East India Company (VOC) rose and then fell. Batavia grew

Left, Jakarta's skyline takes on electric contours. Right, Monas flame, above Medan Merdeka.

rich throughout the 17th century on an entrepôt trade in sugar, pepper, cloves, nutmeg, tea, textiles, porcelains, hardwoods and rice. But after 1700, a series of disasters befell it. Declining market prices, epidemics of malaria, cholera and typhoid, and an unfortunate massacre of the Batavia Chinese in 1740, combined with the frequent wars and official corruption that had plagued the VOC since its inception, cast a pall over the city that had once fancied itself Queen of the East.

At the beginning of the 19th century, Batavia received a much-needed face-lift under Governor-General Willem ("Iron Marshal") Daendels, a follower of Napoleon. The old city was demolished to provide building materials for a new one to the south, around what are now Medan Merdeka and Lapangan Banteng. Two fashionable architectural styles of the period – French Empire and Neo-Classical – blended with many tree-lined boulevards and extensive gardens laid out by Daendels to impart a certain grace and elegance to the city. And with the economic success of the exploitative cultivation system on Java, the colony was once again prosperous. By the turn of the century, Batavia's homes, hotels and clubs were in no way inferior to those of Europe.

During the brief Japanese occupation of World War II, Batavia was renamed Jakarta, dramatically transforming from a tidy Dutch colonial town of 200,000 into an Indonesian city of more than one million people. Following independence, hundreds of thousands more Indonesians flooded in from the countryside and outer islands, and Jakarta quickly outstripped all other Indonesian cities in size and importance, becoming what scholars term a primate city: the unrivaled political, cultural and economic center of the new nation.

Jakarta's old harbor: Starting at sunrise, if possible, visit the picturesque port of **Sunda Kelapa**. This is the name of the original Hindu spice trading post that was conquered and converted to Islam more than four and a half centuries ago. The flavor of ancient times is

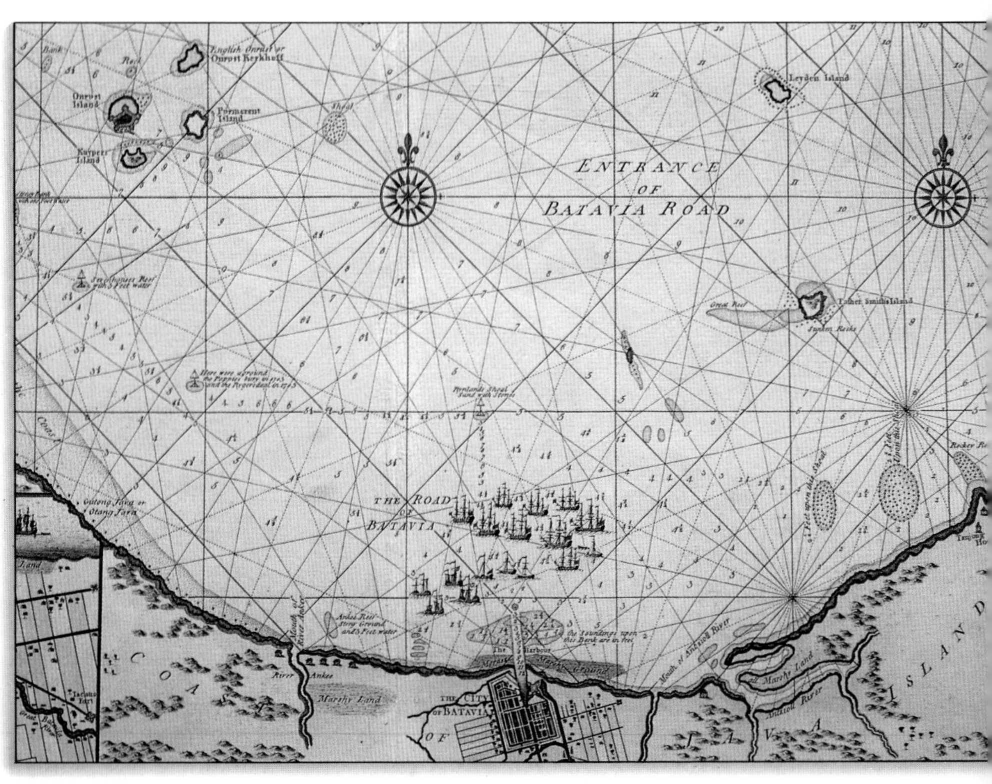

Early map of Batavia Harbor, 1787

preserved in the form of traditional wooden *pinisi* – Buginese sailing vessels that continue to play a vital role in the commerce of modern-day Indonesia. Each day, some 70 or 80 of these craft arrive laden with sawn timber from Kalimantan, which is off-loaded at a two-kilometer-long wharf that has been in continuous use since 1817. A brisk morning walk amidst this nautical bustle, to witness mammoth sails unfurling to the wind, is one of the unforgettable experiences of Jakarta.

The area around Sunda Kelapa is rich in history. Near the river stands a 19th-century **Dutch lookout tower** (Uitkijk), constructed upon the site of the original customs house (Pabean) of Jayakarta. This is where traders once rendered their gifts and tribute to the native ruler in return for the privilege of trading here. The tower is sometimes open and offers a view of the city and the coast.

Behind the lookout stands a long two-story structure dating from VOC times, now the **Museum Bahari**. This warehouse was erected by the Dutch in 1652, and was used for many years to store coffee, tea and Indian cloth. Inside are displays of traditional sailing craft from all corners of the Indonesian archipelago, as well as some old maps of Batavia. Down a narrow lane and around a corner behind the museum lies the **fish market** (**Pasar Ikan**), beyond numerous stalls selling nautical gear.

Further east along the waterfront is a giant seaside recreation area called **Ancol Dreamland**, once swampland and now featuring beach-front hotels, a golf course, bowling alley, arts and crafts market, drive-in theater, and swimming pools. There are also several theme parks, including **Sea World** and **Dunia Fantasi**, Indonesia's only real amusement park with roller coaster and Ferris wheel. Ferries to **Pulau Seribu (Thousand Islands**) leave from the nearby Ancol Marina.

Sights of old Batavia: Now known as **Kota**, the area of the old town of Batavia came to life in the 1620s as a tiny, walled town modeled after Amsterdam. Most of the original settlement – Old

'essels nchored at he port of unda elapa.

Batavia – was demolished at the beginning of the 19th century. Only the town square area survived. It has been restored and renamed **Taman Fatahillah**, and three of the surrounding colonial edifices have been converted into museums: the History Museum, the Fine Arts Museum and the Wayang Museum.

Start at the **Jakarta History Museum** on the south side of the square. This was formerly the city hall (*Stadhuis*) of Batavia, a solid structure completed in 1710 and used by successive governments, right up through the 1960s. It now houses fascinating memorabilia from the colonial period, notably 18th-century furnishings and portraits of the VOC governors, along with many prehistoric, classical and Portuguese period artifacts. Dungeons visible from the back of the building were used as holding cells, where prisoners were made to stand waist-deep in sewage for weeks awaiting their trials. Executions and torture were once commonplace in the main square as judges watched from the balcony above the main entrance.

The **Wayang Museum** on the western side of the square contains many puppets and masks, some of them quite rare. There are buffalo-hide shadow puppets (*wayang kulit*), round-stick puppets (*wayang golek*), flat-stick puppets (*wayang klithik*), Chinese hand puppets (*potehi*), Thai shadow puppets (*wayang siam*), patriotic shadow puppets (*wayang Suluh*), Biblical shadow puppets (*wayang wahyu*), and even a puppet of Batavia's founder, J.P. Coen. Interesting, too, are the simple puppets made of rice straw and bamboo. There is also a collection of *topeng* masks, and tombstones of several early Dutch governors are on display.

The **Fine Arts Museum** (**Museum Seni Rupa**) on the east side of Taman Fatahillah is housed in the former Court of Justice building (completed in 1879). The museum has collections of paintings and sculptures by modern Indonesian artists, and an important exhibition of rare porcelains, including many Sung celadons from the Adam Malik collection, ancient Javanese water jugs

Ancol's Dunia Fantasi.

(*kendhi*), and terracotta pieces dating from the 14th century.

Before leaving the area, walk over to the old 16th-century Portuguese cannon mounted on the north side of Taman Fatahillah. **Si Jagur**, as it is called, is regarded by many as a fertility symbol, perhaps because of the fist that is cast into the butt end of the cannon, with a thumb protruding between its index and middle fingers (an obscene gesture in Indonesia). Occasionally, young couples are seen approaching with offerings. Nearby is a trendy restaurant called Cafe Batavia, once an old warehouse, with window tables that offer excellent views of the square.

Next, walk behind the Wayang Museum to view two Dutch houses dating from the 18th century. Across the canal and to the left stands a solid red brick town house (Jl. Kali Besar Barat No. 11) that was built around 1730 by the soon-to-be governor-general. The design, and particularly the fine Chinese-style woodwork, are typical of old Batavian residences. Three doors to the left stands the only other house from the same period, now the offices of the Chartered Bank. Several blocks to the north, an old red wooden drawbridge straddles the canal, recalling the days when Batavia was a Dutch town laced with waterways. Nearby is the Omni Batavia Hotel.

As is the case in most post-colonial Asian cities, Jakarta's **Chinatown** is immediately adjacent to the old European center – here just to the south of the old city in an area now known as **Glodok**. Unlike Chinatowns elsewhere, you'll see no signs in Chinese here, except in the two Buddhist temples deep within the convoluted back alleys. The public use of Chinese characters was banned decades ago during the failed but bloody Communist insurgency.

Begin at bustling Pasar Glodok shopping center or the City Hotel across the street (Jl. Pancoran) and walk through the maze of narrow lanes winding past shop fronts.

Around Merdeka Square: A circumnavigation of central Jakarta begins at the top of the **National Monument**

Happy faces in fantasy land.

(**Monas**), a 137-meter-tall (450 ft) marble obelisk set in the center of **Medan Merdeka** (**Freedom Square**). The monument is surmounted by an observation deck and a 14-meter (45 ft) bronze flame sheathed in 33 kilograms (73 lbs) of gold. It was commissioned by Soekarno and completed in 1961 – a combination Olympic Flame/Washington Monument with the phallic overtones of an ancient Hindu-Javanese *lingga.* In the basement are dioramas depicting historical scenes from a nationalistic viewpoint. A high-speed elevator shoots to the observation deck, where on a clear day there is a fabulous 360-degree view of Jakarta.

From Monas, travel north along Jalan Gajah Mada to the splendid villa that now houses the **National Archives**. This is the last of scores of 18th-century mansions built by rich Dutch officials of the East India Company. Unfortunately, special permission is needed to tour the building, but even from the street, the beautiful woodwork and manicured gardens that were once the hallmark of old Batavia town are visible.

Double back to Medan Merdeka and pass behind the **Presidential Palace**, situated between Jl. Medan Merdeka Utara and Jl. Veteran. The palace building consists of two 19th-century neoclassical style villas back to back. The older of the two, the **Istana Negara**, faces north and was built by a wealthy Dutch merchant around 1800. It was taken over some years later to serve as the town residence of the governor (whose official residence was then located in Bogor). The south-facing **Istana Merdeka** was added in 1879, as a reception area. Whereas President Soekarno resided in the palace and frequently gave lavish banquets in the central courtyard, President Soeharto prefers to stay in his more modest home in the Menteng area and commutes to work.

Proceeding eastward, one encounters the imposing white marble **Istiqlal Mosque**, with its massive dome and rakish minarets – one of the largest mosques in East Asia. Opposite it are the ultra-modern headquarters of

Prayers in Istiqlal Mosque.

Pertamina, the state oil monopoly that supplies a tenth of OPEC's oil and a large part of the nation's revenue.

Lapangan Banteng (Wild Ox Field) lies just to the east, bounded on the north by the neo-gothic **Catholic cathedral** (completed in 1901; note the rather interesting spires), on the east by the Supreme Court (1848) and the Department of Finance (1982), and on the south by the Borobudur Hotel with its lush gardens. In the center of the square stands a muscle-bound giant bursting from his shackles. This is the **Irian Jaya Freedom Memorial** – placed here in 1963 by Soekarno to commemorate the annexation of Irian Jaya. When the statue was first erected, Jakartans joked that the giant was crying "empty" – refering to the Finance Department behind.

Returning to the eastern side of Medan Merdeka, one passes two more colonial structures: the **Gedung Pancasila** (1830) where Soekarno unveiled the five principles of the Indonesian state, and the small **Emmanuel Church** (1835), resembling a Greek temple.

On the west side of Medan Merdeka lies one of Indonesia's great cultural treasures: the **National Museum**. Opened in the 1868 by the Batavian Society for Arts and Sciences – the first scholarly organization in colonial Asia and founded in 1778 – the museum houses enormously valuable collections of antiquities, books and ethnographic artifacts acquired by the Dutch during the 19th and early 20th centuries. Unfortunately, the displays are not well labeled, although the objects exhibited are fascinating. Hindu-Javanese stone statuary, prehistoric bronze wares and Chinese porcelains are among the exhibits that take hours to see properly. The star collection, however, is housed in the Treasure Room, open only on Sunday mornings – a stupendous hoard of royal Indonesian heirlooms.

Southeast of the square, a short ride down Jalan Cikini, are two other noteworthy attractions. **Taman Ismail Marzuki** (TIM) is a multifaceted cultural center that presents a continuing bill of drama, dance and music from

National Museum.

around Indonesia. Nearby, **Jalan Surabaya** is the city's famous so-called "antique street", with dozens of shops selling everything from wayang puppets to ship fittings, most of it new.

Joyride to south Jakarta: Hail a cab and cruise west across the upper-class residential area of **Menteng** to the **Welcome Statue**, a busy roundabout with a statue of two waving youths and a fountain. **Jalan Thamrin** runs north and south here, turning into Jalan Sudirman a few more blocks south. The roundabout fountain is an urban anchor of Jakarta, built by Soekarno in the early 1960s. Surrounding the roundabout are the Hotel Indonesia, the nation's first international-class hotel, and the ritzy Grand Hyatt, perched atop Jakarta's finest shopping mall, **Plaza Indonesia**.

Further south along Thamrin-Sudirman are numerous monuments to Indonesia's recent economic development, including new banks, hotels, shopping centers and office blocks, as well as the new **Jakarta Stock Exchange**. Twenty years ago, this was a ceremonial boulevard with nothing on either side. Today, the entire street is lined with high-rises and flashy malls.

Blok M is where Jakarta's middle class does much of its shopping. The area bustles with street stalls, hundreds of shops and at least seven modern shopping malls, including two giant shopping centers: Blok M Plaza and Blok M Mall. This is also the home of the famous **Pasaraya** department store, which features two entire floors of clothing and handicrafts from all over Indonesia. After the shopping is done, try one of the trendy restaurants or pubs in the Blok M area.

Lastly, drive through the nearby residential neighborhoods like **Pondok Indah** or **Cipete** to see how the Indonesian wealthy and many expatriates live. Western-style homes rent for as much as US$5000 a month.

Just off the super highway leading south to Bogor is the major theme park called **Taman Mini** – Beautiful Indonesia in Miniature Park – which compresses the entire archipelago into a single attraction. While this is surely an impossible feat, the park does at least permit you to see something of the thousands of Indonesian islands you will not visit. In any case, it is worth a visit, for the fine bird park if nothing else.

Encompassing nearly 100 hectares (250 acres), Taman Mini has 27 main pavilions – one for each of Indonesia's provinces. These are clustered around a lake containing a three-dimensional relief map of the Indonesian archipelago. The pavilions have been constructed using authentic materials and workmanship to exhibit a traditional style of architecture from each province. Inside are displays of handicrafts, traditional costumes, musical instruments and other artifacts for which each region is known. Many items are sold as souvenirs.

In addition, there are at least 30 other attractions, including a tropical bird park, orchid garden, IMAX cinema, cable car ride, transport museum, swimming pool, and the splendid **Museum Indonesia** – a three-story Balinese palace filled with traditional textiles, houses, boats, puppets, jewelry and wedding costumes.

Left, West Sumatran wedding clothes, at Taman Mini. Right, Taman Fatahillah in foreground, central Jakarta in distance.

THOMSON

WEST JAVA AND THE NORTHERN COAST

In the early 1800s, Java had about 3.5 million inhabitants, a population number that had been relatively stable since the time of the great Hindu-Buddhist empires a millennium earlier. Wet-rice cultivation was the basis of civilization, and as long as the population was still fairly small, the Javanese produced vast surpluses. The island's rulers based their power upon the resources that surplus rice afforded, provisioning armies of warriors and laborers to do their bidding, and importing vast riches from overseas through traders.

All of this changed dramatically following the intervention of the Dutch in Javanese economic and political affairs, culminating with the institution, from 1830 to 1870, of the infamous cultivation system (*Cultuurstelsel*) of forced labor and land-use taxes. Under this system, more and more Javanese land was opened to cultivation, the products of which the Dutch sold at a handsome profit overseas. An unforeseen side effect of this policy was a spiraling birth rate. By 1900, the population of Java had soared by 28 million and today it stands at about 110 million people.

Cosmopolitan melting pot: Not everyone on the island is Javanese. In the uplands of West Java, the inhabitants are mainly Sundanese, a people with their own language and identity. The Javanese themselves constitute about two-thirds of the total population and inhabit the fertile plains of central and east Java, plus much of the island's northern coast. Madura and the adjoining coast of east Java are home of the Madurese people. There are also small pockets of Tenggerese and Badui peoples living in isolated highland sanctuaries in east and west Java, respectively. Lastly, the trading ports of the north coast also harbor immigrant Chinese, Arabs and Europeans, as well as other people from the Indonesian archipelago.

Java is also a cultural potpourri. There is a repertoire of dance, drama and comedy that draws its inspiration from the Hindu epics, the exploits of Islamic warriors and tales of ancient Javanese folk heroes. There are mosques where white-capped *haji* finger their prayer beads, Chinese temples where stone lions guard the gates, and churches where choirs sing. There are trance rituals whose origins are as misty as mankind's own beginnings, and puppets of leather and wood who entrance audiences during all-night performances. There is also *gamelan*, a music of gongs and chimes as glistening and fluid as quicksilver, yet as textured as the face of the land.

Sundanese heartland: The Sundanese people inhabit most of the western third of Java, the so-called **Tanah Sunda**, or Sunda Lands. Although physically indistinguishable from the Javanese, they are culturally quite different – known for their mellifluous language, hardy individualism and staunch Islam.

West Java may be roughly divided into two distinct regions: the Parahyangan (Abode of the Gods) or volcanic highlands centered around the

Preceding pages: Banten was the first Dutch settlement on Java. Left, colonial Dutch architecture, Banten. Right, misty montane forest on Mount Gede.

provincial capital of Bandung, and the northern coastal plain. The coast is much more mixed, having absorbed a multitude of immigrants and influences via its trading ports for many centuries. In certain coastal areas (notably around Jakarta and Banten), Javanese and Indonesian are more commonly spoken.

While it may be true that the Sundanese lack the courtly sophistication and architectural monuments of a high civilization, they are certainly no cultural paupers. Their complex gamelan and *angklung* music, popular *jaipongan* dances, and lively *wayang golek* puppet performances have achieved every bit as much recognition as similar art forms in central Java or Bali.

Above all, the Sunda Lands are among the most beautiful and accessible highlands in all of Indonesia, whether for a mountain climb and jungle trek, or an endless round of temples, palaces and dance performances.

Escapes From Jakarta: There are a number of ways to escape from Jakarta without actually leaving west Java. One option is to hop a boat or plane to one of the 600 offshore islands to the north, known collectively as the **Pulau Seribu (Thousand Islands)**. Several of the closer islands, notably Onrust, were used by the Dutch East India Company as warehousing and dry-docking stations, and the ruins of colonial installations can still be seen.

Most of the Thousand Islands are uninhabited and inaccessible except by private boat. Several of the islands contain bird and marine sanctuaries, and the entire northern part of Pulau Seribu has been declared a marine national park – although there are no facilities at present. About a dozen islands have been developed into pleasant beach resorts, which are easily reached by boat from Ancol Marina, in Jakarta. The passage takes anywhere from two to four hours, depending on your final destination, and the marina also offers day trips that visit three of the closer islands.

The more popular resorts include Pulau Seribu Paradise on Pelangi island, Matahari Island Resort on Macan

Muscling a mooring in Pulau Seribu.

Besar island, and Kotok Resort on an island of the same name. Each has fully-equipped hotels, with tiled or thatched roof bungalows overlooking the beach. Activities include scuba diving, snorkeling, swimming and fishing.

Another quick getaway, soon to be made even quicker with the opening of the new Jakarta to Merak expressway, is the jaunt to Java's sandy and secluded **west coast beaches**. Depending on the method of transportation, the route taken and the traffic, you can enjoy a swim and a cool ocean breeze within three to five hours of leaving Jakarta.

Stop along the way at the village of **Banten** – the site, during the 16th century, of one of Asia's largest and most cosmopolitan trading emporiums. Banten town was razed by order of the Dutch governor-general in 1808, and is today but a tiny fishing village straddling a tidal creek. But the ruins of two massive palaces and a Dutch fortress, plus the interesting old mosque (with its adjacent museum) and a Chinese temple, are all well worth the detour.

About 110 kilometers (70 mi) west of Jakarta, the main road branches off to the right at Cilegon and continues another 13 kilometers to **Merak**, where ferries depart for Bakauhuni on Sumatra. Branching south toward the beaches, there are pretty bays and long stretches of deserted beach past the village of **Anyer**, 20 kilometers (12 mi) southwest of Cilegon. Six kilometers past Anyer, at **Karang Bolong**, a huge rock forms a natural archway to the sea and this has become a popular (and crowded) weekend swimming spot for Jakartans.

Twenty kilometers further south is **Carita Beach**, a popular weekend retreat from Jakarta that offers beach-side bungalow resorts with swimming, sailing, diving and dining. In addition to sun, sea, sand and solitude, this palm-fringed coast is famous for its sunset views of the uninhabited volcanic islands of **Krakatau**. Although dormant for centuries, this volcano achieved instant and lasting infamy in 1883, when it erupted with cataclysmic force, ripping out a huge chunk of the earth's

Sunrise at the old mosque, Banten.

crust to form a monstrous 40-square-kilometer (16 sq mi) submarine caldera. The sea rushed in, and tidal waves up to 30 meters (100 ft) high swept the coast, claiming more than 35,000 lives.

In the decades that followed, undersea activity continued, and a new active crater has emerged from the sea – **Anak Krakatau** (Son of Krakatau). Assuming Anak Krakatau is not erupting or spewing poison gases, the four tiny islands of the Krakatau group may be visited by chartering a boat from hotels in Carita or Labuan.

Boats can also be chartered from Labuan to **Ujung Kulon National Park**, at Java's southwest tip, for a tramp through pristine tropical rain forest and a first-hand look at some of Java's rare wildlife species. And there is a scenic back road that winds through the Parahyangan foothills to Rangkasbitung and Bogor, skirting the highland home of the mysterious Badui people. Another narrow, paved road curves up and down across the mountainous southwest coast of Java and ends up at the south coast beach resort area of Pelabuhan Ratu.

Highland garden towns: The third and most scenic of west Java's escape routes is an ascent into the dramatic **Parahyangan Highlands** south of Jakarta. First stop along this route is **Bogor** – only an hour's drive from central Jakarta via the Jagorawi Expressway. Situated about 80 kilometers (50 mi) inland and 290 meters (900 ft) above sea level, Bogor is appreciably cooler (and wetter) than the coast.

The main attraction here are the glorious **Botanical Gardens** (**Kebun Raya**), originally opened by the Dutch in 1817 and world renowned during the 19th century for its range of tropical botanical specimens and its research into cash crops, such as tea, cassava, tobacco and cinchona. The vast park with its rolling lawns, lily ponds and forest groves now contains over 15,000 species of trees and plants (including 400 different types of palms), and special orchid nurseries house more than 5,000 orchid varieties from Indonesia and abroad. There is

Fishing near a smoking Krakatau.

also an excellent zoological museum and a library of richly-illustrated botanical tomes. The elegant white presidential summer palace, constructed by the Dutch in 1856 as the official residence for governors-general of the Dutch East Indies, stands at the northern end of the gardens.

The road east from Bogor up to **Puncak Pass** climbs steadily, winding its way through a crowded highlands resort area and then into a manicured landscape of tea plantations. Stop at the Rindu Alam Restaurant, on the right just before the peak, to enjoy a spectacular view (on a clear day) down to Bogor and toward the coast. Walk across the road and downhill a short distance to find a path leading to tiny **Telaga Warna** (Lake of Many Colors).

Beyond Puncak Pass, a turn-off to the right leads to the **Cibodas Botanical Gardens**, an extension of Bogor's Kebun Raya, and famous for its collection of montane and temperate climate flora from around the world. This is also the starting point for the six-hour climb up to the peaks of Gunung Gede and Gunung Pangranggo, with their fine views, hot springs, waterfalls and interesting wildlife. Excellent accommodation and food are available in the nearby mountain resort of **Cipanas**, a lovely place to spend a few days, hiking through the highland forests and tea estates.

The southern coast of west Java, beautiful but dangerous, is also within easy reach of Bogor (about two hours by car). A good road winds south from Ciawi over the pass between Gunung Pangranggo and Gunung Salak, where the landscape is a lush garden of rubber trees, tea plantations and terraced rice fields. A scenic side road branches off to the right at Cibadak and meanders down to the fishing village of **Pelabuhan Ratu**, where the ragged, wind-lashed Indian Ocean foams and crashes onto smooth black sand beaches.

The village is unspoiled and vital – when the boats moor in the morning, the fish market does a roaring trade in fresh tuna fish, prawns, whitebait, sharks, stingrays and other delicacies. A number

Cibodas Botanical Gardens.

of good swimming beaches and hotels line the coast for several kilometers past the town, but be warned that the surf and the undertow can be treacherous.

A circle drive from Jakarta – up over Puncak Pass and down to the famed rice growing area of Cianjur, then back along the south sides of Gunung Gede and Gunung Pangranggo via Sukabumi to Bogor – is a very enjoyable day-trip from Jakarta. With time out for lunch at one of the Puncak Pass restaurants, the combination of volcanos and lush highlands is an unbeatable alternative to the crowded cacophony of Jakarta.

City of flowers: Only two hours from Jakarta by high-speed train (the "Argo Gede"), four or more by road, the highland city of **Bandung** offers a cool alternative to the capital's oppressive heat. Located in a huge basin 700 meters (2,300 ft) above sea level and surrounded on all sides by lofty volcanic peaks, Bandung is now the population and cultural center of the Sunda Lands, and the capital of West Java Province. It's a burgeoning city with over 1.5 million inhabitants. Before World War II, it was a quaint Dutch administrative and university town of about 150,000, called the Paris of Java because of its broad, shady boulevards and elegant homes. Although it's now a rapidly growing industrial city, Bandung is still green and attractive, often called Kota Kembang (City of Flowers).

Bandung's foremost industry is education, with 27 colleges and universities and thousands of students. But there is plenty for travelers, with an abundance of Dutch-colonial, art-deco architecture, including the magnificent **Gedung Sate**. You can also browse factory outlet shops along **Jalan Ciampelas**, a feast for the eye as well as the pocket book. Many of the shops have quirky facades fashioned from paper mache, chrome and plywood – King Kong peering down from a building or a Jurassic Park dinosaur crashing through a roof.

The **Geological Museum** on Jalan Diponegoro (opposite the imposing Gedung Sate provincial government headquarters) is definitely worth a visit,

Downtown Bandung.

for a look at the extraordinary array of rocks, maps and fossils displayed here – including replicas of the famous Java Man, or *Homo erectus,* skulls found in central Java. (Incidentally, the museum publications department, upstairs in the back building, makes and sells copies of detailed Dutch survey maps for nearly all places in Indonesia.)

The campus of Bandung's **Institute of Technology (ITB)**, Indonesia's oldest and finest university established by the Dutch, is also interesting. The institute's library, built in the 1920s, is a honeycomb of massive wooden girders. Students have a reputation for outspokenness and activism.

There are several other schools in Bandung. Considering the quality of education available in the city, it is no wonder that a significant amount of high-tech industry is based here, as are several research centers. Most notable is Indonesia's aircraft industry; in 1995, an Indonesian-designed and built commuter aircraft took to the air.

Spend some time, too, wandering in the old Dutch shopping district downtown around Jl. Braga, and have a look into the remodelled art-deco Savoy Homann Hotel on Jl. Asia-Afrika. The site of the 1955 Non-Aligned Conference is diagonally across the street. The town's large flower market is also nearby (on Jl. Wastukencana) and if interested in the Sundanese performing arts, then spend a morning observing classes in the **Music Conservatory** (Jl. Buah Batu 212) or at Pak Udjo's private *angklung* school (Jl. Padasuka 118) in Bandung's suburbs. In the evenings, attend one of several local theaters and clubs to observe performances of traditional music, dance or puppet.

Bandung's most exciting excursion is a visit to the nearby volcanic highlands. The nearest and most frequently visited is **Tangkuban Prahu** (Overturned Boat), about 30 kilometers (20 mi) north of the city. A steep, narrow road turns off to the left a short distance past the vegetable growing town of **Lembang** and winds right up to the crater's 1,830-meter (5,700 ft) rim. Here, cold moun-

Tangkuban Prahu.

tain mists and sulphurous fumes swirl up around jagged, scrub-covered ridges, and souvenir sellers offer strange monkey-like objects fashioned from tree-fern fibers. After this rather chilling experience, make your way quickly down to the **Ciater hot springs**, seven kilometers beyond the Tangkuban Prahu turnoff, for a meal and a soothing soak in one of their piping-hot pools. Accommodation is available at Ciater, as well as at Lembang and at nearby **Maribaya** – where there are also hot springs and numerous nature trails.

Several peaks and plateaus south of Bandung are even more spectacular but, higher and more rarely visited, they are somewhat difficult to find. At **Ciwidey**, 30 kilometers (20 mi) southwest of the city, blacksmiths turn out a range of hand-forged knives and daggers.

Alternatively, the town of **Pengalengan**, with its seemingly endless vista of manicured tea plantations covering the rolling hills, 40 kilometers (25 mi) due south of Bandung, is the jumping-off point for visits to the Cileunca Lakes, to the rim of Gunung Wayang, and into the crater of sulphurous, steaming, sputtering Gunung Papandayan. Add to all of these the old Dutch hill station of **Garut**, with its hot springs and reconstructed Hindu temple, and one could easily spend weeks exploring the beautiful southern Parahyangan mountains.

North coast route: The northern coastal ports of Java were once the busiest and richest towns on the island; they served as exporters of agricultural produce from the fertile Javanese hinterland, as builders and outfitters of large spice trading fleets, and as trading entrepôts frequented by merchants from all corners of the globe. Between the 15th and 17th centuries, when Islam was a new and growing force in the archipelago, these ports also flourished as political and religious centers.

First port of call along the northern route east of Jakarta is the ancient sultanate of **Cirebon** – once a powerful royal center and still a fascinating potpourri of Sundanese, Javanese, Chinese,

Distinctive boats of Cirebon.

Islamic and European influences. It's a rather sleepy place now, with a small harbor and a sizeable fishing industry. While famous for its seafood – especially its delicious shrimps and prawns – it is physically indistinguishable from many other mid-sized Javanese cities. As one begins to explore Cirebon's byways, however, the town's colorful past comes to life.

Cirebon's two major palaces were both built in 1678, in order that each of two princes could have his own court. The **Kraton Kesepuhan** (palace of the elder brother) was raised upon the site of the 15th-century Pakungwati palace of Cirebon's earlier Hindu rulers, and one of the royal pavilions occupying the forecourt bears the date 1425. This complex, with its split red brick gate (*candi bentar*) and several elaborately-carved audience pavilions, is undoubtedly one of the finest examples of former Hindu-Javanese architecture in existence.

The palace itself is Javanese in design, but thoroughly composite in its execution. A Romanesque archway framed by mystical Chinese rocks and clouds opens onto a spacious, pillared Javanese *pendopo* furnished with French period pieces. And the walls of the Dalem Ageng (ceremonial chamber) behind it are inlaid with blue-and-white Delft tiles exhibiting biblical scenes. To top it all off, the small adjoining museum contains a coach carved in the shape of a winged, horned elephant grasping a trident in its trunk; it's a glorious fusion of Javanese, Hindu, Islamic, Persian, Greek and Chinese mythological elements.

Just next to the Kesepuhan palace stands the **Mesjid Agung** (**Grand Mosque**) constructed around 1500. Its two-tiered *meru* roof rests on an elaborate wooden scaffolding, and the interior contains imported sandstone portals and a teakwood *kala*-head pulpit. Together with the Demak mosque, it is one of the oldest remaining landmarks of Islam on Java.

Kraton Kanoman (the palace of the younger brother) is nearby, reached via a busy marketplace. Large banyan trees shade the peaceful courtyard within,

Cirebon's cloud motif at the Kraton.

and as at Kesepuhan, the furnishings are European and the walls are studded with tiles and porcelains from Holland and China. The museum has a collection of stakes still used to pierce the flesh of Muslim believers on Mohammed's birthday (*seni debus*), as well as relics from Cirebon's past.

Further evidence of Cirebon's extreme cultural eclecticism is to be found among the restored ruins of **Taman Arum Sunyaragi**, about four kilometers out of town on the southwestern bypass. Although originally built as a fortress in 1702 and used as a base for resistance against the Dutch, this stone-and-coral folly was cast in its present form in 1852 by a Chinese architect, to serve as a pleasure palace-cum-hermitage for Cirebon's rajas. With its many nooks, crannies, tunnels, pools, gardens, gates and sentry cages, it's at once reminiscent of Taoist meditation grottoes and Hindu representations of Nirvana.

Five kilometers north of the city along the main Jakarta road lies the hilltop **tomb of Sunan Gunung Jati**, a 16th-century ruler of Cirebon and one of the nine *wali* who helped propagate Islam on Java. Pilgrims come to burn incense and pray in a shrine at the foot of the hill. Its guardians are said to be descendants of a sea captain who was shipwrecked here, and their shifts are still assigned like watches on a ship. The mausoleum of Gunung Jati's mentor, Sheik Datu Kahfi, sits on another hillside across the road to the east, and at the summit of this hill the grave of Gunung Jati's fifth wife, the Chinese princess Ong Tien, overlooks the sea.

Before leaving Cirebon, be sure to visit one of several artisan villages located just west of the town. In keeping with the area's eclectic past, these villages maintain highly distinctive traditions of calligraphic painting, wayang puppetry, gamelan music and *topeng* mask dancing, in addition to producing some of Java's most unique *batik*.

Traveling east along the coast, the prospect is generally dull. Occasionally, there are small estuarine towns where colorful boats ride easily on the

Pulling fish nets.

tide, and rolled fishing nets shimmer in the bright sunlight like giant cocoons of raw silk. Except as a road junction, **Tegal** has little to recommend it, though pottery and handicraft enthusiasts may be tempted by the excellent ocher and brass wares produced and sold about 10 kilometers south of the town.

Northern coast: What the north coast lacks in scenic beauty, it makes up for in batik. About 220 kilometers (140 mi) and four hours east of Cirebon is **Pekalongan**, a medium-sized town that announces itself on roadside pillars as Kota Batik – batik city. Quite apart from the many factories and retail stores lining its streets, Pekalongan justifies this sobriquet by producing some of the finest and most highly prized batik on Java.

The Pekalongan style, like Cirebon's, is unique – a blending of Muslim, Javanese, Chinese and European motifs, executed in pastel tones of mustard, ocher, olive, mauve, rose, orange and blue. Pekalongan's hallmark is the floral bouquet with hovering hummingbirds and butterflies, a Dutch design.

Semarang: Another 90 kilometers (55 mi) and two hours to the east, the large city of **Semarang** overflows out across a narrow coastal plain and up onto steeply-rising foothills. Known during Islamic times for its skilled shipwrights and abundant supplies of hardwood, this otherwise insignificant town was subsequently chosen as an administrative and trading base by the Dutch, and was one of the few *pesisir* ports to successfully make the transition to steam shipping at the turn of this century. Today, it is the commercial hub and provincial capital of central Java, and the island's fourth-largest city.

Modern Semarang possesses but few relics from the past. Most of them bear witness to the presence, in bygone days, of a large population of Dutch traders and officials, and a generous sprinkling of affluent Chinese merchants. The old **Dutch Church** on Jl. Suprapto downtown, with its copper-clad dome and Greek cross floor plan, was consecrated in 1753 and stands at the center of the town's 18th-century European commer-

Volcanic beach residue.

cial district. During the 19th century, the Dutch built elegant mansions to the west of here, along what is now Jl. Pemuda (Bojong), but most of these were later torn down and replaced by shop fronts. One of the shops, Toko Oen, is now a charming cafe with wicker chairs, ceiling fans and a menu that hasn't changed since colonial times.

Semarang's most interesting district, however, is its **Chinatown** (Pacinan) – a grid of narrow lanes tucked away in the center of the city, reached by walking due south from the old church along Jl. Suari to Jl. Pekojan.

Here, some old townhouses retain the distinctive Nanyang style: elaborately-carved doors and shutters, and delicately-wrought iron balustrades.

Half a dozen colorful Chinese temples and clan houses cluster in the space of a few blocks, the largest and oldest of which is on tiny **Gang Lombok** (turn to the right just by the bridge from Jl. Pekojan). This is the **Thay Kak Sie temple**, built in 1772, which houses more than a dozen major deities. Those with time and an interest in things Chinese will also want to visit the famous grotto **Gedung Batu**, of the deified Ming admiral Cheng Ho (Sam Po Kung), on the western outskirts of Semarang.

From Semarang, there are several towns to the east that may be visited as day trips from the city.

During the early 16th century, a Muslim kingdom centered at **Demak** was the undisputed nonpareil among the coastal states of Java; now only the town's elderly mosque remains. Neighboring **Kudus** was then Demak's holy city, and its Muslim quarter has beautifully-carved teak houses and an early 16th-century mosque, whose red brick *candi bentar* gate and minaret are distinctly Hindu-Javanese in design. Kudus is better known as "Kota Kretek," Java's Kretek cigarette capital.

The village of **Jepara**, 35 kilometers (20 mi) north of Kudus, has long been famous for its teak woodcarvings. Faithful copies of antique chairs and tables are still doweled, slotted, tongued and joined without a nail, and there is apparently also a heavy demand for extremely detailed panels depicting scenes from the *Ramayana* and other Hindu-Javanese tales. Today, some 4,000 carpenters work in 500 shops here.

Farther to the east, the twin towns of **Rembang** and **Lassem** are perhaps the oldest Chinese settlements on Java. Gracious Chinese country homes with upturned eaves, central courtyards and whitewashed outer walls border on a honeycomb of narrow lanes. Both towns have exquisite Chinese temples.

The road south from Semarang climbs quickly up through the stylish Dutch residential suburb of **Candi Baru** into the foothills of Gunung Ungaran.

If there is time, make a detour from the town of Ambarawa to the cool mountain resort of **Bandungan** to visit the **Gedung Songo temples** – some of the oldest and certainly the most spectacularly-situated antiquities in Java. These nine Sivaitic shrines were built sometime in the 8th century and perch on a series of collines overlooking the lofty peaks, verdant valleys and blue skies of central Java.

Left, house woodwork, Kudus. Right, retouching nautical colors on the north coast.

YOGYAKARTA

The green crescent of fertile rice lands that blankets **Gunung Merapi**'s southern flanks – with historic Yogyakarta as its focal point – is today inhabited by about 10 million Javanese, with three million urban residents. Rural population densities here soar above 1,000 people per square kilometer (2,500 sq mi), and in some areas, a square kilometer feeds an astounding 2,000 people with labor-intensive farming.

The area also embraces a seemingly disproportionate number of cultural attractions. The somber stillness of its beautiful Hindu and Buddhist temples – from the 8th, 9th and 10th centuries – is found again in the sequestered courtyards of its 18th-century Islamic palaces, where the liquid cadences of the central Javanese *gamelan* provide a measured counterpoint to the boisterous clamor of colorful city streets and crowded village markets.

Much of interest is concentrated in and around the twin court cities of Yogyakarta (often called Yogya) and Surakarta (often called Solo). It was here, on the well-irrigated banks of several adjacent rivers, that central Java's two great Mataram empires (one ancient and one modern) flourished. The role of the Javanese courts as cultural centers has long been recognized, but their vast catalogue of artistic wealth has only begun to be explored.

Although it was founded only in 1755, the sprawling city of **Yogyakarta** is situated at the very core of an ancient region known as Mataram, site of the first great central-Javanese empires. From the 8th until the early 10th centuries, this fertile and sloping plain between the Progo and the Opak rivers was ruled by a succession of Indianized kings – the builders of Borobudur, Prambanan and dozens of other elaborate stone monuments. In about 900, however, these rulers suddenly and inexplicably shifted their capital to eastern Java, and for more than six centuries thereafter, Mataram was deserted.

Preceding pages: the magnificent main temples at Prambanan. Left, face of royal nobility. Right, Samur Gumuling.

At the end of the 16th century, the area was revived by a new Islamic power based at Kota Gede, east of present-day Yogyakarta. This second Mataram dynasty was founded around 1580 by Panembahan Senapati, and his descendants have ruled central Java up until the present day, although with widely varying degrees of power and influence.

The history of the Yogyakarta sultanate is one of resistance to ever-increasing colonial influence in central Java. The court was twice invaded for failure to comply with colonial instructions – once by the Dutch in 1810, and again by the British in 1812. Later it was swept into the Great Java War (1825–1830), led by the charismatic crown prince of the ruling family, Pangeran Diponegoro.

In more recent times, Yogyakarta served as the capital of the beleaguered Indonesian republic for four long years during the fight against the Dutch, until 1949. This was a time of extraordinary social ferment. Six million refugees, more than one million young fighters and an enlightened young sultan

(Hamengkubuwono IX) transformed the venerable court city into a hotbed of revolutionary idealism.

In many ways, Yogyakarta is still young and restless despite its traditional Javanese past. **Gajah Mada University** is the largest and one of the most respected schools in the nation. Several other institutions of higher learning swell the population of students and teachers to well over 50,000 people.

Yogyakarta's heart: Despite all the extraordinary changes that have taken place here during the past few decades, it is Yogya's traditional attractions that travelers come to see – ancient temples, palaces, *batik* workshops, *gamelan* orchestras, court dances and *wayang* puppet performances.

The first stop for all visitors to Yogyakarta is the royal **Kraton**, a two-century-old palace complex that stands at the very heart of the city. According to traditional cosmological beliefs, the Javanese ruler is literally the "navel" or central "spike" of the universe – anchoring the temporal world and communicating with the mystical realm of powerful deities. In this scheme of things, the Kraton is both the capital of the kingdom and the hub of the cosmos, bringing the two into coincidence through the application of certain elaborate design principles. It houses not only the sultan and his family, but also the powerful dynastic regalia (*pusaka*), private meditation and ceremonial chambers, a magnificent throne hall, several audience and performance pavilions, a mosque, an immense royal garden, stables, barracks, an armaments foundry and two expansive parade grounds planted with sacred banyan trees. All of this is in a carefully conceived complex of walled compounds, narrow lanes and massive gateways, and bounded by a fortified outer wall measuring two kilometers on every side.

Construction of Yogyakarta's Kraton began in 1755 and continued for almost 40 years, throughout the long reign of Hamengkubuwono I. Structurally, very little has been added since his death in 1792. Today, only the innermost com-

Yogyakarta's Kraton.

pound is considered part of the Kraton proper, while the maze of lanes and lesser compounds, the mosque and the two vast squares, have been integrated into the city. Long sections of the outermost wall (*benteng*) still stand, however, and many if not most of the residences inside are still owned and occupied by members of the royal family.

To step within the massive inner Kraton walls is to enter a patrician world of grace and elegance. In the first half of this century, the interior was remodeled along European lines, incorporating Italian marble, cast-iron columns, crystal chandeliers and rococo furnishings into an otherwise classically Javanese setting. The **central throne hall** (Bangsal Kencana) is its most striking feature – a *pendopo* or open pavilion consisting of an ornately-decorated and dramatically sloping roof supported at the center by four massive wooden columns.

There is much else to see within the Kraton, including the museum, the ancient gamelan sets, two great *kala*-head gateways and several spacious courtyards. If possible, try to visit the palace on a Sunday when dancers rehearse to the otherworldly gamelan.

Behind and just west of the Kraton stand the ruins of the opulent and architecturally ingenious royal pleasure garden called **Taman Sari**, constructed over a period of many years by Hamengkubuwono I and then abruptly abandoned after his death. Dutch representatives to the sultan's court marveled at its construction: a large artificial lake, underground and underwater passageways, meditational retreats, a series of sunken bathing pools, and an imposing two-story mansion of European design. They referred to the latter as the *Waterkasteel* (Water Castle), as it was apparently fortified and originally surrounded by an artificial lake.

The **Water Castle** occupies high ground at the northern end of the huge Taman Sari complex, overlooking a crowded bird market and a colony of batik painters. Although its stairways have collapsed, one can still scramble atop the crumbling walls to gain a com-

Left, mask at Kraton entrance scares off evil. **Right**, palace guard.

manding vista of Yogyakarta's downtown and beyond.

A tunnel behind the castle leads to a complex of three partially-restored **bathing pools** (*umbul-umbul*). The large central pool with a *naga*-head fountain was designed for the use of queens, concubines and princesses, while the small southernmost pool was reserved for the sultan. A tower with several interior chambers overlooks the female bathing area; this is where the sultan rested during the day.

Farther south, tucked amid a crowded *kampung,* lies the interesting **Pesarean Pertapaan**, a royal retreat reached by passing through an ornate archway west of the bathing area, then following a winding path to the left. The main structure is a small Chinese-style temple with a forecourt and galleries on either side, said to have been where the sultan and his sons meditated for seven days and seven nights at a time.

The most remarkable structure at Taman Sari is the **Sumur Gumuling** (circular well), commonly referred to by locals as the *mesjid* (mosque), but more likely intended as a trysting place for the sultan and Kyai Loro Kidul, the powerful Goddess of the South Sea, to whom all rulers of Mataram had been promised in marriage by the dynasty's founder (and from whom they are said to derive their mystical powers). Access is by means of an underground (and formerly underwater) passageway, whose entrance lies immediately to the west of the water castle. The "well" is in fact a sunken atrium, with circular galleries facing onto a small, round pool.

Before leaving the area, stroll through the **Pasar Ngasem bird market**, where Javanese bird lovers browse and haggle over a multitude of parrots, cockatoos, macaws, parakeets, thrushes, lories, minivets, sunbirds, guineafowl and more. Birds purchased here are prized more for their singing voices than their colorful plumage.

Next to the bird market and water garden is a **batik painters colony**, home to scores of young and unsung artists of the cloth. Motifs here fall into two distinct categories: traditional *Ramayana* scenes (in non-traditional colors), and attempts at primitive expressionism. Most of it is kitsch, even if of a rather exotic variety; talented artists who succeed quickly move out to set up their own studios. Bargain hard if buying.

"Garland Bearing" Street: Yogyakarta's main thoroughfare, **Jalan Malioboro**, begins directly in front of the royal audience pavilion, at the front of the palace, and ends at a phallic *lingga* some two kilometers to the north, a shrine dedicated to the local guardian spirit, Kyai Jaga. It was laid out by Hamengkubuwono I as a ceremonial boulevard for colorful state processions, and also as a symbolic meridian along which to orient his domain. Folk etymologists insist that the street somehow takes its name from the Duke of Marlborough, perhaps as a consequence of the humiliating English assault on Yogyakarta in 1812. But, in fact, Malioboro derives from Sanskrit words meaning garland bearing – the royal processional route was always adorned with floral bouquets.

Today, Jalan Malioboro is a busy avenue lined with shop fronts and teeming with vehicles and pedicabs; it's primarily a shopping district, but also an area of historical and cultural interest. Begin at the town square (*alun-alun*) and stroll up this latter-day processional, stopping first at the **Sono Budaya Museum**, on the northwestern side of the square. It was opened in 1935 by the Java Institute, a cultural foundation of wealthy Javanese and Dutch art patrons, and today houses important collections of prehistoric artifacts, Hindu-Buddhist bronzes, wayang puppets, dance costumes and traditional Javanese weapons. Visit also the nearby **Grand Mosque**, completed in 1773, and notice the two fenced-off banyan trees standing on either side of the road in the square's center. These symbolize the stable balance of opposing forces within the Javanese kingdom.

Proceed northward from the square through the main gates and out across Yogya's main intersection. Immediately ahead on the right stands the old Dutch garrison, **Fort Vredeburgh**, which is being converted into a cultural center, complete with exhibition and performance halls. Opposite it on the left stands the former Dutch Resident's mansion, used during the revolution as the presidential palace it is now the governor's residence. Farther along on the right, past the fort, is the huge covered central market, **Pasar Beringan**, a dimly-lit women's world of small stalls.

Back out on Malioboro, both sides of the street are lined with handicraft shops selling a great range of traditional textiles, leather goods, baskets, tortoise shell, jewelry and endless knickknacks. Many restaurants here also cater especially to foreign tourists, serving refreshing iced-fruit juices, and Chinese, Indonesian and Western fare. At night, the sidewalks explode into an incredible street market of handicraft stalls running the length of the west side of the street, while the east side sees the emergence of simple food stalls and drink stands. The **Tourist Information Office** faces onto Jalan Malioboro not far from the Hotel Mutiara. Stop in to get up-to-date information about temple tours and dance performances.

Peerless performing arts: In between visits to the palace and the temples, take time off to investigate Yogya's sophisticated performing arts. Of all Java's many art forms, the *wayang kulit* or shadow-puppet play undoubtedly lies closest to the heart of the Javanese. The *dalang* or puppeteer is the key to the performance: a masterly stage hand, actor, impersonator, singer, orchestra conductor, historian, counselor, comedian and storyteller. The basic outlines of the ancient tales, generally episodes from the *Mahabarata* epic, are familiar enough to the audience. But the dalang breathes new life into each re-telling, introducing the present in bawdy asides and outrageous satires while continually reaffirming the harmony and balance between antagonists and protagonists that is a central motif in the Javanese world view.

Despite the increasing encroachment of films and television, wayang kulit still flourishes in and around Yogyakarta.

Colonial Dutch buildings, downtown Yogyakarta.

Performances for *selamatan* ritual feasts, weddings or circumstances occur regularly, often in modest village compounds. The performance always starts around 9pm and continues until dawn. There is a full eight-hour presentation of wayang kulit on the second Saturday of every month at the **Sasana Inggil** performance pavilion, near the Kraton.

Chances are that one's most vivid memory of the wayang, and indeed, of Yogya itself, will be the gentle music of the gamelan. Its insinuating, liquid melodies float over white-washed walls on quiet sunlit streets, or burst forth from a transistor radio at roadside stalls; you may also hear it as you stroll through the Kraton (where there are regular rehearsals), or in a hotel lobby. Entire orchestras may be ordered from gamelan foundries in Yogya, where these ancient bronze instruments are still cast, forged and polished using age-old methods.

Classical Javanese dance: Having originated in the kratons, where they still thrive, court dances are now also taught at a number of private schools and government art academies in the city. The weekly rehearsal within the Kraton itself should not be missed, but there are also a number of regular evening performances, and visitors are welcome to observe dance classes at the schools.

Perhaps the ultimate in Javanese dance spectaculars, however, is the **Ramayana Ballet**, a modernized version of the lavish *wayang orang* dance-drama productions, performed monthly over four consecutive nights during the dry season of May to October, under the full moon in front of the elegant ninth-century Lara Jonggrang temple at Prambanan.

The list of traditional crafts still practiced in the suburbs and towns around Yogyakarta is practically endless, as the court once patronized these village craftsmen. Most villages specialize. Kasongan makes earthenware pottery, Kota Gede is famous for its delicate filigree silverwork, and yet others produce leather bags, weaving, baskets, wooden masks, cane furniture, wayang puppets or hand-forged ceremonial keris blades.

Dancers at Yogyakarta Kraton, around 1860.

Of course, Yogya's most famous handicraft is still batik, and unless amongst the connoisseurs of this involved textile art, it's a good idea to visit the **Batik Research Center** (**Balai Penelitian Batik**), located on Jalan Kusumanegara, east of the main post office. An individually-guided tour costs nothing, and is an excellent introduction to the craft's painstaking manufacturing process, as well as to the staggering variety of patterns and colors to be found throughout Java. (One-month courses are offered for a nominal fee.)

Batik cloth is produced and sold all over Yogya, but especially in the south of the city on **Jalan Tirtodipuran**, a street with over 25 factories and showrooms, most of which are happy to let visitors observe production. But to see a range of finished batik from all over Java, then visit the large **Toko Terang Bulan** shop on Jalan Malioboro, near the central market.

Many of the city's better-known artists, and a number of aspiring ones, also produce batik paintings made with the same resist-dyeing method, but specifically designed for framing and hanging.

The Indian Ocean is less than an hour's drive south of central Yogyakarta. **Parangtritis Beach** is a wonderful stretch of black sand backed by towering bluffs, both a popular recreation spot and a place of worship, where the legendary Queen of the South Seas is said to live. Take a ride along the sand in a pony cart, or watch the sunset from the cliff top bar at the Queen of the South Hotel. The riptides are dangerous here, so be careful if venturing into the water.

Antiquities of central Java: For the Javanese, the *candi* or ancient stone monuments of Java are tangible evidence of the great energy and artistry of their ancestors. For the foreign visitor, communion with one of these 1,000-year-old shrines provides an opportunity to ponder the achievements of a magnificent culture. For just about anyone, a visit to one of the hundred-odd candi, major and minor, that lie scattered about the dramatic volcanic landscapes of central Java is unforgettable.

eft, batik actory. **ight**, amayana allet.

A great deal of effort has been expended since 1900 to excavate, reconstruct and restore their reliefs, study their iconography and decipher their inscriptions. Still, we know little more than the most basic symbolism of these structures. Fundamental questions as to their stylistic affinities with Indian art, and with their function within ancient Indonesian society, remain unanswered. Even their chronology is in doubt. What is known is that they are among the most technically accomplished structures produced in ancient times; and that the awe inspired by their presence has formed a substantial part of their message.

Buddhism's largest shrine: A leisurely one-hour drive across the river beds and rice fields leads to the steps of fabled **Borobudur**, 40 kilometers (25 mi) northwest of Yogyakarta. This huge stupa, the world's largest Buddhist monument, was built sometime during the relatively short reign of the Sailendra Dynasty in central Java, between 778 and 856 – 300 years before Angkor Wat and 200 years before Notre Dame. Yet, within little more than a century of its completion, Borobudur and all of central Java were mysteriously abandoned. At about this time, too, neighboring Mount Merapi erupted violently, covering Borobudur in volcanic ash and concealing it for centuries.

The story of Borobudur's "rediscovery" begins in 1814, when the English governor of Java, Thomas Stamford Raffles, visited Semarang and heard rumors of "a mountain of Buddhist sculptures in stone" near the town of Magelang. Raffles dispatched his military engineer, H.C.C. Cornelius, to investigate. What Cornelius discovered was a hillock overgrown with trees and shrubs, but curiously scattered with hundreds of cut and carved andesite blocks. For two months, he directed a massive clearing operation, removing vegetation and layers of earth, until it became clear that an elaborate structure lay beneath the surface. Cornelius dug no further, for fear of damaging the ancient and unknown monument.

In the years that followed, Borobudur

17th-century drawing of Borobudur.

was fully laid bare and subsequently suffered almost a century of decay, plunder and abuse, during which thousands of stones were "borrowed" by villagers, and scores of priceless sculptures ended up as garden decorations in the homes of the rich and powerful. Typical of the attitude of Dutch officials was the presentation, in 1896, of eight cart loads of Borobudur souvenirs to visiting King Chulalongkorn of Siam, including 30 relief panels, five Buddha statues, two lions and a guardian sculpture. Many of these and other irreplaceable works of Indo-Javanese art ended up in private collections, and now reside in museums around the world.

Finally, in 1900, the Dutch government responded to cries of outrage from within its own ranks and established a committee for the preservation and restoration of Borobudur. The huge task of reconstruction was accomplished between 1907 and 1911 by a Dutch military engineer with a keen interest in Javanese antiquities. Scattered stones were replaced, collapsed walls and stupa were straightened, weak spots were reinforced and the drainage system was improved. It was at this time, too, that Borobudur was discovered to be a fragile mantle of stone blocks built upon a natural mound of earth. Rainwater was seeping through the stone mantle and eroding the soft foundation from within, while mineral salts were collecting on the monument's surface, where they acted in conjunction with sun, wind, rain and fungus to destroy it. Grandiose plans for a permanent restoration were never realized, due to the intervention of two world wars and a depression.

During the 1950s and 1960s, it became increasingly evident that Borobudur was structurally endangered. Parts of the north wall on the lowest terrace began to bulge as a result of internal pressures, and two earthquakes in 1961 created severe cracks and dislocations. Some lower balustrades were dismantled in 1965, but within a year, work was discontinued for lack of funds. Appeals for assistance were made, and UNESCO was called upon to direct a

Borobudur's terraces from above.

rescue operation. Technical assistance and financing became available, and the project officially got underway in 1973.

The scale of the Borobudur restoration project was spectacular. It took 700 men, working six days a week, 10 years to dismantle, catalogue, photograph, clean, treat and reassemble a total of 1,300,232 stone blocks. Each stone had to be individually inspected, scrubbed and chemically treated before being replaced. In addition, a new infrastructure of reinforced concrete, tar, asphalt, epoxy and tin was constructed to support the entire monument, and a system of drainage pipes installed to prevent further seepage.

In the end, the work was completed on time, but at a cost of US$25 million, or more than three times the original estimate. In his speech at the official reopening of Borobudur in 1983, President Suharto explained that his government had decided to underwrite the additional expense so that the Indonesian people would not be deprived of their ancient and glorious heritage. "It is now to be hoped," he said, "the Borobudur will live a thousand years more."

It's unlikely that we shall ever know the full import of Borobudur as a religious monument. It is estimated that 30,000 stonecutters and sculptors, 15,000 carriers and thousands more masons worked anywhere from 20 to 75 years to build the monument. At a time when the entire population of central Java numbered less than one million, this represents a commitment of perhaps 10 percent of the available work force to a single effort. Was it spiritual faith or coercive force that drove so many to create this statement in stone?

What is clear, however, is that the Sailendran rulers of Java were able to command a surplus of rice and labor from the populace. The easiest way to accomplish this was, of course, to convince the cultivators that it was in their own best interest to donate a part of their production to the gods. When we look for the meaning, then, in the monument of Borobudur, we must recognize that its primary function was to embody and

Borobudur was built 300 years before Angkor Wat.

reinforce the very beliefs that created it.

Seen from the air, Borobudur forms a mandala, or geometric aid for meditation. Seen from a distance on the ground, Borobudur is a stupa or reliquary, a model of the cosmos in three vertical parts: a square base supporting a hemispheric body and a crowning spire. As one approaches along the traditional pilgrimage route from the east, and then ascends the terraced monument, circumambulating each terrace clockwise in succession, every relief and carving contributes to the whole.

There were originally 10 levels at Borobudur, each falling within one of the three divisions of the Mahayana Buddhist universe: *khamadhatu*, the lower spheres of human life; *rupadhatu*, the middle sphere of "form"; and *arupadhatu*, the higher sphere of detachment from the world. The lowest gallery of reliefs, now covered, once depicted the delights of this world and the damnations of the next.

The next five levels (the processional terrace and four concentric galleries) show, in their reliefs (beginning at the eastern staircase and going around each gallery clockwise), the life of Prince Siddharta on his way to becoming the Gautama Buddha, scenes from the Jataka folktales about his previous incarnations, and the life of the Bodhisattva Sudhana (from the *Gandavyuha*). These absorbing and delightful tales are illustrated in stone by a parade of commoners, princes, musicians, dancing girls, ships, saints and heavenly throngs, with many interesting ethnographic details about daily life in ancient Java. Placed in niches above the galleries are 432 stone Buddhas, each displaying one of five *mudra* or hand positions, alternately calling upon the earth as witness and embodying charity, meditation, fearlessness and reason.

Above the square galleries, three circular terraces support 72 perforated *dagob* (miniature stupa) which are unique in Buddhist art. Most contain a statue of the meditating *dhyani* Buddha. Two statues have been left uncovered to gaze over the nearby Menoreh moun-

Left, Borobudur under repair. Right, merit in stone.

tains, where one series of knobs and knolls is said to represent Gunadharma, the temple's divine architect. These three terraces are, in fact, transitional steps leading to the 10th and highest level, the realm of formlessness and total abstraction (*arupadhatu*), embodied in the huge crowning stupa, now missing its spire and sunshades.

Borobudur was thus erected for the glorification of the Ultimate Reality – the serene realm of the Buddha – and as a tangible, tactile lesson for priests and pilgrims, an illustrated textbook of the path to Buddhist enlightenment. It was also a massive mausoleum, most likely, and may have once contained the remains of a Buddhist ruler or saint.

Two smaller, subsidiary candi lie along a straight line directly east of Borobudur. The closer of the two is tiny **Pawon** (meaning "kitchen" or perhaps "crematorium"), situated in a shady clearing 1,750 meters from the stupa's main entrance. It is often referred to as Borobudur's "porch temple" because of its proximity, and may well have constituted the last stop along a brick-paved pilgrimage route. Although many theories have been advanced, we know very little about Pawon's actual function or symbolism, other than that the outer walls are covered with heavenly "money trees" and celestial musicians, and that a bearded dwarf above the entrance pours out riches from his bag, perhaps for the benefit of visiting pilgrims.

Just one kilometer farther east, across the confluence of two holy rivers (the Progo and the Elo), lies beautiful **Candi Mendut**. A large banyan tree shades the forecourt, and unlike most other central Javanese monuments that face east, Mendut opens to the northwest. The large central dagob and a series of smaller ones that once crowned the temple's roof are now missing, so that its broad base and high body now seem rather plain from a distance. As it is approached, however, the delightful bas-reliefs on the outer walls come to life.

The base and both sides of the staircase are decorated with scenes from moralistic fables and folktales, many of

Interior of Candi Mendut.

which concern animals. The main body of Mendut contains superbly carved panels depicting *bodhisattva* and Buddhist goddesses – the largest reliefs found on any Indonesian temple. The walls of the antechamber are decorated with money trees and celestial beings, and contain two beautiful panels of a man and a woman amid swarms of playful children. It is thought that these represent child-eating ogres who converted to Buddhism and became protectors instead of devourers.

The Mendut panels are decorative, but they hardly prepare one for the stunning interior, which contains three of the finest Buddhist statues in the world: a magnificent three-meter (10 ft) figure of the seated Sakyamuni Buddha, flanked on his left and right by Bodhisattva Vajrapani and Bodhisattva Avalokitesvara, each about 2.5 meters (8 ft) high. The central or Sakyamuni statue symbolizes the first sermon of the Buddha at the Deer Park near Benares, as shown by the position of his hands (*dharmacakra mudra*) and by a small relief of a wheel between two deer. The two bodhisattva, or buddhas-to-be, have elected to stay behind in the world to help all of Buddha's followers. Four niches around them probably once held meditating dhyani buddhas.

Valley of the kings: East of Yogyakarta, past the airport, the main Yogya–Solo (Yogyakarta–Surakarta) highway slices across a volcanic plain littered with ancient ruins. Because these candi are considered by the Javanese to be royal mausoleums, this region is known by them as the Valley of the Kings or the Valley of the Dead. In the center of the plain, 17 kilometers from Yogya, lies the small town of **Prambanan**. A sign at one intersection points north towards a major temple complex of the same name. For many, this is the finest monument in Java.

Prambanan was completed sometime around 856 to commemorate the victory of Sanjaya's Sivaitic descendant, Rakai Pikatan, over the last Sailendran ruler of central Java, Balaputra (who fled to Sumatra and became the ruler of

Celestial beings, Loro Jonggrang.

Srivijaya). It was deserted within a few years of its completion, however, and eventually collapsed. Preparations for the restoration of the central temple began in 1918, work started in 1937, and it was completed only in 1953. The Indonesian government is conducting a long-term restoration project on the other temples and buildings in the Prambanan courtyard, several of which have already been completed.

The central courtyard of the complex contains eight buildings. The three largest are arrayed north-to-south: the magnificent 47-meter (155 ft) central or Siva temple, flanked on either side by slightly smaller shrines dedicated to Vishnu (to the north) and Brahma (to the south). Standing opposite these, to the east, are three smaller temples that contained the "vehicles" of each god: Siva's bull (*nandi*), Brahma's gander (*hamsa*) and Vishnu's sun-bird (*garuda*). Only nandi remains. By the northern and southern gates of the central compound are two identical court temples, standing 16 meters (50 ft) high.

The largest temple, the masterpiece dedicated to Siva, is also known as **Loro Jonggrang** (Slender Maiden), a folk name sometimes given to the temple complex as a whole. Local legend has it that Loro Jonggrang was a princess wooed by an unwanted suitor. She commanded the man to build a temple in one night, and then frustrated his nearly successful effort by pounding the rice mortar, prematurely announcing the dawn. Enraged, he turned the maiden to stone, and according to the tale, she remains here in the northern chamber of the temple – as a statue of Siva's consort, Durga. In the other three chambers are statues of Agastya, the "Divine Teacher" (facing south); Ganesha, Siva's elephant-headed son (facing west); and a 3-meter (10 ft) Siva (in the central chamber, facing east).

One aspect of Loro Jonggrang's appeal is her glorious symmetry and graceful proportions. Another is its wealth of sculptural detail. On the base of the main terrace are the so-called "Prambanan Motifs" – little lions in niches, flanked by trees of life bearing a lively menagerie of endearing animals.

Above these, on the outer balustrade, are panels of celestial beings and 62 scenes from the classical Indian dance manual, the *Natyasastra.*

Finally, on the inner walls of the balustrade, beginning from the eastern gate and proceeding around clockwise, the wonderfully vital and utterly engrossing tale of the *Ramayana* is told in bas-relief (and completed on the balustrade of the Brahma temple). The movement within each panel is free-flowing, and filled with fascinating detail. Even the most tumultuous scenes contain lovingly rendered touches – monkeys in a fruit tree, birds raiding a granary, a kitchen scene.

Prambanan's beauty and variety demand more than a single visit. One of the most romantic ways to view the temple is by moonlight, during an open-air performance of the *Ramayana,* staged on moonlit nights between May and October. During the rest of the year, abridged performances of the epic are held in the adjacent **Trimurti Theater**.

Left, Prambanan. Right, Loro Jonggrang, Prambanan.

EAST JAVA

Located just 60 kilometers (40 mi) east of Yogyakarta, noble **Surakarta** (also known as Solo) generally receives far less attention from foreign visitors than its distinguished neighbor. This is curious from the point of view of most Javanese, for whom Surakarta is the older and more refined royal center – the arbiter of cultivated speech and aristocratic elegance in traditional Java.

This is partly because Surakarta and its rulers have themselves generally preferred to remain out of the limelight. Indeed, throughout the tumultuous 18th century, they had little choice, for in those years Solo's reigning Pakubuwono line was dependent upon the Dutch for military and economic support. Thereafter, the royal family became well-to-do landowners and sugar magnates – styling themselves, as did most 19th-century Javanese aristocrats, after the manner of European royalty. During the Indonesian revolution, the movement against colonial power was notable in Surakarta by its absence.

Despite some complaining – by Yogyakartans, in particular – the Susuhunan of Surakarta (a titular Muslim prince) can nevertheless claim, with good reason, to be the true and rightful heir to the central Javanese Mataram throne. The court was moved to the Solo River Valley in 1680 from the Yogya area, first to Kartasura and later, in 1745, to Surakarta. Here, the Mataram line has ruled uninterruptedly, despite losing half of the kingdom to the "upstart" ruler of Yogyakarta in 1755, a consequence of a Dutch-negotiated peace.

Perhaps the real reason that Surakarta is less well-known than Yogyakarta is that it has fewer connecting flights and is farther from the ancient monuments of Borobudur and Prambanan. But, in fact, it is only an hour from Yogya by rail or road, and is certainly worth visiting, even if for a single day.

The **Kraton**, or palace of Surakarta, was constructed between 1743 and 1746 on the banks of the mighty Bengawan Solo, Java's longest river. As with the Yogyakarta palace, Surakarta's Kraton simultaneously defines the center of the town and the kingdom, as well as, metaphysically, the hub of the cosmos. Indeed, the similarities between the two courts, built within 10 years of each other, are striking. Both have a thick outer wall enclosing a network of narrow lanes and smaller compounds, two large squares, a mosque, and a central or inner royal residential complex. Perhaps the major difference is that Surakarta has no north-south processional boulevard or pleasure palace.

Entering the Kraton precincts from the north gate, one crosses the main square (*alun-alun lor*) between the two royal banyan trees and stops in front of the pale blue Pagelaran performance pavilion, with its shining expanse of cool marble tiles. Behind the Pagelaran is the royal audience pavilion (*Sitinggil*); behind that is an immense gate leading to the front, or north, door of the palace.

Casual visitors are never permitted to enter this north door, which is kept

Left, inaccessible eastern coastline. **Right**, performance at Pura Mangkunegaran.

closed except on special occasions, but must, instead, walk around to the east and pay a small fee for a guided tour of the museum and the inner sanctum. Here, shaded by groves of leafy leaves, between which flit the bare-shouldered *abdidalem* or female attendants, is the large throne hall of the Susuhunan. The inner columns supporting the roof are richly carved and gilded, crystal chandeliers hang from the rafters and marble statues, cast-iron columns and Chinese blue-and-white vases line the walkways. As if to underscore the sanctity of this place, you are instructed to remove your shoes (to walk on the finely-swept dirt) and refrain from taking photographs. Notice the royal meditation tower to one side – if it looks familiar, that's because it's essentially a Dutch windmill without the arms.

The Kraton museum was established in 1963 and contains ancient Hindu-Javanese bronzes, traditional Javanese weapons and three marvelous coaches. The oldest coach – a lumbering, deep-bodied carriage built around 1740 – was a gift from the Dutch East India Company to Pakubuwono II. The museum also displays some remarkable figureheads from the old royal barges, including Kyai Rajamala, a giant of surpassing ugliness, who once adorned the bow of the Susuhunan's private boat and is said even now to emit a fishy odor when daily offerings are not forthcoming.

After visiting the Kraton, stroll through the narrow lanes outside and be sure to pay a visit to nearby **Sasana Mulya** – the music and dance pavilion of the Indonesian Performing Arts Academy (ASKI), located just to the west of the main or north palace gate. This is an art school with an illustrious history, for it was here that the first musical notation for *gamelan* was devised at the turn of the century. Serious students of gamelan music, traditional dance and *wayang kulit* attend classes and rehearsals here daily. Visitors are welcome to listen and observe, provided done unobtrusively.

Surakarta's "other" palace: About one kilometer (half a mile) to the west and north of the main Kraton, a branch of the

Throne hall.

Surakarta royal family has constructed their own smaller, more intimate palace. Begun by Mangkunegara II at the end of the 18th century and completed in 1866, the **Pura Mangkunegaran** is also open to the public. Upon entering the grounds via the east or west gates, report to the reception office just inside the east gate and pay a small fee for a guided tour.

The outer *pendopo* or audience pavilion of the Mangkunegaran is said to be the largest in Java – built of solid teak wood, and jointed and fitted in the traditional manner, without the use of nails. Note the brightly-painted ceiling, with the eight mystical Javanese colors in the center, highlighted by a flame motif and bordered by symbols of the Javanese zodiac. The gamelan set in the southwest corner of the pendopo is known as Kyai Kanyut Mesem (Enchanting Smiles.) Try to visit the palace on Wednesday mornings, when it is struck to accompany an informal dance rehearsal before noon.

The museum is in the ceremonial hall of the palace, directly behind the pendopo, and it mainly houses the private collections of Mankunegara IV: dance ornaments, *topeng* masks, jewelry (including two silver chastity belts), ancient Javanese and Chinese coins, bronze figures, and a superb set of ceremonial *keris* blades.

Solo is an excellent place for the unhurried shopper who likes to explore out of the way places, in the hope of finding hidden treasures. To begin with, there is a sizeable "antique industry" here – many dealers collect and restore old European, Javanese and Chinese furniture and bric-a-brac. The starting point for any treasure hunt is **Pasar Triwindu**, just south of the Mangkunegaran palace, and behind the electronics shops on Jalan Diponegoro. Five minutes here will whet pack-rat appetites: old bottles, candelabras, Japanese teacups, Chinese coins, Dutch oil lamps, photographs, picture frames, marble-top tables and other odds and ends clutter more than a dozen stalls. Bargain hard, and don't be carried away

Window stuff, Pasar Triwindu.

by the sales pressure. There are many more shops in town where the dealers may be more reputable, the selection just as good and the prices not necessarily any higher.

Solo is also the home of Indonesia's largest *batik* manufacturers, three of whom have showrooms in town with reasonable fixed prices for superb yard goods, shirts and dresses. Many smaller batik shops also line the main streets, but to discover why Surakarta calls itself the City of Batik, pay a visit to the huge textile market, beside the Grand Mosque and near the Kraton. This is where village vendors and housewives converge to buy their cloth, mostly of medium to lower quality, from scores of narrow stalls that are stacked to the rafters with a bewildering array of batik. Just be sure to know what one is doing if buying here – batik can sell for as little as US$1 a yard or US$100, and it takes some experience to know what is what.

As the acknowledged center for the traditional Javanese performing arts, Solo is also the place to see an evening *wayang orang* dance performance or a *wayang kulit* shadow play, or to listen to live gamelan music. It is also the place, not surprisingly, to buy the costumes, puppets and instruments associated with these arts. Ornately-carved and painted leather puppets, contorted wooden masks, gilded headdresses and even monstrous bronze gongs are available and make highly distinctive gifts or house decorations.

East Java's majesty: Although East Java lacks many of the more usual tourist sights and amenities, it's a paradise for unorthodox travelers – rugged individualists who relish the search for obscure but exquisite antiquities, or the breathtaking views from the rims of desolate volcanic craters.

Geographically and historically, the province may be divided into three regions: the north coast (including the island of Madura), with its old Islamic trading ports; the Brantas River Valley, with its ancient monuments and colonial hill stations; and the eastern salient (known to history as Blambangan), with its spectacular volcanoes, secluded nature reserves and unparalleled scenic beauty nearly everywhere.

The broad **Brantas River** traces a circular path through the ancient and fertile rice lands of eastern central Java, and around several adjacent peaks – Arjuna, Kawi and Kelud. For five centuries, after 930 AD, this valley was the undisputed locus of power and civilization on the island. The great kingdoms of this period – Kediri, Singhasari and Majapahit – have bequeathed a rich heritage of art, literature, and music.

With the arrival of Islam as a political force in the 15th century, and with the great fluorescence of the spice and textile trade, a struggle arose between the rice-growing kingdoms of the interior and the new Islamic trading powers of the coast. The Brantas Valley was conquered by Muslim forces around 1530, and many Hindus then fled eastward to Blambangan and Bali. Even today, the highland Tenggerese tribes around Gunung Semeru and Gunung Bromo claim to be the living descendants of these Indo-Javanese exiles, and, of

Wayang kulit puppet.

course, Bali's most powerful rulers trace their genealogies back to the 14th-century line of kings from East Java's Majapahit empire.

City of heroes: Up until the turn of the century, the East Java provincial capital of **Surabaya** was the largest and most important seaport in the archipelago. It still ranks second (after Jakarta's Tanjung Priok), and with more than 400 years of colorful history behind it, one would expect to find much of interest here; unfortunately, this is not so.

Surabaya's rise to prominence began around 1525, when its rulers converted to Islam and then rapidly subdued all neighboring coastal states. However, in the final years of the 16th century, the central Javanese kingdom of Mataram expanded eastward and joined a bloody and protracted struggle with Surabaya for control of the area. Dutch descriptions of the city in 1620 paint it as a formidable adversary surrounded by a canal, and with heavily-fortified bastions measuring some 40 kilometers (25 mi) in circumference. And its army is said to have numbered 30,000 warriors. In the end, Surabaya succumbed, in 1625, only after Sultan Agung's armies had devastated its rice lands and diverted its mighty river.

In the mid 18th century, Surabaya was ceded to the Dutch and soon developed into the greatest commercial city of the Indies – the chief sugar port and rail head on Java. Immortalized in many of Joseph Conrad's novels, this era was characterized by square-riggers in full sail, wealthy Chinese and Arab traders, eccentric German hoteliers, and lusty seamen brawling over the likes of Surabaya Sue (who really existed).

Today's reality is mundane by comparison – Surabaya is a hot, sprawling city of almost 4 million. It is known as a city of heroes because of the momentous first battle of the revolution, fought here in November of 1945. Although the Indonesian rebels were driven from the city by better-equipped British troops, they inflicted heavy casualties and proved that independence could be, and would be, fought for.

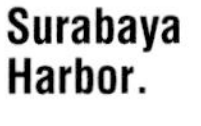

Surabaya Harbor.

The most interesting areas of Surabaya are the old Arab and Chinese quarters at the northern end of the city, not far from the harbor. Spend some time wandering the narrow lanes east of Jalan K.H. Mas Mansyur, around the mosque and the **Holy Grave of Sunan Ampel**, one of the "nine saints" who propagated Islam on the island. Many stalls around the mosque sell handmade textiles from all over Java.

Just to the south of here, at Jl. Dukuh II/2, is the **Hong Tik Hian Temple**, where Chinese hand-puppet (*potehi*) performances are put on daily for the benefit of the assembled deities. And just across Jl. Kembang Jepun, on Jl. Selompretan, stands Surabaya's oldest Chinese shrine – the 18th-century **Hok An Kiong Temple** – built entirely of wood in the traditional manner by native Chinese craftsmen. The temple's central deity is Ma Co, the protectress of waterlogged sailors.

From the Chinese quarter, walk westward along Jl. Kembang Jepun to the famous **Red Bridge** straddling Kali Mas canal. This lies at the very heart of the 19th-century commercial district, where many dilapidated Dutch warehouses and office buildings still stand.

Travel south from here, parallel to the river past the **Heroes Monument**, to see how Surabaya has expanded. From Jl. Tunjungan, the main shopping street, turn left down Jl. Pemuda to the former Dutch **Governor's Mansion**. This stood at what was then the new center of colonial Surabaya, constructed after the turn of the century, and is now a major hotel district. There is a centuries-old statue of King Kertanegara (died 1292) enshrined in a small park directly opposite – called **Joko Dolog** but affectionately known as the "fat boy." From here, continue south through fashionable suburbs to the **Surabaya Zoo** – home of many exotic species, including the famous Komodo dragon.

Beer-drinking bulls: Most visitors, eager to escape Surabaya's heat and bustle, head for the cool and inviting hills to the south of the city, but a few also cross the narrow straits to the neighboring

Dutch warehouses, Kali Mas canal.

Pulau Madura – particularly during August or September, time of the exciting annual bull races.

It's a strange sport, this *kerapan sapi*. According to the Madurese, it began long ago when plow team was pitted against plow team over the length of a rice field. Today's racing bulls are never used for plowing, but are specially bred; they represent a considerable source of regional pride. Only bulls of a certain standard (condition, weight, color) may be entered and they are judged according to appearance as well as speed. In August, district and regency heats are held all over Madura and east Java, building up to the finale in September in **Pamekasan**, the island's capital.

The main event is a thundering sprint down a 100-meter-long field lined by throngs of screaming spectators. Fed on a special diet of beer, eggs and chili peppers, these huge and normally slow-moving creatures attain speeds of over 50 kilometers per hour (nearly 30 mph). Some half-crazed spectators consider it good sport to stand at the end of the track, directly in the path of the onrushing bulls. Accidents do occur.

The Madurese have long enjoyed a reputation for toughness, and Madura's dry limestone terrain may account for this. The major industries here are fishing, tobacco growing and salt panning. The southern coastal fishing villages exude a solid but slightly jaded Mediterranean air. There are some good beaches here and also to the east, where a modest palace at **Sumenep** has a small museum and an important library of manuscripts attached.

Fresh air, cool nights: A quest for antiquities can be one of the great joys of east Java. And even if old stones leave you cold, you'll be on the trail to some beautiful and remote countryside here, with ne'er a tour bus in sight. One of the best bases for temple-tripping (or explorations of any sort) is the delightful mountain resort of **Tretes**, just 55 kilometers (35 mi) south of Surabaya.

The air here is fresh, the nights are cool and the mountain scenery is superb. Walk or ride on horseback in the

Bull hustle at Madura.

morning to one of three valley waterfalls in the vicinity. Then spend the afternoon by a bracing spring-fed swimming pool, or curled up with a good book and a huge pot of tea or coffee. More active souls will perhaps want to hike up **Gunung Arjuna** (3,340 meters/10,950 ft) behind Tretes, through lush montane casuarina forests, or across the Lalijiwa Plateau along a well-worn path to neighboring **Gunung Welirang**, where sulphur is collected by villagers from hissing fumaroles.

This area is also studded with ancient monuments, beginning with **Candi Jawi**, just by the main road 7 kilometers (4 mi) below Tretes. This slender Buddhist shrine was completed around 1300, and is one of several funerary temples dedicated to King Kertanegara, who died in 1292, of the Singhasari dynasty.

Candi Jawi overlooks **Gunung Penangungan** to the north – a perfect cone surrounded on four sides by smaller peaks and regarded, because of its shape, as a replica of the holy mountain, Mahameru. Penanggungan is littered with dozens of terraced sanctuaries, meditation grottoes and sacred pools – about 80 sites in all, most of which are on the mountain's northern and western faces. The most accessible and charming of these is **Belahan**, a bathing pool situated at Penanggungan's eastern foot. It is thought to be the burial site of King Airlangga, who died in 1049. The pool is reached by a dirt road from the main Surabaya highway, only a few minutes' drive north of Pandaan.

Traces of the past: From Tretes or Surabaya, it's about an hour to the village of **Trowulan** near Mojokerto, once the seat of Java's greatest empire, 14th-century Majapahit. Unfortunately, most of Majapahit's monuments were built of wood and soft redbrick, so that only the foundations and a few gateways remain. The **Trowulan Museum**, by the main road, nevertheless has a fascinating collection of terracotta figures and fragments, and a useful table-top map of the area. From here, seek out several nearby ruins: **Candi Tikus** (a royal bathing complex); **Candi Bajang**

Left, 14th-century Candi Jawa. Right, Belahan pools.

Ratu (a tall brick entry way); and **Wringin Lawang** (a palace gate).

Also visit the cemetery of **Tralaya**, two kilometers south of Trowulan, site of the oldest Muslim graves on Java. The most impressive pieces of statuary, however, are kept in the **Mojokerto Museum**, including the famous "portrait sculpture" of King Airlangga as Vishnu mounted on a formidable *garuda* – once the centerpiece at Belahan.

Malang is a pleasant town with a cool climate and a colonial atmosphere. A two-hour drive south of Surabaya, the city is a major regional center. There are three interesting temples nearby. **Candi Singhasari** is on the west side of the main highway from Surabaya, at the town of Singhasari. Just beyond the temple are two huge carved-rock temple guardians. From the village of Blimbing, on the northern outskirts of Malang, take the road to Tumpang, about 20 kilometers (12 mi) away. Just before the Tumpang market, a small road to the left leads to **Candi Jago** – a terraced shrine begun in 1268 as a memorial to the Singhasari king, Vishnuvardhana. All around the terraces are reliefs in the distinctive *wayang* or Javanese shadow puppet style depicting scenes from the *Mahabharata*, and a frightening procession of demons in the underworld (from the *Kunjarakarna*). A little over 5 kilometers southwest of Tumpang is **Candi Kidal**, a tall, slender gem of a temple honoring yet another Singhasari monarch, Anushapati, who died in 1248.

East Java's only sizeable temple complex is **Candi Penataran**, located 80 kilometers (50 mi) west of Malang, just north of the city of Blitar (best reached by taking the longer but more scenic route over the mountains via Kediri). This was apparently the state temple of Majapahit, assembled over a period of some 250 years, between 1197 and 1454. It has no soaring pinnacle or massive stupa, but rather a series of shrines and pavilions arranged before a broad platform. It is assumed that the pavilions were originally roofed with wood and thatch, as was the body of the main temple, now partially reconstructed.

Candi Penataran.

It's interesting that Penataran's architects no longer aimed at formal symmetry, in imitation of Indian models, but instead laid out their temple essentially in the manner of an indigenous palace, with audience pavilions in the forecourt and an ornately-decorated bathing pool at the rear. The main temple is at the back of the complex, closest to the mountain (as in Bali), and its terraces are lined with bold wayang reliefs – scenes from the ever-popular *Ramayana* and the *Krishnayana*, and with many unique animal medallions.

Near Penataran (on the road to Blitar) stands **President Soekarno's mausoleum**, the final resting place of the "Father of Indonesian Independence" who died in 1970. And on the way to or from Blitar via the scenic Malang–Kediri high road, make a detour north from Batu to the mountain resort of **Selekta** – famous for its colonial bungalows, swimming pools and apple orchards.

Tenggerese highlands: The steep slopes of the active volcanos Gunung Semeru and Gunung Bromo have been the home of the Tenggerese people for several hundred years. The region has become a major vegetable-growing area and the spectacular gardens and high-altitude pine trees are a great sight. The region is now accessible by paved roads from Malang, Surabaya, and Probolinggo. New modern hotels and bungalow complexes make the Gunung Bromo area a comfortable and exciting place to visit.

Gunung Bromo itself is a squat volcanic cone inside the much larger Bromo Caldera. The views from the rim of this caldera and from the narrow lip of Gunung Bromo itself are an otherworldly experience, especially if Bromo is belching steam. The traditional visit to Gunung Bromo has been a midnight climb to position oneself on the volcanic lip at dawn. The pink light of the rising sun slowly illuminates the caldera, full of fog at that hour. On clear mornings, the perfectly-shaped cone of **Gunung Semeru**, Java's highest volcano, looms to the south. It is indeed an ethereal experience.

On the way to Bali: The eastern salient of Java is formed by three highly active volcanic clusters, each of which now contains a nature reserve or national park. The most frequently visited of these is Gunung Bromo. The other two, the **Raung Plateau** and the **Ijen Crater**, are also accessible.

There are, in addition, three coastal game reserves in this area that can be visited on the way to or from Bali (by the Ketapang-Gilimanuk ferry).

The most accessible of these is the **Baluran Game Reserve** at Java's northeastern tip. The protruding southeastern tip of Java has also been designated as the **Banyuwangi Selatan Nature Reserve**, and though there are no roads leading into it, surfers have constructed bamboo shacks on the western shore, and often charter boats from Bali for the excellent waves here. Perhaps more enticing is the **Meru Betiri Nature Reserve** on the southern coast around Sukamade, where giant sea turtles lay their eggs on beaches, and where a rain pocket has created unusually dense jungles. This area is also the last refuge of the nearly extinct Javan tiger.

Left, Bromo landscape. **Right**, Banteng bull, Baluran Game Reserve.

THE OUTER ISLANDS

Beyond Sumatra and Java, Indonesia's outer islands are an eclectic group. With a yacht, one could fill a lifetime by cruising amongst Indonesia's island delights: Bali and Lombok, Nusa Tenggara, Kalimantan, Sulawesi, Maluku, and Irian Jaya. A lifetime would probably not be enough.

Bali, of course, is everything that travel guides and explorers and tourists say it is, and then more. There are those who lament its tourist appeal, but others would say that, without the sustaining interest of travelers, many of Bali's arts and rituals might have evaporated over the decades. Like its overshadowed neighbor to the east, Lombok, Bali is anchored by a massive, and still active, volcano that has often defined the lives and culture of its people.

Nusa Tenggara spreads east from Bali like a string of pearls awaiting the traveler. Once called the Lesser Sundas, the islands of Nusa Tenggara include Sumbawa, Flores, Sumba and Timor – all of them exotic enough. But perhaps it is one of the smaller islands that most draws visitors: Pulau Komodo, home of the Komodo dragon.

Kalimantan takes up about 75 percent of Borneo, the third-largest island in the world. (The Malaysian provinces of Sabah and Sarawak make up the remainder.) Mountainous and forested, and with a fringe of coastal swamps, Kalimantan rarely exceeds 1,500 meters (5,000 ft) in elevation, with the typical elevation at less than 300 meters. But it is rugged, having defied Europeans for centuries.

Sulawesi (Celebes) is an oddly-shaped island, much like a convoluted K in shape, a victim of confused and conflicting geological forces. Coral reefs ring the island's unusually long coastline, with deep ocean troughs lying offshore to the south.

Maluku (Moluccas) was long coveted by the Old World colonial powers as the Spice Islands – nutmeg and cloves made European men of those times crazy with desire. All together, there are about 1,000 islands in the Maluku group.

Irian Jaya shares the island of New Guinea with the independent country of Papua New Guinea. Like Borneo, New Guinea is one of the world's largest islands, remote and seductive. Irian Jaya makes up over 20 percent of Indonesia's land area, but less than one percent of its population. The interior is thick with forests and often ruggedly inaccessible; Indonesia's highest point is in Irian Jaya, at 5,030 meters (16,500 ft).

What is simply wonderful about Indonesia's outer islands is the sheer diversity of peoples, cultures, geography and mystery. If a traveler were to compile a dream list of travel experiences, they'd all be found here in these islands.

Preceding pages: beyond Bali by boat is an unparalleled experience. Left, Lombok aristocrat in traditional finery.

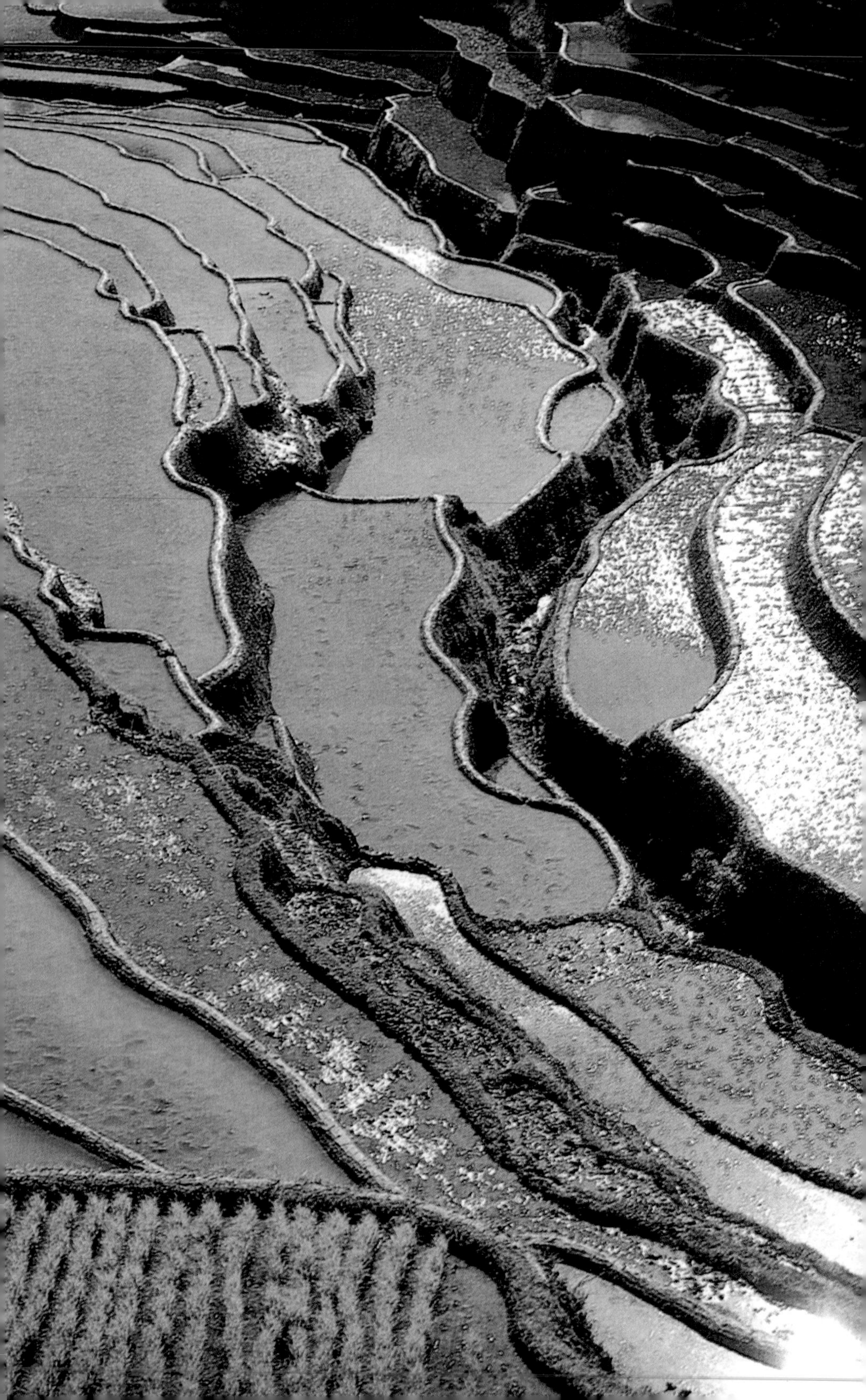

BALI

Bali is, first and foremost, a masterpiece of nature, formed by an east-to-west range of volcanoes and dominated by two towering peaks, Batur and Agung. Bali's volcanic soils are exceptionally fertile, and the reliable northwest monsoon brings abundant rainfall. The Balinese have done much to turn such natural blessings to their advantage. All but the steepest land has been painstakingly terraced with rice paddies that hug the volcanic slopes like steps. Each watery patch is efficiently irrigated through an elaborate system of aqueducts, dams and sluices regulated since ancient times by village agricultural cooperatives called *subak*. The land repays these efforts with abundant harvests, which in turn give the people extra time and energy to devote to their renowned cultural pursuits.

Abundant harvests are attributed to the benign efforts of the goddess of rice and fertility, Dewi Sri. Her symbol is the *cili,* two triangles connected in the form of a shapely woman. Divine spirits dwell in the lofty mountains; dark and inimicable forces lurk in the seas. The human's rightful place is the middle ground between these two extremes, and each home, village and kingdom in Bali has traditionally been aligned along this mountain–sea axis.

Isolation and confrontation: Bali was settled and civilized relatively early, as evidenced by stone megaliths like Gunung Kawi. Around a thousand years ago, Bali became a vassal of the great Hindu empires of east Java.

Yet Balinese culture developed a glittering and sophisticated persona all its own. Bali was united in 1550 under an independent ruler, and for two generations, Bali experienced a cultural golden age in which an elaborate ceremonial life, and also the arts, flourished.

Due to their traditional fear of the sea and suspicion of foreigners, the Balinese lived in virtual isolation from the rest of the world until the early 20th century. Throughout this period, its traditions of dance, music, painting, sculpture, poetry, drama and architecture were refined and elaborated, ostensibly for the benefit of Bali's numerous gods.

Largely spared the ravages of 19th-century colonialism – due, in part, to Dutch respect for the Balinese – the island was nevertheless the scene of horrific mass suicides (*puputan*) at the turn of this century, in which Balinese kings and courtiers threw themselves on *keris* knives, or ran headlong into Dutch gunfire, rather than face the humiliation of surrender.

But Bali has always been skillful, in fact, in absorbing influences from the outside, while retaining, if not strengthening, its local cultural touchstones.

Deep south: As the focus for Bali's tourism, commerce and government, the south is by far the island's busiest region. Screaming jets disgorge thousands of visitors daily at **Ngurah Rai International Airport**, set astride the narrow isthmus that connects the Bukit Peninsula with the rest of the island. Most of these paradise-seekers retire to

Left, irrigated rice fields, central Bali. Right, sun-kissed Sanur.

one of the three nearby beach resorts – Kuta, Sanur or Nusa Dua. Denpasar, the provincial capital, has experienced unprecedented economic and population growth during the past decade.

But don't be deceived by the area's development. The south's temple festivals are legendary for the intensity of their trance dances and the earthiness of their rituals. Denpasar's palace ceremonies rank among the most regal on the island, and Kuta Beach hosts highly-professional dance performances nightly. During Nyepi (Balinese New Year), thousands of villagers, arrayed in their ceremonial finery, flood the southern shores of Kuta bearing offerings of food for the *melis* purification rites.

However, it is the southern beaches that have captivated generations of foreign tourists. **Sanur**, ten kilometers southeast of Denpasar, was once an enclave of fishermen and holy Brahman priests, more famous for its demons and magic than its scenic delights. During the 1930s, however, Sanur's spectacular beaches attracted a colony of western intellectuals and artists that included anthropologist Margaret Mead and painter Walter Spies.

Mass tourism began in the early 1960s, but the real boom got under way only during the 1970s with the development of luxury bungalows along the waterfront, and secluded hotels with lush gardens that now attract a steady stream of visitors from Europe and North America. Perhaps the most famous is Tanjung Sari — nominated for the 1982 Aga Khan Award for Excellence in Islamic Architecture, and the place where Mick Jagger married model Jerry Hall.

North of the Hotel Bali Beach, where sands turn mysteriously black, nestles the **Le Mayeur Museum**. Once the home and studio of the talented Belgian impressionist and his dancer wife, Ni Pollock, the museum now contains luscious images and colors on canvasses framed in an Edwardian chamber.

Southern tip: South of the airport, a bulbous appendage fans out to form the **Bukit Peninsula**, once the hunting grounds of Denpasar's rajas. Geologi-

Sanur Beach.

cally and climatically, this area is Mediterranean, a dry and mostly barren plateau lying well above sea level.

The western and southern shoreline is rimmed with sharp, jutting cliffs, the site of the region's most illustrious temple, **Pura Uluwatu**. Chosen by the Balinese saint Pedenda Sakti Wawu Rauh as the "stage" for his *moksa* reunion with the godhead, Uluwatu is unrivaled for sheer grandeur of site and elegance of architecture. Giant sea turtles swim in the ocean 300 meters (1,000 ft) below the temple's clifftop perch.

The mangroves lining **Benoa Harbor** give way to superb beaches along the northeastern shore of the peninsula – a place called **Nusa Dua**, which has been developed into a massive tourist project over the last decade. There are at least a dozen luxury hotels – including the Amanusa, Grand Hyatt, and Bali Hilton – along with shopping centers and a huge convention center. Roving merchants, hawkers and masseuses are banned from Nusa Dua's streets and beaches. But they're not far away — **Bualu** village, just outside the resort gates, is crammed with souvenir shops and hawker stalls.

Whereas Sanur and Nusa Dua cater to visitors in search of seclusion and quiet, **Kuta**, at the top of the isthmus leading to Bukit Peninsula, has blossomed into Bali's greatest beach party.

First "discovered" by Aussie surfers in the early 1970s, Kuta's chief natural attractions are a broad sloping beach, pounding surf and technicolor sunsets. Accommodation ranges from the delightfully informal, often no more than a concrete block hastily thrown up behind a villager's home, to beautiful new resort hotels with gorgeous manicured tropical gardens facing the setting sun. The streets of Kuta and neighboring Legian are lined with a staggering array of restaurants, cafes, pubs, boutiques, discos, bike rentals, art shops and tour agencies. The result is a kind of tinseltown with a cosmopolitan feel, especially during peak season (July–August and December–January), when Kuta roars into the fast lane.

Left, cliffs at Uluwatu. Right, good fishing.

Secluded escapes: Deserted stretches of sandy beach and the serenity of the Balinese countryside are, thankfully, never more than a few minutes away. Past the Bali Oberoi Hotel is the important estuary temple of **Peti Tenget**. By divine coincidence, this is the spot where both the first Hindu-Javanese priest and the first Dutchman set foot on Bali.

Farther along the main road lies **Kerobokan**, a village of rural charm and as instant a trip into the "real" Bali as one can hope to find. Kerobokan's main road, leading to the richly-carved palace, is lined by a series of three score and ten temples.

Just south of Kuta is **Waterbom Park**, the island's first Western-style tourist attraction: an aquatic theme park with swimming pools, water slides and restaurants. Nearby is the luxury Four Seasons Resort, a magnificent scattering of Balinese-style cottages overlooking **Tuban Bay**.

Denpasar has swollen some tenfold over the years into a metropolis of more than 200,000 people, especially since replacing the northern port of Singaraja as the island's capital in 1945.

Denpasar's **main square** was the scene of the horrific mass suicide of 1906, when almost the entire royal house of Denpasar rushed headlong into blazing Dutch guns. Successive governments have erected monuments commemorating the event.

East of the square stands the town's state temple, **Pura Jagatnata**, a figurine of Tintya, the almighty godhead, glinting from its sea high on the temple's central shrine. The **Bali Museum** next door houses a fine collection of archaeological artifacts and examples of Balinese craftsmanship.

In the morning, visit KOLKAR on Jalan Ratna, the island's foremost conservatory of dance, music and puppet theater. A tertiary level of the arts school (ASTI) is located inside the sprawling grounds of the Werdi Budaya performing arts center, on Jalan Nusa Indah. A masterwork of baroque Balinese recreational architecture, the complex contains museums, open stages and recital

Left, museum, Denpasar. Right, temple offerings at Taman Ayun.

halls. Visitors are welcome to observe dance and music classes in progress.

The most important temple in this area, dating from the 12th century, is **Para Sada**, in Kapal. It has 64 stone seats resembling megalithic ancestral shrines; these are believed to commemorate loyal warriors who fell in battle.

Past Kapal, a turnoff toward the mountains leads to **Mengwi**. In 1634, the Raja of Mengwi, I Gusti Agung Anom, built the magnificent garden temple, **Pura Taman Ayun**. The temple's spacious compound is surrounded by a moat and is adjacent to a lotus lake. In the surrounding pavilions, priests recite their vedic incantations.

Northeast of Mengwi, at Sangeh, is Bali's famed **monkey forest**. According to Balinese versions of the *Ramayana* epic, this is where part of Hanuman's monkey army landed when the monkey king lifted the sacred mountain, Mahameru, and broke it apart in order to crush Rawana. A moss-covered temple lies hidden deep in the jungle. In its courtyard is the 17th-century Pura Bukit Sari, containing a large statue of the mythical garuda bird. The mischievous monkey tribe normally appears whenever there are visitors, in order to divest them of any and all edibles. Hold on tight to your belongings.

Continue along the main highway toward Tabanan, then to the town of Kediri. Here, perched on a large rock just offshore, sits the remarkable temple of **Tanah Lot**, founded by the proselytizing Hindu saint, Naratha, during his wanderings. Like many temples in Bali, it has animal guardians – in this case, snakes who live in caves nearby. At high tide, waves lash the islet, but at other times it is possible to cross over the rocks and ascend to the temple, which at sunset is strikingly silhouetted against a flaming sky. Waves thunder ashore against cliffs west of the temple and splash through natural arches carved by the relentless sea.

Puri Tabanan, the traditional home of the raja, is a striking reminder of the immense wealth once possessed by the Balinese rulers. The regional cultural

ecak dance, anah Lot.

center, **Gedung Mario**, takes its name from the most celebrated dancer of the 1930s and 1940s, the legendary I Nyoman Mario.

All temples in west Bali have shrines dedicated to the spirit of **Gunung Batukau**, the highest peak of the western volcanic range. Past the hot springs at Yeh Panas is Wongaya Gede, the village closest to the temple sanctuary, **Pura Luhur**, high on Batukau's slopes.

Uninhabited jungle encloses the solitary temple, whose single seven-tiered *meru* is the symbolic abode of the mountain deity. Nearby is a square pool symbolizing the ocean, and from the adjacent village of Jati Luwih, there is a stunning panorama of the coast.

Balinese heartland: With more gold leaf per square inch than imperial China, more artists than Montmartre, and the most glamorous traditional culture in the modern world, the magical middle kingdom is Bali's most exotic and artistic region. Ever since the great Hindu-Balinese renaissance of the 17th century, the realm within a 15-kilometer radius of Ubud, north of Denpasar, has been the main center of Balinese art.

The village of **Sukawati** was once an important kingdom and center for Chinese traders during the Dalem dynasty period. A phalanx of shops and a market now conceal the grand **Puri Sukawati** palace. Behind the palace live some of Bali's greatest shadow-puppet masters. Sukawati is the undisputed custodian of the Balinese *wayang kulit* shadow puppet tradition, and a performance by a Sukawati *dalang* (puppeteer) at a wedding or temple festival is considered a major event.

The views of distant Gunung Agung become more spectacular as one enters **Batuan** village, just north of Sukawati. Truly gifted in all the arts, the residents of Batuan are best known for their painting and dance. Under the patronage of Walter Spies, the Batuan School of the 1930s was the first to produce secular Balinese paintings – semi-realistic village scenes and sensitive studies of costumed dancers and musicians.

The *raja* of old, who orchestrated

Rice paddies.

village activities, seem to have parceled out artistic responsibility like today's corporate bosses – with each village as a separate corporate division.

Mas is a village of master carvers. In former times, woodcarvers worked only on religious or royal projects, but now they also produce decorative and "art" works for export. The village's most famous carver was Ida Bagus Nyana, whose visionary modernist sculptures of the 1940s – ethereal maidens with twisted torsoes – are now on display in the vast family gallery.

For many years, **Ubud** has been a mecca for foreign and local artists who enjoy the creative atmosphere in this area of Bali. Although Ubud's main street is now lined with shops selling all manner of paintings, carvings, weaving and bric-a-brac, the surrounding villages and countryside are as charming as ever, and most artists gladly welcome visitors into their home or studio.

Artists have thrived in Ubud since the 1930s, when a local aristocrat named Cokorda Sukawati formed the Pita Maha art society together with German painter Walter Spies and Dutch artist Rudolf Bonnet. Many of the finest works of the early Pita Maha years, which show clearly the transition from traditional to modern Balinese painting styles, are exhibited in the **Puri Lukisan Museum**.

Among the Pita Maha artists, I Gusti Nyoman Lempad was probably the greatest. His ink drawings, cremation towers, Barong heads and temple stone carvings are greatly admired. Lempad died in 1978 at the age of 121; some of his works are on display in his home, at the eastern end of Ubud's main street. Others may be seen at the excellent Neka Gallery, west of Ubud.

In fact, the finest artwork in Ubud is the surrounding countryside, and the only way to see it properly is on foot. Take a walk in the early morning or late afternoon to any of the neighboring villages, or catch a minibus north from Ubud's main intersection for the breathtaking ride to Pujung, from where you can walk to Sebatu village with its split-bamboo roofs, spirit boxes and carved

.otus pond, Jbud.

temple plinths. The more adventurous can take a half-day whitewater rafting trip through the lush **Ayung River** valley, like a trip back in time through a Bali untouched by the 20th century.

Antiquities of central Bali: Most of Bali's ancient remains are found in the narrow region bounded by two holy rivers, the Pekrisan and the Petanu. Crossing the Petanu River immediately to the east of Peliatan on the road to Bedulu, the mysterious **Goa Gajah** (**elephant cave**) is just visible on the lower side of the road, opposite a row of souvenir stands. The cave's gaping mouth is fantastically carved with leaves, rocks, animals, waves and demons, and when it was discovered in 1923, these carvings were apparently mistaken for an elephant, hence the cave's name. Adjacent baths were discovered and excavated in 1954, and, in fact, the site was probably a hermitage used by early Hindu-Buddhist holy men, as the cave contains three joined *lingga* (Shivaitic fertility symbols). Two Buddha statues, as well, have been found only a short distance away. All are believed to date from about the 8th or 9th century.

Just north of **Bedulu** on the main road is an archaeological museum, which houses a collection of neolithic axe heads, sarcophagi, weapons, bronze jewelry and Chinese ceramics.

Several temples just north of the museum contain objects of interest. The **Pura Kebo Edan** (crazed water buffalo) temple houses a 3.6-meter (12 ft) statue. The **Pura Puseing Jagat** (cosmic navel) contains a remarkable stone vessel carved with the tale of the churning of the ocean by gods and demons to obtain *amrta,* the elixir of life.

And the **Pura Penataran Sasih** (lunar governance) temple contains Indonesia's most important bronze-age antiquity: the 2,000-year-old Moon of Pejeng drum. Shaped like an hourglass, beautifully etched and over three meters (10 ft) long, it is the largest drum in the world to be cast as a single piece. According to Balinese legend, it fell from the sky, but the discovery of an ancient, similarly shaped stone mould in Bali

Left, woodcarver. **Right,** entrance to Gao Gajah.

proves that sophisticated bronze-casting techniques were known here from any early time.

A tomb and a spring: From Bedulu, the road winds up towards the crater of Gunung Batur, but about halfway to the peak, just at the source of the Pakrisan River, are two of Bali's holiest spots. **Gunung Kawi** is a spectacular and ancient royal tomb reached by descending a long, steep stairway through a stone arch into a watery canyon. On the far wall, ghostly shrines are hewn out of solid rock, probably memorials to the deified 11th-century Balinese ruler, Anak Wungsu. A complex of monk's cells also line the canyon walls.

The Balinese refer to their religion as Agama Tirta – the religion of the waters. It's not surprising then that a pilgrimage to the **Pura Tirta Empul** spring at Tampaksiring, two kilometers upstream from Gunung Kawi, is an essential part of every major Balinese ceremony and ritual. The waters of Tampaksiring are believed to have magic curative and restorative powers.

North over Batur: After Tampaksiring, the road climbs sharply until cresting finally upon one of the most dramatic sights in Bali: expansive **Danau Batur** and the smoking, black cone of **Gunung Batur**, an active volcano that reaches 1,700 meters (5,600 ft) above sea level. A village called **Penelokan** perches on the lip of the immense caldera – 20 kilometers (12 mi) across as the mythical garuda flies.

From Penelokan, the main road follows the rim of the crater, but there's also a small road that winds down to lava fields and a large crater lake at the bottom of the basin. If the mists have not yet rolled in, hire a motorized canoe to cross the lake to the curious village of **Trunyan**, one of the few pre-Hindu Bali Aga (original Balinese) enclaves on the island. These mountain people still maintain many ancient customs, the most famous of which is the practice of exposing their dead to the elements in a skeleton-filled graveyard by the lake. On the way back, stop at a hot sulphur spring at Toya Bungkah.

Gunung Kawi.

Continue north along the caldera's rim to **Kintamani**, the village closest to Batur's menacing cone. In 1917, the volcano erupted violently, claiming 1,000 lives and destroying a village that clung to its slopes, but miraculously leaving the village temple intact. The survivors took this as an auspicious sign and continued to live there. In 1926, another eruption buried the village and the temple, sparing only the shrine to Dewi Danu, goddess of the lake. The villagers resettled higher up at Kintamani, where the shrine now stands in the Pura Ulun Danu temple.

A short distance past Kintamani, the road veers left and begins the precipitous descent to the north coast. Before descending, however, stop and climb up a long flight of steps visible on the right, to the peak of **Gunung Penulisan**. This is the site of Bali's highest temple, and is believed to have been the mountain sanctuary of the kings of Pejeng.

The north coast: The culture of the north is different in several ways. The language is faster and less refined, the music is more allegro, and the temple ornamentation more fanciful. The port city of Singaraja, the capital of Bali under the Dutch, has sizeable communities of Chinese and Muslims.

From Penulisan, the winding road seems to drop straight out of the sky, flattening out several miles before the village of **Kubutambahan**, on the coast. This village's main temple, **Pura Maduwe Karang**, is dedicated to the animistic ground spirits that ensure good harvests. Partly because the local raja converted to Christianity early this century, leaving temple affairs in the hands of villagers, the carvings at Pura Maduwe Karang are "popular" in the way they depict ghouls, domestic scenes, lovers and even an official riding a bicycle.

A temple at Jagaraga, a short distance inland from the coast, has reliefs depicting Europeans riding in a Model-T Ford, a single-propeller plane diving into the sea, and a steamship attacked by sea monsters. And the Pura Beji temple at Sangsit, just west of Kubutambahan by the sea, is known for its Rabelaisian scenes – complete with flames, arabesques and spirals, and all executed in pink sandstone.

Singaraja, on the north coast and once a thriving center of commerce and government, is now rather sleepy (pop. 25,000). Its tree-lined boulevards and colonial residences tell something of its former glory, but there is relatively little to see or do. The **Gedung Kertya**, on Jl. Veteran near the colonial Hotel Singaraja (once the Dutch governor's mansion), houses a valuable collection of lontar (palm leaf) manuscripts. And at the port are sailing vessels unloading wood and loading coffee, corn or rice.

Heading due south from Singaraja, the road climbs up and up into the lush Bratan plateau, an area fed by numerous mountain lakes and streams.

East Bali: The direction "east" is greatly revered by the Balinese, as the realm of the Hindu god Siwa in his manifestation as Surya, the sun god. Balinese myth tells how the gods set towering Gunung Agung in the east and placed their thrones upon it. Some millennia later, divine providence and a sense for properties

Gunung Batur.

led a party of East Javanese nobles, priests, architects and craftsmen to establish the sanctuary of Besakih, where all Balinese castes and creeds could worship high on the mountain's slopes.

East Bali was also the home of Bali's most powerful kingdoms. Courts at Gelgel, and later at Klungkung and Karangasem, were places of refinement and grandeur, where rajas and noblemen patronized the arts and created traditions of music and dance.

Coming from Ubud or the south, the major roads pass through **Gianyar**, center of Bali's famous weaving industry. Many workshops and factories still produce a variety of beautiful hand-woven and hand-dyed textiles, although the use of machine-spun cotton thread, quick chemical dyes and tinsel foil cannot possibly match the quality of the older cloths, with their hand-spun threads, elaborate vegetable dyes and gold and silver ornamentation.

Beside the town square of Gianyar is the royal palace, one of the few that's still inhabited by a royal family. The intricately-carved wooden pillars, the stonework and generous proportions of its various courtyards are representative of the style to which all Balinese rulers were once accustomed. The Raja of Gianyar conducted a dual royal cremation ceremony for his mother and wife in 1992, one of the most dazzling – and probably one of the last – traditional cremation ceremonies held on Bali in many years.

Klungkung, 20 kilometers to the east, was once the political center of Bali. The descendants of the great Hindu-Javanese Majapahit court settled in this area after fleeing Java in the 15th century. The raja of Klungkung was regarded, by virtue of his illustrious genealogy, as the most senior of all Balinese rulers, and played an influential role in government and the arts.

Holiest of the Holy: The mountain road north from Klungkung climbs through some of Bali's most spectacular rice terraces, passing through several villages on the way to the island's holiest spot, the temple of **Pura Besakih**. With

Pura Besakih.

the massive peak of **Gunung Agung**, the Balinese Olympus, as a backdrop, the broad, stepped granite terraces and slender, pointed black pagodas of this 60-temple complex are a fitting residence for the gods.

Regarded as a holy place since prehistoric times, the first record of Besakih's existence is an inscription dating from 1007 AD. From at least the 15th century – when Besakih was designated as the sanctuary of the deified ancestors of the Gelgel god-kings and their very extended family – this has been the "mother" temple for the entire island. All the allegiances of the Balinese come together here: every god in the extensive Balinese pantheon is represented, gathered in one vast meeting place in the clouds, and Balinese make periodic pilgrimages to worship them.

Several kilometers after Kusumba, at the foot of a rocky escarpment, gapes the entrance to **Goa Lawah**, one of the nine great temples of Bali. Goa Lawah is said to be the terminus of an underground passageway leading to distant Besakih temple up on Agung. Many Balinese temples have resident beasts, the so-called *duwe* (possession) of the temple, and apart from the thousands of small black bats that inhabit Goa Lawah and give it its name, the cave is also believed to be the abode of Naga Basuki, the sacred dragon of Gunung Agung.

About 15 kilometers (9 mi) past Goa Lawah, a side road to the right leads to the picturesque harbor town of **Padang Bai**. This is where the Lombok ferry departs, and where cruise ships anchor – a perfectly-shaped bay, cradled by white sand coves and grassy hills.

Candi Dasa is a perfect base for exploring Tenganan, home of a pre-Hindu Bali Aga tribe. Located several kilometers inland in an area of lush bamboo forests and mystical banyan trees, **Tenganan** was for some reason never assimilated to the island's Hindu-Balinese culture, and thus has retained its own traditions of architecture, kinship, government, religion, dance and music, supplying the rest of the island with several valuable items, notably the sacred double-ikat *geringsing* fabrics.

Palaces of Karangasem: Twenty-five kilometers (16 mi) farther east, the road crosses a wide lava bed and enters **Amlapura**, a medium-size town formerly known as Karangasem and once the capital of Bali's most cultured king.

Puri Agung Karangasem, the traditional home of the Karangasem kings, is an austere compound surrounded by a thick redbrick wall, penetrated only by a three-tiered gate.

Puri Kanginan, the palace where the last raja was born, is an eclectic creation reflecting the strong European influence of his education, and of his architect – a Chinese by the name of Tung. The main building, with its lavish Edwardian moldings and long veranda, is called the Bale London. The furniture, curiously, bears the crest of the British royal family.

From Subagan, a village in the solidified lava flows on the western outskirts of Amlapura, the mountain road climbs due west through **Sibetan**, a village famous for its *salak* – a teardrop-shaped fruit with the sweet-sour texture of an apple and skin resembling that of a cobra. Past Sibetan the road levels out, winding across an exciting landscape of sculpted rice terraces and river valleys of great dramatic beauty.

The idyllic mountain village of **Iseh** was chosen by painter Walter Spies as the site for his country home. It gazes over an uninterrupted vista of mighty Gunung Agung – acclaimed by many as the great Bali view.

Bulls to the west: The district capital of **Negara**, near the western end of Bali and on the southern coast, is famed mostly for its bull races. A secular entertainment introduced from east Java and Madura less than a century ago, bull racing takes place regularly between July and October.

As on Madura, the bulls are specially-bred for speed and color (no ordinary plowing bulls, these), then decked out in silk banners and enormous wooden bells and paraded before being raced down a two-kilometer track. They are judged for speed (up to 50 kilometers per hour) and style. It's a spectacular sight, and that's no bull.

Ornamental kala-head gateways are distinctive on Balinese temples.

LOMBOK

East of Bali, across a deep strait seething with whirlpools and dolphins, lies Lombok. The island is quite different its world-famous neighbor. Its climate is certainly drier and the land more rugged, and it is only about half as crowded.

Lombok was formerly a day-trip destination from Bali. But its lovely rugged scenery, beautifully white beaches, and unique culture and traditional architecture combine to make Lombok a unique destination in its own right.

Like Bali, Lombok is dominated by a towering northern volcanic range, with 3,800-meter (12,300 ft) Gunung Rinjani, the second-highest peak in Indonesia outside of Irian Jaya, at its center. A non-volcanic mountain range traverses the barren southern side of the island. Most of Lombok's arable land and population occupy a narrow 25-kilometer-wide (16 mi) strip in between.

The western third of this plain, in many ways similar to east Bali, is well fed by mountain streams and artesian springs. Here, Balinese and Sasaks have sculpted handsome rice terraces into the fertile sloping alluvial fan at the foot of Gunung Panacean, and Hindu temples vie for attention with glistening white mosques amidst the picturesque rural villages.

Lombok exudes an aura of the genteel and the rural. It is an island of startling contrasts: Hindu rituals incorporated into Muslim ceremonies, and lush rain forests backing arid plains. The island's polyglot populace – Sasak, Balinese, Chinese and Arab – continues its paced, traditional ways. Tourism is still in its infancy here, although government-sponsored development of resorts on both the west and south coasts have brought increasing numbers of international visitors.

The island's people: Only about 10 percent of Lombok's inhabitants are Hindu Balinese, and almost all of them live in towns and villages on the island's tiny west-central plain. The vast majority of Lombok's inhabitants are Sasak, dividing themselves into two more or less distinct groups: the Waktu-telu – whose customs are still basically pagan with some Muslim influence – and the Waktu-lima, who inhabit the lowlands and the coasts and are devout Muslims.

A touch of history: Early native chronicles confirm that Lombok was colonized from East Java, and the Sasak people perhaps take their name from a type of bamboo raft (*sesek*) used to cross the straits. According to a 14th-century lontar-leaf text found here in 1894 (the famous *Negarakertagama*), the island was brought under direct Javanese control by Patih Gajah Mada, powerful prime minister of the Majapahit kingdom, before his death in 1365.

In the 17th century, Lombok was invaded and colonized from two directions. The western plain was annexed by the Balinese. The east coast, which had been the political center of the native Sasak inhabitants, was conquered by Makassarese traders operating from Sumbawa, and the Sasak aristocracy was converted to Islam. In 1677, the

Left, odalan ritual at Pura Meru. Right, sacred stone, Hindu temple.

Makassarese were expelled from eastern Lombok, and for the next 150 years, the native Sasak aristocracy resisted numerous Balinese advances. Meanwhile, west Lombok came into a Balinese-inspired golden age, with a local architectural style and court pageantry that rivaled Bali's own.

In 1849, Lombok and eastern Bali were united under the rule of the Balinese raja of Karangasem. But Balinese hegemony lasted less than half a century; in 1894, a large Dutch military expedition landed at Ampenan. Aided by Sasaks trying to liberate themselves from Balinese rule, the Dutch managed to wrest control of the island – but not without bitter fighting and over 1,000 Dutch casualties.

Urban hustle and bustle: The island's three main towns cluster in a long, six-kilometer-long urban strip, running inland from the western coast. Ampenan is the old port town, Mataram the government center, and Cakranegara the commercial center.

Ampenan, formerly the main port of Lombok and once a vital link in the spice trade, is now little more than a broken-down wooden jetty with rows of deserted warehouses. At the main crossroads stands the **Maritime Museum**, which attempts to recount the colorful history of Ampenan's overseas trade.

Neighboring **Mataram** is the modern provincial capital of West Nusatenggara Province, with government buildings and large well-kept houses to prove it. Yet, other than providing banking, ticketing and other services, the town offers little for the visitor. One shop that should not be missed, however, is the New Zealand government-sponsored ceramic project on the main highway bypass. Delightful ochre pottery ranging in size from small jam pots to huge water jars are on sale, and proceeds go to the villagers, who make the ceramics.

Cakranegara, just east of Mataram, is the most interesting of the island's towns. Raja Agung Made Gege Ngurah established his royal capital here in 1744, and the town still boasts many 18th-century landmarks. It's also the island's

Kuta Beach.

major market town. The crowded Arab quarter bustles with activity – this is the place to shop for an intricately-patterned cotton *sarung*. And the Balinese quarter, to the north of the town across the Ancar River, has many splendid courtyard homes in the unique Lombok-Balinese style. The old covered market adjacent to Sweta Bus Station is one of the best places in Lombok to buy local arts and crafts.

Pura Meru, central temple for Lombok's Hindu population, overlooks Cakranegara's main crossroads. Built in 1720 to unify the island's various Hindu factions, the three courts symbolize the *tri loka* or three-tiered division of the Hindu cosmos: the earth, the human realm and the divine. In the innermost courtyard stand three pagodas representing the Hindu trinity – Brahma, Vishnu and Siva. Each of the 33 smaller shrines is cared for by a different Hindu community in Lombok.

Opposite the temple, a vast pond filled with lilies surrounds a pavilion that may be reached by crossing over a stone causeway. This is the **Puri Mayura royal garden**, constructed in 1744. The pavilion is known as the Bale Kambang and formerly served as both a court of justice and a meeting hall for Lombok's lords. Gen. Van Ham, leader of the Dutch military expedition of 1894, was killed here, along with all his men.

The **Royal Palace** behind the garden is surprisingly modest – a part-Dutch, part-Balinese bungalow surrounded by a moat. The house is now a kind of museum, filled with old photographs and memorabilia from the Dutch times.

To the north and south of Mataram and Ampenan, there are several sights worthy of investigation, though few tourists take the time to seek them out. Seven kilometers south of Mataram, white shrines glint like calcified stalagmites on the rocky outcrops of **Gunung Pengsong**. The temples are reached by climbing a long flight of stairs that rises from the road between ancient banyan trees; the 360-degree view from the top is superb. Tribes of monkeys, the temple guardians, play and pester.

Left, Kecodak dance, Tanjung. Right, Pura Meru.

The small village temple in nearby **Pagutan** once housed a priceless 14th-century palm-leaf manuscript version of the *Negarakertagama* – the major source of knowledge concerning the great Majapahit empire in Java. The manuscript was discovered here by a Dutch scholar in 1898 and now resides in the National Museum, in Jakarta.

From Ampenan, a road leads north across river estuaries and through coconut groves to the **Batu Bolong** cliff temple. Situated high upon a rock formation that juts out into the Lombok Strait, the temple is reached by passing over a natural stone arch. From this unique vantage point, experience the magnificent setting of the sun as it picks up specks of color from the sails of passing boats.

Further north along the coast is **Senggigi Beach**, where a plethora of modern luxury resort hotels take advantage of the beautiful and sandy beach, along with a fantastic view of Gunung Agung on Bali. More than a dozen large hotels and bungalow complexes stretch along the white sands, intermixed with traditional fishing communities.

Narmada and Suranadi: Small white mosques speckle the terraced rice fields between Cakranegara and **Narmada**, 10 kilometers (6 mi) to the east. Stop at the sprawling market on the right, reputed to be Lombok's largest, and shop for baskets, earthenware and other village handicrafts.

The small town of Narmada is dominated by a human-made plateau, upon which stands the late 19th-century summer palace that was designed and built by the king of Karangasem. It is a vast complex of tiered gardens that descends sharply into a river valley below. Western-style ponds, fountains and arbors are built into traditional Balinese compounds of interlocking courtyards and pavilions. The king was evidently influenced by wealthy Dutch merchants, who told him of the great palaces of Europe; his eclectic summer palace ranks as one of the great achievements in the history of Balinese architecture.

The temple at **Suranadi**, seven kilometers above Narmada, is a pilgrimage point for Hindus from Lombok and Bali on account of its holy springs. Like Tampaksiring on Bali, the waters here (Suranadi is the name of the river that flows through Nirvana) are sought for the performance of important rituals. The springs were created, according to local legend, by the Hindu saint Niratha, who led a group of village elders to the spot and thrust his staff in the ground five times.

The neighboring Suranadi Hotel, once a royal pleasure garden, is now a delightful small hotel, with a large spring-fed swimming pool and an excellent restaurant. There are trails leading up into mountain villages, where traditional stilt houses line small clearings in the rain forest. And just to the west, at the temple of **Lingsar**, albino fish swim in the ponds of the inner sanctum, a sure sign of elevated spirituality, according to ancient Javanese belief.

From Narmada, travel south through Mangang and Praya to the sandy shores of the southern coast. The round trip takes between four and five hours, so

Narmada.

get an early start. At **Sukarere**, stop to see Lombok *ikat* and *lambung* cloths being woven.

Farther south, the road gently rolls through miles of wet-rice paddies – a sea of lime-green shoots or cracked brown earth, depending upon the season. Along the road are several traditional Sasak villages with uniquely-shaped houses and rice barns. Finally, **Kuta** is a small solitary village that guards access to a magnificent 100-kilometer (60 mi) stretch of deserted golden beach. As on the south coast of Bali, waves crash ashore on exposed rocky points. The coast is a series of small protected bays and coves, where calm turquoise water and sandy sloping beaches are a natural magnet for development. The government has designated a long stretch of this beautiful indented coastline for official tourist development, and several modern hotels have already been planned. By the turn of the century, this area is fated to be "developed," so hurry to see it in a more pristine condition.

On the way home from Kuta, or on the way to the east, visit the Dutch hill station of **Tetebatu**. Here, in the midst of fruit orchards and vegetable gardens, a pre-World War II villa with a spring-fed pool has been transformed into a small hotel and picnic stop.

Scaling the heights: Those who have made the climb to the top of 3,800-meter (12,300 ft) **Gunung Rinjani** claim that it's the ultimate Lombok experience. The climb is a strenuous one and is certainly not for everyone, and can only be attempted during the dry season (April to October).

A police permit is required from the main office in Mataram. Take warm clothing, food and water for the two-day expedition. There are two approaches, one running south from Bayan and up the western slopes, the other from the village of **Sapit**. Guides and porters can be hired at either point. Ascend the slopes just below the caldera, then camp and climb the last stretch in the pre-dawn hours in time for the sunrise – an unveiling of the eastern islands.

Crater lake, Gunung Rinjani.

NUSA TENGGARA – THE LESSER SUNDAS

In Old Javanese, Nusa Tenggara means southeastern islands, referring to the tightly-packed necklace of sparsely-inhabited islands stretching east from Bali. In the Dutch days, these islands were known as the Lesser or Eastern Sundas – a grouping that then included Bali. In 1951, Bali was made a separate province of the new Republic of Indonesia, and the other islands were organized into two distinct provinces: West Nusa Tenggara (comprising Lombok and Sumbawa) and East Nusa Tenggara (Sumba, Flores, Timor and the adjacent islands). In 1976, Indonesia annexed the former Portuguese colony of East Timor, gaining its 27th province.

The islands of Nusa Tenggara are formed by the protruding peaks of a giant submarine mountain range that runs from Sumatra to Timor. East of Lombok, the range splits into two distinct chains: a southerly group that is older and non-volcanic (forming the islands of Sumba, Sawu, Roti and Timor), and a northerly, intensely volcanic range that dominates Sumbawa and Flores, and then curves up to end in the peaks of the Banda Islands.

Moving eastward in the Sunda archipelago, the climate becomes markedly drier due to the action of hot, desiccating winds that blow up from the Australian land mass. The moisture-laden northwest monsoon fights against these dry winds in November and December, reaching the easternmost islands of Nusa Tenggara relatively late, and sometimes only for a period of weeks. Yearlong droughts are common on Sumba and Timor. Rainfall falls on the windward slopes, creating pockets of lush forest and vegetation amidst parched grassland and savannah.

Beasts of Wallacea: The depth of water separating the islands of Nusa Tenggara is such that even at the height of the Ice Age – when the sea level was about 200 meters (450 ft) lower – there were no land bridges between the islands.

A 19th-century naturalist, Sir Alfred Russell Wallace, spent several years studying these islands and noted a marked difference between the Eurasian animal species of the Greater Sundas (monkeys, elephants, tigers, pigs, rhinoceroses, buffalo, deer) and the Australian species of the eastern islands. He drew a line (now called the Wallace Line) separating Bali and Borneo from Lombok and Sulawesi, postulating this a boundary between two faunal groups.

More recent studies have shown that many Eurasian species, particularly birds and insects, persist throughout the islands of Nusa Tenggara and disappear only in New Guinea and Australia. Nusa Tenggara thus lies within a transitional zone called Wallacea, in which the fauna of Eurasia and Australia coexist. The islands still harbor a great variety of interesting wildlife: Australian marsupial species, colorful New Guinean plumage birds and large primitive reptiles like the legendary Komodo dragon.

Trade and conquest: Coastal areas of Nusa Tenggara have participated in re-

Preceding pages: horsemen from Sumba. **Left**, wrapped in weavings, Sumbawa. **Right**, young dancers, Sumbawa.

gional trade since very early times. Although the islands produce no spices, they have been a major source of sandalwood and other aromatic and hardwood products for nearly 2,000 years. Small coastal kingdoms dominated the region until the 14th century, when the Majapahit empire claimed the entire Nusa Tenggara chain as part of its realm. Islam arrived in the 15th and 16th centuries, via Java and Ternate.

The first Portuguese ships reached the area in 1512 and, by the end of the century, they had hijacked the Timorese sandalwood trade and established fortresses on Flores and Solor. The Dutch wrestled much of the spice trade away from their European rivals in the 17th century, but the area's sandalwood was nearly depleted by then. Consequently, the Dutch didn't take much interest in Nusa Tenggara until the early 20th century, when military expeditions were dispatched to impose Dutch rule.

Subsistence economics: Today, Nusa Tenggara is among the poorest and least-fertile regions of Indonesia. Most of the almost 10 million inhabitants of Nusa Tenggara are subsistence farmers or fishermen. Fish, livestock and some agricultural products (coffee, copra, rice, beans, onions) are exported to other islands, while manufactured goods and some food products are imported, mainly from Java. Recently, the Indonesian government has invested heavily to improve communications, establish schools and provide health facilities. This is bringing rapid change to some of the urban areas. Yet partly because the population is so scattered, many villages remain remote and relatively untouched by modern civilization.

Worship of nature and ancestral spirits is still common in Sumba and Timor. Elsewhere, ancient beliefs are often disguised by a thin veneer of Islam or Christianity. Supernatural beings are thought to control harvests, bring disease, and guard against disaster. Chickens, pigs and water buffalo are frequently sacrificed to the spirits, and then consumed in communal feasts. Human blood often flows in ritualized

Roman Catholic missionary at Lela, South Flores.

contests – boxing matches, whip duels or cavalry bouts – associated with planting, harvesting and marriage.

Most people of Nusa Tenggara fitted, until recently, into one of three distinct social categories: noble, commoner or slave. The ruler of a trading port frequently styled himself raja or sultan, although in most areas, tribal organization prevailed and the leaders were often quite indistinguishable from the other members of the community.

Nobles have been distinguished instead by ritual practices and status items. The bride price was an essential cultural and economic factor – an aristocrat would need to provide money and exotic items such as bronze drums (on Alor), ivory tusks (on Flores and Lembata), or ivory bracelets and water buffalo (on Sumba) in order to secure a bride of high social standing. The bride's family would reciprocate with fine woven *ikat* cloths, which often had ritual significance. Indeed, the ikat weavers of Nusa Tenggara are famed throughout the archipelago and their products are now highly prized by textile collectors around the world.

Sumbawa: The island of **Sumbawa** is larger than Bali and Lombok combined, its contorted form the result of violent volcanic explosions. It's divided into three administrative districts or regencies that correspond roughly to the former sultanates: Bima in the east, Sumbawa in the west, Dompu in the middle.

Most of Sumbawa's 800,000 inhabitants farm or fish. The island's exports are almost entirely agricultural: rice, peanuts, beans and cattle, although timber is becoming more important.

The people of Sumbawa are devout Muslims. Indeed, the eastern regency of Bima sends a higher percentage of pilgrims to Mecca than any other area in Indonesia. The *kerundang* or orthodox Islamic dress for women is very much in evidence in Bima, and powerful loudspeakers amplify the *muezzin*'s predawn call to prayer in all major towns on the island. Yet even though Islam is firmly implanted on Sumbawa, there is

Market at Sape.

a strong undercurrent of ancient customs and beliefs. One of the most important traditions is the *dukun* or shaman, who can cure disease or make water buffalo run faster.

Most visitors speed through Sumbawa Besar or Bima, the island's two main settlements. Nevertheless, both towns are worth a sojourn. Each has a royal palace museum where the sultan's sacred *pusaka* or insignia of power can be seen. And each town has an ancient harbor where skilled shipwrights construct large wooden vessels.

In **Sumbawa Besar**, the sultan's former residence is made entirely of wood. Built in 1885 and called the Dalem Loka, the palace is raised on stilts in the traditional manner and crowned by two unusual carvings. The palace in **Bima** houses a fantastic collection of royal crowns and *keris* with gem-studded gold and ivory hilts. It's possible to see these, but you must contact the city government and negotiate a fee. Near Bima, there are several significant Muslim tombs. The most important is the grave of the first sultan who embraced Islam.

Fertile river valleys with shimmering velvet-green rice fields surround the towns, but as one moves out across Sumbawa along the single paved highway, the monotony of rolling scorched brown hills is alleviated only by a stretch of dramatic coast. Picturesque bays and harbors shelter *bagan* – twin-sailed catamaran fishing boats with a small hut in the middle. Fishermen cast off at night, using powerful lanterns to attract fish.

Outside of urban areas, most houses are made of wood and raised one or two meters above the ground on stilts, to catch the breeze and avoid flooding during the rainy season. Men and women wear wraparound *sarung,* and in Sape it's not unusual to see conical, brilliantly-painted, plaited-leaf sun hats.

From Sumbawa Besar's harbor, one can charter a motorized fishing boat for the three-hour voyage to **Pulau Moyo**, an island populated by deer, wild boar and other game. Hunting is permitted, but requires a police permit. For non-hunters, there is excellent scuba diving. The superbly luxurious **Amanwana** resort, with modified villas using tent toppings of canvas, is on Moyo, undoubtedly the most expensive night under canvas in the world. Access is by prearranged boat transfers from the Sumbawa airport. The isolation is total.

Hikers and climbers may want to ascend **Gunung Tambora**, site of the world's greatest volcanic explosion. In 1815, approximately 100 cubic kilometers of debris were ejected into the atmosphere with a force equivalent to that of several hydrogen bombs, creating the "year without summer" of 1816. Located on the northern peninsula of Sumbawa and due east of Pulau Moyo, the gaping, 2,820-meter-high (9,250 ft) caldera offers a spectacular view.

The hills east of Sumbawa Besar contain many large stone sarcophagi, carved in low relief with human forms and crocodiles, and scattered around **Batu Tering** village, in Semamung district. It's assumed the megaliths are the royal tombs of a neolithic culture that thrived here about 2,000 years ago.

While waiting for the Komodo ferry

Looking for a good time.

in **Sape**, at the east end of Sumbawa, it's possible to charter a minibus for the 25-kilometer (15 mi) ride northward to several coastal villages, where white beaches, crystal-clear water and coconut trees contribute to an idyllic setting.

Island of dragons: Directly in the center of the island-strewn strait between Sumbawa and Flores lies **Pulau Komodo**, home of the world's largest reptile, the Komodo dragon (*varanus komodoensis*). This giant monitor lizard (called *ora* by the locals) is one of the world's oldest species, a close relative of the dinosaurs that roamed the earth 100 million years ago.

Komodo island lies 500 kilometers (300 mi) east of Bali, and is 30 kilometers (20 mi) long on its north-south axis and 16 kilometers (10 mi) at its widest point. The island's parched hills are covered with scrub brush and small palm trees.

There is only one village on Komodo, a small community of 500 people clinging precariously to the shore. Requested earlier by the government to abandon their inland gardens in the name of conservation for the national park, the people now make a living fishing by night from graceful catamarans.

Several hundred adult lizards live on Komodo. The adult males can reach three meters (10 ft) in length and weigh 150 kilograms (330 lbs). Females attain only two-thirds of this size and lay up to 30 eggs at a time.

The greatest threat to the monitors comes now from deer poachers, who kill off the animals upon which the lizards feed. Dogs are sometimes abandoned on the island and compete with the dragons, and eat the dragons' eggs.

The highlight of a Komodo visit is to see the dragon in its natural habitat. Although you may spot one by walking around the island, a safer and surer way is to let the Indonesian Directorate of Nature Conservation (known by its Indonesian initials PPA) arrange your visit. For a fee they will bring a goat to the PPA campsite on Komodo, and from there walk you to a vantage point some two kilometers away. Here, the goat will be slaughtered, and from the shade and

Komodo dragon on the prowl.

safety of an elevated observation area is an excellent view of dragons devouring the bait. Be sure to keep well away from the lizards – their tails are lethal weapons and their saliva is extremely toxic. By the time the lizards are finished, the entire goat will be gone.

Aside from the dragon tour, there are designated trails for hiking, accompanied always by a guide. These lead into the hills above the national park headquarters, where there are exquisite panoramas of the surrounding emerald-blue seas. One may also hire a boat to **Red Beach**, east of Loho Liang, or to **Pulau Lasa**, across from Komodo village. The snorkeling and swimming are superb, but keep an eye out for the Komodo dragons – they can swim and sometimes move back and forth between Komodo and nearby small islands.

When visiting Komodo, whether arriving by government ferry or by a private boat chartered on Sumbawa or Flores, be aware that the currents around Komodo are very strong and the seas usually rough. When swimming, keep an eye out for sea snakes, which are plentiful in these waters, and always be mindful of currents and riptides.

Sumba: Well to the south of the main Nusa Tenggara chain, **Sumba** has always been one of the major backwater regions of the archipelago. Barren throughout the long dry season and lacking modern tourist facilities, Sumba does offer the opportunity to see remnants of an ancient pagan Indonesian culture. Because Sumba never had much historical significance and few resources, it escaped the waves of Hindu, Muslim and Christian influence that washed over neighboring islands.

Known in past centuries as a source of sandalwood, slaves and horses – and as a land of cannibal tribes and rugged horsemen – Sumba is famous today for its sculptured megalithic tombs, tribal wargame rituals and intricate hand woven ikat textiles. The island is almost oval shaped, about 300 kilometers (180 mi) long and 80 kilometers (50 mi) wide, and divided politically and climatically into two quite distinct halves.

Traditional Sumban village.

West Sumba, with a population of 350,000, is the more prosperous half, higher and thus lush and green during the rainy season, and culturally diverse, with two separate linguistic groups speaking at least eight dialects. West Sumbans live in thatched huts with high conical roofs raised on stilts. Agricultural communities flourish, and ancestral and land worship are still strong, with about two-thirds of the population observing traditional religious practices such as the *pasola* (in which hundreds of mounted warriors fling spears at one another) and the communal construction of stone slab tombs.

East Sumba is dry, rocky and inhospitable, with 250,000 inhabitants who speak the same language. Most people live near or on the coast, and an extensive hand-loom industry has flourished for several centuries, producing distinctive, high quality ikat weavings.

Traditional villages with elaborate megalithic tombs are scattered throughout West Sumba. **Waikabubak**, the small district capital, boasts a number of ancient mausoleums. **Tarung** village, an important hilltop ceremonial center just west of Waikabubak, has tombs and houses decorated with water buffalo horns – souvenirs of sacrificial feasts.

There is another tomb with unusual carvings at the village of **Pasunga** in Anakalang district, 20 kilometers (14 mi) east of Waikabubak on the main road to Waingapu. A bit farther east and a few minutes off the road, the Resi Moni grave is the burial site of a former raja of Anakalang – one of the largest megaliths on the island. Nearby, the village of Lai Tarung boasts many old graves and an important ceremony called the *purunga ta kadonga,* which is held every two years. **Wanukaka** district, 18 kilometers (12 mi) south of Waikabubak, has the oldest megaliths in the area, the *hatu kajiwa* (spirit stones) at Prai Goli.

Sodan is perhaps the most interesting traditional village in West Sumba, located 25 kilometers (16 mi) southwest of Waikabubak, a few kilometers from Lamboya. An important lunar new year ceremony takes place each October, and

Left, a weaving such as this can take several months to complete. **Right**, megalithic carving.

the village possesses a sacred drum whose playing surface is covered with human skin.

Bemo from Waikabubak will get you close to all the places mentioned above. It's a good idea to ask which village is holding its weekly market and head in that direction. Adventurous visitors may want to hike to even more remote villages away from the roadways. The best bet is to head south from Waikabubak towards Wanokaka, Lamboya or Padedewatu, where smaller settlements are as close as half an hour's walk.

The *pasola* is West Sumba's most exciting ritual – scores of colorfully-arrayed horsemen on bareback, battling with spears. The ceremony is held during February in **Lamboya** and **Kodi** (on the western tip of the island), and during March in **Gaura** and **Wanokaka**. It begins several days after the full moon, and coincides with the yearly arrival to the shore of strange, multi-hued sea worms called *nyale*. Riders charge one another and fling spears. The law says that the spears must be blunt.

To relax in West Sumba while waiting for the *pasola* or other rituals, swim at the white-sand beach at **Rua**, 21 kilometers (13 mi) south of Waikabubak, or at the spring-fed pools at Haikelo Sawah, 10 kilometers west of the town. Both places may be reached by bemo. A small luxury hotel has opened on the lovely beach south of Waikabubak.

East Sumba weavings: East Sumba has been known for centuries as a center for its warp, or ikat, weavings patterned by dyeing the warp threads before the weft is introduced. The entire process is long and tedious, taking several months to complete a single piece. First the cotton is carded and spun, then the threads are stretched on a frame and tied with dye resistant fibers to create the pattern. Then they are immersed in pots of dye, such as indigo, and then sun dried.

Subsequent rebinding and redyeing creates the final design, usually featuring bands of blue and red with bold animal and human figures. Sumba *hinggi* come in pairs, one as a body wrap and one as a shawl.

The pasola.

You can observe women dyeing and weaving in Praliu village just outside of **Waingapu**. Other major ikat production centers are down on the southeast coast. Take a bus from Waingapu to **Rende**, 70 kilometers (40 mi) and two hours to the southeast, where megalithic tombs with unusual carvings may be seen. Farther down the coast, in the vicinity of Ngallu and Baing, 125 kilometers (80 mi) from Waingapu, whole villages produce the famous *hinggi kombu* weavings. There is also great surfing at **Kalala Beach**, five kilometers from Baing, between December and May. Australian interests have built a small resort on the coast to take advantage of the outstanding sport fishing in offshore waters.

Flores: The largest island in the eastern Nusa Tenggara chain, **Flores** received its name in 1512 from passing Portuguese explorers who christened it *Cabo das Flores* (Cape of Flowers). Before then it was known to traders as Stone Island.

Flores has absorbed foreign influence from many quarters. Its ports once formed a vital link in interisland trade, and during the 1500s, it was drawn into the commercial and political sphere of the Hindu-Javanese empire of Majapahit. Some coastal communities began to convert to Islam in the 15th and 16th centuries, as a result of contacts with the far-flung trading sultanate of clove-producing Ternate.

Then, in the mid 16th century, the Portuguese arrived. They established a mission at Larantuka and built a fort on Solar Island, east of Flores, primarily to protect their trading interests in Timor. By the 1570s, there was already a seminary in Larantuka, and Catholicism was spreading quickly to other areas.

In 1664, Muslim invaders from Goa in South Sulawesi took control of Ende, ostensibly to stem the tide of Catholic conversions. Subsequent Makassarese immigrations created a strong Islamic community here, and the Endenese raided Sumba for slaves and traded sandalwood from Timor.

The Dutch acquired the Portuguese settlements on Flores in 1859, with a proviso that the Catholic church be encouraged. They also bombarded Muslim Ende twice and exercised increasing authority there, but fully controlled the island only after subduing a bloody rebellion in 1907–1908. Catholic missionaries flooded into Flores in this century, sparking a new wave of conversions that continues.

Catholicism claims 90 percent of Flores's one million inhabitants. The church has put heavy emphasis on improving living conditions through its schools, health services and agricultural programs. And although the clergy in Flores is well aware of the continued existence of many traditional beliefs and customs, they make no systematic efforts to eliminate them. The ancient traditions that have survived are many and varied, and constitute much of the island's fascination for the visitor.

Many people still believe that *nitu* or ancestral spirits reside in trees, stones, rivers and mountains. These spirits once were – and perhaps still are – propitiated with offerings to ward off illness and

Koran lesson.

encourage bountiful harvests. The nitu employ snakes to warn their descendants of impending danger, and pythons were worshipped on Flores, lending the island's former name: Snake Island.

In many areas, the bride price is still of paramount social importance. Items given to the father of a bride determine the status of all individuals involved, and can include fine handwoven textiles, money, water buffalo, horses, pigs and ivory tusks. Church wedding or no, a marriage cannot be consummated until the bride price has been paid and certain ancient rituals performed.

And in various parts of Flores, one can still find traditional style houses, called *kada,* where offerings are made and relics are preserved. In one such kada, the beams are carved with serpents and life-sized male and female figures. These are interpreted variously as Jesus and the Virgin Mary, or as the male principle of the sun and the female principle of the earth, showing clearly the coexistence of Catholicism and traditional cosmology.

A 670-kilometer (420 mi) road, paved for about half the distance, runs the length of Flores, from Labuhanbajo in the west to Larantuka in the east. To travel the entire route is long and exhausting, but can also be exciting, particularly if a visit coincides with a major ritual somewhere on the island.

The western third of Flores is called Manggarai and contains almost half the island's population. Manggarai is self-sufficient in rice, and exports fine coffee and livestock. The agricultural economy suffers somewhat from a lack of adequate roads, as will become painfully obvious during a journey, but progress is being made.

Labuhanbajo is the western-most of three main port towns on the island, a beautiful harbor filled with catamarans. The road winds up to **Ruteng**, a pleasantly cool town situated up in the western hills. There are fairly good hotels in Ruteng, and in the market one will find many colorful embroidered sarung.

With luck, travelers may see a spectacular *caci* whip duel, held occasion-

Portuguese cannon.

ally as part of a wedding or other important ceremony. Combatants are outfitted with head-wrappings and buffalo-hide shields, attacking each other with long leather whips. The aim is to overcome the physical and spiritual defenses of one's opponent. Resulting welts and scars are admired, and blood drawn during the caci becomes an offering to the ancestral spirits.

The next stop, following a slow but scenic ride (the highway is paved for most of the way from Ruteng east to Ende), is the town of **Bajawa**, scene of the annual Maha Kudus mass. The mass itself is essentially Catholic in form and content. Afterwards, swordsmen lead a lively procession of dancing villagers around the town bearing the holy cross. The date of this event is determined according to the traditional calendar, and it immediately precedes a ritual deer hunt in nearby **So'a**, to the north.

The deer hunt is a fertility ritual associated with puberty rites: circumcision for the boys and tooth filing for the girls. Strong taboos against sex are enforced throughout the hunt, including a prohibition against the consummation of recent marriages. After the hunt, young women dip their hands into the blood of slain deer to enhance their fertility.

The area around Bajawa is one of the most traditional of Flores, and several old megaliths are found. Exquisite yellow-on-black embroidered sarung are also produced here. The accommodations are basic, as is the food; dog meat is a local delicacy. Losmen in Bajawa can provide a jeep and guide for a circular trip to several traditional villages around the region.

From Bajawa it is 125 kilometers (80 mi) and about five hours to **Ende**, the principal city of Flores. Ende has a distinctly Islamic flavor; it was an important Islamic trading port from the late 17th to the 19th centuries. During the Japanese occupation, the city was the regional capital for the eastern archipelago. Sukarno was exiled here for a time, and the town was later bombed by the Allies. Today, Ende's commerce is largely in Chinese hands. Good ac-

Left, a whip warrior. Right, Easter procession.

commodation and delicious Chinese food are available.

Sorcerers, sinners, virgins: A couple of hours northeast of Ende (off the main road to Maumere) are three adjacent multicolored volcanic crater lakes called **Keli Mutu**, the island's main tourist attraction. The lakes are separated only by low ridges, and curiously they are of different colors: blue-green and turquoise, or dark burgundy or brown. But like chameleons, they appear to be changing all the time, and postcard photos taken in different years show the lakes in dramatically different colors.

No scientific study of the lakes has been made, but one possible explanation is that the coloration results from dissolved minerals, and that the water eats through different mineral layers of varying rates, perhaps due also to changes in acidity. The natives of this area say that one red lake holds the souls of sorcerers, the other the souls of sinners, while the third lake holds the souls of infants and virgins.

Hotels in Ende can arrange early morning departures to the summit of Mount Kelimutu (before the daily clouds role in), or travelers can stop at the road junction and hire jeeps or trucks for the ride to the summit.

Twelve kilometers east of Keli Mutu, at Wolowaru, turn south to the coastal village of **Japo** to see superb weavings being produced, often with vegetable dyes. Similar weavings are available in Ende, but the quality is often lower and the prices higher than in the village.

From Ende to Maumere, the road cuts diagonally across the island toward the north coast. The distance is 150 kilometers (90 mi), but the winding, scenic drive can take seven hours.

Maumere is experiencing something of an economic boom as a result of increased copra and coffee exports. The Catholic Church, with its large coconut and coffee holdings, is behind much of the development. The town and nearby Catholic seminary were severely damaged in a 1992 earthquake and tidal wave that killed hundreds along the north coast of Flores. The Indonesian

Keli Mutu.

army played a major role in reconstruction houses and business buildings in Maumere. The surrounding area looks like a gigantic coconut factory, with vast groves and drying racks. Trucks carry copra to the harbor.

The last leg of the journey is a hot and dusty 140-kilometer (80 mi) stretch of road to **Larantuka**, on the eastern tip of Flores. Larantuka's history is intimately bound up with the fortunes of the Portuguese and the spread of Catholicism on the island. It was a Portuguese colony for about 300 years, and Catholic rituals here reflect a great deal of Iberian influence. As in Seville, men dressed in white hoods carry the black coffin of Jesus through the streets during the daytime Easter procession. At night, another procession bears Jesus's coffin through the eery blackness, stopping along the way for prayers and hymns, in a modified form of the *Via Dolorosa*. There are many local Christian elements, including a black Virgin Mary statue said to have been washed ashore at a spot designated by a beautiful woman in a local man's dream. Another statue of Jesus is washed each year before Easter, and the water is kept to cure sick children and to ease difficult childbirth.

East of Flores: At the eastern end of the Lesser Sunda archipelago lie a number of smaller islands: Solor, Adonara, Lembata, Pantar and Alor (east of Flores), as well as Sawu and Roti (south and west of Timor). The inhabitants have been in contact with the larger islands and each other since ancient times, and over the centuries have developed sophisticated cultures based on palm and taro cultivation, and trade in sandalwood, textiles and slaves.

Larantuka is the gateway to these tightly-packed islands. Small boats of all shapes and sizes leave daily from Larantuka harbor, plying the interisland trade routes. Plenty of time and patience is needed to explore this area, but the fares are cheap.

On the island of **Solor** is an old Portuguese fort, constructed in 1566 and still in surprisingly good shape. Massive stone walls, some two meters thick and

Lembata harpooner.

four meters high, encircle a rectangular interior. The entryway is covered by an impressive arch, and in one corner of the fort, rusting cannon have survived and stand guard over the approaches from the seaward side.

Pulau Lembata (also known as Lomblen) is noted primarily for its primitive whaling industry. Shallow-draught, sail-and oar-propelled wooden boats are used for whale hunting. When a whale is sighted, a harpooner balances precariously on a narrow plank extending from the bow of the boat and then jumps with his harpoon, thrusting it accurately into the whale's back. The islanders also weave fabulously intricate ikat cloths from homespun threads.

The islands of **Pantar** and **Alor**, farther to the east, are known for their bronze kettle drums.

Hundreds and perhaps thousands of these drums, called *moko* by the local residents, are still kept as heirlooms. They are often used to pay the bride price. They are also similar to 2,000-year-old Dong Son bronze drums unearthed in these islands, and to those uncovered in Vietnam.

Timor: The island of **Timor** has been known throughout its history as a source of fragrant sandalwood. Chinese, Javanese and Islamic traders frequented the island for many centuries to obtain the wood; the Portuguese and the Dutch later fought to control the trade and subsequently divided the island into two colonies: the Dutch West Timor and Portuguese East Timor.

After Indonesia's independence, East Timor remained a Portuguese possession until 1975. Politics overtook the island in 1976, when a left-wing movement threatened to take control of a newly-independent East Timor; Indonesia decided to annex the territory. Isolated fighting continues in the remote interior of the island, but East Timor is open to travelers, although facilities are limited. **Dili**, the East Timor capital, is a languorous imitation of a small Mediterranean seaport. Several good hotels are available and can arrange trips outside town. The hinterlands offer spectacular rocky mountain landscapes and some lovely but isolated beaches. Leftist Fretilin guerrillas destroyed most of East Timor's unique high-roofed homes, but several still stand by the road near the eastern inland district capital of **Los Palos**.

The West Timorese city of **Kupang** (capital of East Nusa Tenggara Province) is an international entry point with direct flights from Australia, and regular ferry and air service to the rest of Indonesia. The city has a number of small hotels, as well as shops to stock up on supplies before sailing to smaller outlying islands like Roti and Sawu. Kupang's attractions include the town market and the **Museum of East Nusa Tenggara**, where one can ask about cultural performances. There are several ikat weaving villages in the vicinity of Kupang, and a wonderful white-sand beach at **Pantai Laisiana**, 12 kilometers north of the city center. The modern, paved Trans-Timor highway connects Kupang with Dili, and includes a spectacular shelf road just inside the border of East Timor Province.

Left, West Timor. Right, Flores is an ivory-carving center.

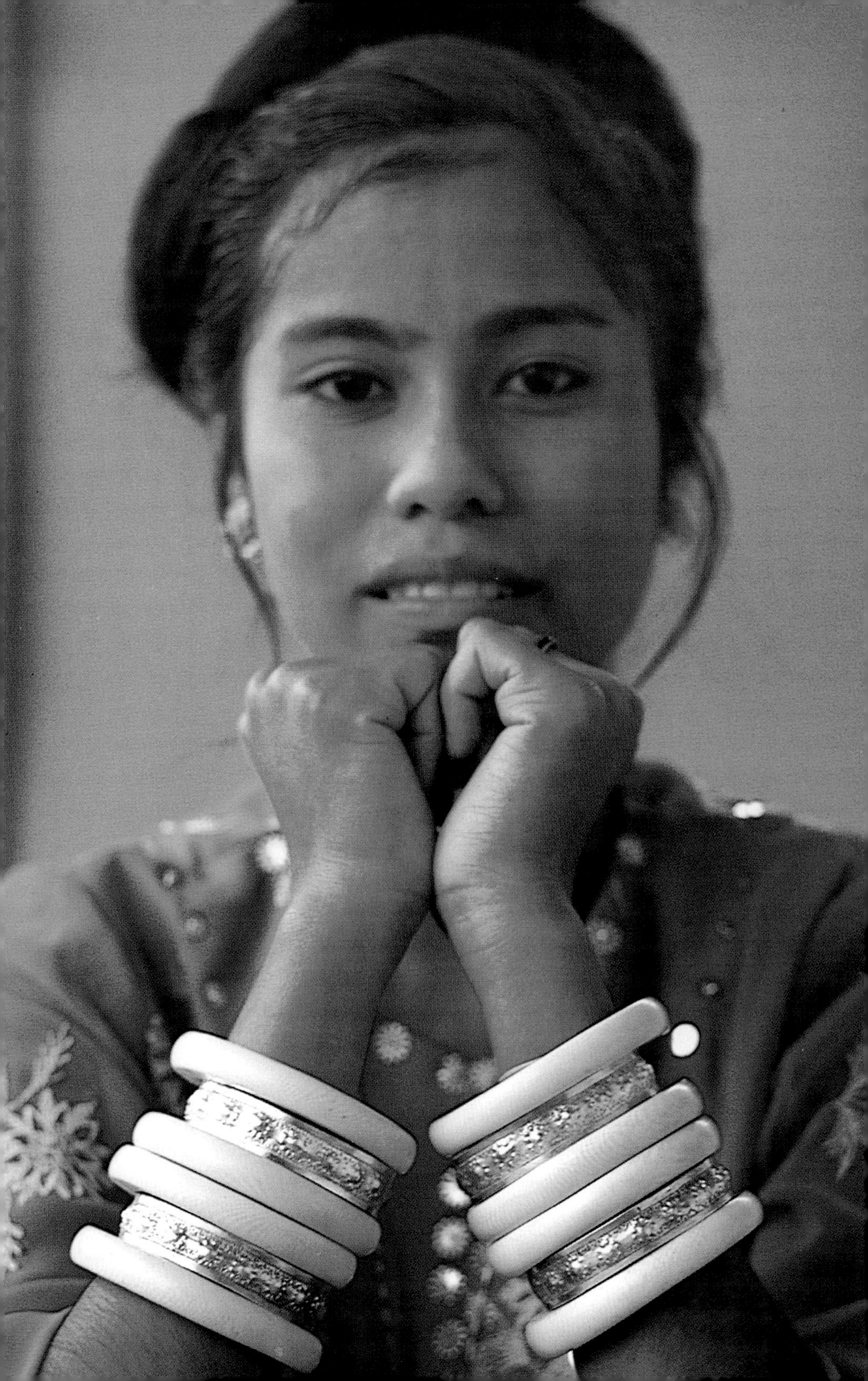

KALIMANTAN

Kalimantan is Indonesia's name for its two-thirds of Borneo, the world's third-largest island. The other third of Borneo is divided into the East Malaysian provinces of Sarawak and Sabah, plus the tiny oil-rich sultanate of Brunei. Kalimantan, with an area of 540,000 square kilometers (200,000 sq mi), represents nearly 30 percent of the nation's land area, but less than five percent of the population.

The central section of Borneo is made up of several mountain ranges. The highest peak is 4,100-meter (13,450 ft) Gunung Kinabalu, in Malaysia's Sabah, but summits seldom exceed 1,500 meters (5,000 feet). Great rivers cascade down from the highlands and they are often navigable for hundreds of kilometers – crucial channels of communications between the coast and the interior in a vast land where there aren't many roads.

Geology is the key to Kalimantan's economy. The eastern coastal region produces petroleum and natural gas, processed at Balikpapan and Tarakan with a huge LNG plant at Bontang. Diamonds have been mined in west and south Kalimantan since pre-colonial times; an area near Banjarmasin still yields many gems. Mining companies have tapped into gold reserves far inland, while local people still pan rivers for the valuable yellow flecks. Large-scale coal mining started in the 19th century and continues unabated. Valuable deposits of uranium and other minerals await exploitation.

Logging has been a major industry since the 1960s. Mills have been developed on the lower reaches of many rivers, notably near Samarinda and Banjarmasin. Logs are floated downstream to be processed into planks, plywood, and other wood products.

There are other cash crops – pepper, rubber and oil palm – but most people survive on subsistence farming, supplemented by hunting and fishing.

As long as population pressures are not great, the land can recover from slash-and-burn farming – if the plots are left fallow for sufficient time. This method has been used in Kalimantan for many centuries.

But large-scale logging, with little replanting, has done much harm to the ecology. The rain forest just doesn't regenerate fast enough. The luxurious vegetation rests on laterite soils, poor in both organic and inorganic nutrients. The thin topsoil is held in place by a shallow network of roots, where furious bacterial action quickly recycles all fallen leaves and trees. There is little undergrowth, as the canopy of trees filter out the sunlight essential for photosynthesis. When logging strips away the vegetation cover, a combination of increased bacterial action, intense sun and rain leads to quick erosion.

Flora and fauna: Kalimantan's coast features mangrove swamps and low-grade forest. An inland belt of gentle hills and alluvial plains marks the start of the rain forest. The main forest canopy is about 25 meters (80 ft) above the

Preceding pages: rain forest in Kalimantan. Left, orangutan. Right, Mandor Nature Reserve houses the orchid gardens.

ground, occasionally punctured by huge tapang trees with crowns reaching 70 meters (230 ft). Valuable ebony and ironwood trees are scattered through the forest. In the colder reaches of the central highlands, branches and trunks are covered with tufts of moss and decorated with strands of lichen.

The island's wildlife is just as exotic. Orangutans, found only in Sumatra and Borneo, head the list of unusual animals, along with the endemic proboscis monkey. Other forest denizens include the clouded leopard, leaf monkeys, crab-eating macaques, the pangolin anteater and the tiny tarsier, with its huge eyes and the ability to swivel its head 180 degrees. The orangutan – "man of the jungle" – is an endangered species. There are only about 5,000 left in the wild and their habitat is increasingly threatened by humans. The aptly-named proboscis monkey sports a huge red nose, which in adult males can reach 15 centimeters (6 in). This disproportionate proboscis adds tonal qualities to the voice as well as strengthening the vocal powers.

There are about 600 species of birds. The reclusive, magnificent Argus pheasant takes the top prize in plumage. Some experts considered it as even more showy than the peacock. Hornbills are considered sacred by several Dayak groups, perhaps because of its unusual appearance, the sound made during flight and the strange habit of sealing up the female in a tree trunk while eggs incubate.

Kalimantan's past: Around 3,000 BC, the first immigrants reached Borneo from the Asian mainland, a steady trickle that continued for hundreds of years. All of the island's current resident population traces its ancestry to this Austronesian migration.

While the Malay peoples of Borneo brought along domestic animals and irrigated rice-growing techniques, it was under the influence of northern Vietnam's Dong Son culture that the metal age began around 400 BC. Hindu influence penetrated coastal areas around AD 100, arriving from Java. Indonesia's earliest written record, dated from around 400, comes from eastern

Dutch engraving depicting the people of Borneo.

Kalimantan and describes offerings to Hindu deities by the ruler of the Mulawarman kingdom. Although Borneo doesn't surface in Chinese annals until the eighth century, it's likely that trade existed between China and India well before that date.

By the 17th century, the coastal kingdoms had converted to Islam, about the same time as increased contact with Europeans. Although the Dutch established forts along the Kalimantan coast, the impenetrable jungle and hostile tribes kept them at bay for several centuries. But the situation changed drastically in the early 1800s. Singapore was founded, the Opium Wars opened China to international trade, and Borneo's location became strategic.

The British adventurer James Brooke set up an independent fiefdom on the northeast coast of Borneo. The Dutch had to take some action or lose any claims on Kalimantan.

The Dutch signed a series of agreements with the most important rulers in Kalimantan, while other Europeans were excluded from these areas. This was fairly well accepted in east and west Kalimantan. But the Banjarese waged a long, vicious and costly war against Holland. The Dutch also vanquished a huge community of Chinese gold miners in west Kalimantan who had threatened their authority. By the close of the 19th century, the Dutch had established numerous administrative posts and garrisons, and in due time, Kalimantan was part of Holland's East Indies colony.

Much like central Africa, the interior of Borneo wasn't conquered by Europeans until the 19th century. George Muller was the first to attempt a trans-island trip. He traveled up the Mahakam River and crossed the central mountain range in 1825, before dying at the hands of Dayak headhunters. The first successful inland trip came in 1846, when a German geologist covered a large area between the south coast and Pontianak. In 1894, a Dayak peace gathering under Dutch auspices allowed an expedition to journey from Pontianak to Samarinda, a 15-month journey from coast to coast.

anjung Isuy, iverside own.

Oil and gas towns: East Kalimantan – Kalimantan Timor or **Kaltim** for short – is the most popular destination of Indonesian Borneo. The province is huge, embracing the Mahakam River and its various tributaries as well as several river basins to the north. With over 200,000 square kilometers (77,000 sq mi), the district covers an area similar to England and Scotland combined. Yet it holds only 1.5 million people, many of whom are farmers from Java.

Much of the land is uninhabited jungle, and the population is mostly concentrated in the coastal areas. Besides oil, Kaltim also produces natural gas, processed into methanol and fertilizers at **Bontang**. However, most jobs are in the timber industry, which has been booming since the early 1970s. The province also exports gold, shrimp, pepper and other agricultural products.

Balikpapan is the usual port of entry to Kaltim. This busy oil town, with a population of nearly half a million, holds little interest to travelers unless on business. One can take in the hilltop view of Pertamina's sprawling oil installations, do some souvenir shopping and sample local nightlife in the company of burly oil workers. But that's about it. Independent travelers head straight to Samarinda on one of several daily flights or the 115-kilometer (70 mi) paved road.

Samarinda, with about 300,000 people, is the capital of Kaltim province. There aren't many attractions here either. But it might be worthwhile to hire a boat and observe activity along the waterfront: freighters loading or discharging, coal barges shoved around, rafts of logs towed to nearby lumber mills. Early morning or late afternoon hours are best for these jaunts. A half day is enough in Samarinda, including time to check out schedules for planes or boats heading inland.

Mahakam river trips: Dayak country is accessible via the great **Mahakam River** and its tributaries, although missionary planes and Merpati flights offer a quicker alternative. If there is time, consider taking a river boat as far up the Mahakam as possible. A Dayak village called

Balikpapan.

Tanjung Isuy sits next to Danau Jempang, about one and a half days upriver from Samarinda. However, this setup is geared for package tourists. Travel agencies, using special boats outfitted for Westerners, run tours to various destinations along the Mahakam.

It's possible to reach, in three or four days, a Dayak village in the mid Mahakam area. With a day or two more, visit the nearest authentic longhouses, located in the **Barong Tongkok** area. With a week, it's possible to get up to Long Iram and Long Bagun, just below the rapids. But if the river level drops – especially in summer months – normal boats cannot chug beyond Long Iram.

Beyond Long Bagun, logistics become difficult due to the rapids. There are occasional twin-outboard-engine canoes that do the run, but it's usually a long wait or an expensive special charter. Otherwise, fly from Samarinda to Data Dawai, past the rapids.

Some of the larger passenger boats, making the Samarinda-Long Iram run in about 36 hours, offer bunks and mattresses for a small surcharge, and have kitchens serving simple meals. The several larger riverside towns offer basic accommodations and restaurants offering rice-based meals. Beyond Long Iram, there is only the hospitality of the Dayaks or government officials.

For all river boats, the first major stop out of Samarinda is **Tenggarong**, the former sultan's capital. There is a museum well worth a visit, but one's boat might not stop long enough (or the museum could be closed). A paved road snakes from Samarinda to Tenggarong, so travelers can travel this sector overland, visit the museum, then join a boat.

The next major stop, **Kota Bangun**, lies six hours upstream from Tenggarong. Nothing extraordinary here, but nearby, from a rented boat, one can see freshwater dolphins, proboscis monkeys, kingfishers and many other birds. The animals are easier to spot at dawn or dusk. This is the last chance for Western-style accommodation.

The riverside town of **Muara Muntai**, two to three hours from Kota Bangun, is

Samarinda.

the point of departure for exploring the mid-Mahakam lakes region, the beginning of Dayak country. Small motorized canoes can be rented here for the two-hour run to **Tanjung Isuy**, a Dayak village on Danau Jempang. Welcome rituals and dances are often put on for tourists here, the most popular destination in Kaltim. At the village of **Mancong**, a rebuilt longhouse gives an idea of past splendors.

Melak, a day out of Samarinda, marks the first stage inside Dayak-dominated areas. There is a local road system out of Melak with transportation (usually jeeps or motorcycles) for visiting the **Padang Luwai Nature Reserve**, famous for its orchids, and nearby Dayak villages with lived-in longhouses. Ask around if there are any funerary ceremonies in progress – this ritual features killing a water buffalo with spears.

Six hours' upstream from Melak, year-round river navigation stops at **Long Iram**, over 400 kilometers (250 mi) from the coast. Many of the Dayaks in this area and also further upstream belong to the Roman Catholic Church, which tolerates and even encourages some traditional rituals.

If the river level isn't too low – or flooding – cargo and passenger boats can reach **Long Bagun** in four to six hours from Long Iram. Several Dayak groups are settled along this stretch of the Mahakam, including the Kenyah, who are known for their huge sculptures and paintings in communal buildings.

Beyond Long Bagun, a series of rapids choke off most river travel, with only an occasional powerful twin-outboard longboat roaring through. It's a great experience, but unless one has plenty of time, the best way to reach the uppermost areas of the Mahakam is by flying on scheduled planes from Samarinda to **Data Dawai**.

For Kaltim's Apokayan region, homeland of the Kenyah Dayaks, flying is the only means of access, other than mounting an expedition and trekking for weeks. Located on the uppermost reaches of the Kayan River, a dozen villages are strung out on either side of the landing

Logging fuels the economy.

strip at **Long Ampung**. Due to its isolation and the difficulty in obtaining essentials (soap, medicines, cooking oil), most of the Apokayan's inhabitants have migrated to more accessible locations. Those who remain often live in longhouses, and the prolific baroque artwork of the Kenyah is still in evidence. There are good trails for trekking and villages are a few hours apart.

Although the chances of seeing wildlife are fairly good on hikes in the Apokayan and the upper Mahakam areas, the best bet to see animals is in the **Kutai Nature Reserve**. To get there, travel either by road from Samarinda, or fly from Balikpapan to Bontang, the natural gas port on the coast.

At Bontang, contact the nature reserve office so that they will radio ahead to the park rangers. Then hire a boat for the sea-and-river journey to the reservation, which can take two to eight hours, depending upon the boat. The principal attraction in the park are the orangutans. The park offers only the most basic and essential of facilities.

Southeast Kalimantan: Kalimantan Selatan (Kalsel) is a small province on the southeast coast of Borneo. There are frequent flights to **Banjarmasin**, the capital city, famous for its colorful floating market and bustling canals.

There are a couple of places (under the Yani bridge and at Kuin Pertamina) where travelers can rent motorized canoes, or *klotok,* for a tour of Banjarmasin and the Barito River. Start early for the **floating market**. It gets under way before dawn and the activity peters out a couple of hours after sunrise. Produce is brought to the market in small boats, from which it is sold directly to women in tiny, hand-paddled canoes. The women then glide on the canals to sell the fruit and vegetables directly to housewives, whose front (or back) doors are on the water. There are also little boats serving coffee, tea and snacks to canoes for a quick breakfast.

Further upstream from the floating market, the traditional lumber mills are worth a look (modern lumber mills are located downstream). Along the Barito

Banjarmasin.

Dayak Remembrances

The term "Dayak" is an amorphous one, somewhat akin to "Indian". Genetically, they are identical with the Malays. Before the arrival of missionaries, most Dayaks followed animist religions, and prior to enforceable government authority, many Dayaks practiced head-hunting. These and other traditional practices were partially due to their relative isolation. In contrast, the coastal Malays, with continuous trade contacts, tended to assimilate outside influences, the most important of which was Islam. There are exceptions, but we can partially define Dayaks as non-Muslim peoples living in the interior areas of Kalimantan.

Within the Dayak group, there is much linguistic diversity, as well as different art styles, customs and lifestyle. For years, Dayak groups migrated on occasion and waged war out of necessity or exuberance. Tribes adopted the languages, rituals and customs of their victors, then moved on with a mixture of tongues and traditions. Migrations continue today as villages shift in search of goods, markets and jobs.

Some Dayak groups retain aspects of a hereditary class structure of aristocrats, commoners and slaves. Although there are no slaves today, the aristocrats maintain some of their former privileges, such as free labor in their fields and control of trade. Other groups are more egalitarian.

The Dayaks were romanticized in the past – and with good reason. They were noted head-hunting jungle warriors, and they possessed an art of intricacy, built massive longhouses, and protected their women – all combined into an exotic subject. European explorers, too long on expedition, also pondered Dayak breasts. "One is never tired of watching the rhythmic movements of nearly nude women" (while pounding rice) or "...it is strikingly evident that the mammae of Dayak women retain firmness and shape much longer than is the case with white women."

If European explorers were fixated on breasts, the Dayak women preferred males who sported a *palang*, the ultimate sexual enhancer. This was recorded by a British expert from first-hand experience: "The basic operation simply consists of driving a hole through the distal end of the penis. In this hole, a small tube of bone, bamboo or other material can be kept so that the hole does not grow over and close. It is of no inconvenience once the initial pain of the operation has been overcome. When the device is put into use, the owner adds whatever he prefers to elaborate and accentuate its intention. One lively range of objects can be so employed – from pigs' bristles and bamboo shavings to pieces of metal, seeds, beads and broken glass. The effect, of course, is to enlarge the diameter of the male organ inside the female. And so to produce accentuated points of mobile friction, quite evidently giving a particular sort of sexual satisfaction to the female recipient."

While the palang, (used mostly by the Kenyah and Kayan) never hurt a man's chances with women, there was, however, a bride price to come up with. Back in the old days, no suitor needed to apply to marry the chief's daughter unless he could produce several freshly-severed heads. These heads were believed to be essential for the spiritual and material welfare of a village. A newly-severed head possessed a powerful force that transfused energy and spiritual strength to the village, as well as to its warrior captor. Events like the building of a longhouse, erection of an important carving, or the ceremony of marriage or funeral needed heads to function properly. ■

River is a place called **Pulau Kembang** – Monkey Island – which houses a Chinese shrine with large numbers of simians. To see the famous proboscis monkeys, putter downstream to **Pulau Kaget**. Dawn and dusk are the only times to see these unusual primates, found only in Borneo.

Closer to town, take a *klotok* up a branch of the Martapura River just beyond the Trisakti docks, which are for large ships, and a modern lumber mill, where cranes lift tree trunks out of the river. A short way up the Martapura, open-fronted stores replete with brightly-colored plastic items cater to water-borne shoppers. A bit further, graceful Bugis-style schooners are constructed along the river bank. Just beyond, a fish market (working at night till dawn), a red-light district, then the not-to-be-missed Bugis schooner dock amidst a beehive of activity of loading and unloading.

Left, hunting with a blowpipe. **Below**, hazardous Dayak country crossing.

The **Sabilal Muhtadin**, or **Grand Mosque**, is one of Asia's largest places of worship. It's clearly visible from the river, but a visit inside is very rewarding. Beautifully-finished stone panels, with inscriptions from the Koran, line a spacious open space for praying. To visit this mosque, dress decently and remove footwear before entering.

For a visit to the Dayaks of this province, travel to **Loksado**, which is off the main road between Banjarmasin and Balikpapan, near Kandongan. The trip usually takes one to three days.

Heart of Dayak country: Central Kalimantan (Kalteng) is the Dayak province par excellence. Long dominated by Islamic Banjarmasin, the local Dayaks – led by war hero Tjilik Riwut – fought a short guerrilla conflict to obtain separate provincial status, granted by President Sukarno in 1957.

The Ngaju Dayaks predominate among the province's several groups. Many were converted to the Protestant faith and became aware of their cultural identity thanks to German missionaries in the late 19th century. Many other Ngaju, along with their more isolated cousins, retained the ancient Dayak faith,

called *kaharingan.* One of the demands of the autonomy movement was to obtain official recognition for this traditional religion, finally granted in 1980.

The *tiwah,* or funerary ritual, is the kaharingan's most spectacular feature. This series of rites cleanses the bones of the deceased and guides the soul to paradise. Funerary structures are erected for the ceremonies, including a carved ironwood coffin and a totem-like pole used to tie up animals for sacrifice. A properly-conducted tiwah insures the spirit's intervention with the supernatural in helping to produce abundant harvests and good health for descendants.

The tiwah set of ceremonies lasts up to one month and is expensive for the family of the deceased. Unless the family is wealthy, several groups get together for a collective tiwah. Dozens of souls can be dispatched simultaneously.

Palangkaraya, the capital of Kalteng, has a population of less than 100,000. Most of the commercial and business activities are concentrated in the **Pahandut district**, where a village once existed on the Kahayan River before the place was selected as the provincial capital. Newer and larger hotels are located in the center of the new city.

There are two docks on the river: the lower one (Rambang) serves boats heading downriver; the upper one (Flamboyant) is for upstream passengers. While in Palangkaraya, see Dayak artifacts at the **provincial museum**, located near the Pasar Kahayan market at the 2.5-kilometer mark, just off the paved road running parallel to the river.

Dayak country is up the **Kahayan River**. There are daily passenger boats heading upriver as far as **Tewah**. One can also charter a speedboat that allows stops along the way. From Tewah, where regular river traffic stops, hire a motorized canoe to **Tumbang Mire** and beyond, to the traditional Ot Danum Dayak land with longhouses and funerary structures. Travel here depends essentially on water levels. Try to reach **Tumbang Korik**, on a tributary, or **Tumbang Maharoi**, last village on the river.

Visiting the local orangutans is a bit

Dayak war preparations.

more tricky. Guided tours are now available through adventure travel agents in Jakarta. But if going solo, first charter a small plane in Banjarmasin and fly to **Pangkalanbun**. After obtaining permits from the nature conservation office, purchase supplies in town before flying overland to **Kumai**, a riverside village just outside the **Tanjung Puting Nature Reserve**.

At Kumai, rent a boat to travel around the reserve. There is no commercial accommodation inside the park; you must sleep in the boat, or perhaps in one of the guardhouses.

While animals can be seen from either the boat or an observation tower (early morning or late afternoon are best), Tanjung Puting's highlight is the **orangutan rehabilitation center**, at Camp Leakey. Tame orangutans that have been confiscated are turned over to the center, where they are taught to live once again in their natural environment.

Equator crossing: Western Kalimantan (Kalbar) covers another huge area, essentially the basin of the Kapuas River. Unlike the Mahakam River, there has been very little tourism in this province. Consequently, there are fewer English speakers and no tourist facilities. Local travel agencies that deal with foreign tourists offer only city tours or jaunts along the coast, but not to the inland areas where the Dayaks live.

Pontianak, the provincial capital, lies near the sea at the juncture of a branch of the Kapuas and the Landak rivers. The thriving town boasts an international airport with regular flights to Jakarta, Singapore and Kuching (Sarawak), as well as the inland landing fields at Sintang and Putussibau.

While the city's **state museum** might be worth a visit if there is time, the old sultan's palace on the far side of the Kapuas from downtown must not be missed. **Istana Qadariyah** belongs to the descendants of Abdul Rahman, an Arab rover who founded the city in the late 18th century, with Dutch backing. The city's name – Pontianak – refers to evil spirits who inhabited the area before Abdul Rahman scattered them with

Dayak beadwork.

a sustained and persuasive cannon barrage. Nearby is the 250-year-old **Abdur Rachman Mosque**.

The coast road heading north from Pontianak passes a strange-looking monument marking the equator. Coconut plantations hem in the road that heads for **Singkawang**.

Just outside this town are a couple of huge ceramic kilns turning out Chinese-style items. The large Chinese population in this area descends from the gold miners who arrived in a rush at the beginning of the 19th century. Setting up independent, self-sufficient enclaves around the gold fields, the industrious miners came up with one-seventh of the yearly world gold production in the early 1800s. But by the mid 19th century, the gold reserves were dwindling and the Dutch put an end to local independence.

Most of the Chinese miners remained and intermarried with locals. Their progeny represents one of the largest ethnic Chinese enclaves in Indonesia. There are several striking Chinese temples in the Singkawang area.

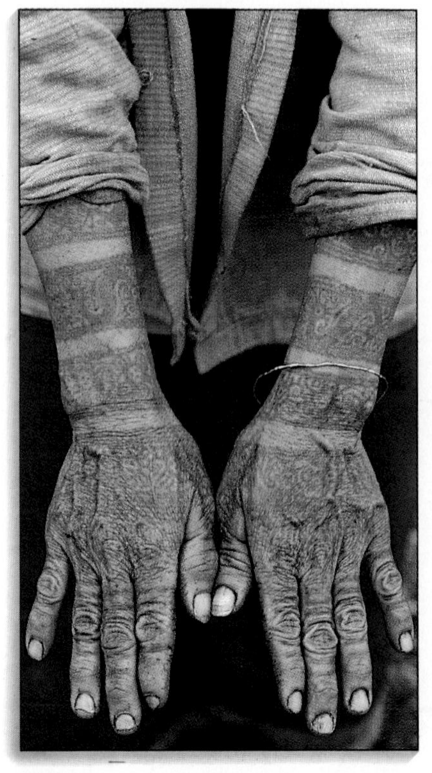

Further north is **Sambas**, a former sultanate and pirate's lair that produces fine weaving called *kain sambas,* made with gold and silver threads.

Many of the homes hold simple weaving looms where women turn out the kain sambas, in their spare time or as essential income. Sambas also has a gracefully-decaying sultan's palace and adjacent mosque, similar but less grand than the ones in Pontianak.

For trips inland to Dayak country, try flying to either Sintang or Putussibau. One can also go by river boats, but facilities are geared for local travelers and it takes two to three days to reach Sintang, five to six days to Putussibau. River boats depart from downtown Pontianak, near the ferry landing.

Be prepared for long and tedious lines in front of the onboard toilets (a simple hole, no paper) and nothing but rudimentary meals.

The town of **Sintang** dominates the middle portion of the Kapuas Basin. It can be reached by road, small plane or river boat from Pontianak.

Nearby **Gunung Kelam**, a superb sheer-walled rock, dominates the countryside and challenges climbers. For traditional Dayak country, head up the Melawi River, which flows into the Kapuas at Sintang. Take either the Kayan River, a tributary of the Melawi close to Sintang, or else head up the main stream of the Melawi, past the town of **Nanga Pinoh** and to the Schwaner Mountains. In the far upriver villages, there are carved funerary structures. These trips require planning and supplies.

Putussibau, the last town on the Kapuas River, can only be reached by plane or boat. From here, visit traditional Dayak villages such as those of the Kayan on the Mendalam River, or the Maloh longhouses a short way upstream on the Kapuas.

Further inland, in the Muller Mountains, most Dayaks have been proselytized by American fundamentalist missionaries, who frown on just about all aspects of traditional life. For the adventurous, it's possible to make the week-long trek from the upper Kapuas to the upper Mahakam.

Left, a woman's hands show the intricate tattoo work of the Dayaks. Right, homes of a Dayak village line a tributary.

SULAWESI

Although primarily known as the home of two flamboyant ethnic groups – the highland Torajans and the seafaring Buginese – the oddly-shaped island of **Sulawesi** offers a startling array of landscapes: steep mountains, deep gorges, fast flowing rivers, highland lakes, lush rain forest, *lontar* palm savannahs and white-sand beaches. The island also tenders a fascinating range of unusual flora and fauna, including many species found nowhere else, like the black macaque monkey, the *babirusa* wild boar, the *anoa* dwarf buffalo, the eccentric *maleo* bird, the saucer-eyed tarsier, and many beautiful butterflies. The island's nine million people are equally diverse, speaking more than 40 languages.

Such astonishing diversity is partially a product of Sulawesi's tortured geography. The island's four outstretched arms all rise from a deep seabed formed by contiguous folds in the earth's crust, but which are isolated from one another by steep ravines, dense forests and forbidding peaks. Unlike many other Indonesian islands, only Sulawesi's northeastern and southwestern extremities (the Minahasa and Makassar regions) are volcanic. And instead of gently sloping contours and broad plains, most of the island consists of jagged uplands and rugged plateaus lying 500 meters (1,600 ft) or more above sea level.

Sulawesi's central position within the Indonesian archipelago – a focus for interisland migrations and trade – has also contributed to its heterogeneity. The northern Sangihe-Talaud archipelago forms a natural link with the Philippines, while the eastern Banggai and Sula archipelagos connect Sulawesi to the spice islands of Maluku. Borneo and Flores, Sumbawa, and Lombok are only a short sail from southern Sulawesi's excellent natural harbors.

Complex history: A neolithic settlement discovered on Sulawesi's west coast – together with numerous cave stencils, megaliths, sarcophagi and other prehistoric artifacts – reveals mankind's long presence on the island. South Sulawesi, with its excellent anchorages, was a key stop on the international spice trading routes over two thousand years ago.

When the island's Islamic conversion began at the end of the 16th century, there were already a dozen major ports – cosmopolitan entrepots where Chinese, Indian, Siamese, Malay, Javanese and Portuguese traders exchanged fine textiles and metal goods for precious cloves, nutmeg, pearls, gold, copper and camphor of the eastern islands.

The first Western visitors were the Portuguese, who ventured in this direction soon after their conquest of Malacca in 1511. They called the island Celebes, a corruption of Ponto dos Celebres (Cape of the Infamous) on the Minahassan coast, where several Portuguese ships wrecked in 1521. Spanish missionaries soon followed, preaching in Minahasa and the neighboring islands from their base in the Philippines. But early in the 17th century, the Dutch arrived and eventually drove out all competition – European and Asian. The

Preceding pages: panorama from Sulawesi. **Left**, a traditional Bugis house on stilts. **Right**, a reminder of past Portuguese and Spanish colonial presence.

Dutch tried and failed to impose monopolistic treaties on the South Sulawesi sultanates. Then in 1667, a large Dutch fleet subdued the Makassarese and put a stop to the "smuggling" of spices. Although the Dutch were able to enforce an external trading monopoly, it wasn't until the early 20th century that they secured political control over the island.

South Sulawesi: Striking landscapes and remarkable people are the hallmarks of **South Sulawesi** – a province that is rapidly becoming one of Indonesia's major tourist destinations. This is a region of steep volcanoes, fast-flowing rivers, fertile plains, broad savannahs, uneven coasts and white-sand beaches.

Such geographical diversity has led to the development of divergent lifestyles among the province's six million inhabitants. South Sulawesi is one of the most heavily populated regions of Indonesia, with an average density of more than 125 people per square kilometer (300/sq mi) – considerably lower than in Java and Bali, but much higher than in most other areas. The staple food is rice, grown in lowland irrigated paddies; maize and sago are the preferred highland crops. Tall pandanus, lontar and banana palms abound, as do wild pineapples – providing a varied diet as well as many natural fibers for the highly-developed native arts of weaving and plaiting.

The coastal and lowland regions of South Sulawesi are today inhabited by many Mongoloid-type peoples generically known as the Bugis. It's generally assumed they settled along these shores well over 1,000 years ago, and since that time, they have had one of the more colorful histories of any Indonesian ethnic or social group.

The Bugis have always been great seafarers and shipbuilders. From South Sulawesi, it is thought that they sailed as far afield in ancient times as Madagascar and northern Australia, leaving behind artifacts and loan words and returning with foreign trade goods and treasures. Buginese settlers almost certainly lived in some of the region's great Hindu-period maritime capitals, such

Prahu in the Java Sea.

as Sumatra's Srivijaya (7th–13th centuries) and East Java's Kediri, Daha and Majapahit (11th–14th centuries), bringing new beliefs and practices back to Sulawesi after their sojourns abroad.

These connections lasted for many centuries, and various Bugis kingdoms – Luwu (Palopo), Bone, Soppeng, Goa, Supa and Mandar – rose to power in South Sulawesi between the 12th and 15th centuries as a result. After 1500, trading relations with the Islamic sultanates on Java's north coast were strong, and with the emergence of the Makassarese kingdom of Goa-Tallo as the preeminent power in the early 17th century, South Sulawesi officially converted to Islam.

Though the Bugis kingdoms were later subdued and dominated by the Dutch, their influence was felt throughout the Malay world. Even in the 18th and 19th centuries, Bugis groups were still founding new sultanates on the Malay peninsula and in the Riau archipelago. Today, there is hardly an estuary or a bay without a Buginese settlement.

The Bugis courtly heritage is preserved today only imperfectly in South Sulawesi's villages. And visitors often misinterpret their traits of aggressiveness, outspokenness, perseverance and pride. Most tourists, therefore, bypass the Bugis homelands en route to the highland Torajan communities in the north. There is much to see in the south, nonetheless, and the dynamism of the Bugis is serving them well in the modern world, gearing the province for rapid economic development.

Ujung Pandang is today a modern city of 700,000 – the business and administrative center of Sulawesi. Called Makassar by the Dutch after they conquered the Kingdom of Goa and established a fortified trading post here in 1667, the current name (which means pandanus cape) was restored following Indonesian independence. Like all major Indonesian cities, it has undergone its share of growing pains in recent years, as the grandeur of the colonial town has given way to concrete buildings, roads and drainage ditches that

This Bugis prahu is being built to specifications introduced by the Dutch.

create a rather bland contemporary look.

The town flourished as the port and trading center for the medieval kingdom of Goa. The old fort (*benteng*) of Ujung Pandang was one of the eleven Goanese strongholds when it was first erected in 1545. The Dutch conquered and reconstructed it in 1667, renaming it **Amsterdam Castle**. With its interior church and trading offices, it today stands as one of the outstanding examples of 17th-century Dutch fortress architecture. The fort now houses the **Ujung Pandang Provincial Museum**, with many fine displays of old ceramics, manuscripts, coins, musical instruments and ethnic costumes. The **Conservatory of Dance and Music** is also located here – drop in to observe rehearsals in progress. And there is a famous dungeon where one of Indonesia's national heroes, Prince Diponegoro of Yogyakarta (1785–1855), was imprisoned for 27 years.

Prince **Diponegoro's grave**, and those of his family and followers, is located in the middle of town on a street named after him. He was exiled after defying both the Dutch and his own royal family, leading a series of popular uprisings in Central Java between 1825 and 1830. None of the prince's relatives or descendants ever returned to Java. His grave is now a pilgrimage point for many Indonesian visitors.

Another interesting stop is the residence of Dutchman C.L. Bundt, at No. 15 Jalan Mochtar Lufti. His house, with its spacious gardens, contains a private collection of sea shells, coral rocks and rare orchids.

In the late afternoon, it's pleasant to stroll along the Makassar Straits and watch the sunset from the **Pantere Anchorage** along Jalan Penghibur, at the north end of the city and berth for many *pinisi* schooners. The seafront promenade south of the Makassar Golden Hotel is another popular sunset gathering place, with food and drink vendors vying with families and lovers for a place to watch the sun sink.

Just south of Ujung Pandang lies **Sungguminassa,** the former capital of the sultanate of Tallo. Today, the wooden palace is the **Ballompoa Museum**, containing many weapons and royal costumes, which includes a gem-studded gold crown weighing 15.4 kilograms (34 lbs). It may be seen on request.

Near Sungguminassa are tombs of the kings of Goa, of whom Sultan Hasanuddin (1629–1670) is the most famous for his bravery and leadership in the struggle against the Dutch. Just outside the walls of the cemetery, a small fenced-off plot holds the **Tomanurung stone**, upon which the kings of Goa were once crowned. On a side road nearby lies the tomb of Aru Palakka, the King of Bone – related to and yet the arch enemy of Sultan Hasanuddin.

Southern round-trip: To escape the lowland heat of Ujung Pandang, travel 70 kilometers (45 mi) to **Malino**, on the slopes of Gunung Bawakaraeng, some 760 meters (2,500 ft) above sea level. This cool, quiet resort in a pine forest is noted for its orchards of *markisa* (passion fruit) trees. The fruit is pressed locally to produce a refreshing drink that is marketed all over Indonesia. The

Laeng Pataere Caves.

lovely **Takapala Waterfall** is an easy four-kilometer walk south of the town.

A road from Malino leads across to **Sinjai** on the eastern coast of the peninsula, facing the Gulf of Bone. From there, a coastal road – breathtaking for its steep precipices and spectacular views – leads south to the tip of **Cape Bira**, heart of the Bugis shipbuilding industry. Round-bellied *prahu* are still fashioned here with ancient tools and without the use of metal or nails of any sort. Teak logs are hewn into planks, then fastened with wooden pegs according to an ancient design retained in the communal memory. Sails were once made of plaited banana and pineapple fibers, then later of woven cotton and ironed silk. Rituals are employed in all phases of construction, from the selection of the tree to the final launching, to ensure that the craft will be seaworthy. The huge 200-ton *pinisi,* and a lighter vessel called the *bago,* are unstable and ungainly till fully loaded with copra or timber – then they are one of the best ships afloat and may be seen today from one end of the archipelago to the other carrying vital cargoes.

Turning westward along the southern **Bulukumba Coast**, the road leads back to Ujung Pandang through small towns like Bantaeng, Jeneponto and Takalar, whose names were mentioned six and seven centuries ago in Chinese texts. The road then passes through Baronghong, a popular seaside resort with white-sand beaches.

A mountainous 180-kilometer (100 mi) road takes one northeast from Ujung Pandang towards **Watampone**, the former capital and port city of the Bugis kingdom of Bone. En route it passes a telecommunications station at Maros and a series of gushing waterfalls at Bantimurung. This rocky karst area is also famed for the variety of common and rare butterflies found there. Nearby are the **Leang-Leang Caves** containing 5,000-year-old blood-red henna hand stencils. To the east is the brisk mountain resort of **Camba**, where the views are superb and there are many mysterious caves. A side road north from Camba

Ferry boat amongst the islands.

leads to **Ujunglamuru**, noted for its holy graveyard – site of the tombs of Bone's early Muslim teachers and rulers. The main road descends to the coast.

The once-bustling port town of **Watampone** (also called Bone) is quiet now, but retains its dignity. Notice the architecture of the houses in the Bugis section of town. The tympanum-like triangles over the doorways are composed of three, five, seven, or nine parts, indicating the social rank of inhabitants. Nine parts were reserved for royalty.

The **Museum Lapawawoi** houses the regalia of the kings of Bone, as well as a copy of the 1667 Treaty of Bonggaya with the Dutch that ended their economic dominance over the area. Both may be seen only on request. Watampone's harbor is still a center for interisland shipping, and a ferry leaves here for Kolaka in Southeast Sulawesi, across the Bay of Bone. Boat building and fishing are the principal industries. Beautiful cotton and silk weaving are also produced, as well as some unusual plaiting made with orchid fibers.

South Sulawesi's largest cave system, **Goa Mampu**, is located about 30 kilometers (20 mi) away. Stalactites and stalagmites here resemble animals and humans, and give rise to local legends.

On the mountain plateau northwest of Watampone, nestled on the shores of Danau Tempe, lies **Sengkang-Soppeng**, seat of another feudal kingdom of old. It is best known today for its handloomed silk weaving. Fishing in **Danau Tempe** was formerly an important industry until the lake began to dry up in recent years. South of Sengkang in the hill country is the town's twin-court center, **Watang-Soppeng**. The regalia of the kings of Soppeng are kept in a small pavilion and may be seen on request.

From Watang-Soppeng, a road leads northwest to the coast and port town of **Parepare**. This was once the site of the powerful trading kingdom of Supa, connecting Ujung Pandang in the south and the ports of the Kingdom of Mandar in the north with the highlands. In the days of sailing pinisi and Portuguese galleons, Parepare's deep natural harbor was

Bugis hair piece.

always busier than Ujung Pandang's. Farther to the north and west, the old kingdom of Mandar once stretched all along the coast of what is now Mandar Bay. The Mandarese, who are distinct from the Bugis yet often confused with them, are also great sailors. Their shipbuilding tradition still rivals that of their southern neighbors, and is centered now around **Balangnipa**, between Polewali and Majene.

The last Bugis stronghold to the northeast of Parepare before entering Torajaland is **Enrekang**, separated from neighboring towns by a deep ravine.

Central Sulawesi: On the east coast of the peninsula, the Bugis kingdom of Luwu – with its harbor, **Palopo** – is Toraja's closest neighbor. Luwu is regarded as the oldest of all Bugis kingdoms; Palopo is today a busy commercial center, gateway to southern Sulawesi and to the nickel mining areas around Malili, at the northern end of the bay.

Between southeastern and central Sulawesi lies the nickel mining township of **Soroako**, the headquarters for the International Nickel Co. (INCO) mining operations. About 45,000 tons of nickel – nearly 10 percent of the world's total supply – are extracted here each year. The mine site is 50 kilometers (30 mi) inland by an all-weather road, on the shores of huge Danau Matana.

The best reason to visit this area to see the two lakes, Matana and Towuti. **Danau Matana** is incongruously covered with sailboats and speedboats, part of INCO's employee recreation facilities. Visitors are sometimes permitted to use the facilities. There are ancient burial caves around the lake, especially near Soroako village (accessible by boat). **Danau Towuti**, at 50 kilometers (30 mi) wide the largest lake in Sulawesi, surrounded by rain forest.

Torajaland tribes: Tucked away amid the rugged peaks and fertile plateaus of southcentral Sulawesi live many isolated tribes, who share a common ancestry with the seafaring Bugis, Mandar and Makassar. Coastal dwellers refer to these tribes collectively as the Toraja, or highland peoples. Their homeland is

Sunset above Sulawesi.

called Tanah Toraja, or **Torajaland**. According to traditional accounts, the Toraja left the island of Pongko, located to the southwest, some 25 generations ago and crossed the ocean in canoes (*lembang*). Arriving in Sulawesi, they made their way up the Sa'dan River (which now cuts diagonally across Torajaland) and settled on its banks.

The Toraja have remained in this land-locked region, growing rice and vegetables. Clove trees and coffee were also introduced as cash crops. A certain degree of outside influence was brought by traders and missionaries, but, for the most part, Torajan tribal customs and social structures endure as before.

The Toraja traditionally lived in a small settlements perched on hilltops and surrounded by stone walls. Each village is composed of several extended families who inhabit a series of houses, called *tongkonan,* arranged in a circular row around an open field. In the middle stands a sacred stone or banyan tree used for ritual offerings, and granaries (*lumbung*) face the dwellings.

The roofs of tongkonan rise at both ends like the bow and stern of a boat; ritual chants compare these dwellings to the vessels that carried their ancestors here. House panels are exquisitely carved with geometric and animal motifs executed in the sacred colors of white, red, yellow and black. The house symbolizes the universe. The roof represents the heavens, and it is always oriented northeast to southwest – the directions of the two ancestral realms, according to Torajan cosmology.

Although villages were self-contained and often warred with one another, larger federations called *wanua* eventually formed. These were headed by a council of elders (*puang*). At one time, there were as many as 40 wanua, dominated by the powerful southeastern wanua of Sangalla, which maintained relations with the Buginese coastal kingdoms, and even later converted to Islam.

In the early 20th century, Dutch missionaries penetrated to the highlands of Torajaland, and in 1905 many Torajan villages were brought under direct Dutch control. To facilitate their administration, they were ordered to move from their hilltop perches and settle in more accessible valleys and plateaus. Instead of stone walls, these villages are now ringed by hedges. In the post-independence era, the Toraja were organized into a single *kabupaten* (district), with Makale as its capital.

Since the late 1970s, traveling in Torajaland has become much easier due to the installation of new roads and transportation systems. Tanah Toraja is generally reached from Ujung Pandang via Pare-Pare and the inland river town of Enrekang. From here, the road enters a land of steep terraced slopes, tall bamboo forests and high mountain peaks. Across the Sa'dan River from Salubarani, the road passes under a large boat-shaped arch, marking the entrance to Tanah Toraja. The road continues through Bambapuang Valley and past the shapely **Buttu Kabobong (Erotic Hills**). After 310 kilometers (200 mi) and eight hours, the traveler arrives at **Makale**, the district capital.

Eighteen kilometers farther on lies

The architecture of Ke'te village is typical.

Rantepao, the center of the Torajan tourist trade. Small hotels in all price ranges, restaurants and shops cater to foreign visitors. The surrounding villages contain markets and traditional houses, where Torajans practice their crafts of weaving and woodcarving, and stage rituals and folk dances for themselves and for tourists. There are several cave tombs (*liang*) in the vicinity, with effigies that stare out from suspended balconies like guards.

The best-known grave site is at **Londa**, about two kilometers off the main road connecting Makale with Rantepao. Here, the effigies are those of noblemen and other high-ranking community leaders. Similar tombs can be seen at **Lemo**, about five kilometers from Rantepao, where the burial chambers are carved out of a sheer rock face. The effect of the near life-size effigies staring unblinkingly into the distance is distinctly eerie. On a hillside behind nearby **Ke'te**, coffins are guarded by life-size statues.

Especially beautiful *tonkonan* houses grace the village of **Palawa**, on a small hill facing lumbung granaries. This village, which has a traditional feel to it, is located about nine kilometers from Rantepao. Other traditional villages are located north and east of Rantepao.

All these places are easily reached by hired vehicles. Unfortunately, though, because of the proximity to Rantepao, many traditions in this locality seem to be waning.

A journey from Makale to **Sangalla** is worth the effort. Older *tonkonan* houses here provide a more traditional atmosphere. And the 80-kilometer (50 mi) trek west through the mountains to **Mamasa**, or 120 kilometers (75 mi) north to **Rongkong**, will introduce the traveler to other facets of Torajan life.

The southwest or Mamasa Toraja area has been opened to better access by the paving of the road up from the Mandar coast west of Pare-Pare. The mountainous road climbs and winds its way between and upriver valleys, and is one of the most scenic drives in all Sulawesi. A comfortable bungalow hotel and a few country inns in Mamasa itself provide

Toraja homes.

accommodations. Mamasa's spectacular villages, with roofs and decor even larger than those in the Rantepao area, lie on rugged tracks, but several are accessible to jeeps with a guide. Mamasa is the only place in Sulawesi where copper is worked. Here is produced a dazzling array of jewelry with unique Dong Son-type designs. Rongkong weaving, with their characteristic colors and bold motifs, are used throughout the area as ancestor cloths.

Feasts for the dead: The Toraja are perhaps best known for their elaborate, colorful feasts for the dead, offered to ensure that souls of the dead may pass to the afterworld (*puya*) in a manner appropriate to the status they enjoyed in this world. Only when these rites have been performed, it is believed, will the ancestors bestow their blessings upon the living, thus maintaining the fragile balance between the various realms of the cosmos.

These feasts require an enormous outlay of material wealth – kin groups will often save and work for many years to prepare a suitably elaborate funeral. Many are held from August to October, following harvest time. Visitors should be sure to contribute food, cigarettes, soap or money to assist the family.

A man is considered dead only when his funeral feast is held. In the meantime, the deceased is regarded as merely "sick" and the corpse is kept in the southern end of the *tongkonan*, where it is fed and visited as if still alive. The corpse is first ritually cleansed and dressed in fine weaving, and made to sit up. After some days, it is wrapped in specially woven fabrics.

When enough goods have been set aside to send the soul off, the funeral ceremonies are performed in two stages over a period of about a week, presided over by a "death" specialist, or *tombablu*. Buffaloes and pigs are first slaughtered, and offerings of betel nut, fruits and *tuak* (palm wine) are made. The corpse is then moved to face north and is now officially dead. The kinsfolk must observe a number of taboos, including a rice fast that lasts several days.

Torajan burial ceremony.

The *ma'bolong* ceremony follows, for which a pig and a buffalo are again slaughtered and the relatives wear black. The body is placed in a sandalwood coffin in the shape of a *tongkonan*, then brought out of the house draped in a glittering death shroud and placed on an open platform beneath the granary. Meanwhile, an effigy (*tau-tau*) and funeral tower (*lakkian*) are prepared, and a large stone is placed in the center of the village ceremonial field (*rante*).

The second phase of the funeral takes place in the *rante,* decorated for the occasion with banners and the funeral tower. The coffin is borne from the house to the field and suspended in the lakkian. Feasting, chanting and dancing continue through the night, and buffalo fights and boxing matches take place during the day.

The funeral culminates with the ritual slaughter of up to 50 water buffalo, each by a single stroke of the sword. The blood is collected in bamboo containers to be cooked along with the buffalo meat, and distributed among the guests. On the last day of the feast, the coffin is lowered from the funeral tower and carried up to the mountainside family grave site amid great shouting and excitement. From here, the soul of the deceased ascends to the realm of the deified ancestors (*deata*) and its tau-tau effigy is installed on a high balcony overlooking the green valleys.

North Sulawesi: Something of an anomaly, **North Sulawesi** is a fertile, snake-like volcanic peninsula outstretched in the middle of the vast Maluku Sea, more than 1,000 kilometers (600 mi) from the nearest major population center. It is one of the most Christianized places in Indonesia.

About 2.3 million people make their homes here, more than 200,000 of them in **Manado**, the pleasant provincial capital. This city lies at the top of the lovely mountainous **Minahasa region**, with its active volcanoes, clear highland lakes, hot water springs and sandy beaches. Coconut plantations stretch for miles along the coasts (18,000 tons of copra are produced in North Sulawesi every

Toapekong Chinese festival.

month), and inland there are terraced rice fields, vegetable gardens and patches of cultivated maize. Minahasans also love flowers, and brightly colored bunches line the roads of the region.

The Minahasans: Originally of Mongoloid stock, and as with most coastal Indonesians, the Minahasan peoples migrated here several thousands of years ago. Their languages most closely resemble those spoken in the Philippines, however, and over the past few centuries, large numbers of Chinese and Europeans have settled in the area and intermarried with them.

It's said that the earliest Minahasan port was situated on Manado Tua, an extinct volcanic island on the north side of Manado Bay. Perhaps 500 years ago, the town was moved across to the site of modern-day Manado and flourished thereafter as a stop on the spice route.

Portuguese traders arrived here early in the 16th century, and were soon followed by Spanish missionaries from Manila, who landed at Manado and persuaded many Minahasans to convert to Catholicism. Dutch Calvinist missionaries in turn converted most of them to Protestantism in the mid-19th century.

Most of the traditional crafts of Minahasa have been lost, including the Bentenan weaving for which the area was once renowned. Folk dances are the most attractive of the surviving arts, though they lose much of their meaning when performed out of context for tourists. The Cakalele war dances are often performed today, a rather pale imitation of what they once must have been.

In agricultural areas, various seasonal events are worth watching for. At the beginning of the planting season and at harvest time, villagers march to the fields singing songs in a festival known as the Mapalus. Following the harvest, thanksgiving feasts last for several days and nights. They are inaugurated with a religious convocation but consist mainly of eating, *saguer* (palm toddy) drinking and dancing. Adults prefer the traditional European waltz, polka and quadrille, while the younger generation indulges in more modern gyrations. The

North Sulawesi war dance.

lack of a dance hall is no problem – an open coconut-palm clearing or sandy beach provides an ideal setting.

Seaside city: Alfred Russell Wallace called Manado "one of the prettiest towns in the East", a description that still fits given the area's abundance of coconut palms and turquoise water. Although the capital of North Sulawesi has grown into a commercial hub in recent years (with a population of more than 200,000), it retains much of its languid charm. Manado doesn't offer much in the way of urban attractions – except for **Ranotana market** and the quaint horse-drawn carriages, *bendi*. The real attraction here is the sea, both the beaches and the nearby reefs.

Manado is an excellent staging point for scuba diving and snorkeling trips to **Pulau Bunaken** and its superb marine national park, 15 kilometers (10 mi) offshore. Millions of marine creatures call the area home, including dolphins, sharks, barracuda, manta rays, sea turtles and countless species of neon-colored tropical fish. There are also World War II wrecks to explore, and a spectacular 200 meter (600 ft) coral wall. In fact, Bunaken is rated as one of the best dive spots in the Western Pacific. Boats to Bunaken and other offshore islands like Siladen and Manado Tua can be hired from the wharf at Manado harbor, or at the diving center in **Malalayang** village northeast of town. The Manado Beach Hotel, a modern resort establishment has been built 18 kilometers (12 mi) west of the city, is, unfortunately, the wrong way from the Bunaken diving area. Other smaller modern hotels are reportedly planned for the Malalayang area, closer to the key diving sites around Bunaken Island.

A horse and cart is still a common form of transport.

An excellent road network radiates from Manado. One interesting route runs east through the Tonsea area to **Bitung** on the east coast of the peninsula, a distance of 55 kilometers (35 mi). Along the way it passes through **Airmadidi** (Boiling Water) and the coastal town of **Kema**, populated by *burghers* (Minahasan-Dutch settlers) who all have Dutch surnames.

South of Kema there is a lovely stretch of coastline that is ideal for water sports, with many coral gardens in the neighborhood of **Pulau Nona**. Beyond Bitung lies **Aertembaga**, focus for the region's tuna fishing industry. From Bitung one may hire a boat for the journey up the coast to Batuputih village and the **Tangkoko-Batuangus-Dua Saudara Nature Reserve.**

A road south from **Lembeyan** (near Airmadidi) winds up through the Minahasan hills to the lake side district capital of **Tondano**, an attractive town with wide boulevards and surrounded by rice fields and forested hills. Just before Tondano, the road passes a park full of *waruga* – stone sarcophagi engraved with interesting reliefs and capped with statues. From prehistoric times into the early 20th century, Minahasans buried their dead in such sarcophagi, in a crouching position, together with their most valuable possessions. Traditionally they were placed around the family house; now they are gathered in one place to preserve them.

On a hill just outside of Tondano lies

the mausoleum of Kyai Maja, a Javanese leader who fought in Diponegoro's army during the Java Wars (1825–1830) and was exiled here by the Dutch. Even now, his **Kampung Java** is a Muslim enclave in a Christian region.

There are a number of interesting towns around **Danau Tondano**, including **Passo** and **Remboken** (noted for their hot springs and ceramics), and **Tandengan** and **Eris**. At the southern end of the lake is the village of **Kolongan Kawangkoan**, site of *kolintang* performances, bullock cart races and an underground Japanese fortress.

Southwest of Danau Tondano, near Langowan, a sign gives directions to the ancient megalithic monument known as **Watung Pinabetengan**, a short distance off the main road. A huge anvil-shaped stone thought to mark the territorial boundary of three tribal areas, it is covered with hitherto undeciphered hieroglyphics. Pre-Christian traditional heroes are still worshipped here.

Beaches and springs: West from Tondano, the road cuts through more hills on the way to **Tomohon**, a busy center for trade, education and missionary activities. There are hot springs nearby, at **Lahendong**, amidst a clove tree forest, and at **Kinilow**. From here the road descends to the coast of **Tanawangko**, a popular beach resort.

Traveling south along the coast, you soon arrive at **Amurang**, a small harbor town 80 kilometers (50 mi) from Manado that has a thriving trade with East Kalimantan, across the Sulawesi Sea. Surrounded by lovely hills, this is the gateway to southern Minahasa and **Gorontalo** (a day's drive west) via the Trans-Sulawesi Highway. And the **Gunung Ambang Nature Reserve** near the town of **Kotamobagu** offers excellent hikes amid forests, lakes and coffee plantations.

Starting at **Pineleng,** entering Manado, villages and houses become tightly packed – this is the most heavily populated rural area in the region. Near Pineleng is the mausoleum of Tuanku Imam Bonjol, a Sumatran leader who led a revolt against the Dutch in the mid-19th century and was exiled here.

Southeastern and central Sulawesi: The island's southeastern and central provinces (**Sulawesi Tenggara** and **Sulawesi Tengah**) are rarely visited and have not developed tourist facilities of any significance. Because of their distance from the beaten track, however, they retain a charm and a traditional lifestyle not found in more developed areas.

The capital of Southeast Sulawesi is **Kendari**, whose craftsmen were famed for their silver filigree work. Facing onto the Banda Sea, the town is a port of some importance and a gateway to Maluku. Sheltered by myriad small islands, Kendari often appears, when viewed from the sea, of lying on a lake.

A 12-hour boat trip to **Bau Bau** on Buton Island is highly recommended. Overlooking Bau Bau is the **old royal Kraton** – an ancient fortress with a commanding view of the sea and adjacent islands. Inhabiting remote shorelines all along this coast, the Bajau people hunt the giant stingray, using its poisonous spine for their harpoons.

A good road from Kendari leads across the peninsula to the nickel mining area of **Kolaka**, where a ferry crosses over to Watampone, in South Sulawesi.

The provincial capital of Central Sulawesi is **Palu**, a trading city located on the west coast at the tip of a deep, narrow bay. Palu is also the gateway to the beautiful **Lore Lindu Nature Reserve**. Here, there are dozens of statues of "grandfathers", phallic-shaped human images larger than life-size.

Most of central Sulawesi takes the form of isolated peaks, rain forest and remote tribal settlements. The Trans-Sulawesi Highway now connects **Tentena** and **Pendolo** near scenic Danau Poso, so it's possible to drive the length of Sulawesi, from Ujung Pandang to Manado, in about one week. The most scenic part of the entire trip is the mountainous section between Malili at the top of the Gulf of Bone, across the thick waist of Sulawesi and past Danau Poso. The long stretch up the northern-most "arm" of Sulawesi is the most recent to be opened, after the building of dozens of bridges across the many short rivers running down to the sea.

Right, an entire Torajan "graveyard" with galleries for effigies of the dead.

MALUKU

The fabulous so-called Spice Islands were avidly sought by Europeans for many years before their actual "discovery" by Portuguese mariners. Columbus and Magellan dreamed of finding their wealth. In fact, one of the main incentives for Europe's Age of Discovery was this zealous search for spices – easily worth their weight in gold.

Three of the most prized spices – clove, nutmeg and mace – grew only on a few tiny islands in the Moluccas chain. For centuries, the world's total clove production poured forth from five small islands off the west coast of Halmahera. And the Banda Islands, 350 kilometers (220 mi) to the southeast, supplied every last ounce of nutmeg and mace. Control of these islands assured vast fortunes.

The English word Moluccas is derived from Maluku, the Arabic term for "land of kings". This originally applied only to the five clove islands, but today, **Maluku** refers to an entire province dotted with a thousand islands spread over a huge area, almost 1.5 million square kilometers (600,000 sq mi). That works out to about one square kilometer for each of the province's inhabitants. But most of that is, in fact, water. The total land area covers only 87,000 square kilometers (33,600 sq mi), half of it the islands of Seram, Halmahera and Buru.

Curse of the spices: Exchanging silk, rice, metal tools, porcelain and other luxury items, Javanese, Chinese, Indians and Arabs traded for spices long before the first Europeans appeared.

In 1511, the Portuguese laid siege and stormed Malacca on the Malay Peninsula, Southeast Asia's principal trade center. Within a year, Portuguese ships had reached Banda and Ambon. Soon thereafter, the Portuguese believed the spice trade to be monopolized by themselves. Not quite.

Soon Magellan's motley ships arrived, the remnants of the once-proud fleet that had left Spain more two years earlier. The expedition had just lost its leader, with Magellan's untimely and violent death in the Philippines. But that didn't stop the Spaniards from claiming the Spice Islands as their own. The English, following in the footsteps of intrepid Sir Francis Drake (who called at Ternate in 1579), were not far behind. And neither were the Dutch. With methodical organization and determination, the Dutch eliminated the Portuguese and other European rivals. Local competition was also squashed in bloody engagements with local inhabitants.

From their stronghold on Ambon, the Dutch reinforced their clove monopoly by dispatching *hongi* expeditions of local war canoes to uproot clove trees elsewhere, and to execute illegal spice traders. Nutmeg and mace were easy to monopolize, as they had always been concentrated only in the Banda Islands. For a while, the English held on. But, eventually, the only island held by the English was traded with the Dutch for Manhattan Island, now part of New York City. Thus, the spice monopoly was complete. Toward the end of Dutch East Indies Company (VOC) rule, prof-

Left, tribal elder from Pulau Tanimbar. **Right**, nutmeg tree on Banda.

its fell far short of meeting expenses. But, overall, the monopoly was fairly well enforced and maintained, with no serious competition until the third decade of the 19th century.

By the 19th century, about half of Ambon's population had converted to Christianity. The converted Ambonese availed themselves of educational opportunities, forming the backbone of the Dutch colonial army.

Not even World War II could shake the loyalty of the Ambonese to Holland. The Moluccas were overrun by superior Japanese forces in spite of heroic Australian resistance in Ambon, and the area became a central Japanese base.

After the war, the Dutch returned to a welcome in Ambon. When Indonesia became independent a few years later, Ambon resisted, with thousands fleeing to Holland, while others fought a nasty guerrilla war.

Flora and fauna: The ecology of Maluku is one of feast and famine. Of the dozen species of land mammals, the placental half were probably introduced by people, with most restricted to the eastern portion of the archipelago. The indigenous marsupials include the squirrel-like flying opossum; three kinds of wide-eyed, prehensile-tailed furry cuscus; and the wallaby or tree-climbing kangaroo. There are also over 25 species of bats.

The 300-odd species of bird life include over 40 different kinds of birds-of-paradise, which are concentrated in the Aru archipelago; a couple of dozen species of parrot, headed by the large, handsome red-crested cockatoo, and beautiful crimson lorries. The strange megapods, using large feet and strong claws, build immense mounds of vegetable matter up to 10 meters in diameter and over 3 meters high. The large eggs laid inside this nest hatch from the heat generated by the decomposing plants.

Underwater, Dutch ichthyologists identified 780 species of fish around Ambon alone, a number almost equal to that of all Europe's rivers and seas.

Most people here live from fishing and subsistence gardens of vegetables,

Mosque near Ambon.

bananas, yams, cassava and sweet potatoes. Although cloves, nutmeg and mace retain a measure of importance, the cash economy is based on copra, dried coconut meat. Large companies are exploiting the islands' timber resources for the Japanese market, processing logs into sawn planks and plywood. The seas yield important harvests of tuna, shrimp, *trepang* (a sea cucumber), mother-of-pearl shells and pearls.

Except for about 10,000 people in the interior of the large islands of Seram, Buru and Halmahera who still adhere to ancestral beliefs, the rest of 1.5 million Moluccans are almost evenly divided between Christian (mostly Protestant) and Muslim. But supernatural practices are still practiced among those who profess Christianity or Islam.

Ambon: With nearly a quarter million inhabitants, **Ambon** is the metropolitan focus of Maluku and an important transportation hub. The city's architecture is functional but nondescript, as it was heavily bombed in 1944. The entrance to 18th-century Fort Victoria, which now backs an army barracks, is the only worthwhile colonial relic. But it's difficult to find, and taboo to photograph, unless one has a permit from military security in Jakarta. The picturesque **Gotong Royong market** in the harbor area is slowly being replaced by the sanitized setting of the newly-built **Merdeka market**, a short way down the waterfront. For last minute shopping try **Jalan Patty**, lined with shops. Look for framed montages from shaped pieces of mother-of-pearl, *ikat* cloth from Tanimbar and miniature ships cleverly made from wire and cloves. At the end of Jalan Patty there are the **Al Fatah Mosque**, next to the old **Jame Mosque**.

There are several attractions around Ambon, and the one that should not be missed is the **Siwalima Museum**, located on a hill just beyond the urban area. (Off the paved road on the way up, take a look at the impressive Japanese shore battery, still protected by its concrete bunker.) The Siwalima Museum displays aspects of Maluku's natural history and geology, but the emphasis is

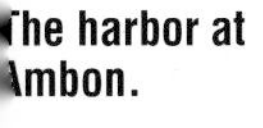

The harbor at Ambon.

on the ethnographic, with many fine objects, including ancestral carvings from the southern islands. Unlike many other museums in Indonesia, most of the showcases have an English description. On another paved road in the same direction as the museum, near the TV tower on a hill called **Gunung Nona**, is the best view of the bay and Ambon town. The bay looks better from a distance than underwater. The once-beautiful coral banks and marine life have been destroyed, the ecological price paid for the town's growth.

On the outskirts of town, in the opposite direction from the museum, a large, well-manicured **cemetery** holds the remains of Australian and other Allied troops who died during World War II. Maintained by the Australian government, the cemetery is open to the public. Many of those buried here were prisoners of war who perished in spite of the heroic aid given to them by the Ambonese. The special bond between Ambon and Australia is reinforced by the yearly Darwin-to-Ambon yacht race, held in late July or early August. Dozens of yachts from many countries participate, with a bash at the end to celebrate.

Beyond the city: The village of **Soya Atas** is less than half way up the slopes of 950-meter (3,100 ft) **Gunung Sirimau**. There's a fine church there, but be sure to also check out the *baileo* – a ritual meeting place with sacred megaliths. From Soya Atas, a well-kept path leads up to a sacred hilltop site with more megaliths, and a water container that never dries out. Drinking this water brings health, love and prosperity. Footpaths from Soya Atas lead down to some of Ambon's most traditional villages. A guide is recommended. Beware of a spirit residing in the area, the ghost of a former raja's daughter with a predilection for handsome foreign men.

A couple of popular beaches lie off the paved road west of town. **Amahusu** is seven kilometers (4 mi) away on the bay side, while **Namalatu**, 16 kilometers (10 mi) out, faces the island's southwestern shore. In the other direction, east of Ambon, the **beach at Natsepa** offers protected, shallow water. These beaches are crowded on weekends. Beyond Natsepa, the road leads to **Tulehu** village, the point of departure for passenger boats to central and east Seram, as well as to Haruku, Saparua and Nusa Laut islands. To the north past Tulehu, the village of **Waai** boasts sacred eels that live in a spring-fed cave, whose waters flow into a crystal-clear pool. Their keeper entices the eels to slither out of the cave by flicking his fingers or the palm of his hand on the water surface, then cracking open raw eggs. At the end of the paved road, the village of **Honimua** has a ferry service to western Seram and its booming lumber industry. Near Honimua, there is a long and deserted beach, but the best swimming and snorkeling is off **Pulau Pombo**, accessible by boat from either Tulehu or Honimua.

Rounding the bay out of Ambon City, a paved road cuts across Hitu to the island's north coast. On either side of this road are clove plantations, occasional stands of nutmeg and – with some luck – the processing of sago tree trunks

Women picking cloves.

into the starchy paste, the staple for many people. On the north coast, the road swings to the west. At Hila village, look for the neat **Immanuel Church**, built in 1780, and the **Mapauwe Mosque**, whose foundations were laid in 1414. A short stroll away are the seaside ruins of the majestic but neglected **Fort Amsterdam**.

Diving, magic and the Naulu: Among the islands close to Ambon and reachable by inexpensive passenger ferries, **Saparua** offers the most attractions. Two or more boats each day make the two-hour run from Tulehu to Saparua. The ride reveals lush tropical islands emerging from shallow seas.

There is a paved road, of sorts, winding around most of Saparua, and two acceptable, simple hotels. Time a visit to coincide with the Wednesday and Saturday market days, so as to sample some of the delicious smoked fish and to see the variety of tropical produce. There are many clove spreads on Saparua, along with strands of sago palms and the occasional nutmeg. **Ouw** village produces pottery – simple, elegant and functional – for use in this area and for sale in Ambon, as well. **Fort Duurstede**, restored and bristling with cannon, is a top attraction, along with the turquoise bay it dominates. Try to find the keeper of Pattimura's war paraphernalia, said to have acquired a sacred character because of the hero's prowess in fighting the Dutch. In addition to accommodations and meals, the Mahu Village Resort also provides boats, snorkeling equipment and scuba gear. Several spots off Saparua, as well as nearby Nusa Laut, are reputed to be world-class diving spots.

Seram, the largest and among the least-known islands in Maluku, hovers over Ambon, Saparua and lots of sea. Many of Ambon's traditions are said to have originated in Seram, including the division into two sets of customs, the *patasiwa* and the *patalima*, as well as the *pela* alliances between two villages, often located far apart. Seram is also replete with magic, for the Ambonese anyway, with many anecdotes of men

Gentlemen of a conch orchestra from Ambon.

who can fly, kill at a distance and change their shape at will. While the western part of the island has lost its mystery, thanks to a thriving lumber industry, the remote eastern mountains is where the magic is now concentrated.

Masohi, the capital of the central Maluku district, is on Seram's southcentral coast. The plains around the town have received a population boost, with migrants from overcrowded Saparua and some of the isolated islands to the south, as well as resettled mountain dwellers from Seram itself.

One group of mountain people – the Naulu, with their familiar red headbands – live fairly close to Masohi and can be reached by road, unless a heavy rain has washed out one of the none-too-sturdy bridges. Of the few remaining groups in the Maluku who closely adhere to ancient traditions, and without the veneer of a foreign religion, these paganistic coastal Naulu are the easiest to reach. The men's distinctive red headband, first worn after initiation rituals, distinguish the Naulu from their Christian and Muslim neighbors. The young men's initiation requires a five-day trek in the mountains of their ancestral homeland, where they must kill a deer and a boar with spear, and the tree-dwelling marsupial cuscus with a single arrow. With sufficient notice – a day or two – the Naulu can perform a rousing *cakalele* war dance for visitors. Those who wish to explore further into Naulu lands must hike (with a guide) inland to the mountainous Manusela Reserve. There are several Naulu villages there, along with exotic birds and other fascinating wildlife. Attempt it only if in good physical condition and with a week to spare.

Banda and beyond: South of Seram and Ambon, **Pulau Banda** were "founded" by the Portuguese in 1512, but it was the Dutch who arrived a century later to set up a spice monopoly. The English, who came later, undercut the Dutch efforts of price control by shipping nutmeg and mace to Europe from Rum Island, in the Bandas. The Dutch monopoly was restored when Manhattan was traded for Rum. But as spices were increasingly

Women of Ambon performing a welcome dance.

produced elsewhere, the Bandas faded into obscurity.

Forgotten or not, few spots on earth can surpass the Banda islands in tropical scenery. The reconstructed **Fort Belgica** that dominates Banda Neira is not reserved for history buffs. Closer to the sea, **Fort Nassau** crumbles in neglect. The Bandas' string of forts continue on **Pulau Lontar** with Concordia and Hollandia and Fort Revingil (Revenge) on Pulau Ai.

Energetic and active souls will want to climb **Gunung Api**. This active volcanic island is directly opposite Banda Neira. It last erupted in the late 1980s, but fortunately almost all of the lava and ash fell on the side away from the town. The view from the summit is spectacular. Attempt this with a guide and get an early start to beat the heat of the day.

In Banda Neira, the **Rumah Budaya Museum** holds many historical artifacts. Other places include the church, its interior stone slab graves inscribed with the names of Dutch colonialists, and the **Hatta-Syahrir mosque**.

There are excellent diving spots in the Bandas that offer incredible coral and marine life. The Bandas also have seasonal fishing and windsurfing.

Heading east or southeast from Banda, things get a bit more complicated; foreigners seldom travel this way. Yet both Tual in the Kei Archipelago as well as Saumlaki in the Tanimbars offer attractions and passable tourist facilities. The airstrip near Tual was built by the Japanese during World War II. Close by, on the grounds of the Roman Catholic mission, a long relief-sculpture depicts the history of the church in this area, starting with the first Jesuit missionaries who arrived in the latter part of the 19th century. During World War II, the Japanese invaded the Kei islands, murdering the bishop and 13 foreign priests here.

Tual is the capital of the district of Maluku Tenggara (Southeast Maluku) and the transportation hub for an extensive network of roads and sea lanes. A half-hour ride away is **Dullah** village, where the **Belawang Museum** boasts a splendid ceremonial canoe, complete

Gunung Api volcano.

with carved decorations. From Tual, motorized canoes depart daily to the mysterious island of **Kei Besar**. Occasional boats from Tual also head for **Dobo**, the largest town of the Aru archipelago. This spread of some 25 islands, all mangrove swamp and low-lying palm forest, is the home of unusual butterflies and flocks of birds-of-paradise.

South of the Keis is the **Tanimbar group** of islands. This area was brought under Dutch control only in the first years of this century, during the final phase of Holland's colonial expansion in Indonesia. Saumlaki was a Japanese air base during World War II. Tanimbar artists carve strange, small statues of human figures with big heads and tiny stick-like arms and legs.

In the village of **Sanglia Dol**, there is a wide megalithic staircase that leads to the village ceremonial ground, which features a huge stone boat with carved prow. It is believed that the ancestors arrived in this sacred craft. Near Saumlaki is an island known for its rare species of orchids. There is also a pearling operation, where tanks can be rented by visitors for scuba diving.

Ternate and Halmahera: The administrative and geographical district of the northern third of Maluku, north of Seram, is dominated on maps by Pulau Halmahera. But tiny **Ternate** is the real center of power and communications. Although it has lost its preeminent role in Maluku to Ambon, Ternate remains the second-most important town in the province. Two-thirds of the island's 80,000 people live in Ternate town, the business and market center of the whole region. A visit to the market will give an idea of some of the area's products.

Fort Oranje, built by the Dutch and currently used by the Indonesian police and military, is open to the public. There are many ancient cannons in this large complex. On the outskirts of town, in the direction of the airport, there is a **mosque** whose foundations date back to the 15th century. Its multitiered roof covers an airy space, beautifully designed for prayer and meditation.

A bit further out, the *kedaton,* or sul-

Overgrown Dutch fort.

tan's palace, houses a museum. Prior arrangements can be made through the local tourism office to view the museum's jewel: the magical crown, said to be a personal gift from Allah to the first sultan who submitted to Islam. Some hair attached to the crown is said to grow and needs periodic trimming. A few years ago, when the Gamalama volcano threatened to erupt, the son of the last officially-recognized sultan took the crown on a boat ride around Ternate to calm the impending eruption. It worked. Three times a week the crown and the resident spirits receive offerings of flowers, holy water and betel nuts.

A 45-kilometer-long (30 mi) paved road encircles Ternate, never wandering very far from the coastline and the volcanic slopes of the 1,720-meter (5,640 ft) **Gunung Gamalama**. In a counter-clockwise direction from town, the first stop is **Dufa-Dufa** village. **Fort Toloko** stands on a seaside cliff, in surprisingly good shape and with a still-legible seal on its main entrance. The next stop, **Batu Angus**, is a former lava flow, now jagged rock, which continues underwater for quite a distance. On the northeast coast, the steep slopes of **Pulau Hiri** pop into view. Nearby, there are two lakes, both called **Danau Tolire**. The smaller one is near the sea, while the other is a short distance inland.

After rounding the north of Ternate, the crumbling **Portuguese fort of Kastela** comes into view. From here, there is a path to the sacred royal springs of Akerica and to the huge old Afo clove tree (also reachable by a different path from town). Past Kastela and just before the village of Ngade is **Danau Laguna**. This lake, partially covered with lotus plants, is home to the sacred crocodiles who trace their ancestry to a princess. Seeing one of these is said to lead to a lifetime of luck. A path along one side of the lake rises to give a splendid view of the Danau Laguna, with Maitara and Tidore islands in the background. The last stop, **Fort Kayu Merah**, offers a sea-level view of the same islands.

Gamalama volcano has an excellent view from the top on a clear day. To beat

World War II tank, Morotai.

the heat, start early, take a hat and plenty of water. A guide is also necessary.

Pulau Tidore, a bit larger than Ternate, is for the less energetic. Frequent boats leave Bastion to Rum, where there is a weekly Sunday market. Tidore is dominated by Kiematubu volcano. A paved road goes around most of the island, but beyond the main town of **Soa Siu**, the surface degenerates considerably. The best views of Ternate are from Tidore's north coast.

Battle sites and bases: The infrastructure of **North Halmahera** has improved over the past few years, making it easier for visitors to get to North Halmahera from Ternate. This is largely due to the government's program of resettling farmers from overcrowded Java to the outer islands, coupled with a thriving economy based on cash crops such as copra and cacao.

The principal town of **Tobelo** lies on the eastern shore of Halmahera's northern peninsula. Small sand-and-palm-fringed islands, set off by gliding canoes, make a wonderful dawn or dusk sight. Boats can be rented from Tobelo for picnics and snorkeling off the uninhabited islands.

The village of **Daru** is several hours of bumps, mudholes and nerve-rattling bridges south of Tobelo. From here, there is a boat to **Pulau Bobale**, where there are two local diving operations that bring up mother-of-pearl, with an occasional authentic pearl, for a hefty profit. Pulau Bobale also has a large, well-kept Japanese bunker.

Some 80 kilometers (50 mi) south of Tobelo and near the bottom of the bay, the town of **Kao** hosted some 80,000 Japanese troops during World War II, earning itself the name of Little Tokyo. Prior to landing on Morotai, Allied planes bombed the installations.

A few anti-aircraft guns still guard the landing strip, now used by commercial flights from Ternate. Just offshore, the superstructures of a couple of sunken Japanese ships can be seen protruding above the water surface.

Pulau Morotai was the site of a major battle during World War II. The task force led by Gen. Douglas MacArthur swept ashore after destroying the light Japanese defenses there, as well as the concentration of power at Kao Bay. Morotai was quite vital to MacArthur's island-hopping strategy towards the Philippines, and onward to Japan, if necessary.

The landing strips built by the Allied forces on Morotai could handle today's jumbo jets, but serve only small Twin Otters. Although much of the relics from the war were carted off to the maws of the Krakatau steel mill, in Java, there are still remnants of war machinery.

In 1973, a Japanese soldier came out of the jungle, nearly three decades after Japan surrendered and after three decades of hiding; the local government official is convinced that there are still some Japanese survivors on the island. **Daruba** town, where the scheduled flights land and passenger boats call, has a small family style losmen. A local diving operation has a compressor and tanks available for rent. Many islands and reefs offer superb diving in waters full of unusual marine life.

Left, King of Tidore puts on a show for visiting traders. Right, nutmegs.

IRIAN JAYA

Irian Jaya, which represents 22 percent of Indonesia's total land area, spreads over the western half of New Guinea – the second-largest island in the world after Greenland. The shape of this 800,000-square-kilometer (300,000 sq mi) island resembles a squatting bird with a neck that narrows to a few kilometers, before joining a large peninsula called the Bird's Head. A cordillera of mountains runs the length of New Guinea, topped by Puncak Jayawijaya, at 4,884 meters (16,000 ft) the highest peak between the Himalayas and the Andes. The rugged highlands that surround the mountains hold most of the population. Closely packed, radically different ecological zones result from the combination of tropics, steeply rising elevations and weather patterns.

New Guinea and Australia share the Sahul continental shelf, which was never linked to the Asian land mass during the Ice Ages, even when sea levels dropped some 120 meters (400 ft). Mammals, mostly marsupials, thus evolved in isolation. People introduced the common placentals like dogs, pigs (and recently, deer) to complement native kangaroos, bandicoots and cuscus.

Saltwater crocodiles, some over seven meters (20 ft) in length, are Irian's largest animals. One such monster was credited in the 1950s with 55 confirmed human victims. Other awesome reptiles include tree pythons and the death adder, whose bite brings almost instant death. Huge bird-eating spiders grace sticky, sheet-like webs.

Irian's largest bird, the flightless cassowary, can handle spiders of any size as well as careless hunters, who are disembowelled by a swift kick and sharp claws. There are also parrots, lorries, cockatoos, the Victoria crowned pigeon and the birds-of-paradise with their spectacular plumage.

The soils of Irian are thin and susceptible to erosion despite a luxurious cover of vegetation. While logging has started in earnest, the spread of tropical vegetation is still huge, second only to the Amazon. Plant life includes insect-eating pitcher plants, phosphorescent fungi and 2,700 species of orchids.

In the past: The first inhabitants of Irian arrived from the west perhaps 60,000 years ago. While the sea level was considerably lower when people first migrated to Australia and New Guinea, there were still stretches of ocean to cross. Rising seas eventually cut off Australia from New Guinea.

Small groups settled along the seashores and short distances inland, living from hunting, fishing and gathering. There must have been but slight contact between these groups on what was to emerge as New Guinea. On this island, with only 0.01 percent of the earth's population, 15 percent of the world's languages are spoken. Out of an almost incredible 800 languages – not dialects – about 550 are found in Papua New Guinea, an independent country, and some 250 in Indonesia's Irian Jaya.

More newcomers arrived, originating from southern China and Taiwan on a

Preceding pages: Placcid Danau Habbena. Left, free-fall on Pulau Biak. Right, tribesman from Pulau Numfor.

2,000-year settling of the Philippines, Indonesia, Malaysia, Micronesia and Polynesia. In most areas, these people replaced existing populations thanks to their more advanced tools, weapons and agricultural skills. But in New Guinea, the majority of the long-established Papuans successfully resisted assimilation by the newcomers, who established themselves only on some nearby islands and coastal strips.

Plant geneticists still have not established an accurate date for the introduction of the sweet potato to New Guinea, but the impact of this new tuber altered population distribution. The sweet potato, unlike taro and other previously-planted crops, grows well above 1,500 meters (5,000 ft). This placed its cultivators beyond the normal range of the malarial mosquito, which had previously limited human numbers. Intensive cultivation resulted in great yields, which also helped to increase the highland population.

New Guinea was visited by Europeans in the early 16th century, who mostly stayed away until the 19th century. When Britain, and later Germany, started claiming parts of eastern New Guinea, Holland asserted possession of the island's western half. Most of Irian's interior was a cartographic blank until the early years of this century, when a series of Dutch military expeditions ventured inland. The Baliem Valley – with over 50,000 inhabitants – was not visited by Westerners until 1938, and even today many areas are still *terra incognita*.

After World War II, Holland retained its half of New Guinea. However, strong diplomatic pressures and a persistent guerrilla resistance forced Holland to cede West Irian to Indonesia in 1963, after which it was given its new name of Irian Jaya, and its capital changed its name from Hollandia to Jayapura.

Gateway to Irian: Off Irian's north coast, **Pulau Biak** has the province's best air connections: international flights to North America, as well as jets to Bali, Jakarta and other points west.

Other tropical islands lie scattered around Biak. **Pulau Yapen**, long and mountainous, boasts birds-of-paradise, a decent little hotel and daily flights from Biak. **Pulau Numfor**, flat with a couple of deep lagoons, also receives flights from Biak but holds no commercial facilities for travelers. **Supiori**, separated from Biak by a long narrow sea passage, can only be reached by boat, and, once there, visitors must depend on local hospitality.

Although thoroughly missionized, many villages on all the islands can perform traditional dances with a day's notice. On Biak, this includes fire-walking, an ancient ritual revived at Adoki village, close to town. Also near Biak town, visit a cave called **Goa Binsari**, one of many used by the Japanese in World War II during the furious battle for control of this island.

Biak Island can easily be explored, as three paved roads head out of town: to Bosnik in the east, Wardo in the opposite direction, and Korem in the north. From Bosnik, take a canoe to one of the nearby **Pulau Padaido**, little jewels in the sea. Near Wardo, hop into any outrigger for the best magical trip up a

A resident of Irian Jaya wearing a combination of modern and primitive garb.

river, to **Wapsdori Falls**. From Korem, the paved road continues along Biak's northeast coast for the most wonderful seascape and village scenery in this part of the world. Stop at **Warsa** village, where boys gleefully jump off the top of a 15-meter (50 ft) waterfall.

There are frequent minibuses everywhere on market days, and a chance to catch a boat ride from the end of the road to those villages, which can only be reached by sea. Markets are usually on Wednesday and Saturday, but check before heading out. Another alternative is to hire a local boat. Try the fishermen's cooperative or a travel agency in Biak town for a double-hulled outboard-powered catamaran. Take along a sack of rice, mask, snorkel and fins. The crew will provide the fish. Go exploring for several days – but not between November and March, the season of heavy seas. Or just relax in the new Biak Beach Hotel and enjoy the quiet.

Sorong and **Manokwari** are located on the lush Bird's Head (Vogelkop) Peninsula of western Irian Jaya. Sorong, an old oil town, has a great seascape and offers access to the Bird's Head region. Manokwari, the site of the first mission in Irian, boasts of a couple of beautiful islands just outside its bay. There are also flights from there to the **Danau Anggi**, two beautiful bodies of water located in the Arfak Mountains.

North-coast capital: The capital of the province of Irian Jaya, **Jayapura** is the gateway for the Baliem Valley. The flight schedules make it impossible for travelers, even if already possessing the necessary *surat jalan* or travel permit, to plan a same-day connection from anywhere to Wamena, Baliem's principal town. And the fact that the airport is located some 40 kilometers (25 mi) from town doesn't simplify life either.

The logical way to proceed is to land as early as possible in the day to allow enough time to obtain the *surat jalan* and a ticket to Wamena. The police station for the travel permit, as well as the Merpati Airlines office, are located in downtown Jayapura, near the Hotel Matoa. The daily flight to Wamena tends

Jayapura Harbor.

to be full and one might not be able to obtain a ticket for the next day; plan a few days in Jayapura. But don't despair: the Baliem is worth the wait and the Jayapura area itself holds enough interest to keep you gainfully occupied.

The main part of Jayapura, a city with a population of about 100,000, lies on **Yos Sudarso Bay**. The city's constricted site along several indented, steep-walled coves is the most gorgeous of any provincial capital in Indonesia. There is a splendid view of the city from the base of a communications tower, on a steep hill just in back of the harbor.

To the east, the suburb of **Hamadi** offers numerous souvenir stalls, and Yotefa Bay and Engros village, where the church and all the houses are built on stilts. To the west, there's a decent swimming beach called **Base G** (pronounced as *bestegi*), a popular spot on weekends.

A short distance from town are several crocodile farms. Along the road to the airport, there is a good museum of artifacts located at the **University of Cenderawasih**. On the same road, the **Museum Negeri** features excellent ethnographic displays. Boats are available to motor around **Danau Sentani** – try to land on Apayo Island, where local craftsmen produce bark-cloth paintings and carvings in the traditional Sentani style.

Into the highlands: The fertile **Baliem Valley** lies in Irian's highlands, a one-hour flight from Jayapura. At 1,500 meters (4,900 ft), the valley is cool, especially at night. But the midday sun can still burn. The fertile, heavily-cultivated 525-square-kilometer (200 sq mi) valley floor is surrounded by steep mountains on all sides. Early morning clouds and mist often hide the surrounding heights, giving a timeless and mystical atmosphere that slowly dissipates with the sun's rays. These clouds kept the valley hidden from Westerners' knowledge until the 1930s. The Baliem River, with its rich and creamy brown tone, snakes through the valley before pouring out through a southern gorge to the Arafura Sea.

This is home to the Dani tribe, the most famous of Irian's interior people.

Lowlands and Freeport Bridge.

These farmer-warriors lived in isolation until they were "discovered" in 1938. They grew stupendous harvests of their staple sweet potatoes in the rich valley soil, with the help of an efficient irrigation system. As the men had plenty of time left over after the gardening chores (most of which were done by the women anyway), ritual warfare developed to a degree seldom matched anywhere.

Today, after over 50 years of contact with the outside world, the Dani's lifestyle has changed somewhat. But many of the men still wear only distinctive penis sheaths, and the women only grass skirts; agriculture is still centered around sweet potatoes. Pigs and women remain a man's most valued possessions. Occasional ritual battles result in casualties from arrows, spears and the odd imported axe. Funerals and marriage rites have changed little over the years.

A visit to the Baliem Valley can be tame or adventurous. For those who need creature comforts, Wamena has acceptable hotels and meals, and locally-organized day trips that may include a Dani ritual. Hardier souls can set out by public transport, then trek to fascinating villages. Guides are essential for these jaunts, relying on local hospitality (small payment is appreciated) and a straight diet of yams.

Wamena, with several thousand people, is the only urban center in the Baliem Valley. All flights land here, the highlands' main airstrip. Foreigners will have their travel permits checked upon arrival. The district's principle officials live in Wamena, along with students of the high school and teacher college. The Catholic Church has its highland headquarters here. There's a post office, a bank and telephone service.

And best of all, there's the daily market. In the early hours of dawn, Dani from miles around begin to drift to the market. Most of the locals bring surplus sweet potatoes and tomatoes, carrots, cucumbers and cabbage, along with pineapple and a variety of bananas. Bows and bunches of multipurpose arrows, each for a different kind of game – including humans – can be bought. Other

An Asmat armada.

items include penis sheaths, stone axes and cowrie shells, formerly used as money. Easily the best attraction, however, are the people. Few wear western dress. Instead, the Dani traditional dress of penis sheath and feathers for the men and grass skirts and the traditional woven-string *noken* bags of the women provide an astonishing cultural melange.

There are a few traditional Dani villages near Wamena. The nearest, **Pugima**, can be reached in an hour's stroll. **Jiwika**, some 20 kilometers (12 mi) away, is linked by a good road and frequent public transportation.

En route to Jiwika, all tours stop to see the **mummy of Akima**, the smoke-dried remains of a powerful war chief who has access to the world of spirits. There is also another mummy, not so popular as the war chief, but considerbly cheaper to photograph.

An hour's steep climb leads to a brine pool, from where salt is extracted in the traditional way. The road continues from Jiwika, with caves and villages along the way.

South of Wamena, a road leads part of the way to **Kurima**, at the head of the Baliem Gorge. Paths along the gorge lead to the Yali tribe, who saw their first missionaries only a generation ago.

On the other side of the Baliem Valley from Jiwika, a newly-upgraded road leads to Pyramid, at the northern entrance to the valley. Before Pyramid, side paths head into the mountains, past Dani villages to uninhabited lands where Danau Habbema and the snow-capped Mt. Trikora are located. **Pyramid**, a Protestant missionary center, lies on the main path leading out of the Baliem Valley to the territory of the Western Dani. The sub-district center of **Karubaga** can be reached in three or four days on a good path. There are scheduled flights each week from Karubaga to Wamena, and the occasional missionary flights. Or else, hike out of Karubaga to Bokondini and Tiom.

Asmats and gold mines: The lands of the Asmat tribe, centered around the town of **Agats**, has been off-limits to travelers in the past. Only Agats itself has been opened up recently. There is an excellent museum with world-class carvings, but it's hardly worth the trip if one can't explore around.

Most of the swamp-dwelling Asmat are converted Christians and wear tattered Western clothing. Other interesting tribes live far inland and are very inaccessible. High transportation costs in outboard-powered dugouts, and days of monotonous motoring in malarial swamps, make these places for explorers and adventurers only.

Below Puncak Jayawijaya is the world's most spectacular mine, a massive **copper-and-gold complex** managed by an American-Indonesian joint venture called Freeport Indonesia. (In the mid 1990s, there were numerous problems with Irian separatists in this area, including the kidnapping of foreigners. The mine was sometimes the focus of separatist anger.)

Sheraton recently opened an "eco-resort" at **Timika** on the south coast of Irian Jaya, a good base for exploring the Asmat lands, Puncak Jayawijaya and **Lorentz Nature Reserve**.

Left, bow and arrow are both tool and weapon. Right, Irian colors.

INSIGHT GUIDES

Travel Tips

FOR THOSE WITH MORE THAN A PASSING INTEREST IN TIME...

Before you put your name down for a Patek Philippe watch *fig. 1,* there are a few basic things you might like to know, without knowing exactly whom to ask. In addressing such issues as accuracy, reliability and value for money, we would like to demonstrate why the watch we will make for you will be quite unlike any other watch currently produced.

"Punctuality", Louis XVIII was fond of saying, "is the politeness of kings."

We believe that in the matter of punctuality, we can rise to the occasion by making you a mechanical timepiece that will keep its rendezvous with the Gregorian calendar at the end of every century, omitting the leap-years in 2100, 2200 and 2300 and recording them in 2000 and 2400 *fig. 2.* Nevertheless, such a watch does need the occasional adjustment. Every 3333 years and 122 days you should remember to set it forward one day to the true time of the celestial clock. We suspect, however, that you are simply content to observe the politeness of kings. Be assured, therefore, that when you order your watch, we will be exploring for you the physical—if not the metaphysical—limits of precision.

Does everything have to depend on how much?

Consider, if you will, the motives of collectors who set record prices at auction to acquire a Patek Philippe. They may be paying for rarity, for looks or for micromechanical ingenuity. But we believe that behind each $500,000-plus bid is the conviction that a Patek Philippe, even if 50 years old or older, can be expected to work perfectly for future generations.

In case your ambitions to own a Patek Philippe are somewhat discouraged by the scale of the sacrifice involved, may we hasten to point out that the watch we will make for you today will certainly be a technical improvement on the Pateks bought at auction? In keeping with our tradition of inventing new mechanical solutions for greater reliability and better time-keeping, we will bring to your watch innovations *fig. 3* inconceivable to our watchmakers who created the supreme wristwatches of 50 years ago *fig. 4.*
At the same time, we will of course do our utmost to avoid placing undue strain on your financial resources.

Can it really be mine?

May we turn your thoughts to the day you take delivery of your watch? Sealed within its case is your watchmaker's tribute to the mysterious process of time. He has decorated each wheel with a chamfer carved into its hub and polished into a shining circle. Delicate ribbing flows over the plates and bridges of gold and rare alloys. Millimetric surfaces are bevelled and burnished to exactitudes measured in microns. Rubies are transformed into jewels that triumph over friction. And after many months—or even years—of work, your watchmaker stamps a small badge into the mainbridge of your watch. The Geneva Seal—the highest possible attestation of fine watchmaking *fig. 5.*

Looks that speak of inner grace *fig. 6.*

When you order your watch, you will no doubt like its outward appearance to reflect the harmony and elegance of the movement within. You may therefore find it helpful to know that we are uniquely able to cater for any special decorative needs you might like to express. For example, our engravers will delight in conjuring a subtle play of light and shadow on the gold case-back of one of our rare pocket-watches *fig. 7.* If you bring us your favourite picture, our enamellers will reproduce it in a brilliant miniature of hair-breadth detail *fig. 8.* The perfect execution of a double hobnail pattern on the bezel of a wristwatch is the pride of our casemakers and the satisfaction of our designers, while our chainsmiths will weave for you a rich brocade in gold *figs. 9 & 10.* May we also recommend the artistry of our goldsmiths and the experience of our lapidaries in the selection and setting of the finest gemstones? *figs. 11 & 12.*

How to enjoy your watch before you own it.

As you will appreciate, the very nature of our watches imposes a limit on the number we can make available. (The four Calibre 89 time-pieces we are now making will take up to nine years to complete). We cannot therefore promise instant gratification, but while you look forward to the day on which you take delivery of your Patek Philippe *fig. 13,* you will have the pleasure of reflecting that time is a universal and everlasting commodity, freely available to be enjoyed by all.

Should you require information on any particular Patek Philippe watch, or even on watchmaking in general, we would be delighted to reply to your letter of enquiry. And if you send us

TRAVEL TIPS

Getting Acquainted

Time

With its considerable spread from east to west, Indonesia covers three time zones. When it's 0100 in Jakarta, it's:

0100 Sumatra, Java, Madura

0200 Kalimantan, Sulawesi, Bali/ Lombok, Nusa Tenggara

0300 Maluku, Irian Jaya

Jakarta is 7 hours ahead of GMT.

Climate

All of the archipelago's islands lie within the tropical zone, and the surrounding seas create a homogenizing effect on temperatures and humidity. Consequently, local variables like topography, altitude and rainfall produce more variation in climate than do latitude or season. Mean temperatures at sea level vary by only a few degrees throughout the region (25–28°C, or 78–82°F). In the mountains, however, the temperature decreases about one degree Celsius (two degrees Fahrenheit) for every 200 meters (65 ft) of altitude, which makes for a cool, pleasant climate in upland towns like Java's Bandung and Sumatra's Bukittinggi.

Much of the archipelago also lies within the equatorial ever-wet zone, where no month passes without several inches of rainfall. The northeast monsoon means that many islands receive drenching precipitation between November and April. Moreover, the tropical sun and the oceans combine to produce continuously high humidity everywhere. Due to local wind patterns, a few places like Bogor in West Java receive as much as 400 centimeters (200 in) of rain annually.

The southeast monsoon tends to counteract this generally high humidity by blowing hot, dry air up from over the Australian landmass between May and October. Although much depends upon local topography, on most islands this produces a dry season of markedly reduced precipitation, and as one moves south and eastward in the archipelago, the influence of this desiccating dry monsoon increases.

Economy

Indonesia's rise in average per capita income – from only US$50 in 1966 to just over US$1,000 today – has been impressive. Moreover, the number of people living below the poverty line has dropped from around 50 percent at the end of World War II to just 15 percent in 1996. Indeed, as a diversified economy with an annual growth rate of about 7 percent, Indonesia has much to crow about. The benefits of this growth can be seen in daily life. Nearly all children now attend primary school, compared with about half three decades ago. The days when food shortages were the norm and triple-digit inflation made a mockery of the rupiah's value are long gone, a further sign that the government, for all its shortcomings, has more than delivered on the economic front.

In a broad sense, the Indonesian economy appears to be on track, due in no small part to deregulation. Such economic shock tactics have not been taken lightly by a country which was once all but closed to foreign imports and investment.

It is estimated that to maintain its present rate of growth, Indonesia must invest US$53 billion in infrastructure projects alone to meet the requirements of an industrialized society.

A sustained effort to diversify away from the country's traditional dependence on oil revenues and develop export manufacturing is bearing fruit. As recently as the early 1980s about 80 percent of revenue came from the oil and gas sectors, compared to less than 30 percent today. Indeed, labor-intensive exports of goods such as shoes, textiles and televisions are rapidly replacing foreign-exchange earnings from oil and gas as production falls and domestic consumption rises.

For all the glowing predictions about the Indonesian economy in the years ahead, there are a few issues bubbling under the surface that may need attention in the future. One sensitive issue with the middle classes is the lack of political opening to match the country's economic and financial liberalization. Resentment felt by ordinary people towards rich, ethnic Chinese Indonesians – a distinct minority – is a further source of tension. Apart from these social issues, there is a need to put a more up-to-date legal system in place for business. The existence of highly favored, official state-owned monopolies is also leading to an erosion in Indonesia's competitiveness.

Compounding these concerns is the need to balance conflicting demands. There are increasing calls, for instance, for a more equitable distribution of wealth and income in the country. Most analysts agree that Indonesia must accelerate economic reform, continue to upgrade its physical infrastructure – roads, power stations, ports and telecommunications – and foster a pool of managerial talent if growth is to be sustained in the long term. The country's endemic corruption and cumbersome bureaucracy – it has a reputation for the highest hidden business costs in Asia – is another worry for foreign investors.

Etiquette

- Do not shout or show anger, and never direct displeasure at any individual in particular, especially in public. Bad news or displeasure should be conveyed in private.
- Never use red ink. It suggests that the writer is angry with the reader or recipient.
- Never give or receive anything with the left hand. For Muslims, it is used for bodily cleaning and thus inappropriate. Similarly, eat using only the right hand.
- When given food or drink, don't start until actually asked to do so. Don't empty your glass or cup unless you want a refill.
- Once you have entered somebody's home, do not leave until they have served a refreshment, regardless of how long it may take them to prepare it. Otherwise, you shame them.
- Never point at people or things. If beckoning someone, don't rake the air with a crooked finger; use a downward wave of the hand.
- Hands on the hips indicates defiance or arrogance, especially if standing with legs apart, gunslinger style.
- When sitting, feet should be tucked away, not propped up and the bottoms

INSIGHT POCKET GUIDES

North America
Atlanta
Boston
British Coumbia
Florida
Florida Keys
Hawaii
Miami
Montreal
New York City
North California
Quebec
San Francisco
South California
Toronto

Latin America and The Caribbean
Bahamas
Baja
Belize
Bermuda
Jamaica
Mexico City
Puerto Rico
US Virgin Islands
Yucatan Peninsula

Europe
Aegean Islands
Algarve
Alsace
Athens
Barcelona
Bavaria
Berlin
Brittany
Brussels
Budapest
Corsica
Costa Blanca
Costa Brava
Cote d'Azur
Crete
Denmark
Florence
Gran Canaria
Hungary
Ibiza
Ireland
Lisbon
Loire Valley
London
Madrid
Mallorca
Malta
Marbella
Milan
Moscow
Munich
Oslo/Bergen
Paris
Prague
Provence
Rhodes
Rome
Sardinia
Scotland
Seville
Sicily
Southeast England
St Petersburg
Tenerife
Tuscany
Venice
Vienna

Middle East and Africa
Istanbul
Kenya
Maldives
Morocco
Seychelles
Tunisia
Turkish Coast

Asia/Pacific
Bali
Bali Birdwalks
Bangkok
Beijing
Bhutan
Canton
Chiang Mai
Fiji
Hong Kong
Jakarta
Kathmandu, Bikes & Hikes
Kuala Lumpur
Macau
Malacca
Nepal
New Delhi
New Zealand
Penang
Phuket
Sabah
Sikkim
Singapore
Sri Lanka
Sydney
Thailand
Tibet
Yogyakarta

United States: **Houghton Mifflin Company, Boston MA 02108**
Tel: (800) 2253362 Fax: (800) 4589501

Canada: **Thomas Allen & Son, 390 Steelcase Road East**
Markham, Ontario L3R 1G2
Tel: (416) 4759126 Fax: (416) 4756747

Great Britain: **GeoCenter UK, Hampshire RG22 4BJ**
Tel: (256) 817987 Fax: (256) 817988

Worldwide: **Höfer Communications Singapore 2262**
Tel: (65) 8612755 Fax: (65) 8616438

"I was first drawn to the Insight Guides by the excellent "Nepal" volume. I can think of no book which so effectively captures the essence of a country. Out of these pages leaped the Nepal I know – the captivating charm of a people and their culture. I've since discovered and enjoyed the entire Insight Guide Series. Each volume deals with a country or city in the same sensitive depth, which is nowhere more evident than in the superb photography."

Sir Edmund Hillary

FLY SMOOTH AS SILK TO EXOTIC THAILAND ON A ROYAL ORCHID HOLIDAY.

Watching exquisite cotton and silk umbrellas being hand-painted in Chiang Mai. Lazing in the shade in sun-drenched Phuket. This

THA6059H

s what holidaying in Thailand is all about. Book the holiday of your choice now, flying Thai. Smooth as silk.

INSIGHT GUIDES

COLORSET NUMBERS

North America

160 Alaska
173 American Southwest
184I Atlanta
227 Boston
275 California
180 California, Northern
161 California, Southern
237 Canada
184C Chicago
184 Crossing America
243 Florida
240 Hawaii
275A Los Angeles
243A Miami
237B Montreal
184G National Parks of America: East
184H National Parks of America: West
269 Native America
100 New England
184E New Orleans
184F New York City
133 New York State
147 Pacific Northwest
184B Philadelphia
172 Rockies
275B San Francisco
184D Seattle
Southern States of America
186 Texas
237A Vancouver
184C Washington DC

Latin America and The Caribbean

150 Amazon Wildlife
260 Argentina
188 Bahamas
292 Barbados
251 Belize
217 Bermuda
127 Brazil
260A Buenos Aires
162 Caribbean
151 Chile
281 Costa Rica
282 Cuba
118 Ecuador
213 Jamaica
285 Mexico
285A Mexico City
249 Peru
156 Puerto Rico
127A Rio de Janeiro
116 South America
139 Trinidad & Tobago
198 Venezuela

Europe

155 Alsace
158A Amsterdam
167A Athens
263 Austria
107 Baltic States
219B Barcelona
1187 Bay of Naples
109 Belgium
135A Berlin
178 Brittany
109A Brussels
144A Budapest
213 Burgundy
122 Catalonia
141 Channel Islands
135E Cologne
119 Continental Europe
189 Corsica
291 Côte d'Azur
165 Crete
226 Cyprus
114 Czech/Slovak Reps
238 Denmark
135B Dresden
142B Dublin
135F Düsseldorf
149 Eastern Europe
148A Edinburgh
123 Finland
209B Florence
154 France
135C Frankfurt
135 Germany
148B Glasgow
279 Gran Canaria
124 Great Britain
167 Greece
166 Greek Islands
135G Hamburg
144 Hungary
256 Iceland
142 Ireland
209 Italy
202A Lisbon
258 Loire Valley
124A London
201 Madeira
219A Madrid
157 Mallorca & Ibiza
117 Malta
101A Moscow
135D Munich
158 Netherlands
111 Normandy
120 Norway
124B Oxford
154A Paris
115 Poland
202 Portugal
114A Prague
153 Provence
177 Rhine
209A Rome
101 Russia
130 Sardinia
148 Scotland
261 Sicily
264 South Tyrol
219 Spain
220 Spain, Southern
101B St. Petersburg
170 Sweden
232 Switzerland
112 Tenerife
210 Tuscany
174 Umbria
209C Venice
263A Vienna
267 Wales
183 Waterways of Europe

Middle East and Africa

268A Cairo
204 East African Wildlife
268 Egypt
208 Gambia & Senegal
252 Israel
236A Istanbul
252A Jerusalem-Tel Aviv
214 Jordan
270 Kenya
235 Morocco
259 Namibia
265 Nile, The
257 South Africa
113 Tunisia
236 Turkey
171 Turkish Coast
215 Yemen

Asia/Pacific

287 Asia, East
207 Asia, South
262 Asia, South East
194 Asian Wildlife, Southeast
272 Australia
206 Bali Baru
246A Bangkok
234A Beijing
247B Calcutta
234 China
247A Delhi, Jaipur, Agra
169 Great Barrier Reef
196 Hong Kong
247 India
212 India, South
128 Indian Wildlife
143 Indonesia
278 Japan
266 Java
203A Kathmandu
300 Korea
145 Malaysia
218 Marine Life in the South China Sea
272B Melbourne
211 Myanmar
203 Nepal
293 New Zealand
205 Pakistan
222 Philippines
250 Rajasthan
159 Singapore
105 Sri Lanka
272 Sydney
175 Taiwan
246 Thailand
278A Tokyo
255 Vietnam
193 Western Himalaya

facing or pointed at another person.

• When visiting mosques and other places of worship, remove shoes and assure that you are dressed appropriately, especially if female, ie, minimal exposed skin.

Indonesians are generally mild-mannered and polite, and are extremely reluctant to give offence. They usually hide negative feelings like jealousy, envy or anger, and prefer the roundabout way to doing business.

Government officials and bureaucrats should be accorded a lot of respect. Be polite, persistent and patient, although you may have to be assertive at times, as government offices are usually busy.

Social hierarchy is important in Indonesian society, and considerable respect is accorded to status, position and age. When greeting a group of people, for instance, you should always start with the boss or the host.

Business

At first meetings, business may not be discussed at all, or it may be mentioned briefly or in general, paving the way for another consultation later.

Meetings usually begin with the conversation centering on social or predictable topics. Specific or personal enquiries are avoided. The best way to air a grievance is to politely talk around the subject until your business partner sees your point of view. It is not a good idea to be direct. Rather than saying no directly, Indonesians will say *belum*, which means not yet.

The notion of consensus is fundamental to both business as well as one's personal relationships. Harvey Goldstein, six-term president of the American Chamber of Commerce in Indonesia, observes: "Business deals are not so much based on carefully crafted legal documents (though these are certainly drawn up) as they are on the relationships and bonds of trust that arise between partners in a venture... Eschewing litigation, the Indonesians prefer to solve disputes through what they term *musyawarah* and *mufakat*, deliberation and consensus."

Indonesia has been described as a face-to-face society, where courtesy calls on business counterparts can help to cement a working relationship. Indonesians prefer personal contacts to the hassles of written communication. Faxes and letters may go unanswered without a telephone call or personal visit.

Doing business in Indonesia is a lot about connections. Wherever possible, try to start at the top and work your way down through the rest of the business groups or personalities.

Tied to the concept of hierarchy are a number of other face-giving or face-saving contortions. Senior levels of the hierarchy, for example, demand respect. It would not do for them to deal directly with a person of a lower hierarchy or a foreigner. Thus, it is usual for a go-between or middleman to be used for such negotiations. This traditional practice is important in facilitating business transactions.

The terms *Bapak* (or *Pak*) and *Ibu*, meaning Sir and Madam, are universally applicable in Indonesia and are used to address business counterparts.

It is customary to exchange business cards on introduction. Titles and position should be clearly stated, as Indonesians accord due respect to people in senior positions. Indonesians offer their business cards with their right hand or with both hands to be polite. The use of the left hand to give or receive is taboo.

Handshaking is customary for both men and women on introduction. Drinks are usually served for business guests, but one should not reach for the drink until the host gestures to do so. You also have to observe the formalities until your Indonesian counterpart gives the lead to be more relaxed.

Be neat, clean and fairly careful about what you wear, as Indonesians are conservative. Office or business attire for men is usually a lightweight shirt and slacks. A tie and a jacket may be worn on official meetings or functions. Long-sleeved batik shirts are an acceptable alternative as formal wear. Women may wear anything so long as it is modest.

Dealing with Indonesians requires patience and endurance, as most business in Indonesia will take far longer than hoped or planned. Indonesians have a more elastic concept of time – rubber time or *jam karet*. Your Indonesian counterpart may arrive half-an-hour late for an appointment, but he or she would expect you to be punctual. This elasticity stretches beyond the meeting itself.

A businessperson may come to Indonesia with something to offer, but may not find the right person to discuss it with, and no one will tell him or her that they are dealing with the wrong person.

Planning The Trip

Electricity

Electricity in Indonesia is at 50 Hz, and usually 220 volts, although 110 volts is sometimes found.

Entry Regulations

Visas & Passports

All travelers to Indonesia must be in possession of a passport valid for at least six months after arrival and with proof (tickets) of onward passage. Many nationalities do not require a visa prior to arrival; for those that do, tourist visas can be easily obtained from any Indonesian embassy or consulate.

There are some restrictions on the entry and exit points in Indonesia, so it best to check this with the nearest Indonesian embassy or consulate.

Each visitor is required to pay an airport tax of Rp 21,000 for international departures; and an average of Rp 8,000 for domestic flights depending on the airport of departure.

Surat jalan: A *surat jalan* is a letter from the police permitting the bearer to go to certain places. It is advisable to carry one when traveling in some of the outer islands, such as Irian Jaya. If in doubt, check with a good travel agent or else with an Indonesian embassy. In Jakarta, a surat jalan may be obtained in an hour or two at Police Headquarters, or *Markas Besar Kepolisian Republik Indonesia,* on Jalan Trunojoyo (Kebayoran Baru).

Health

Yellow fever vaccinations are required if you arrive within six days of leaving or passing through an infected area. It is also advisable to be vaccinated against cholera, typhoid and paratyphoid.

If intending to stay in Indonesia for sometime, particularly outside of the big cities, gamma-globulin injections are recommended; they won't stop hepatitis, but many physicians believe that the risk of infection is greatly reduced. Diarrhoea may be a problem; it can be prevented by a daily dose of doxycycline, an antibiotic used to prevent "traveler diarrhoea". Obtain this from your doctor. At the first signs of stomach discomfort, try a diet of hot tea and a little patience. Stomach upsets are often a reaction to a change in food and environment. Proprietary brands of tablets such as Lomotil and Imodium are invaluable but temporary solutions, best taken only while on public transport, or where toilet facilities are lacking. Malaria prophylactics are increasingly questionable; strains are developing in Southeast Asia that are resistant to most medications. Consult your physician. Minimize contact with mosquitoes with repellent; as mosquitoes are most active around dawn and dusk, wear long-sleeved shirts and long pants at these times.

Outside of the best hotels, all water, including well water, municipal water and water used for making ice, MUST be made safe before consumption. Bringing water to a rolling boil for 10 minutes is an effective method. Iodine (Globoline) and chlorine (Halazone) may also be used to make water potable. All fruit should be carefully peeled before eaten and no raw vegetables should be eaten.

Protect yourself against the sun *and* the heat. Tanning oils and creams are expensive in Indonesia. Drink more water than you think you'll need. For, indeed, you'll need it unless thoroughly acclimated.

Security

Jakarta is certainly safer, on the whole, than most European or North American cities. There are the usual pickpockets in crowded areas, thieves in cheap hotels, and the occasional scam artist. But one can find these anywhere. Simply follow the precautions that one would take elsewhere, and don't fret.

Women who fail to dress modestly, especially outside of urban areas, can expect problems. Indonesia is primarily Muslim, and women with bare legs and minimal tops are considered to be lacking in respect for both themselves and Indonesian morals and expectations. Dressed in what Muslims consider an immodest fashion, and women can expect to be harassed and treated with little respect. Similarly, beach nudity is not permitted, although the beaches of Bali increasingly flaunt this local norm.

Show respect for Indonesian sensibilities. This is their home.

Money Matters

Changing Money

Foreign currency, in bank notes and traveler's checks, is best exchanged at major banks or leading hotels (though hotel rates are slightly less favorable than bank rates). There are also registered money changers who offer fair rates, but avoid unauthorized changers who operate illegally. There is no gain in using them; a black market in money changing is nonexistent. Banks in many smaller towns are not necessarily conversant with all foreign bank notes, so it is advisable to change most currencies in the cities. Rupiah may be freely converted to foreign currencies when leaving.

Rupiahs come in bank note denominations of 50,000; 20,000; 10,000; 5,000; 1,000; 500 and 100. Coins come in 1,000, 500, 100, 50, 25, 10 and 5 rupiahs.

Traveler's checks

Traveler's checks are a mixed blessing. Major hotels, banks and some shops will accept them, but even in the cities, it can take a long time to collect money (in small towns, it is impossible). The US dollar is recommended for traveler's checks. Credit cards are usable in the big hotels, International airline offices, city restaurants and shops. Don't count on using them in the hinterlands.

Getting There

By Air

Coming from outside the Indonesian archipelago, arrival is at two main airports: Soekarno–Hatta International Airport, 20 km (13 mi) west of Jakarta, or Ngurah Rai Airport, near Denpasar on Bali, and with connecting flights to Yogyakarta. The government has announced that nearly two dozen more airports will eventually serve as international gateways, but most of them are only able to accommodate smaller jets, not jumbo jets.

A highway links Soekarno–Hatta airport with Jakarta. Buses operate at regular intervals to Gambir – itself the location of a railway station and only a few minutes by road from the city.

A majority of visitors arrive in Jakarta from Singapore. Garuda, Merpati, Sempati and Singapore Airlines have multiple daily flights between the two destinations. Other flights from within the region include daily flights from Kuala Lumpur in Malaysia on Garuda and MAS, as well as flights from Penang and Kuala Lumpur on Sempati. Flights from Hong Kong are served by Garuda and Cathay Pacific. Thai International and Royal Brunei fly from their home capitals to Bali. There are flights from Japan on Garuda and from Taiwan on Garuda, Sempati and EVA Air. In Australia, Qantas and Garuda fly from Perth, Sydney, Melbourne, Cairns and Adelaide; Merpati from Darwin and Port Hedland and Sempati from Perth.

In an effort to increase tourism, Indonesia is actively trying to expand air links, now offering landing rights without the necessity of reciprocal arrangements to some airlines. Service to the archipelago should continually improve in the future.

Departure and Arrival Information
Soekarno-Hatta Int'l Airport
Tel: (021) 550-5307–9

By Sea

If you're one of the lucky ones with plenty of time (and money), an ocean cruise to Indonesia should not be missed. Luxury cruise lines offer fly/cruise arrangements that allow you to fly to Bali and other ports, then catch a ship on the way home, or vice versa. Contact a travel agent to see who is presently offering Indonesia as part of their itinerary.

If traveling with the footloose budget travelers, you can hop on a motor launch leaving Finger Pier, Prince Edward Road, in Singapore for Tanjung Pinang, where you can catch one of PELNI's (Indonesia's national shipping line) several passenger ships serving Indonesia's main ports. Check at Finger Pier in the morning for schedules and tickets. Packages are also available from tour agencies that include the boat ride from Singapore, the transfer from Tanjung Pinang to the PELNI ship by sampan, and accommodation on board according to the class booked. Food and drinks can be purchased on board but may be costly. It is an unforgettable two-day trip across the Java Sea. It is advisable to leave Singapore two days before the ship departs and spend time on Tanjung Pinang. Cabins must be booked one to two weeks in advance. Deck class can be obtained at short notice.

Domestic Air Travel

Indonesia, for those who can afford it, is aviation country. The national carrier, Garuda, serves both international and domestic routes. Garuda also offers an air-pass program that makes domestic flights cheaper, overall. Merpati and Sempati also offer regular services to a multitude of destinations within Indonesia. Merpati and Sempati are particularly useful, serving the smaller islands and more remote destinations. Besides Garuda and Merpati, there are also several privately-owned airlines with both scheduled and charter services. Rides with missionary planes can sometimes also be arranged for reasonable fees.

Water Transport

PELNI, the state-owned shipping company, serves about 30 ports in 20 of Indonesia's 27 provinces with six ships. Each is built to accommodate 1,000 to 1,500 passengers in four classes; they are comfortable but not luxurious.

For information and sailing schedules in Jakarta, contact the PELNI office at Jl. Gajah Mada 14, Jakarta 10130. Tel: (021) 343-307, Fax: 381-0341, 345-605 or the sales office at Jl. Angkasa 18. Tel: 421-1921, Fax: 421-1929. In Bali, the sales office is at Jl. Pelabuhan Benoa, Denpasar. Tel: 38-962, Fax: 28-962.

For a more luxurious cruise, **P&O** offers an island-hopping cruise that includes stops at Bali, Lombok, Sumbawa, Komodo, Flores, Lembata, Timor, Sawu and Sumba, as well as a volcanoes-and-wildlife cruise. Contact P&O Spice Islands Cruises, Jl. S. Parman, Slipi, Jakarta. Tel: 567-3401. From Bali, the **Bali Hai** makes stops at Bali, Nusa Lembongan and Nusa Penida. Other international companies (like the floating Club Med) offer cruises within Indonesia from time to time. Contact a travel agent for more details.

For the more adventurous, the **Indonesian Sea Safaris** (Tel: (65) 337-4836, Fax: 337-4904 in Singapore) offers a cruise through the Spice Islands on a 31-meter, traditional Buginese sailing schooner.

There are also regular ferries between the islands, but these tend to be a bit rough.

Useful Addresses

Tourism Promotion Board

Bank Pacific Building 9F, 8 Jalan Jenderal Sudirman, Jakarta 10220. Tel: (021) 570-4879/4917, Fax: (021) 570-4855.

Indonesia Tourist Offices

Australia: Indonesia Tourist Promotion Office, c/o Garuda Indonesia, 4 Bligh Street, P.O. Box 3836, Sydney 2000. Tel: 334-9944, Fax: 233-2828.

Germany: Indonesia Tourist Promotion Office for Europe, Wiessenhuttenstasse 17, D. 6000, Frankfurt/Main 1 Germany. Tel: (069) 233-677, Fax: 230-840.

Singapore: Indonesia Tourist Promotion Office for ASEAN, 10 Collyer Quay, #15-07, Ocean Building, Singapore 0104. Tel: 534-2837, Fax: 533-4287.

Taiwan: Indonesia Tourist Promotion Office for Taiwan and Hong Kong, 5th Floor, 66 Sung Chiang Road, Taipei, Taiwan ROC. Tel: (02) 537-7620, Fax: 537-7621.

United Kingdom: Indonesia Tourist Promotion Office for UK, Benelux and Scandinavia, 34 Hanover Street, London WIR 9 HH, UK. Tel: (0171) 493-0334, Fax: 493-1747.

United States: Indonesia Tourist Promotion Office for North America, 3457 Wilshire Boulevard, Los Angeles, California 90010, USA. Tel: (213) 387-2078, Fax: 380-4876.

International Airline Offices

Air New Zealand, Chase Plaza, Jl. Jend. Sudirman Kav 21, Jakarta Selatan. Tel: 570-4024, Fax: 570-3439.

British Airways, 10th Floor, World Trade Center, Jl. Jend. Sudirman, Kav. 29-31, Jakarta 12910. Tel: 521-1500/1490, Fax: 521-1494.

Cathay Pacific, Borobudur Intercontinental, Jl. Lapangan Banteng Selatan, Jakarta 10710. Tel: 515-0777/1747/2747, 380-6660, Fax: 380-6533.

China, M1 Floor, Wisma Dharmala Sakti, Jl. Jend. Sudirman 28, Jakarta 12920. Tel: 251-0790/0789, 521-2211.

EVA Air, 10th Floor, Price Waterhouse Center, Jl. H.R. Rasuan Said, Kav. 3, Kuningan, Jakarta Selatan. Tel: 520-5808, Fax: 520-5828.

Garuda, BDN Building, Jl. M.H. Thamrin, 5. Tel: 230-0925/0892; Wisma Dharmala Sakti, Jl. Jend. Sudirman. Tel: 251-2229/2286/2242/0577; Borobudur Intercontinental, Jl. Lapangan Banteng. Tel: 231-0023/0339/1991; Hotel Indonesia, Jl. M.H. Thamrin. Tel: 230-0568/0356.

Japan, Ground Floor, Mid Plaza, Jl. Jend. Sudirman Kav 10-11, Jakarta Pusat. Tel: 572-3211/3226, 570-3169.

KLM, Plaza Indonesia, Jl. M. H. Thamrin, Jakarta Pusat. Tel: 310-7666, 252-6730/6735, Fax: 336-636.

Korean, Wisma Bank Dharmala, Jl. Jend Sudirman Kav 28, Jakarta 12920. Tel: 521-2211/2180.

Lufthansa, 2nd Floor, Panin Center Building, Jl. Jend. Sudirman 1, Jakarta Pusat. Tel: 570-2005, 739-6767, Fax: 571-1476.

Malaysian (MAS), Hotel Indonesia, Jl. M.H. Thamrin, Jakarta Pusat. Tel: 320-909, 522-9682/9690/9701.

Philippines, Borobudur Intercontinental, Jl. Lapangan Banteng Seletan, Jakarta 10710. Tel: 380-5555, 526-7780/7784.

Qantas, BDN Building, Jl. M.H. Thamrin 5, Jakarta Pusat. Tel: 327-707, 230-0277/0702/0866 Fax: 310-5788, 326-707.

Singapore, Chase Plaza, Jl. Jend. Sudirman, Jakarta 12910. Tel: 570-4411, 520-6899/6933.
Thai, BDN Building, Jl. M.H. Thamrin, Jakarta Pusat. Tel: 320-607, 314-0607.

Domestic Airline Offices

Bouraq, Jl. Angkasa 1-3. Tel: 659-5179/5194.
Garuda, BDN Building, Jl. M.H. Thamrin 5. Tel: 570-6105/6155.
Mandala, Jl. Veteran 1/34. Tel: 368-107.
Merpati, Jl. Angkasa 2. Tel: 424-3608.
Sempati Air Jl. Merdeka Timur 7. Tel: 231-1612, 384-8760.

Diplomatic Missions In Jakarta

Australia, Jl. H. R. Rasuna Said Kav C. Tel: 522-7035.
Austria, Jl. P. Diponegoro 44. Tel: 338-090, 338-101.
Belgium, 15th Floor, Wisma BCA, Jl. Jend. Sudirman Kav 22-23. Tel: 571-0510.
Burma (Myanmar), Jl. H. Agus Salim 109. Tel: 320-440, 327-684.
Canada, Jl. Jend. Surdirman, Kav. 29, d/a Wisma Metropolitan I, 1st–5th Floor Tel: 510-709.
China, 26 Jl. Jenderal Sudirman Kav 69. Tel: 714-596.
Denmark, Jl. H.R. Rasuna Said Kav. 10, d/a Bina Mulya Building, 4th Floor Tel: 520-4350.
Finland, Jl. H.R. Rasuna Said Kav. 10, d/a Bina Mulya Building, 10th Floor Tel: 516-980.
France, Jl. M.H. Thamrin 20. Tel: 332-807.
Germany, Jl. M.H. Thamrin 1. Tel: 323-908.
Great Britain, Jl. M.H. Thamrin 75. Tel: 330-904, 310-4229 (Answer phone).
India, Jl. H.R. Rasuna Said 51, Kuningan. Tel: 520-4150.
Italy, Jl. Diponegoro 45. Tel: 337-445.
Japan, Jl. M.H. Thamrin 24. Tel: 324-308.
Korea, South, Jl. Jend. Gatot Subroto, Kav. 57-58. Tel: 520-1915.
Malaysia, Jl. H.R. Rasuna Said, Kav. X-6. Tel: 522-4947.
Netherlands, Jl. H.R. Rasuna Said, Kav. S-3, Kuningan. Tel: 511-515.
New Zealand, Jl. P. Diponegoro 41. Tel: 330-680.
Norway, Jl. H.R. Rasuna Said Kav. 10, d/a Bina Mulya Building, 4th Floor. Tel: 511-990.
Pakistan, Jl. Teuku Umar 50. Tel: 310-4011, 310-4008.
Philippines, Jl. Imam Bonjol 6-8. Tel: 348-8917.
Singapore, Jl. H.R. Rasuna Said, Block X, Kav. 2/4. Tel: 520-1489.
Spain, Jl. Agus Salim 61. Tel: 335-771, 335-937.
Sweden, Bina Mulia Building 1, 7th Floor, Jl. H.R. Rasuna Said, Kav. 10. Tel: 520-1551/3.
Switzerland, Jl. H.R. Rasuan Said, Block 1, Kav. X/3. Tel: 520-7451.
Thailand, Jl. Imam Bonjol 74. Tel: 390-4225.
United States of America, Jl. Medan Merdeka Selatan 5. Tel: 360-360.
Vietnam, Jl. Teuku Umar 25. Tel: 310-0357/8/9.

Hospitals in Jakarta

The following hospitals and clinics are popular with expatriates living in Jakarta and Indonesia. They will have staff that can handle problems in English.
S.O.S. Medika (**AEA Int'l Clinic**), Jl. Puri Sakti 10, Cipete, Jakarta, Tel: (021) 750-6001.
Medical Scheme, Setiabudi Bldg. 11, Jl. H.R. Rasuna Said, Jakarta, Tel: (021) 525-5367.
Medikaloka, Jl. H.R. Rasuna Said, Times Square Bldg., Kuningan, Jakarta, Tel: (021) 526-1118.
Pondok Indak Hospital, Jl. Metro Duta Kav. UE, Jakarta. Tel: (021) 750-2322.

Health Info Hotline: (0900–1200 MWF) Tel: (021) 754-5486/5488 ext. 1424.
Ambulance service (SOS Medika): (021) 750-6001.

Practical Tips

Business Hours

Government offices are open from 8am to 3pm, close at 11.30am on Fridays. On Saturdays, they are often open until around 2pm. **Business** offices are open from between 8 or 9am, until 4 or 5pm. Some companies work Saturday mornings, as well. **Banks** are open from 8am until 3pm on weekdays, and sometimes on Saturday mornings. Foreign banks are closed on Saturdays.

Media

Surprisingly, there is a wealth of English-language publications available in Indonesia, especially in Jakarta. There are three English-language daily newspapers: *The Jakarta Post, Indonesian Observer,* and *Indonesia Times.* In addition, most international newspapers – English-language and others – are available in hotel newsstands. Business magazines published in English include *Indonesia Business Weekly, Economic Business Review Indonesia, Indonesian Quarterly,* and *Products & Industry.*

Several publications with listings of city events and restaurants are available, including *Jakarta Now* and *What's On.* These are usually available in hotels and other tourist-related locations.

Television is everywhere, even in the most remote locations, offering both Indonesian television channels and, via satellite, Star TV, CNN, Asia Business News, CNBC, HBO, ESPN, Discovery and on and on.

Telecoms

Telephone service is rapidly being modernized and overhauled, particularly in urban areas. As the phone system is brought into the 21st century, however, **telephone numbers are often changed**, especially in Jakarta and other urban areas.

If a number listed in this guide doesn't work, most probably it has been upgraded – and changed. (Between 1994 and 1999, five million telephone lines are slated to be installed – an ambitious target considering that only 900,000 lines were installed between 1968 and 1988.)

Moreover, most hotels have several different telephone lines, obtained at different times – in Jakarta, some of them are six digits, others seven digits. Thus, comparisons of listings never seem to match one another. The telephone and fax numbers in this book are as accurate as possible, but they may have changed – or will change one day.

Hotels offer IDD service, with the usual surcharges. Public telephones often accept convenient telephone cards (these phones seem to work better than coin phones) and international calls can be made at a number of exchanges.

HOME COUNTRY DIRECT DIAL

In general, dial 001 801, followed by your country's area code.

Australia (Optus) 001 801 0611
Australia (Telstra) 001 801 61
Canada 001 801 16
Denmark 001 801 45
France 001 801 331
Germany 001 801 49
Italy 001 801 39
Malaysia 001 801 60
Netherlands 001 801 31
New Zealand 001 801 64
Singapore 001 801 65
UK (BT) 001 801 44
UK (Mercury) 001 801 0441
USA (AT&T) 001 801 10
USA (Sprint) 001 801 15
USA (MCI) 001 801 11

Indonesia's country code: 62

Domestic Area Codes

Jakarta 021
Ambon 0911
Balikpapan 0542
Banda Aceh 0651
Bandung 022
Bogor 0251
Denpasar 0361
Dili 0390
Jayapura 0967
Manado 0431
Medan 061
Padang 0751
Palembang 0711
Parapat 0625
Sanur 0361
Surakarta (Solo) 0271
Surabaya 031
Ternate 0921
Wamena 0969
Yogyakarta 0274

Attractions

Suggested Itineraries

For those with limited time to spend in Indonesia, below are some suggested itineraries that can be done solo, or with a group through a tour agent.

Bali (4 days)

Day 1: Morning departure from Jakarta to Denpasar.

Day 2: Full-day excursion. Barong dance, where good fights evil in an ancient Ramayana story. Then to Mas, the village of the woodcarvers; to Ubud, where many well-known painters live; to Tampaksiring with its holy springs and the elephant cave temple. Visit Kintamani with its beautiful view of Gunung Batur and its lake.

Day 3: Excursion along the East Coast. Visit the Palace of Justice in Klungkung, the temples of Besakih on Gunung Agung (the highest and most holy volcano of Bali), the Bat Cave Temple and the Bay of Padang.

Day 4: Leisure. Return to Jakarta.

Excursions In Bali

Full day: See the colorful *barong* and *kris* dances, then drive to Tegal Tamu, center of the sandstone sculpturing; Celuk, silver-and-gold village; Mas, famous for its wood carvings; the ancient elephant cave at Bedulu; the rice terraces at Gunung Kawi; the Tampaksiring holy springs and the breathtaking view of the semi-active volcano of Gunung Batur.

Full day: Excursion along the East Coast. Visit the Palace of Justice in Klungkung, the temples of Besakih on Gunung Agung (the highest and most holy volcano of Bali). Visit the Bat Cave Temple and the Bay of Padang.

Half-day sailing tour: Join a large sailing vessel around the harbor, then visit the village of Tandjung and Turtle Island if the tide permits, dropping anchor for swimming, snorkelling, sunbathing or fishing.

Bali Diving Tour (6 days)

Day 1: Arrive in Denpasar.

Day 2: Early morning, coach to Padang Bay, to start with the first dive around Gili Tepekong island group.

Day 3: After breakfast, coach to Tulamben, on the eastern tip of the island. Shore as well as boat dives can be done. In the afternoon, drive westward along the northern road to Teluk Terima. Overnight.

Day 4: After breakfast, enjoy a drive around Menjangan island group, with large numbers of fish.

Day 5: After breakfast, Tabuhan island group is the destination. Coral reefs, tropical fish and shark sites are the main diving draws.

Day 6: After breakfast, a chance to have another dive, in a different location, yet still around the island group. In the afternoon, drive to Denpasar.

Lombok (3 days)

Day 1: Arrive in Lombok. Stroll through the streets and markets of Cakranegara and Ampenan.

Day 2: Visit the main market of Cakranegara, with its bird market, then on to Getap, a village where knives are made and horseshoes fitted. Proceed to the weaving village of Sukarasa. From Praya, the capital of central Lombok, through the flat rice fields to Nyale Beach. On the return trip, visit a typical Sasak village.

Day 3: Early afternoon, return by air or ferry to Bali.

Pulau Komodo (4 days)

This tour is typically arranged from Denpasar or Jakarta.

Day 1: By air to Lombok. Overnight.

Day 2: Fly to Bima in early morning, transfer by public transport to the town. Leave by road for Sape, about 2 hours away. Due to the strong current, the crossing can only be made at night. After dinner, leave by boat for an 8-hour trip to Komodo.

Day 3: Early morning arrival in Komodo. Pay respect (and money) to the village head. Walk to Waing Galung to watch the giant lizards. Picnic lunch, brought from Bali. Return to Komodo. Dinner on board boat.

Day 4: Arrive after midnight. Breakfast on board, do not miss the beautiful sunrise at 4.30am. Drive to Bima. Rest at the Hotel Komodo. Afternoon

visit to town by pony cart. Then watch the sunset at Bima Beach. Overnight.
Day 5: Return to Denpasar via Lombok.

Yogyakarta-Bali (5 days)

Day 1: Arrive Yogyakarta.
Day 2: Morning excursion to Borobudur, a Buddhist temple dating from the eighth century. En route visit temples of Mendut and Pawon. Afternoon, a look at some of the art and culture for which Yogya is famous.
Day 3: Morning at leisure. Early afternoon flight to Denpasar.
Day 4: Full-day excursion to Mas, the village of the woodcarvers, and then Ubud, where many well-known painters live; to Tampaksiring with its holy springs and the elephant cave. Finally, visit Kintamani with its beautiful view of Gunung Batur and its lake.
Day 5: Afternoon return to Jakarta.

Bali to Jakarta (10 days)

Day 1: Bali–Tretes. Early departure for Gilimanuk to take the ferry to Java, then travel along the northern coast to Tretes, in the mountains of East Java.
Day 2: Afternoon visit to Surabaya, Indonesia's second-largest city. City sightseeing, including a visit to the zoo to view a Komodo dragon. Return to Tretes.
Day 3: Tretes–Yogyakarta. Drive through the Javanese countryside with a stop for lunch. Prior to arriving at Yogyakarta, visit Prambanan.
Day 4: Visit batik factory, the Sultan's Palace, Water Castle and a silver workshop.
Day 5: Yogyakarta. Shopping, relaxation or sightseeing.
Day 6: Yogyakarta–Batu Raden. In the morning, leave Yogyakarta to visit Borobudur, the magnificent Buddhist temple complex. Overnight in Batu Raden.
Day 7: Batu Raden–Bandung. Continue along the delightful scenic route, with regular stops, and visit the village of Naga, where the villagers have retained their traditional ways. Overnight in Bandung.
Day 8: Tangkuban. Excursion into the countryside to visit Tangkuban Prahu, and the active volcano. Assisted by guides to the crater. Visit a nearby hot spring before lunch. In the afternoon, return to Bandung.
Day 9: Bandung–Jakarta. In the morning, drive down from the highlands to Bogor. Lunch, and visit the famous Botanical Gardens.
Day 10: Jakarta. Readjust to life.

Medan–Danau Toba (4 days)

Day 1: Arrival in Prapat by bus. En route to Prapat, panoramic view of Danau Toba. Overnight in Prapat.
Day 2: After breakfast, embark launch for cruise on Danau Toba to visit Ambarita and Tomok on Samosir Island, to see the original home of the Batak people and the tombs of Batak King Sidabutar. Back to Prapat, shopping. Overnight in Prapat.
Day 3: Depart for Medan. After lunch, city tour visiting the Palace of Sultan Deli, Mesjid Raya and shopping at Jl. A. Yani. Overnight in Medan.
Day 4: Depart.

Torajaland (5 days)

Day 1: After arrival in Ujung Pandang, drive directly through the typical Bugis and Makassarese villages, fish farms, and rice fields to Tana Toraja. Lunch in Parepare. Break with fresh fruits in Kotu Enrekang. Arrival in Tana Toraja in the late afternoon. Overnight.
Day 2: Tour Toraja villages, the grave caves at Marante, the hanging grave of Lemo, the old Toraja village at Palawa. Also visit the handicraft center and souvenir shops at Kete.
Day 3: Full-day tour to explore Batutumonga, Lemo and Loko' mata, and to the most scenic rice terraces in Indonesia. Visit the typical Toraja market and the ancient grave of Londa. Art-carving houses in Siguntu and Manggala.
Day 4: Return to Ujung Pandang. Stop at the beach in Lumpue. Overnight in Ujung Pandang.
Day 5: Morning sightseeing in old Makassar, Port Rotterdam and the museum. See the harbor from where the Bugis sail to all islands of Indonesia. Orchids garden and seashell collection.

Nature Reserves/Nat'l Parks

Indonesia has been ahead of most of the world in preserving its natural wonders. In fact, 10 percent of its land area is under protection. The range of protected areas extends from volcanoes to orangutan habitats and coral reefs, nearly 200 reserves and parks.

Nevertheless, understaffing and aggressive loggers threaten many of the parks.

Local porters can be hired and park guards may often accompany visitors as guides. They should be tipped, plus reimbursed expenses. To avoid misunderstandings, it is advisable to negotiate fees clearly before setting out.

The listing below, though not comprehensive, covers some of Indonesia's finest reserves and parks.

Java

Ujung Kulon: At Java's western tip, Ujung Kulon is Indonesia's first and premier reserve. You will have to be lucky to see one of the park's 60 remaining Javan rhinos, but there are many other fascinating animals, including leopards, gibbons, long-tailed macaques, leaf monkeys, crocodiles, muntjaks, mouse deer and herds of grazing wild oxen (*banteng*).

There are two types of accommodation available: most visitors stay at the guesthouses on Peucang Island, but its also worthwhile to stop over for a night or two at the older guesthouse on Handeleum Island to visit the Cigenter River, a favorite rhino haunt just across the strait. Bedding, furniture and cooking facilities are provided at both guesthouses, but you must bring your own food.

Ujung Kulon is accessible by motorbike track from Labuan via Sumur to Taman Jaya, where the park headquarters is located (about a six-hour ride). From here, it is a leisurely two-day ride to Kalejetan and Peucang Island via the south coast. Or else charter a boat from Labuan directly to Peucang or Handeleum, a five-hour voyage each way. While there, visit the volcanic island of Krakatau, 40 kilometers (25 mi) northwest of Labuan, in the middle of the Sunda Straits separating Java from Sumatra.

Cibodas/Gede and Pangranggo: A spectacular mountain reserve just two hours south of Jakarta, long the main Bogor–Bandung road. The well laid-out Cibodas Botanic Gardens are an extension of the Bogor Gardens, specializing in sub-montane, montane and alpine species. From the garden, climb to the summit of Mt Gede (5 to 6 hours each way), passing through several interesting vegetation zones, including alpine meadows and thickets of Javan edelweiss near the peak. About halfway up, there is a side trail leading to the Cibeureum waterfall, where leaf monkeys and rare Javan gibbons are often spotted. The surrounding forest is rich in bird species. To witness the spectacular sunrise, camp overnight at a hut in the saddle between Mt Gede and Mt Pangranggo and climb the final stretch just before dawn. Excellent accommodation can be had in the Botanic Gardens, and also at nearby Cipanas, a weekend mountain resort.

Bromo-Tengger: A volcanic area of incredible scenic beauty, about four hours from Surabaya in eastern Java. There are several lodges and restaurants, with guides and horses for hire at the top. Descend on horseback into the Tengger caldera and climb a flight of steps to the summit of Mt Bromo to watch the sun rise over the sea, or simply watch the sunrise from the caldera's edge. Bring warm clothing.

Baluran: located at the northeastern tip of Java, four hours from Denpasar (including the ferry crossing). Report first to the PHPA office in Banyuwangi, eight kilometers (5 mi) south of the ferry. This reserve, with its monsoon forests, acacia bushes and open grasslands, and dominated by the volcanic cone of Mt Baluran, reminds one of Africa. There is a guesthouse and a lookout tower at Bekol, with marvelous views over grazing lands where herds of banteng, feral buffalo and deer feed. Along the coast are nice beaches and mangroves, where mudskippers can be seen.

Bali and Nusa Tenggara

Bali Barat: lies in the western part of Bali, with temporary accommodations and a guard post at Terima Bay, 20 kilometers (12 mi) east of the ferry terminal at Gilimanuk. This is the last refuge of the endangered Rothschild's starling and of wild oxen. The marine portion of the reserve around Terima Bay and neighboring Menjangan Island has some spectacular reefs, particularly on Menjangan's north shore, and there are no strong currents with which to contend. There is a shelter for divers on Menjangan Island's western tip; more facilities are planned.

Komodo: located between Flores and Sumbawa, offers the ultimate thrill for naturalists – the Komodo dragons, latter-day relatives of dinosaurs, in their arid and natural habitat. Although the park is now being developed as a tourist attraction, access is still complicated.

Sumatra

Mt Leuser: Contains some of Sumatra's most spectacular forest, centering around the Alas River Valley on the western side of northern Sumatra. Orangutans, Sumatran rhinos, gibbons, leaf monkeys, macaques, elephants, tigers, and countless other animals, birds, butterflies and plants are found in the park. For a day-trip from Medan, visit the Bohorok Orangutan Rehabilitation Center near Bukit Lawang (two hours from Medan via Binjai), where confiscated pet orangutan are encouraged to return to the wild. Visitors with permits are welcome at feeding times.

Way Kambas: located on Sumatra's southeast coast, only a few hours' journey from Jakarta. Though much of the original swamp forest has been felled and replaced by open grassland, this is the best place to see wild elephants. The reserve is packed with interesting animals – gibbons, tapir, leaf-monkeys, macaques, otters and many birds. Fly from Jakarta to Tanjung Karang, or take the Merak-Bakauheni ferry, report to the PHPA office at Tanjung Karang, then drive via Sukadana right to the reserve guest house at Way Kanan. Hire canoes to explore the river, or travel to the estuary of the Kambas River, with its sand spit and fishing village, or visit the swamps and mud flats at Wako, where elephants graze and shore birds feed.

Kalimantan

Mt Palung: Offers a complete range of rain forest vegetation types, including mangrove and swamp forests. It also offers a chance to see orangutan, gibbons and the silver and red proboscis monkeys found only on this island. Check in with the PHPA office in Pontianak and travel south by boat from Pontianak to Melanu Bay. Here, charter a river barge for the four-hour journey up river to a point where you can walk up Mt Palung for a closer look at the rain forest.

Tanjung Puting: On the south coast of Kalimantan, remote but accessible. At the northern end of the reserve lies Camp Leakey, a research station and orangutan rehabilitation center with a guesthouse and a network of forest trails. See orangutans, gibbons, macaques and crocodiles. Fly first to Pangkalanbun via Banjarmasin and check here with the PHPA office. From here travel by road 15 kilometers (9 mi) to Kumai and by boat (about three hours) to Camp Leakey. Bring your own provisions and allow at least four days from Banjarmasin.

Sulawesi

Tankoko-Batuangus-Dua Saudara: In northeastern Sulawesi, the most convenient place to see a cross-section of Sulawesi's most unique animal species: crested macaques, tarsiers, cuscus, anoas and maleo birds, all in a geologically interesting area of volcanic craters and hot springs. Travel by road to Bitung, a port town about one hour to the east. Hire a boat from Bitung up the coast to Batuputih village, 25 kilometers (15 mi) away, on the reserve's northern fringe. Stay at the nearby guest bungalow. Bring your own food and spend several days walking the reserve.

Mt Ambang: A picturesque region of mountain forests, crater lakes and sulphur fumaroles (hot mud pools) at an altitude of between 1,100 and 1,800 meters above sea level. There are many well-used paths through the forests, which are filled with lovely tree ferns. Pigafetta palms and flowering shrubs. Stay in Kotamobagu (two hours by bus from Manado) and make day hikes to the beautiful crater lakes – Moaat, Alia and Payapaya – and throughout the surrounding coffee plantations.

Lore Lindu: The largest reserve at 2,500 square kilometers (970 sq mi) in Sulawesi, located only a few hours south of Palu, the provincial capital of Central Sulawesi. Lore Lindu has it all: high, heavily-forested mountains and a large highland lake (Danau Lindu) in the north; and gently sloping open grasslands, home of the interesting Torajan peoples in the southern valleys. See black macaques and many birds, perhaps also *anoa* (dwarf buffalo) and wild babirusa pigs.

Depending upon whether you want to see the northern mountains or the southern valleys, travel to Sidaunta on the western side of the park, or Wuasa on the eastern side, both about three hours by good roads from Palu. Bring along camping gear and provisions, and hire porters/guides to camp at many excellent sites along the rivers of the area. At least a week is needed to explore the southern valleys of Besoa and Bada (where there are ancient megaliths and water cisterns), but it is possible to cross from Sidaunta to Wuasa via Danau Lindu in two or three days.

Places

Jakarta

There are many "musts" in Jakarta, but be forewarned about trying to do too much in one day. It is hot and the air is thick and usually polluted. Two major sights or areas of the city a day are enough. Take a siesta or a swim in between to recover from the heat. Get an early start in the cool morning hours, then get out of the noonday sun before venturing out again in the late afternoon and early evening.

Arriving In Jakarta

Air: All flights in and out of Jakarta use the **Soekarno-Hatta International Airport**, about 20 km to the west of the city. Domestic flights also use this airport.

Transportation to and from the airport by taxi is made somewhat expensive by the connecting expressway's toll. Nonetheless, taxi fare will be between US$10–15. Alternatively, hop on one of many convenient DAMRI Airport buses, which run between 0300 and 2200 from one of several strategic points in the city. The buses are air-conditioned and run every half hour between the city and airport. Cost is less than US$5. At the airport, the bus stand is in front of Arrival Terminal A.

For more information, see entry on page 330.

Sea: See entry on page 330.

Train: There are five major train stations in Jakarta, but only two serve the first-class intercity trains. **Kota Station** in the north of the city is the gateway for Central and East Java, whereas **Gambir Station** on the eastern side of Medan Merdeka serves trains bound for Bogor and Bandung.

Train tickets can be purchased on the morning of your departure from the station ticket window. Allow 1 hour to reach the Kota Station during business hours, because of the heavy traffic in that part of town. Most trains depart in the afternoon, although the Parahiangan trains to Bandung depart several times daily.

Train tickets may also be reserved at least a day in advance through hotels or travel agencies.

Gambir Station: Jl. Merdeka Timur, Tel: (021) 342-777, 352-981.

Kota Station: Jl. Station 1, Tel: (021) 679-194.

Bus: There are three bus terminals for buses operating to the west, the south, and the east of Jakarta. Buses to Sumatra and Java's west coast operate from **Grogol Terminal** on the western edge of Jakarta. Those to Bandung, Bogor and other points south operate from **Kampung Rambutan** just beyond the old Halim Airport. Those to Central and East Java operate from **Pulo Gadung Terminal**, where Jl. Bekasi Timur Raya meets Jl. Perintis Kemerdekaan. All bus terminals are connected by local city buses to the city center. Intercity buses also pick up passengers at their offices in the city, so if you know the address and don't mind getting there early and waiting on the bus, you can save the trip out to the terminal.

Mini-buses/intercity taxis: Best way to get to nearby cities like Bogor, Bandung or Cirebon. They will pick up and deliver directly to one's destination, for about the same fare as the train and slightly more than an air-conditioned bus. They do not operate directly to more distant destinations. Ask your hotel to book seats a day or more in advance.

"4848" intercity taxis, Jl. Prapatan 34. Tel: 364-488.

Media, Jl. Johan 15. Tel: 320-343.

Parahyangan, Jl. R.H. Wahid Hasyim 13. Tel: 424-0148, 420-2748/9.

City Orientation

At Jakarta's center lies **Medan Merdeka** (Freedom Square), a vast parade ground crisscrossed by broad ceremonial boulevards, with the National Monument towering in the middle. Going north, the major artery is Jl. Gajah Mada/Jl. Hayam Wuruk, two one-way roads with a canal separating them. This is the older, commercial area of town, horribly congested throughout much of the day and practically deserted at night. At the north end of this artery lies the old colonial city **Kota** and the old harbor, now both major tourist sights. To the east along the coast are **Ancol**, a sprawling entertainment complex, and Tanjung Priok, the port.

The "main street" of Jakarta is now **Jl. Thamrin/Jl. Sudirman**, which connects Medan Merdeka (the central square) with Kebayoran Baru (the satellite suburb). Many international hotels, office buildings, theaters, restaurants and nightclubs are on this boulevard. To the east of Jl. Thamrin lie the older colonial residential areas of **Menteng**, **Cikini** and **Gondangdia**, with their luxurious mansions and tidy, tree-shaded streets. **Jl. Imam Bonjol/Jl. Diponegoro** is Embassy Row, lined with many of the finest mansions in Jakarta and worth a quick drive or walk-through. Many shops, boutiques and restaurants are in this area, as is **TIM**, the arts center of Jakarta.

Telephone Numbers

Note: Jakarta's telephone system has been undergoing renovation since 1994. Many businesses have had, or will have, numbers changed. Moreover, most hotels have several different telephone lines, obtained at different times – some of them are six digits, others seven digits. Thus, comparisons of listings never seem to match one another. The numbers below are as accurate as possible, but they may have changed – or will change one day.

Police: 110
Fire: 113
Ambulance: 118
City Health Service: 119
Police Foreign Affairs: 523-4202

Jakarta City Tourist Office: Jl. Kuningan Barat No. 2, Jakarta 12710. Tel: (021) 520-5455/9671, 525-0738, Fax: 520-9677, 522-9136.

Indonesia Tourism Board: Bank Pacific Building 9F, 8 Jl. Jend. Sudirman, Jakarta 10220. Tel: (021) 570-4879/4917, Fax: 570-4855.

Visitor Information Center: Jakarta Theater Bldg. (across from Sarinah), Jl. M.H. Thamrin No. 9, Jakarta 10340. Tel: (021) 332-067, 364-093, 315-4094.

Getting Around

Taxis: By far the most practical way of getting around the city is by taxi, and fares are cheap. Cabs are available at any hotel and easily hailed on major roads. President and Bluebird are the largest and generally the most reliable companies. All taxi fares are paid by meter; don't accept a "broken" meter. Some cabbies will try and take you for a ride. It is a good idea to rent a cab by the hour if intending to make a lot of stops. Tipping is not customary, but drivers rarely have change; round off upwards to the nearest Rp 500.

Rental cars: Available with or without drivers from Avis and Hertz, or with a driver from any major hotel. Hourly or daily rates are available within the city; trips out of town are charged on a round-trip basis according to a fixed schedule.

Avis, Jl. Diponegoro 25. Tel: 314-2900, Fax: 331-845.

Hertz, Chase Plaza Podium. Tel: 332-610, 332-739.

National, Jl. M.H. Thamrin No. 10, Kartika Plaza Hotel. Tel: 333-423/425.

Bluebird Taxi, Jl. H.O.S. Cokroaminoto No. 107. Tel: 333-461/485, 325-607.

City buses: Cheap, but often crowded and sometimes dangerous as they do not stop completely when picking up and discharging passengers. Beware of pickpockets, especially during peak hours.

The orange "Metro Mini" buses have a particularly bad reputation, and it's recommended that visitors avoid them.

Hotels

Jakarta has come a long way since the 1960s, when the only international-class hotel in town was the Hotel Indonesia, built by the Japanese as a war reparation. Some of Asia's finest hotels are now found in Jakarta.

Deluxe

Aryaduta Hotel, Jl. Prapatan 44-48, Jakarta 10110. Tel: (021) 386-1234, 231-1234, Fax: 380-9900. Managed by Hyatt, located near Medan Merdeka and many key government offices and embassies. It has undergone a major renovation, and is undoubtedly one of Jakarta's best deals. Restaurants serve Indonesian, Italian (superb), Japanese, Chinese and Western food.

Borobudur Intercontinental, Jl. Lapangan Banteng Selatan, P.O. Box 1329, Jakarta. Tel: (021) 380-5555, Fax: 380-9595. Located on 23 acres of beautifully-landscaped gardens, the hotel has an Olympic-sized swimming pool; nine-hole mini golf course; tennis, badminton and squash courts; fitness club. Eight restaurants.

Grand Hyatt, Jl. M.H. Thamrin, P.O. Box 4546, Jakarta 10045. Tel: (021) 390-1234, 310-7400, Fax: 390-6426. Centrally located on Jl. Thamrin and directly above the fashionable Plaza Indonesia mall, the hotel has unquestionably the most majestic lobby in Jakarta. The lagoon-like swimming pool is expansive.

Hilton International, Jl. Gatot Subroto, P.O. Box 3315, Jakarta 10002. Tel: (021) 570-3600, Fax: 573-3089. Situated next to the Jakarta Convention Center, this locally-flavored hotel is made up of three different units – the main hotel and two towers. Nine restaurants including Japanese, Chinese, and Asian.

Le Meridien, Jl. Jend. Sudirman Kav. 18-20, Jakarta 10220. Tel: (021) 251-3131, Fax: 571-1633. Located across the boulevard from the World Trade Center, this hotel is a bit off the Jl. Thamrin, but close enough to be convenient. French, Japanese and Asian cuisine available in the five restaurants.

Mandarin Oriental, Jl. M.H. Thamrin, P.O. Box 3392, Jakarta 10301. Tel: (021) 314-1307, Fax: 314-8680. Across the street from the British Embassy, the hotel offers Italian, Chinese, Asian and Western cuisine.

Regent, Jl. H.R. Rasuna Said, Jakarta 12920. Tel: (021) 252-3456, Fax: 252-4480. Located at the northern end of the Kuningan business district. As with all Regents, this one is a pristine oasis. Restaurants offers Asian and Western dining.

Sahid Jaya, Jl. Jend. Sudirman 86, Jakarta 10220. Tel: (021) 570-4444, Fax: 573-3168. Centrally located, just off Jl. Thamrin. One of Jakarta's largest hotels. Restaurants offer Indonesian, Indian, Japanese, Chinese seafood.

Shangri-La, BNI City, Jl. Jend. Sudirman Kav. 1, Jakarta 10220. Tel: (021) 570-7440, Fax: 570-3530. This 32-story centrally-located hotel offers French, Chinese, Asian and Western restaurants and a lobby lounge.

Expensive

Citraland, Jl. S. Parman, Jakarta 11470. Tel: (021) 566-0640, Fax: 568-1616. Located midway between the airport and the downtown business district, situated atop of a large shopping mall.

Horison Hotel, Jl. Pantai Indah, Taman Impian Jaya Ancol, P.O. Box 3340, Jakarta. Tel: (031) 640-6000, Fax: 640-6123. Located in the seaside recreation area of Ancol, this hotel has everything for tourist and businessperson.

Hotel Indonesia, Jl. M.H. Thamrin, P.O. Box 1054, Jakarta 10310. Tel: (021) 230-1008, Fax: 230-1007. Indonesia's first international-standard hotel. Faces the Welcome Statue and Jl. Thamrin.

Imperial Century, Village Boulevard Central 1501, Lippo Village 1500, near Jakarta. Tel: (021) 546-0101, Fax: (021) 546-0224. About half an hour out of Jakarta in the midst of Lippo's well-planned satellite town.

Jayakarta Tower, Jl. Hayam Wuruk 126, P.O. Box 5024 JKT, Jakarta 11180. Tel: 649-6760, 629-4408, Fax: 629-3000. Situated in Kota, north Jakarta, the hotel has Cantonese seafood, Asian and Western restaurants.

Kartika Chandra, Jl. Gatot Subroto, Jakarta 12060. Tel: (021) 525-1008, Fax: 520-4238. Situated in southern Jakarta, and home to the Planet Hollywood restaurant.

Sari Pan Pacific, Jl. M.H. Thamrin, P.O. Box 3138, Jakarta 10340. Tel: (021) 390-2707, Fax: 323-650. Central location, walking distance to government ministries and embassies.

Moderate

Arcadia, Jl. K.H. Wahid Hasyim 14, P.O. Box 10340, Jakarta, 10340. Tel: (021) 315-3380, Fax: 384-6252. Interesting retro art deco design differentiates this centrally located, boutique hotel from the others.

Atlet Century Park, Jl. Pintu 1, P.O. Box 6608 JKBSI, Jakarta 10270. Tel: (021) 571-2041, Fax: 571-2191. Situated in southwest Jakarta, across from the Senayan Sports Complex.

Garden Hotel (116 rooms), Jl. Kemang Raya, P.O. Box 6741, Kebayoran Baru, Jakarta 12730. Tel: (021) 798-0760, Fax: 798-0763. Centrally located.

Laki Island Resort, Jl. H.O.S. Cokroaminoto 116, Jakarta, 10310. Tel: (021) 323-678, 314-4885, Fax: 320-496. Beach hotel on Laki Island. Air-conditioned, clean but basic chalet accommodation. Water sports.

BUDGET

Most budget lodging is centrally located around **Jalan Jaksa**, to the south of Medan Merdeka. Other streets with backpacker lodgings include Jl. Kebon Sirih Barat Dalam and Jl. Sultan Hasanuddin.

Bali International, Jl. K.H Wahid Hasyim 116, Tel: (021) 334-967, 325-067.

Borneo Hostel, Kl. Kebon Sirih Barat Dalam No. 35. Tel: (021) 320-095.

Cipta Hotel, Jl. Wahid Hasyim No. 53. Tel: (021) 390-4701. 330-424.

Djody Hostel, Jl. Jaksa No. 35. Tel: (021) 346-600.

Jusenny, Jl. Senayan Bl S3/29. Tel: (021) 720-5379.

Tambora, Jl. Sultan Hasanuddin No.70. Tel: (021) 715-771.

Wisma Delima, Jl. Jaksa No. 5. Tel: (021) 337-026.

Yannie Int'l Guest House, Jl. Raden Saleh Raya 35. Tel: (021) 320-012, Fax: 327-005.

Eating Out

Indonesian food is, of course,. the smart traveler's first choice in Jakarta, particularly as one may indulge in gastronomic island-hopping on consecutive nights.

Beginning with the northern tip of Sumatra, try the Acehnese restaurant, Sinar Medan, conveniently located on Jl. Sabang. Acehnese food is displayed and served cold on many small plates, in the same way as Padang food. But some say it is more delicately spiced, with a wider range of flavors.

The best Padang food is found at **Sari Bundo**, Jl. Ir. H. Juanda 27, Tel: 358-343. Here, as in all Padang restaurants, between 10 and 15 spicy dishes are placed in front of diners, who pay only for what is eaten. For slightly more atmosphere and a view (and higher prices), try The Pepper Pot.

Javanese cuisine may be divided into four categories: Sundanese (West Javanese), Central Javanese, East Javanese and Madurese cooking. For an excellent Sundanese meal of grilled carp (*ikan mas bakar*), grilled chicken (*ayam bakar*), prawns (*udang pancet*), barbecued squid (*cumicumi bakar*) and a raw vegetable salad with shrimp paste chili sauce (*lalap/sambal cobek*), try the popular Sari Kuring. This is, incidentally, one of the best seafood places in town, and serves a deliciously cooling cucumber-and-lime juice drink.

Central Javanese delicacies are fried chicken and *gudeg*. Javanese chickens are farmyard chickens, allowed to run free in the village. As a result, they are full of flavor but very tough in comparison with factory-fed chickens. The Javanese boil their chickens first in a concoction of rich spices and coconut cream for several hours, before deep frying them for about a minute at very high temperatures to crisp the outer coating. Two famous fried-chicken places in Jakarta are both in Kebayoran: Ayam Bulungan and Ayam Goreng Mbok Berek.

Gudeg is the specialty of Yogyakarta, consisting of young jackfruit boiled in coconut cream and spices, served with buffalo hide boiled in chili sauce, chicken pieces, and egg. The best gudeg is at Bu Tjitro's.

East Java and Madura are known for their soups and sate. For *soto madura* (spicy chicken broth with noodles or rice), the best place is **Soto Madura** on Jl. Ir. H. Juanda. For chicken or mutton sate (barbecued meat skewers), the Senayan Satay House has a near monopoly in Jakarta, with its three locations.

INDONESIAN

Ayam Bulungan, Jl. Bulungan No. 64. Tel: 714-962. Fried chicken is the house specialty.

Ayam Goreng Mbok Berek, Jl. Prof. Supomo SH 14, south Jakarta. Tel: 829-5366. Famous for its traditional Javanese-style fried chicken (7 other locations in Jakarta).

Bakmi Gajah Mada, basement, Studio 21 cinema comples, Jl. Thamrin and Jl. Melawai IV, Blok M. Indonesian and Chinese-style noodles served up cafeteria-style.

Bengawan Solo, Sahid jaya Hotel. Tel: 570-4444. Upmarket cuisine specializing in dishes from Central Java.

Natrabu Indah Agung, Jl. H. Agua Salim, 29A, Jakarta 10340. Tel: 335-668. Hot and tasty, good and cheap award-winning Padang food.

Oasis, Jl. Raden Saleh No. 47. Tel: 327-818. Housed in an old Dutch-style villa, this restaurant's specialties are *flambes* and *rijstaffel* (rice table). A must visit.

Raden Kuring, Jl. Raden Saleh 62, Jakarta 10330. Tel: 314-0744. Traditional Indonesian menu in tourist-type setting. Daily traditional dances in evenings.

Sari Kuring, Jl. Batu Ceper 55 A, Jakarta 10120. Tel: 341-524. Excellent Sundanese (West Java) food. Try the *ikan mas bakar* (grilled carp), *cumicumi bakar* (barbecued squid) to *ayam bakar* (grilled chicken).

Senayan Sate House, Jl. Cokroaminoto and Jl. Kebon Sirih in Menteng. House specialty, delicious sate. Inexpensive.

SEAFOOD

Perahu Bugis, Horison Hotel, Ancol. Tel: 680-008. Nice atmosphere, right by the sea.

Nelayan, Gedung Manggala Wanabhakti, Jl. Jend. Gatot Subroto, Jakarta Pusat 10270. Tel: 570-0248. One of the best places to go for seafood in a local setting.

Seafood Terrace, Grand Hyatt hotel. Tel: 390-1234. Top of the line in an elegant and international setting.

Yun Njan, Jl. Batu Ceper 69. Tel: 364-063. Busy atmosphere, plastic plates but delicious crab, fish, prawns and squid. Reasonable prices.

CHINESE

Blue Ocean, Jl. Hayam Wuruk 5. Tel: 345-6650. A good place for *dim sum*.

Cahaya Kota, Jl. K.H. Wahid Hasyim 9. Tel: 333-077, 335-331. One of Jakarta's premier banquet house.

Dragon City, Lippo Plaza Podium Block Ground Fl, Suite P101, Jl. Jenderal Sudirman KAV 25, Jakarta 12920. Tel: 522-1933. Szechuan and seafood delicacies, popular business lunch locale.

Marquee, BNI Tower. 100 top-of-the-line Cantonese dishes from which to choose. Panoramic view of the city from 32 stories up.

Paramount, Jl. R.P. Soeroso 35. Tel: 323-111. Family-type Cantonese restaurant.

Summer Palace, Tedjabuana Building, 7th Floor, Jl. Menteng Raya 29. Tel: 333-899, 332-970. A must for lovers of Szechwan dishes. Medium priced.

THAI

Thai Garden, Jl. Cideng Timur 58. Tel: 386-0455. One of two branches serving all the favorites.

Siam Garden, Wisma Hayam Wuruk, 3rd Floor, Jl. Hayam Wuruk 8, Jakarta Pusat 10120. Tel: 358-300. Medium-priced restaurant serving a wide range of dishes.

Sawasdee, Jl. Batu Tulis 57B, Jakarta 10120. Tel: 385-7602. Possibly one of the more authentic Thai restaurants. It receives menu and cooking advice from an award-winning Bangkok restaurant and imports the key ingredients. Seafood specialties.

Tamnak, Jl. H.O.S. Cokroamintoto 78, Jakarta. Tel: 334-243. Cafeteria-style, bright, busy, reasonable prices. Seafood specialties.

VIETNAMESE

Hayam Wuruk, Jl. Hayam Wuruk No. 5, Jakarta. Tel: 365-544.

Paregu I, Jl. Sunan Kalijaga 64-65, Jakarta Selatan 12160. Tel: 713-266.

INDIAN

Eastern Promise, Jl. Kemang Raya 5, kemang, South Jakarta. Tel: 799-6151. Reasonably priced North Indian food. The buffet is a good deal. Also serves Indonesian, Italian and British dishes.

Hazara, 112 Wahid Hasyim, Jakarta 10340. Tel: 315-0424. Good North Indian frontier food presented in magical setting amongst antiques and curios.

Mutu, Jl. Tanah Abang Timur 14 Jakarta Pusat 10110. Tel: 380-5233. Southern Indian dishes served on banana leaves.

Palki, Mulia Center, 4th Floor, Jl. H.R. Rasuna Said Kav. X-6 No.8, Jakarta Selatan. Tel: 522-9447. North Indian cuisine cooked the traditional way. Relaxed atmosphere.

MIXED ASIAN

Koi Gallery, Jl. Mahakam 1 no 2, South Jakarta. Tel: 722-2864. An ever changing menu from six Asian countries to complement the exhibits in this gallery-cum-eatery.

Shopping

Jakarta is not known as a shopper's paradise. Imported goods are heavily taxed and domestic manufacturers rarely can compete in quality, though they are cheap. The good buys are hence limited mainly to two categories: handicrafts and antiques, with exceptions – notably pirated cassette tapes and locally-produced designer clothes.

HANDICRAFTS

These are produced outside of Jakarta (with the exception of cane furniture and some batik). Nevertheless, all are available in the city, and short of going to the original producer, you cannot get them cheaper elsewhere.

Pasar Raya near Blok M is the best one-stop shop for the full gamut of Indonesian products. Don't be put off by the lower floors, which look just like a Western department store. Head for the upper floors to the handicrafts. Good, but smaller are **Sarinah** on Jl. Thamrin and **Keris Gallery** in Menteng. In these stores are everything from baskets, cane chairs, and leather sandals, to placemats, paintings, carvings, clothes, toys, and batik.

At the **Jakarta Handicraft Center**, 12A Jl. Pekalongan, you'll find a large collection of high-quality handicraft. As most of the merchandise was manufactured for export, the wood has been treated for climatic changes.

Many of the antique and art shops along **Jl. Kebon Sirih Timur Dalam, Jl. Majapahit and Jl. Paletehan (Kebayoran)** also sell handicrafts. A few shops, such as the **Irian Art and Gift Shop**, Jl. Pasar Baru. Tel: 343-422, specialize in tribal handicrafts and primitive art.

ANTIQUES AND CURIOS

Although some copies are difficult to detect, you have a better chance of getting a genuine article if you go to reputable dealers who offer refunds.

Gallery 50B, Jl. Ciputat Raya 50B. Tel: 749-2850. This three-story shop has some fine pieces. Free hotel collection for serious buyers.

Cony Art, Jl. Melawai Raya 189E. Tel: 720-2844. Two floors of antique ceramics, mainly from Sulawesi. Near Blok M.

Johan Art Curio, Jl. Salim 59A. Tel: 336-023. One of the largest collections of old Chinese porcelains and statues.

Other shops are scattered throughout the city, but especially on **Jl. Kebon Sirih Timur Dalam**, where there are several tiny shops with names like **Bali**, **Bima**, **Djody** and **Nasrun** – all stocked with old furniture, weavings, masks, puppets and porcelains. Djody is especially well-respected.

The so-called "antique" market on **Jalan Surabaya**, near Embassy Row (Jl. Diponegoro), consists of numerous stalls selling porcelains, puppets, tiles, brass and silver bric-a-brac. Most of it is new, but made to look old.

Ciputat Village, Jl. Ciputat Raya, may be a little out of town, but it's well worth a visit if you are looking for larger pieces like furniture.

JEWELRY

Many jewelry shops in Jakarta design and produce their own gold and silver work. Prices are higher than in Yogyakarta and Bali, but the quality and designs are vastly superior – especially if interested in Indonesian gems: Borneo diamonds, purple amethyst, natural pearls and the West Javanese black opal. This can also be a good place to buy chains, filigree and repousse work. Labor is cheap and workmanship can be good. Check the papers for the current cost of gold and silver per gram before shopping. Many of the quality shops are in the hotels. However, **Djaya Jewelry** on Jl. Gunthor is an excellent place to buy gold, and is popular with the expatriate community in Jakarta.

Ana Gold, Gajah Mada Plaza 1F 39, Jl. Gajah Mada.

Christian Diamond, Ratu Plaza G35-36, Jl. Jend. Sudirman.

Classic Jewelry, Plaza Indonesia 2F 12, Jl. MH Thamrin Kav. 28-30.

Djaya Jewelry, Jl. Guntur No. 4-D.

Jays' Jewelry, Mandarin Oriental Hotel, Jl. MH Thamrin.

Jakarta Pearl Center, Plaza Indonesia, St. Floor No.111.

Joyce Spiro Jewelry, Sari Pan Pacific Hotel, Jl. MH Thamrin.

SCL Jewelry, Gajah Mada Plaza 1F 4-5, Jl. Gajah Mada.

ART

For works of serious artists, go to Oet's Gallery, which features the work of a different artist every few weeks.

Check *What's On* magazine for up-to-date exhibition dates. The elegant but difficult-to-find **Koi Gallery Restaurant**, Jl. Mahakam, Tel: 722-2864, is a great place to view the latest art while enjoying an excellent meal.

The best place to see kitsch is at Taman Suropati in Embassy Row. The Art Market in Ancol has several shops where you may watch artists at work and commission a portrait.

Art Market in Ancol also has several shops where one may watch artists at work and commission a portrait.

Harris Art Gallery, Jl. Cipete 41, Kebayoran Baru. Tel: 769-6860. For the serious collector.

Kings Gallery, Jl. K.H. Hasyim Ashari 36. Tel: 345-602.

Oet's Gallery, Jl. Palatehan I/33, Kebayoran Baru. Tel: 713-632. Features revolving exhibitions.

Taman Suropati, Embassy Row. A paradise for kitsch lovers.

Shopping Centers

A visit to some of the shopping centers in Jakarta is a good way to pass time and to indulge in some people-watching. The newer malls are just like those you may have left at home.

Blok M. Everything from jeans to cassettes to designer goods and handicraft. Four cinemas and amusement arcade on the top floor.

Glodok Shopping Center, in the middle of Jakarta's Chinatown.

Pasar Baru, several square blocks of shops, where everything and anything can be bought.

Pasar Tanah Abang, not far from Sarinah Department Store, this shopping center provides all kinds of textiles and batiks.

Plaza Indonesia, below the Grand Hyatt. One of the more upmarket plazas in Jakarta.

Pondok Indah, located in an exclusive housing estate in suburban South Jakarta.

Nightlife

Unlike most other Indonesian cities, Jakarta rages on into the night. This is perhaps one more reason to have a nap in the afternoon, so that you can get out on the town in the evening, when a cool breeze blows in from the sea.

There are far too many night spots in Jakarta to mention. Suffice it to say that there are enough venues to accommodate any breed of night creature.

CLUBS

Bats, Shangri-la Hotel, Jl. Jend. Sudirman. Tel: 570-7440.

Cafe Batavia, Jl. Pintu Besar Utara No.14, Taman Fatahilla, Jakarta Barat. Tel: 691-5531.

Hard Rock Cafe, Sarinah Bldg., Jl. Thamrin. Tel: 390-2766.

Jamz Jazz Club, Jl. Panglima Polim Raya No. 11 LM. Tel: 720-6043.

M Club, Blok M Plaza, 76 Jl. Bulungan. Tel: 720-9103.

Oriental Discoteque, Hilton Hotel. Tel: 570-3600.

Pitstop, Jl. MH Thamrin. Tel: 323-707.

Planet Hollywood, 16 Jl. Gatot Subroto. Tel: 526-7827.

Stage, Ratu Plaza L6 01-07. Tel: 739-7505.

Tanamour, 14 Jl. Tanah Abang Tmr. Tel: 380-5233.

BARS AND PUBS

Blue Note, Atria Square, Jl. Jend. Sudirman Kav 334. Tel: 573-2883.

Green Pub, Jakarta Theater Bldg., Jl. MH Thamrin 9. Tel: 359-332.

Jaya Pub, Jaya Bldg., Jl. MH Thamrin No. 12. Tel: 327-508.

Koi Gallery Restaurant, Jl. Mahakam. Tel: 722-2864.

Metropolis Dine and Dance, Niaga Tower, Jl. Jend. Sudirman. Tel: 2505-5713.

News Cafe, Setiabudi, Jl. H.R. Rasuna Said. Tel: 525-7378.

O'Reilly's, Grand Hyatt Hotel. Tel: 335-551.

Tavern, Aryaduta Hotel, Jl. Prapatan 44-48. Tel: 386-1234.

Zanzibar Cafe, Victoria 2F, Jl. Sultan Hasanuddin, Kebayoran Baru. Tel: 725-5527.

Cultural Events

For culture in any form, the first place to check is **Taman Ismail Marzuki (TIM)**, the cultural and performing arts center of Jakarta. TIM hosts an eclectic variety of Indonesian dance performances, *wayang kulit* and *wayang orang*, singing groups, poetry readings, modern and traditional theater productions, as well as visiting performances of ballet, modern dance, and classical and jazz music.

Wayang orang: If not planning to visit Central Java, then attend the popular Javanese wayang orang performances at **Baharata Theater**, Jl. Pasar Senen 15. The audience is almost entirely Javanese and is generally very appreciative – often more so than in Yogyakarta and Surakarta these days, where there is rarely a good turnout and tourists often outnumber the locals. This in itself is a good reason to see wayang orang in Jakarta. Performances nightly.

Folk theater: If fascinated by folk theater, visit the **Teater Miss Tjihtjih** on Jl. Stasion Angke in a poor, western suburb of the city. It's rather dark and dingy inside, and you won't understand a word unless you speak Sundanese, but the audience seems to enjoy the traditional folk tales being enacted.

Night shopping: Visit the **Art Market** (Pasar Seni) at Ancol, where three or four nights a week there are live, open-air performances of one sort or another, and one may walk leisurely about the pavilions inspecting the handicrafts and paintings for sale. Chat with the artists and then sit down at one of the sidewalk cafes for a tasty bowl of soup, a hamburger or a plate of noodles. Ancol is about 10 kilometers (6 mi) from the center of town.

CULTURAL CENTERS

The French, British, Dutch, American, Australian and German embassies all maintain cultural centers with scheduled exhibitions, tours, films and lectures. Call them for details.

Alliance Francaise (French Cultural Center). Central Jakarta: Jl. Salemba Raya 25. Tel: 390-8585. South Jakarta: Jl. Senopati No. 23. Tel: 720-3081.

Australian Cultural Center, Jl. H.R. Rasuna Said Kav. C15–16, Kuningan.

British Council, S. Widjoyo Center, Jl. Jend. Sudirman 57. Tel: 587-4411.

Erasmus Huis (Dutch Cultural Center), Jl. H.R. Rasuna Said Kav. S-3. Tel: 51-2321.

Goethe Institute (German Cultural Center), Jl. Matraman Raya 23. Tel: 858-1139/850-9719.

Indonesia-America Friendship Society, Jl. Pramuka Kav. 30. Tel: 881-241, 883-536, 883-867.

Sumatra

GETTING THERE

Air: If intending to start one's trip to Indonesia in Sumatra, Medan is the natural choice. Medan and Palembang are international airports with regular flights from Singapore and Malaysia, as well as service now from Holland and Germany. Garuda and Malaysian Airlines fly in from Penang and Kuala Lumpur, and Silk Air has daily flights in from Singapore.

Padang is another main gateway into West Sumatra, with flights from Singapore and Malaysia, as well as from Jakarta and Medan.

Sea: A ferry makes the crossing from the port of Merak on the northwest tip of Java to Panjang, near Telukbetung at the southern tip of Sumatra. The trip takes 4 hours. Krakatau, the infamous volcanic island, can be seen off the port side of the boat in good weather. Sibolga is the port for Nias and the journey takes about 16 hours. PELNI ships connect Medan with Jakarta, and Padang with Jakarta. There is also regular ferry service between Singapore and Medan.

Road: The 2,500-km (1,550-mi) Trans-Sumatran Highway runs from Tanjung Karang in the south to Banda Aceh in the north, greatly reducing the driving time. Other roads – except in the Medan and Danau Toba area, or the Padang and Bukittinggi areas – are in poor condition. During the rainy season, expect many smaller roads to be entirely impassable, while even in the dry season motoring will only be possible with a four-wheel-drive vehicle.

Rail: There are three separate rail systems in Sumatra; none connects with another. In northern Sumatra, a line runs from Medan north to Banda Aceh and south to Rantauprapat. In West Sumatra, there's rail from Padang and its port of Teluk Bayur to Padangpanjang, then north to Bukittinggi and Payakumbuh, and south to Solok and Lunt. In south Sumatra, the rail line begins at Tanjung Karang and runs north to Parabumulih, east to Palembang and west to Lubulkinggau.

Tourist Offices

Medan: Diparda Tk. I Sumatra Utara, Jl. Jend. A. Yani 107, Medan 20151. Tel/Fax: (061) 538-101.

Banda Aceh: Diparda D. I. Aceh, Jl. TGK Chik Kuta Karang 3, Banda Aceh 23121. Tel: (0651) 23-692, Fax: 33-723.

Padang: Diparda Tk. I Sumatra Barat, Jl. Jend. Sudirman 43, Padang. Tel: (0751) 34-231.

Palembang: Diparda Tk. I Sumatra Selatan, Jl. PON IX (Taman Budaya), Palembang 30137. Tel: (0711) 357-348.

Pekanbaru: Diparda Tk. I Riau, Jl. Diponegoro 24A, Pekanbaru 28141. Tel: (0761) 31-562, Fax: 31-565.

Medan

ACCOMMODATION

Deluxe

Danau Toba International, Jl. Imam Bonjol 17. Tel: (061) 557-000, Fax: 530-553.

Dharma Deli, Jl. Balai Kota. Tel: (061) 327-011, Fax: 327-153.

Dirga Durya, Jl. Imam Bonjol 6. Tel: (061) 321-555, Fax: 513-327.

Emerald Garden Hotel, Jl. Yos Sudarso 1. Tel: (061) 611-888, Fax: 622-888.

Garuda Plaza, Jl. Sisingamangaraja 18. Tel: (061) 716-255, 711-411, Fax: 714-411.

Novotel Seochi, Jl. Cirebon 76A. Tel: (061) 561-234, Fax: 572-222.

Hotel Polonia, Jl. Sudirman 14. Tel: 542-222, 535-111, Fax: 519-553.

Hotel Tiara, Jl. Cut Mutiah. Tel: (061) 516-000, 523-000, 538-880, Fax: 510-176.

Intermediate

Dhaksina, Jl. Sisingamangaraja 20. Tel: (061) 720-000

Elbruba, Jl. Perintis Kemerdekaan (Jl. Jati) 19. Tel: (061) 530-476, 520-119.

Garuda City Hotel, Jl. Sisingamangaraja 27-39. Tel: (061) 718-553, 717-975, Fax: 714-411.

Hotel Sumatera, Jl. Sisingamangaraja 35. Tel: (061) 718-807.

Pardede International, Jl. Ir. H. Juanda 14. Tel: (061) 543-866, Fax: 553-675.

Sumatra Village, Jl. Djamin Ginting Kilometer 11. Tel: (061) 720-964.

Wai Yat, Jl. Asia 44. Tel: (061) 718-975, 718-575.

Wisma Benteng, Jl. Kapt. Maulana Lubis 6. Tel: (061) 518-426.

EATING OUT

Medan is a good place for eating. The **Tip Top Restaurant** is noted for its excellent Padang food, curried mutton brains and ice cream. The **Garuda Restaurant**, on Jl. Pemuda, also serves excellent Padang food, along with a wide choice of thirst-quenching fruit juices.

At night, one of the best places to visit is at **Selat Panjang**, an alley behind Jl. Pandu, with stalls serving Chinese food, sate and fruit juices. Another open-air eatery is at the swimming pool on Jl. Sisingamangaraja.

Medan is also highly regarded for durians. August and September are the best months, when street stalls offer the fruit in abundance and at unbeatable prices.

SHOPPING

Medan is a large trading town whose markets offer handicrafts from all over Sumatra and Java. There are several antique shops that will give you a good choice of purchases.

Borobudur, Jl. A. Yani. Batak textiles, masks and statues.

Arafah Art Shop, Jl. A. Yani 66.

Asli Art Shop, Jl. A. Yani 62.

Rufino Art Shop, Jl. A. Yani 64.

Selatan Art Shop, Jl. A. Yani 44.

Along Jl. A. Yani there are a number of other souvenir shops selling a variety of arts and crafts.

For batik you should go to **Pasar Ikan Lama**, located on Jl. Perniagaan between Jl. A. Yani and the railway tracks. Most of the souvenir shops along Jl. A. Yani sell batik, as do some shops on Jl. Arifin. A number of shops sell batik by the meter or ready-made, including:

Batik Keris, Jl. Arifin 200.

Batik Semar, Jl. A. Yani 128.

Seni Batik Indonesia, Gedung Perisai, Jl. Pemuda 7.

Iwan Tirta, Jl. Sriwijaya Ujung Utara 1.

Banda Aceh

GETTING AROUND

The Banda Aceh Express bus service links Medan with Sumatra's northernmost city. Numbered seats, reclining chairs, fans and nonstop, all-night videos of kungfu and Indonesian rock bands are the norm on this route.

Other services, which start in the morning and arrive mid-afternoon, connect the following destinations: Blangkeseren–Kutacane, Takingon–Bireuen, Sigli–Aceh.

Accommodation

Kuala Tripa, Jl. Mesjid. Tel: (0651) 21-455, 21-879.
Rasa Sayang Ayu, Jl. Teuku Umar. Tel: (0651) 21-983, 21-379.
Sultan, Jl. Panglima Polim. Tel: (0651) 22-581, 23-633.
Pavilion Seulawah, Jl. Masjid Ibrahim II/3. Tel: (0651) 22-788, 22-872.
Aceh, Jl. Mohammed Jam 1. Tel: (0651) 21-354.
Medan, Jl. A. Yani 15A. Tel: (0651) 21-501.
Prapat, Jl. A. Yani 17. Tel: (0651) 22-159.
Sri Budaya, Jl. Masjid Ibrahim III/5e. Tel: (0651) 22-919.

Eating Out

The food in Aceh offers a chance to try something other than the ubiquitous Padang food. Aceh food is usually served with steamed rice, and common dishes include: fish (*ikan panggang*), papaya flower salad (*sambal bunga kates*) and egg cooked in spinach (*sayur bayam*). Squares of twice-cooked black rice (*pulot hitam dua masak*) serve as sweets. Tea with honey, ginger and condensed milk (*serbat*) is an alternative. Batak restaurants at Kutacane serve dog curry (*cicang anjing*) and palm wine (*tuak*). Good coffee is available everywhere in Aceh; bitter coffee is *kopi tok*, and coffee with milk is *kopi susu*. A coffee with a half-boiled egg (*telur setengah malang*) is the usual breakfast fare.

Shopping

Special items to look for in Banda Aceh include *rencong* (traditional Acehnese daggers) and delicate filigreed jewelry. The best place to shop for *rencong* is in the market. A shop on Jl. Kartini offers Acehnese and Dutch antiques for browsers and collectors.

The whole province of Aceh offers a variety of textiles, with each locality having its own special pattern of *kain adat* or *opo adat*.

Danau Toba

Accommodation

In Prapat:
Hotel Patra Jasa. Tel: (0625) 41-796, or (061) 323-535 in Medan.
Hotel Prapat. Tel: (0625) 41-048.
Hotel Tara Bunga Sibigo. Tel: (0625) 41-089, 41-700.
Danau Toba Cottages. Tel: (0625) 44-172.
Niagara Hotel. Tel: (061) 521-128 in Medan

In Samosir:
Tuk Tuk Toledo Inn. Tel: (0625) 41-181, 513-561.
Hotel Silintong. Tel: (0625) 41-345, or (061) 529-265, 511-497 in Medan.
Hotel Toba Beach. Tel: (0625) 41-275.

Batak Handicrafts

Fifteen years of tourism has, unfortunately, almost exhausted the supply of genuine antiques in the Toba and Karo districts. Reproductions of Batak calendars and buffalo-horn medicine pouches are all too common.

A real antique is just as likely to turn up in Medan, at the **Toko Bali** located on Jl. Jend. Jani 68, or the **Indonesian Art Shop** also on Jl. Jend. Jani.

Some Toba entrepreneurs will take visitors on "antique safaris" around the country, but prices are likely to be high. Good Chinese porcelain and Dutch silver coins are still available.

The greatest, although certainly the most macabre, find is a Tungkat carved magic wand. Real wands contain a vial of slaughtered baby's blood, and they are considered to be very powerful. Genuine Batak spirit figurines can still be found, although the mini Batak houses are invariably contemporary carvings. Batak weaving and *kain ulos* are also extremely good buys, but bargain very hard for them.

West Sumatra

Arts & Crafts

West Sumatra is renowned for its beautiful hand-loomed *songket* cloth, fine embroidery, silverwork and woodcarving.

Weaving is practiced in a number of communities, and the best known is **Silungkang**, a small town on the Agam plateau where the brightly-colored silk songket sarongs, scarves and headwear – all interwoven with gold – are loomed. Another popular center is **Pandai Sikat**, on the main road from Padang to Bukittinggi. Women in small cottage industries take from a few weeks to a few months to finish a set consisting of a sarung and scarf. Pandai Sikat is also known for its embroidery and woodcarving.

Silversmiths working in **Kota Gadang**, near Bukittinggi, produce fine filigree work. In **Sangaipuar**, a small village 20 minutes from Bukittinggi, blacksmiths still make anything from spoons to agricultural equipment.

Riau Archipelago

Pulau Bintan and **Pulau Batam** can be reached by sea from Jakarta, Pekanbaru, Palembang and Singapore. Batam, Bintan and Karimun also have airports. Once there, you can travel easily to neighboring islands. For **Pulau Penyengat** and the **Snake River**, as well as number of nearby beaches, charter a *prahu* from the wharf.

Several Singapore-based travel agents organize tours to **Tanjung Pinang**, on Pulau Bintan, including excursions to **Pulau Penyengat** and other areas.

Accommodation

On Batam:
Batam View, Jl. Hang Lekir, Nongsa. Tel: (0778) 453-740, Fax: 453-747.
New Holiday, Jl. Imam Bonjol, Nagoya. Tel: (0778) 459-308.
Nagoya Plaza, Jl. Iman Bonjol, Labuk Baja. Tel: (0778) 459-888.
Batam Jaya, Jl. Raja Ali Haji. Tel: (0778) 458-707, Fax: 58-226.
Ramayana, Jl. Pembangunan, Komplek Batam Blok B 1, Labuk Baja. Tel: (0778) 456-888.

On Bintan:
Sempurna, Jl. Yusuf Kahar 15, Tanjung Pinang. Tel: (0771) 21-555.
Garuda, Jl. Gatot Subroto, Tanjung Pinang. Tel: (0771) 22-344.
Pinang Island Cottages, Jl. Gudang Minyak 133, Tanjung Pinang. Tel: (0771) 21-307.
Wisma Panorama, Jl. Haji Agus Salim 12, Tanjung Pinang. Tel: (0771) 22-920.

Java

Each part of the island is different, with distinctions in dialect, custom and food.

The areas around the old court cities (Yogyakarta, Surakarta and Cirebon) are culturally much richer than other areas. In general, the lowlands are more crowded (and hotter) than the uplands.

- All of Java's hill resorts are deliciously cool and spectacularly scenic – every major city has one.
- The only well-developed tourist beaches are found in western Java.
- For handicrafts, ancient temples, palaces, dances and wayang puppet shows, the Yogyakarta/Surakarta central Javanese heartland is best.

The standard two-week "package tour" of Indonesia has, up to now, included only Jakarta, Yogyakarta and Bali. Visitors with more time to spare generally add a few more days in Bandung, Yogyakarta and Surakarta before continuing on to Bali. Only a handful of adventurous travelers explore the north coast of the island or the eastern highlands around Malang and Bromo.

Domestic tourism has opened up many new areas on Java – mainly hill stations and beaches around the major cities – and these are now served by good roads, with convenient public transportation, and clean, comfortable accommodation.

Familiarize yourself with the intricate geography of the island. Although the distances aren't great – the island is only 1,100 km (650 mi) long – remember that roads here, though generally good, are made slow by heavy traffic.

Bus fares and schedules are too numerous to list. Remember that buses operate on all major highways, linking together the cities in a comprehensive and inexpensive travel network. Mini-buses (known here by the Mitsubishi brand-name "Colt" or the Dutch word *oplet,* which means "to flag down") ply the by-roads, providing a local network of transport to and from smaller towns and villages.

Local Transport

Air: By far the quickest and easiest way to get around the island. Numerous daily flights. One can go from Jakarta to Yogyakarta, for example, in only half an hour, as opposed to the 10 or even 12 hours if by bus or train. Air tickets are invariably two or three times the price of a first-class train ticket and as much as 10 times more than the bus.

Intercity trains: They are quite comfortable, if a bit slow. First-class carriages have air-conditioning and a dining car that serves meals. Javanese trains are often late – sometimes many hours late, as only a single track connects many major cities. If one train is held up, they are all late.

Intercity buses: Generally faster and more punctual than trains, and cheaper. Most Indonesians travel this way. Long-distance express buses operate at night, leaving major cities at either end of the island in the late afternoon, stopping to pick up and discharge passengers in Central Java in the middle of the night, and arriving at the other end of the island early in the morning. Seats are narrow – six across in a bus that in West would only seat four across. Some have air-conditioning and video movies. Bus drivers drive like maniacs; accidents are not uncommon.

Rented mini-bus ("colt"): The most comfortable and practical way to go on a limited budget. For trips out of town or across the island, the only extra you need pay is for the driver's food and lodging, and you may have to buy some or all of the petrol. Still, with a group of four or five people, you can go from Jakarta all the way to Yogyakarta via Bandung and the north coast for about the same cost as flying. Be sure that the agreement is all worked out clearly in advance, including the amount you will give the driver every day for food and lodging (tips are not expected, though they would be appreciated). You may have difficulty finding a driver who speaks some English, so expect to pay a premium for this. Count on one extra day's rental fee and a full tank of gas for the driver to get home.

Banten and the West Coast

The excursion out to Java's sparsely-populated west coast is made easier by the Jakarta-Merak expressway. The surf and the sand are not as fine as in Bali or Pelabuhan Ratu, but a visit to the historic ruins at Banten or the active volcano, Anak Krakatau, or the Ujung Kulon Nature Reserve, more than makes up for this. Go during the week, when it is less crowded and hotels offer a discount rate.

Getting There

To visit the ruins at Banten, which are some distance from the main road, hire a car or taxi. It will take the better part of a day. Otherwise, take a bus from Jakarta's Grogol Terminal to Serang (any bus bound for points west: Merak, Labuan or Sumatra will pass through Serang) and alight at the center of town. Then locate the small road leading north to Banten, and wait at the intersection for a local mini-bus ferrying passengers up to the village, or walk the remaining 10 km (6 mi). A slow, local train also goes to Serang from Jakarta's Tanah Abang Station.

A taxi or rental car to the west coast beaches at Anyer or Carita will take about 4 hours. A chartered minibus (*colt*) will cost less and carry more people (ask someone in your hotel in Jakarta to arrange this for you). In either case, make the detour to Banten along the way, this should be negotiated as part of the fare in advance.

Intercity buses run hourly from Jakarta's Grogol Terminal to the port of Labuan on the west coast (about 5 hours), via the inland route through Serang and Pandeglang. From here, catch a colt going north along the coastal road to the beach areas. Or take the slow, local train from Tanah Abang Station in Jakarta to Cilegon, and from here catch a colt on the main road going south. Remember that if intending to visit the nature reserve at Ujung Kulon, first get a permit and make arrangements through the PPA head offices in Bogor.

Alternatively, phone the Jakarta booking office of any west coast hotel to make all the arrangements for you. They will arrange transportation (generally at a slightly higher cost than if you do it yourself) if you plan to stay at the hotel. Private tours to Ujung Kulon, Krakatau and the west coast can also be arranged.

Tourist Office: Diparda Tk I Jawa Barat, Jl. Cipaganti 151-153, Bandung 40161. Tel: (22) 231-490, Fax: 237-976.

ACCOMMODATION

The coastal towns of Anyar and Carita are where you'll find the main concentration of accommodation – but there are also a few comfortable places to the north and south.

Anyer Beach Motel, Jl. Raya Karang Bolong, Anyer, Serang Banten, Jakarta. Tel: 81-376 or 510-503 ext 166. Tidy little concrete bungalows set in a grove by a broad, secluded beach.

Carita Beach Resort, Jl. Raya Carita, P.O. Box 12, Labuhan 42264, Pandeglang, West Java. Tel: (0254) 202-222, Fax: 202-444. Four-star hotel with beach-front rooms.

Mabruk Quality Resort, Jl. Raya Bolong, Anyer Kidul, P.O. Box 10, Anyer, West Java. Tel: (0254) 601-602, Fax: 601-723. The decor reflects the motifs of the nearby ancient kingdom of Banten. Children's playground and camp program.

Merak Beach Hotel, Jl. Raya Merak 65, Merak 42438, West Java. Tel: (0254) 71-015, Fax: 71-450. Located right on the water just next to the Merak Bakauhuni ferry terminal.

SIGHTS

From Serang, a town 90 km (56 mi) west of Jakarta, a surfaced road leads north to Banten village. Just before the village, on the right-hand side of the road, is the tomb of Maulana Yusup, the second Muslim ruler of Banten, who died around 1590.

Crossing a bridge and turning off to the left down a direct track is the old Banten town square. The remains of Surasowan Palace line the south side of the square and the Grand Mosque stands to the west.

Banten used to be protected by a thick outer wall enclosing the fortified palace, with the square at its center and surrounded by a large market and a number of crowded ethnic quarters inhabited by Malay, Chinese, Gujarati, Abyssinian and Annamese traders. The palace was excavated and an elaborate system of terracotta pipes was discovered, complete with two filtering reservoirs, linking the sunken royal baths with Tasik Ardi, an artificial lake and pleasure garden just to the southwest. Just to the northwest of the square are the ruins of Fort Speelwijk, built by the Dutch in 1682 and expanded in 1685 and 1731. To the west of the fort, a road leads across a bridge to the red-and-yellow Wan-De Yuan temple, one of the oldest and largest Chinese temples on Java. The Goddess of Mercy, Kuan-yin or Avalokitesvara, is enshrined here along with several other deities, and a steady stream of devotees burn incense and consult the temple's fabled divination sticks.

Pulau Seribu

GETTING THERE

Motorboat launches may be hired to all the islands from the Ancol Marina, located within the vast Ancol amusement park on Jakarta's north shore. Pulau Onrust and the other islands closest to the mainland are only 20 to 30 minutes away, making this an easy and relaxing escape from the city to the beach. Pulau Rambut is about an hour away; Pulau Puteri and Pulau Melinjo, about 3 hours. A regular morning ferry leaves from Sanggar Bahari pier at Tanjung Priok harbor for several of the closer islands, returning in the afternoon. For the farther islands, such as Pulau Puteri, Pulau Genteng and Opak Bersar, boats leave from the Kartika Bahari pier.

SIGHTS

There are three groups of frequently-visited islands in this 600-island chain that scatters across the Java Sea to the north of Jakarta. The first is a cluster of tiny islands located just a few kilometers offshore, directly to the north of the city: Onrust, Kelor, Kahyangan, Bidadari (also known as Sakit), and Damar.

Pulau Onrust was formerly the Dutch East Indies Company's (VOC) dry-docking station for the entire Asian fleet. Capt. Cook had his ship, HMS *Endeavour,* repaired here in 1770 and praised the island's caulkers and carpenters as the best in the East. Today, there are several houses dating from a later period, and a fort.

On neighboring Pulau Kelor and Pulau Kahyangan, the remains of Dutch forts are also visible. Pulau Bidadari (Heavenly Nymph Island) was once the site of a leper colony, and Pulau Damar (Torch Island) houses a powerful beacon used to guide airplanes into Jakarta at night. Also on the latter are the ruins of a Japanese-style house constructed in 1685 by Governor-General Camphuijs, one of the few VOC leaders known for his intellectual endeavors.

Much farther out to sea, about 100 km (65 mi) from Jakarta, two islands have been developed into a private scuba-diving resort: Pulau Puteri (Princess Island) and Pulau Melinjo. Pulau Melinjo has a divers camp – simple thatched huts with toilets, fresh water, showers, barbecues and tables.

The main attractions on both islands are crystal-clear waters and the spectacular coral reefs offshore. Diving equipment, food and evening entertainment are available on Pulau Puteri; on Pulau Melinjo, you're on your own, though there are resident attendants who maintain radio contact with the main island.

Large, five-foot-long black lizards inhabit these islands, but they're harmless. Be careful, however, to wear protective footwear and to avoid the razor-sharp coral when in the water. There are sea urchins and poisonous stone-fish, and cuts fester very quickly in the tropics. Mosquitoes.

Lastly, there is the Pulau Rambut (Hair Island) bird sanctuary, two tiny islands lying some distance to the west of Jakarta, about 15 km (10 mi) from shore. These islands serve as a nursery for seabirds during the breeding season (March–July), and also have a large permanent population of herons, storks and cormorants. Two chalets on the island may be rented from the resident forestry guards. Many of the Thousand Islands are crowded on weekends, though much less so during the rainy season, November to March, when the strong northwest monsoon winds bring daily afternoon showers, making the return boat journey precarious. The best time to visit is during the dry summer months, May to September.

ACCOMMODATION

Matahari, Pulau Macan Besar, Thousand Islands, Jakarta Bay. c/o P.T. Jakarta International Hotels management, Hotel Borobudur, Jl. Lapangan Banteng, Selatan, Jakarta 10710. Tel: (021) 380-0521, Fax: 344-6731. This comprehensive resort occupies an entire island.

Pulau Ayer Resort, c/o PT Sarotama Prima Perkasa, Jl. Juanda 111/6 Jakarta 10120. Tel: (021) 384-2031, Fax: 384-6580. Island beachfront hotel in Jakarta Bay, 30 minutes from Ancol. Rooms on stilts over the water.

Pulau Bindadari, c/o Marina Ancol, Taman Impian Jaya Ancol, Jakarta 14430. Tel: (021) 680-048, Fax: 690-3028.

Pulau Laki, PT Fadent Gema Scorpio, Wisma Fadent, Jl. HOS Cokroaminoto 116, Jakarta 10310. Tel: (021) 314-4885, Fax: 692-5048.

Pulau Pelangi Island, c/o PT Pulau Sribu Paradise, Jl. Wahid Hasyim 69, Jakarta 10350. Tel: (021) 335-535, Fax: 384-8533. A floating restaurant, watersports, tennis courts.

Pulau Putri, c/o PT Buana Bintang Samudra, Jl. Sultan Agung 21, Jakarta 12980. Tel: (021) 828-1093, Fax: 829-9002.

Pulau Puteri or **Pulau Melinjo**, c/o P.T. Pulau Seribu Paradise, Jakarta Theater Building, Jl. M.H. Thamrin, Jakarta. Tel: 348-533. Book deluxe bungalows or space in a divers camp.

Pulau Sepa, c/o Pulau Sepa Permai, Jl. Kali Besar Barat 29, 2nd Floor, Jakarta 11230. Tel: (021) 690-5935, Fax: 692-5048.

Bogor

Surprisingly few foreign tourists visit Bogor, despite the quick and easy connection from Jakarta. Those who finally do make it often wish they had come earlier, to spend more time in the orchid houses or in the library by the entrance to the gardens, pouring over the beautifully-illustrated botanical tomes.

Another little-known feature of Bogor is that it has one of the few remaining gamelan foundries left on Java, and probably the only one in West Java, located at Jl. Pancasan. From the center of Bogor, go left down Jl. Empang and bear right at the next intersection. Cross over the bridge and after several hundred meters you will see carpenters working by the left side of the street making the frames. The foundry is across the street.

Getting There

Most Jakarta taxis will take you to Bogor and back, waiting while you spend a couple of hours in the Botanical Gardens. For a more leisurely visit, rent a car or mini-bus for the day.

Buses leave for Bogor very frequently from Jakarta's Kampung Rambutan Terminal (in the south of the city). Express buses marked "Jl. Tol Jagorawi-Bogor" are the fastest (1 hour) and cheapest, stopping at the Ciawi terminal just above the town to the south. From here, mini-buses circulate into Bogor, going right by the Kebun Raya entrance.

The Jabotabek commuter train is a slower but cheaper way to get there. Board the train at Gambir, Pegangsaan or Mangarai stations in Jakarta.

Bandung

There are two views of Bandung, either as a charming old colonial town with a cool mountain climate – the capital of Sundanese culture – or a bustling industrial and technical metropolis. Certainly the city's ambiance has suffered immensely with the influx of industry and the dramatic increase in population, from just 150,000 before World War II to nearly two million today. On the other hand, some of the city's colonial charm is still in evidence, and the arts are not doing too badly, either.

Getting There

Bouraq, Merpati and Garuda operate frequent flights to Bandung from Jakarta, but it's so close and the mountain scenery and terraced rice paddies so spectacular that it seems a pity to fly.

Most Indonesians take the bus or train. The **Parahiangan Express** takes just over 3 hours from Jakarta to Bandung. A one-way ticket costs about US$15 (first class). There are several trains a day leaving from Jakarta's Gambir Station. Tickets can be arranged one day in advance through a travel agent, or else directly at the station several hours before departure.

The Parahiangan Express is comfortable enough, but for top-notch train travel, ride the **Argo Gede Executive Express**, which will get you to Bandung in just over 2 hours, with comfortable reclining seats, music videos, movies and meal service at your seat. A one-way ticket costs about US$15.

Another way to get to Bandung is by shared intercity taxi. A ride that takes four hours costs about the same as the train but brings you to your doorstep. The express bus is a bit slower, but cheaper – less than US$5 with air conditioning. Buses leave from Jakarta's Cililitan Station in the south of the city.

Orientation

For all sorts of information about Bandung, visit the tourist information kiosk on Jl. Asia-Afrika at the north-eastern corner of the town square, staffed by helpful young students. They will be glad to arrange a personal guided tour of Bandung and transportation to fit your budget.

Any travel agent in Bandung can arrange a guided tour of the city, with a car and an English-speaking guide, for a reasonable price.

Getting Around

There are no cruising metered cabs in Bandung as yet. A car must be rented from the hotel or from one of many rental companies – by the trip, by the hour or by the day, with a 2-hour minimum. For excursions outside of the city, a minibus will be cheaper and roomier.

Airline Offices

Bouraq. Tel: 58-061.
Garuda. Tel: 420-9467/9468.
Mandala. Tel: 411-868, 411-768.
Merpati. Tel: 439-742.

Accommodation

Deluxe

Chedi, 56-58 Jl. Ranca Bentang, Ciumbuleuit, Bandung 40142. Tel: (022) 230-333, Fax: 230-633. Casual but stylish. Brasserie-style restaurant serves Continental and Indonesian food.

Grand Preanger, Jl. Asia Afrika, No. 81, Bandung. Tel: (022) 430-682. Deco design with Sundanese touches. Grill and buffet restaurants. Pool, fitness center.

Jakarta Suites Hotel, Jl. Ir. H Juanda 381 A (Dago), Bandung 40135, West Java. Tel: (022) 250-5888, Fax: 250-5388. On the main street, on the north side of the city, Cafe serving Indonesian and Continental food.

Panghegar, Jl. Merdeka 2, P.O. Box 506, Bandung 40111, West Java. Tel: (022) 432-286, Fax: 431-583. Revolving roof-top restaurant serving Sundanese cuisine. Near golf courses.

Savoy Homann, Jl. Asia Afrika, No. 112, Bandung 40261. Tel: (022) 432-

244, Fax: 436-187. Opened in 1939 and refurbished, this tribute to deco has two restaurants serving Indonesian and Western food.

Sheraton Inn, Jl. Ir. H. Juanda, No. 390, Bandung 40135. Tel: (022) 250-0303, Fax: 250-0301. Casual but comfortable. Restaurant serving Indonesian and Western food, bar, pool.

Moderate

Arjuna Plaza, Jl. Ciumbuleuit, No. 152, Bandung. Tel: (022) 84-742.

Braga, Jl. Braga, No. 8, Bandung. Tel: (022) 51-685.

Bumi Asih, Jl. Cisitu 45-B, Bandung 40135, West Java. Tel: (022) 443-419.

Chrysanta, Jl. Pasteur, No. 35, Bandung. Tel: (022) 437-733.

Cihampelas, Jl. Cihampelas, No. 240, Bandung 40131. Tel: (022) 233-425, Fax: 235-914.

Cisitu GH Sankuriang, Jl. Cisitu 45 B, Bandung, West Java. Tel: (021) 82-420.

Cortina, Jl. Ir. H. Juanda, No. 32, Bandung. Tel: (022) 56-778.

Istana 1, Jl. Lembong, No. 21. Tel: (022) 436-079.

Patrajasa Motel, Jl. Ir. H. Juanda 132, Bandung, West Java. Tel: (022) 250-2664, Fax: 250-4995.

Dining

The dining scene in Bandung promises something for everyone. Considering that Bandung is home to the National Hotel School, the chances are that your meal will be more than satisfying. In any case, no trip to Bandung would be complete without a sampling of local Sudanese fare.

Most hotels offer one or two Sudanese items on their menu or buffet table. Some popular dishes include grilled carp (*ikan mas bakar*) and barbequed chicken in sweet soya (*ayan panggang*). The **Sindang Reret** on Jl. Naripan 9 and the open-air **Babakan Siliwangi** on Jl. Siliwangi (below the ITB campus) are local favorites for Sudanese cuisine. For a nice mix of Indonesian food and live music, try the **Handyani** on Jl. Sukajadi.

The **Bamboo Kafe** on Jl. Chiampelas 222 is staffed by Hotel School students and offers tasty food, low prices and friendly service – all in a relaxing bamboo setting. For Chinese, the **Queen Restaurant** on Jl. Dalem Kaum 79, **Tien Tien** on Jl. ABC 82, and the **Mushika Sari** on Jl. Ciambeluit come highly recommended.

German cuisine can be found at **Glosis** on Jl. Gunung Agung 2. The **Warung Steak-Glory** restaurant on Jl. Cihampelas offers a great selection of steaks in a very clean and home-style atmosphere.

While Bandung lacks the party pulse of Jakarta, there is still a healthy variety of night spots. The **Laga Pub** on Jl. Dr. Junjunan 164 is very popular with university students and serves up good food and local live music nightly. Other popular spots include **O'Hara's Tavern** on Jl. Jend. Sudirman, **Fame Station Club** in the Lippo Bank Building, and the **Polo Club** in the BRI Building.

Another of Bandung's treats is the **Dago Tea House** – turn left at the top of Jl. Ir. H. Juanda and follow a narrow winding road to a lovely vista of the city.

Shopping

Bandung is a good place to buy baskets and mats (woven in nearby Tasikmalaya), bamboo *angklung* instruments, and *wayang golek* puppets (old and new, though most old-looking puppets are 'antiqued' by hanging them over the kitchen stove). High-quality ceramics (including imitation Chinese antiques) are produced in the nearby village of Plered and sold in Bandung. Good leather shoes can be made in many shoe stores – they will copy your favorite pair for a fraction of what you would pay at home. Bandung is also the denim jeans center of Indonesia, with store after store dedicated to this clothing item.

Souvenir and Art Shops

Balai Penelitian Keramik (Ceramic Research Office), Jl. A. Yani 390. Visit in the mornings to observe the whole process and buy the finished products. There is a textile institute in the same complex.

Batik Semar (paintings, batik, embroidered textiles, angklung, flute, ceramics). Jl. Dalem Kaum 40.

E Sukatma Muda Studio (wayang golek) Jl. Mohammad Ramdan 4.

M. Sukama (statues, traditional headdresses, wayand golek). Jl. Braga 88.

Cibaduyut shoe industry, Jl. Cibaduyut.

Cihampelas jeans shopping, Jl. Cihampelas.

Sanggar Awi Wulung (paintings, lampshades, bamboo furniture). Jl. Raya Cibeureum 31.

Performing Arts

The Sundanese are known for their folk literature (especially sung poetry), music, wayang golek puppet plays and popular dances.

Wayang golek (*golek* means round) are three-dimensional puppets carved from wood, then painted and adorned with traditional clothing. There are frequent wayang golek performances in Bandung at Yayasan Pusat Kebudayaan (the city's cultural center), Jl. Naripan 7-9 (just a few doors down from Jl. Braga).

The cultural center also holds *jaipongan* dance evenings regularly, in which slim dance hostesses (seated along one side of the hall and dressed like brides in the traditional Sundanese *sarung kebaya*) invite the male patrons (seated along the other side of the hall and dressed in street clothing) to dance. Before they leave, the men pay a cashier in the corner who keeps track of with whom the man has danced. Jaipongan is also held nightly at the Sanggar Tari Purwa Setra, Jl. Otto Iskandardinata 541A.

Angklung (hand-held bamboo chime) performances are held regularly in the afternoons at Pak Ujo's Saung Angklung (Jl. Padasuka 118). This is both an angklung school and a workshop; wayang golek and dance performances are also put on by request. Instrument sets may be purchased here.

Bandung Highlands

Tangkuban Prahu volcano, Ciater hot springs, Lembang and the waterfall at Maribaya are all less than an hour by vehicle to the north of Bandung.

The highlands to the south of Bandung are even more spectacular, and anyone seriously interested in exploring them should get a copy of Bandung and Beyond, by Richard and Shila Bennett, available from Bandung Man (Jl. Cihampelas 120). This little booklet has detailed instructions to a wide variety of mountain destinations, and descriptions.

Cirebon

Cirebon (pronounced *cheer-i-bon*) has begun to receive a bit more attention from scholars and artists, mostly because of its colorful past and wealth of traditional performing arts and crafts.

GETTING THERE

Cirebon is about 4 hours (260 km/160 mi) overland from Jakarta, only 3 hours by road from Bandung. There is a small airport, but trains and mini-buses are generally more convenient. The Bima Express and the Mutiara are air-conditioned first-class trains operating on the Jakarta-Cirebon coastal route, leaving from Jakarta's Kota Station. Second-class trains also serve Cirebon. The Gunung Jati leaves from Jakarta's Pasar Senen Station, and the Senja Utama departs from Jakarta's Gambir Station.

A more convenient way to go is by nine-seater mini-bus. They will fetch you in Jakarta and deliver you to the hotel in Cirebon approximately 4 hours later. Some companies offer air-conditioned buses.

Numerous eastward-bound intercity buses leave Jakarta in the late afternoon from Pulo Gadung Terminal, arriving in Cirebon 4 hours later. From Bandung's Cicaheum Terminal, buses to Cirebon generally depart in the early evening and arrive 2 hours later.

GETTING AROUND

Most everything in town is within walking distance, or take a pedicab (*becak*). For trips out to Gua Sunyaragi, Trusmi and Gunung Jati, rent a car from the hotel, or simply catch one of the local mini-buses headed in that direction.

ACCOMMODATION

Patrajasa, Jl. Tuparev II, P.O. Box 68, Cirebon 45153. Tel: (0231) 209-401, Fax: 207-696. Modern but tacky rooms.

Park, Jl. Silwangi 107, Cirebon 45124. Tel: (0231) 205-411, Fax: 205-407.

Cirebon Plaza, Jl. Kartini 64, Cirebon 45122. Tel: (0231) 202-061, Fax: 204-258.

Grand Hotel, Jl. Siliwangi 110, Cirebon. Tel: 20-14-5. A variety of rooms from huge to tiny.

EATING OUT

Cirebon is famous for its seafood (the city's name means "shrimp river"), and the best seafood restaurant in town is **Maxim's** (Jl. Bahagia 45-7), just a short walk back along the road next to the Thay Kak Sie Chinese temple. Giant steamed crabs and prawns here are fresh and cheap. They also serve tasty Chinese food.

For spicy Padang food, there's **Sinar Budi** (Jl. Karang Getas 20), where they also serve good fresh fruit drinks. For a simple lunch, try the local specialty, *nasi lengko* (rice with bits of fried tempe, tahu, vegetables and sambal) at the **Kopyor** across the street (Jl. Karang Getas 9).

SHOPPING

To get the best batik, visit **Ibu Masina's** studio in Trusmi, 12 km to the west of Cirebon, just off the Bandung road. Ibu Masina has revived many of the traditional Cirebon court designs, which incorporate a variety of Chinese, Javanese, Indian, Islamic and European motifs.

For Cirebonese *topeng* masks, visit Pak Kandeg at Suranenggala Lor village, about 5 km north of Cirebon on the road to Gunung Jati. Topeng masks and paintings on glass using Arabic calligraphy are also produced in Palimanan and Gegesik villages, to the northwest of Cirebon.

Pekalongan

Known as a center of batik, Pekalongan is between 3 and 4 hours from Cirebon by bus or colt, two hours from Semarang. The best way to get around town is to walk or take a becak.

BATIK SHOPPING

Besides shops on Jl. Hayam Wuruk and Jl. Hasanuddin where fabrics are sold, seek out individual batik makers.

Tobal Batik at Jl. Teratai 24, Klego, specialists in export clothing. Many of the batik sundresses and shirts in boutiques in California and Australia are drawn, dyed and sewn here. While they produce to order for wholesale customers and do not normally sell individual pieces, they often have overstocks of certain items they sell to casual visitors.

Ahmad Yahya at Jl. Pesindon 221. Enter the small lane near the bridge on Jl. Hayam Wuruk, next to the Sederhana Restaurant. His fabrics have been selling in New York for many years, and have been used to decorate the bathrooms and kitchens of Hollywood celebrities.

Achmad Said, at Jl. Bandung 53, is another producer well-known to foreigners, producing brightly-colored cap fabrics under the Zaky label.

Salim Alaydras at Jl. H. Agus Salim 31 produces some floral piece goods and has antique fabrics for sale.

For higher-quality, hand-drawn tulis work, visit **Jane Hendromartono** at Jl. Blimbing 36. Her superb work is in the permanent collection of the Textile Museum in Washington D.C., as well as in many private collections around the world. She generally has a variety of original *sarung* and *kain* pieces, as well as some Chinese altar cloths done in batik, and several types of less-expensive batik cap.

Perhaps Pekalongan's most famous batik artist is **Oey Soe Tjoen**, who bought over and continued many of the designs of the great Eliza Van Zuylen, an Indo-Dutch woman whose rare batik, produced in the 1920s and 1930s, now fetches thousands of dollars from avid collectors in Holland and New York. Oey Soe Tjoen's wife and son now continue the business at their home and workshop in Kedungwuni, south of Pekalongan (Jl. Raya 104).

Yogyakarta

Emerging from the shadow of an increasingly touristed Bali, it has been some years since Yogyakarta was discovered as a tourist destination. Indeed, more and more visitors are finding that Yogyakarta's majestic temples and palaces, traditional crafts and performing arts provide a fascinating counterpoint to those of Bali. Many who have spent time in both places profess to prefer this laid-back city.

A modest tourist boom has overtaken the venerable Javanese court center as a result; the standard and availability of hotels, restaurants, and other services has improved greatly.

GETTING THERE

A majority of foreign visitors to Yogya arrive by air. There are several daily flights from Jakarta. Fares average US$125 round-trip.

The first-class **Bima Express** train that plies the Jakarata–Yogyakarta–Surabaya route nightly is Java's finest: comfortable, air-conditioned sleeper cars with small two-mattress compartments, a sink and a table. Fares for executive class average US$50 one-way. The train leaves Jakarta's Kota Station in late afternoon and arrives the following day at the crack of dawn. The second-class **Senja Utama** and **Senja Yogya** trains from Jakarta cost much less, but they are slower and not air-conditioned.

Intercity buses always travel at night. The Jakarta-Yogyakarta trip takes about 9 hours; from Bandung, 6 hours. Fares average US$15 or so.

Orientation

Yogya's main street is Jl. Malioboro, which runs north-south from the front steps of the Kraton palace all the way up to the Tugu monument, which is in the middle of the intersection with Jl. Jend. Sudirman and Jl. Diponegoro.

Jl. Pasar Kembang is a small street lined with inexpensive hotels and shops – once Yogya's red-light district, but now taken over by budget travelers. Jl. Sosrowijayan, the next small street to the south, also has budget hotels, as do several of the lanes connecting these two streets.

The more fashionable suburbs of Yogyakarta are located across the river to the east of Jl. Malioboro/ Mangkubumi. From here, it is about a mile north to the campus of Gajah Mada University. Farther down is Jl. Solo, which is a busy shopping area lined with stores, restaurants and hotels. The Ambarrukmo Palace Hotel and the Adisucipto Airport are several miles out of town to the east.

Tourist Office: Diparda D.I. Yogyakarta, Jl. Malioboro 14, Yogykarta 55213. Tel: (0274) 62-811 ext: 218, 224.

Getting Around

Taxis and Mini-Buses: Taxis and mini-buses are expensive in Yogya because of the tourist demand. Drivers have come up with fixed fares, although a few will accept less after bargaining. Some will demand more.

Most hotels, including the budget guesthouses on Jl. Prawirotaman, will meet you at the airport or train station with transportation, if informed before arrival.

Pedicabs: Pedicabs, or becaks, are convenient for short distances in town. Yogyakartans use them for their daily transportation, and some tourists have taken to chartering one for touring. Becak drivers sometimes try to charge outrageous amounts to tourists, and often won't come down to a reasonable price. Bargaining for becak rides is something of an art anyway, and this makes it doubly difficult for foreigners to use them. The key to good bargaining is to smile and joke about how high the first offer is, then to walk away once you have stated your final price. If it is reasonable, he will usually accept and call you back.

City buses: Within the city, buses circulate all day along fixed routes. In addition, there is a whole fleet of smaller pick-up micro-buses that are perhaps more convenient, as they travel in smaller circuits.

Andong: Lastly, you can hire an *andong* or dokar pony cart for trips into the country along scenic back roads – a very nice and slow way to get out to Kota Gede or even to Imogiri or Parangtritis. Not recommended on major highways, however. Dokars generally wait to the east of the post office, along Jl. Senopati, or on side roads at edge of town; villagers still use them to get to and from the city.

Tours/Travel Agents

Bhayangkara Tour, Jl. Jend Sudirman 3. Tel: (0274) 566-763, 561-088, Fax: 566-418.

Borobodour Pahala Wisata, Sriwedari Hotel, Jl. Adisicipto Km. 6. Tel: (0274) 566-424, ext: 609, Fax: 566-415.

Citra Sahabat Wisata, Phoenix Heritage Hotel, Jl. Jend Sudirman 9-11. Tel: (0274) 566-845, 566-717, Fax: 562-836.

Dewata Sakti, Jl. Cenderawasih 8. Tel: (0274) 566-249, 515-934, 513-781.

Grand Sunshine Prima, Aquila Prambanan Hotel, Jl. Adisucipto Km. 8. Tel: (0274) 565-005, ext: 10834, Fax: 515-010.

Intan Pelangi, Jl. Maliboro 18. Tel: (0274) 562-895, 565-279.

Intras Travel, Jl. Maliboro 177. Tel: (0274) 513-189, 576-792.

Pacto Travel, Gandok Ambarukmo Palace Hotel. Tel: (0274) 566-488, ext: 7130, Fax: 561-050.

Royal Holidays, Arcade APH. Tel: (0274) 566-488, ext: 7142, Fax: 563-282 (ATT Royal).

Sahid, Sahid Garden Hotel, Jl. Babarsari. Tel: (0274) 587-078, ext: 222, 223, Fax: 563-183.

Tourindo, Jl. Mangkubumi 11 B. Tel: (0274) 566-629, Fax: 566-673.

Trans Java Holidays, Gedong Kuning KG 1/48, 49. Tel/Fax: (0274) 374-503.

Accommodation

Yogya has room for everyone, from the Presidential Suite at the Ambarrukmo to the closets at the Home Sweet Homestay on Gang Sosrowijayan I. There is even one agency, Indraloka, that will place you in the home of an English- or Dutch-speaking family, where you share home-cooked meals.

Deluxe

Ambarrukmo Palace, Jl. Laksda Adisucipto Km. 5, P.O. Box 10. Tel: (0274) 566-488 (9 lines), Fax: 563-283.

Aquila Prambanan, Jl. Adisuciptio 48, P.O. Box 82. Tel: (0274) 65-005, Fax: 65-009.

Garuda (Natour), Jl. Maliboro 72. Tel: (0274) 586-491, 586-457, 586-353, Fax: 563-074.

Melia Purosani, Jl. Suryotomo No. 31, P.O. Box 1246. Tel: (0274) 589-521, 589-523, Fax: 588-070.

Queen of the South (beach resort), Parangritis. Tel: (0274) 367-196, Fax: 367-197. Located on a cliff overlooking Parangtritis Beach.

Sahid Garden, Jl. Babarsari, Yogyakarta 55281. Tel: (0274) 564-596, 587-078, Fax: 563-183.

Santika, Jl. Jend. Sudirman 19, Yogyakarta 55233. Tel: (0274) 63-036, Fax: 62-047.

Yogja Palace Hotel, Jl. Laksda Adisucipto (Jl. Solo) Km. 8. Yogyakarta, P.O. Box 90 YKBB. Tel: (0274) 566-418, Fax: 566-415.

Intermediate

Duta Garden Hotel, Timuran MG 111/ 103. Tel: (0274) 373-482, Fax: 372-064.

Gaja Mada Guesthouse, Jl. Bulaksumar, Kampus Universitas Gajah Madha. Tel: (0274) 88-461, 88-688, ext: 625.

Hotel Kota, Jl. Jlagran Lor No. 1. Tel: (0274) 515-844, Fax: 513-586 (near train station).

Jogja Village Inn, Jl. Menukan 5. Tel/Fax: (0274) 373-031.
Mutiara, Jl. Malioboro 18, P.O. Box 87. Tel: (0274) 63-814, Fax: 61-201.
Phoenix Heritage, Jl. Jendral Sudirman 9-11. Tel: (0274) 66-617, 66-856. The oldest hotel in the area.
Puri Artha, Jl. Cendrawasih No. 36. Tel: (0274) 563-288, Fax: 562-765.
Sejatera Comfort Suites Yogjakarta, Jl. Pringodanni 22 Demangan Baru. Tel: (0274) 519-336, Fax: 519-338 (serviced apartments).
Sriwedari, Jl. Adisucipto, P.O. Box 93. Tel: (0274) 88-288, Fax: 62-162.
Sri Manganti, Jl. Urip Sumoharjo, P.O. Box 46. Tel: (0274) 2881.

EATING OUT

The pilgrimage point for **fried chicken** lovers from all over Java (and all over the world) is **Nyonya Suharti's** (also known as Ayam Goreng "Mbok Berek," after the women who invented this famous fried-chicken recipe), located 7 km to the east of Yogya on the road to the airport. Nyonya Suharti's chicken is first boiled and coated in spices and coconut, then fried crisp and served with a sweet chili sauce and rice. Excellent when accompanied by pungent *petai* beans and raw cabbage. Indonesians patronize the place in droves; Jakartans in the airport lounge clutch their take-away boxes of the special chicken for friends and family back home.

Nasi padang fanatics also rave about the fare at **Sina Budi** Restaurant, at Jl. Mangkbumi 41, about 500 meters north of the railway tracks on the left (opposite the cinema). Mutton's brain *opor,* beef *rendang* and *gulai ayam* (chicken curry) await at a moment's notice. Be sure to ask for their spicy potato chips (*kentang goreng*) – Sinar Budi's answer to the barbecue-flavored variety in the West.

The Yogya specialty is *gudeg* – a combination plate consisting of rice with boiled young jackfruit (*nangka muda*), a piece of chicken, egg, coconut cream gravy and spicy sauce with boiled buffalo hide (*sambal kulit*). **Juminten** at Jl. Asem Gede 22, Kranggan 69, just north of Jl. Diponegoro, is known for its gudeg. The other gudeg restaurant is **Bu Citro's**, just opposite the entrance to the airport out on Jl. Adisucipto (a good place to eat while waiting for a flight). Most restaurants in Yogya also serve the dish, and there is excellent gudeg just north of Taman Sari on the eastern side of Jl. Ngasem. Other restaurants worth a try include **Andrawinaloka Gudeg Bu Citro**, Jl. Laksda Adi Suciptio 29; **Natour**, Bandara Adi Sucipto; and **Pesta Perak**, Jl. Tentara Rakyat Mataram 8.

There are several fine **Chinese** restaurants in town. The old standby and the favorite of the local Chinese community is the **Tiong San**, at Jl. Gandekan 29, a block west of Malioboro. **Moro Senang**, Jl. Solo 55 (on the north side next to Miroto's Supermarket), is also very good. The best seafood, however, and probably also the best Chinese food, is to be had at **Sintawang**, several doors north of Jl. Diponegoro at Jl. Magelang 9, on the west side of the street. For slightly more upmarket surroundings, try **Valentino International**, Jl., Magelang 57, or **Colombo**, Jl. Malioboro 25.

SHOPPING

Yogyakarta is commonly said to be a shopper's paradise, but be careful – some of the stuff sold here is pretty tacky. Nevertheless, it is all extremely cheap, and for this reason alone tourists seem to buy it.

Batik

They don't sell much *tulis* work here; most of the batik is made by the quicker copper-stamp (*batik cap*) method. They do have good yard-goods, including some that are on heavier cotton, to be used for curtains and upholstery.
Batik Juwita, Jl. A.Y. ani 64.
Batik Plentong, Jl. Tirtodipuran 29.
Batik Soemihardjo, Jl. Mangkuyudan 15A.
Batik Surya Kencana, Jl. Ngadinegaran M.J. VII.
Batik Tirto, Jl. Tirtodipuran No. 56.
Batik Winotosastro, Jl. Tirtodipuran 54.

Silver

Kota Gede, to the southeast of Yogya, is the center of the silver industry. There are two major workshops, **M.D. Silver** and **Tom's Silver**, and a number of minor ones where (buying or not) you can pass an intriguing half-hour watching the hammering, beating, heating, cleaning and polishing of the precious metal. Deft fingers create spider-web filigree; anvils clang till your ears ring; gentle hammer-blows tap out elegant repouss work.

Do not be constrained to buy only what is on display. Any workshop will produce pieces to specifications. All that is needed is a drawing or a specimen to copy. In most workshops, prices are calculated strictly according to the weight and grade of the silver used (generally either 80 percent, or sterling, 92.5 percent), except for certain exceptional or original designs.

It is said that some shops stamp their products with "925" with total disregard to the true purity of the silver content. Shop around for products that "feel" (heavy) and look like good quality silver (no pinkish or dull tones).

Most of these larger shops accept major credit cards; prices are usually in rupiah.
Ansor's Silver, Jl. Tegalgendu No. 28, Kota Gede. Friendly – big selection.
Asri Silver, Jl. Mondorakan No. 5A, Kota Gede. Nice items including accessories for traditional Javanese dress, ie, crowns, gold costume jewelry.
Bagus & Co, Pura Jenggala Bld, Jl. Mondorakan 252 Kota Gede. Multilingual and friendly staff have a new "exclusive design" fixed-price gallery next to this shop.
Narti's Silver, Jl. Tegalgendu No. 22, Kota Gede. Prices in US$.
Tom's Silver, Kota Gede 3-1A.

Leather Goods

Yogya's buff-colored, hand-tooled suitcases, overnight bags, briefcases, pocketbooks, sandals, belts and money pouches produced from buffalo hide are slowly improving in quality. But the tanning process employed here is still crude, so there is no fine, softer grades of leather. Another problem is the finishing – flimsy brass or tin clasps and hinges, and poor stitching.

There are many shops on Malioboro. One of the better ones is **Toko Setia**. For a bit better quality, though, try **Kusuma** just off Malioboro, or **Moeljosoehardjo's** near Taman Sari.

Buffalo hide is also the starting point for making wayang kulit puppets, although the thin, translucent kulit used to make them is not tanned at all and should properly be called parchment. For the best quality puppets, try **Ledgar** and **Swasthigita**.

Aris Handicraft, Jl. Kauman 14.
Benir Setiyo, Lingkungan Industri Magwoharjo.
Ledgar, Jl. Mataram DN I/370.
Swasthigita, Jl. Ngadinegaran MD 7.
Toko Setia, Jl. Maliboro 79 and 165 (2 outlets).

Antiques & Curios

Hunting grounds for so-called antiques include the many shops that line Jl. Malioboro. Try also the streets to the south and west of the Kraton, and the handful of small shops near the Ambarrukmo Palace Hotel. Most of the batik galleries listed above also sell antiques. Among the things that may catch your eye are carved and gilded chests for herbal medicines, or a pair of polychrome *loro blunyo,* or seated wedding figures, that were traditionally kept in the ceremonial chamber of an aristocratic Javanese home. A handful of 18th-century copper coins with the Dutch East Indies Company's (VOC) insignia can be fashioned into interesting decorations. Elaborately-carved Dutch and Chinese teakwood furniture is available, along with roofed and walled wedding beds, gilded panels, wicker chairs, massive chests and delicate vanities.

Then there are *naga*-wreathed stands for gamelan instruments; bronze statuettes of Durga, Nandi, Siva, Ganesa, Agastya, Buddha and innumerable bodhisattvas; crude *wayang klitik* figures; fake blue-and-white Ming porcelains.

Ardianto, Jl. Magelang Km. 5.8. Top-quality antiques.
Asmopawiro, Jl. Letjend. Haryono 20.
Edi Store, Jl. Malioboro 13A.
Ganeda Art Shop, Jl. Abdul Rahman 69.
Ken Dedes, Jl. Sultan Agung.
La Gallerie, Jl. Kota Gede, Kota Gede.
Pusaka Art Shop, Jl. Taman Garuda 22.
Seni Jaya Art Shop, Jl. Taman Garuda 11.

Paintings

Affandi, Jl. Laksda Adisucipto. Indonesia's "grand old man" has a large studio-cum-gallery overlooking the river on Jl. Solo, close to the Ambarrukmo Palace Hotel. Fame has brought fortune in its wake: the starting price for an original is in the thousands of dollars, which may be considered a bargain by international standards. In 1973, Affandi acquired the status of "painter laureate" when his egg-shaped concrete dome received the blessing of the government as a permanent private museum (the first of its kind in Indonesia). The works of other artists are also displayed.

Academy of Fine Arts (ASRI) on Jl. Gampingan. Pay a visit to find out where the up-and-coming generation is moving in painting, sculpture and handicrafts. This is considered one of the top art academies in the country.
Amri Gallery, Jl. Gampingan 6, Yogyakarta.
Kabul, Jl. Timoho 29-A. Good quality batik paintings from the artist.
Kuswadji K., Jl. Alun-Alun Utara, Pojok Barat Daya.
Nyoman Gunarsa Gallery, Jl. Wulung 43 Papringan Depok, Sleman. Specialists in oils.
Taman Sari batik painters complex
Yani's Gallery, Jl. Kmasan 178.

Masks & Wooden Puppets

For the finest work made by one of the few remaining craftsmen who still carves for the actors and *dalangs,* rather than for casual visitors, visit **Pak Warno Waskito**, a shy, gentle old man who's been playing his craft for more than 50 years. He is self-taught.

To reach Pak Warno's secluded hideaway, take the Bantul road south from Yogya, turn right at the 7.6-km marker, walk about 300 meters, turn left, stop at the first house on the right.

Performances in Yogyakarta

There are two types of performances: those that are put on especially for tourists, and those that are put on for the Javanese.

Tourist performances are not necessarily any less authentic or in any way inferior (as some people insist), even though they are frequently shortened or excerpted versions of the originals, adapted for the benefit (and short attention span) of foreigners.

What they do lack, of course, is a Javanese audience, and as the audience is as much a part of the performance as the players (especially in Java), try if at all possible to catch a village or *kampung* shadow play or dance-drama. Being here at the right time is just a matter of luck.

Gamelan: A gamelan orchestra is struck to accompany all of the dances and puppet shows listed below.

Visit the **Kraton Gamelan Rehearsals** on Monday and Wednesday mornings from 10.30am to noon. And if somehow you seem to be missing all the other performances, then try the hotels, you are sure to find one that has a performance when you want Hotels will have a detailed schedule of daily cultural events held on the hotel premises.

Wayang Kulit: This is truly the most influential Javanese art form, the one that traditionally has provided the Javanese with a framework through which to see the world and themselves. Not surprisingly, many foreigners have become fascinated by the shadow play (even if few are able to understand the dialogue), and there is quite a voluminous literature in Dutch and English on the subject. Traditional performances are always at night, beginning at 9pm and running until dawn.

The Agastya Art Institute (Jl. Gedong Kiwo M.D. III/237), a private *dalang* (puppeteer) school located to the southwest of Taman Sari, stages rehearsal-excerpt performances for the benefit of tourists most days in the afternoon.

Another tourist excerpt performance is at **Ambar Budaya**, in the Yogyakarta Craft Center opposite the Ambarrukmo Palace Hotel every Monday, Wednesday and Friday from 9.30 to 10.30pm.

Other venues for wayang kulit:
Sasana Hinggil, South Palace Square (Alun Alun Selatan). Performed every second Saturday of the month, 9pm–5.30am.
Sonobudoyo Archaelogical Museum, Jl. Trikora. Daily except Saturday, 11am–1pm.

Wayang golek: These are three-dimensional round puppets that are less popular in Central Java than in West Java. The movements, voices and staging, however, are very similar to that of the wayang kulit.

Agastya Art Institute (school for narrators), Jl. Gedong Kiwo MJI/996. Every Saturday 3–5pm.

Nitour Inc, Jl. KHA Dahlan 71. Daily except Saturday, 11am–1pm.

Javanese dance: The most wonderful time to experience the art of Javanese dance is on a moonlit evening in May at **Prambanan**. The famous *Ramayana* epic is performed between 7pm and 9pm. Season lasts from May to October – the dry season.

Other places to attend the Ramayana are:

Puruwisata Open Theatre, Jl. Brigjen Katamso. Nightly performances from 8–10pm. The introduction to the performance and characters is in English. Most hotels offer transportation.

Trimurti Theatre, Prambanan. Performances every Tuesday, Wednesday and Thursday from 7.30–9.30pm.

Many of the finer hotels, such as the **Melia Purosani**, will organize a dinner and Ramayana ballet bus tour. They can also find out the latest information on special seasonal and monthly cultural performances.

Wayang orang: Finally, you might also want to catch a folk version of the courtly dance-dramas. There are performances nightly at the **Taman Hiburan Rakyat** (THR), in the People's Amusement Park, on Jl. Brig. Jend. Katamso.

If looking for the most innovative Javanese dancing in Yogyakarta, visit the **Indonesian Dance Academy** (**ASTI**). This is one of five government tertiary-level schools in the nation, and with the most promising young dancers from the Yogyakarta area. Visit the school on Jl. Colombo.

For more information on dance schools, performances and puppet plays, pick up a copy of the "Yogyakarta Calender of Events" brochure published by the tourist office, or visit the Yogyakarta office on Jl. Maliboro.

The **Purowista Cultural Workshop** offers one-day workshops in traditional costume, Javanese dance training, gamelan music training, batik, and *Ramayana* ballet. The Purowisata also offers more thorough six-day workshops. For more information, contact or visit Purowisata 1. Brigjen Katamso, Yogyakarta 55152. Tel: 374-089, 380-642, Fax: 378-905.

Trips from Yogyakarta

Besides the famous temple complexes of **Borobudur** and **Prambanan**, there are many other lesser-known, but equally spectacular, temple sites within easy reach of Yogyakarta. These include the monuments of the **Dieng Plateau**, **Gedung Sanga**, and a handful of sites around Prambanan, including **Sewu**, **Plaosan**, **Ratu Boko**, **Kalasan**, **Sari** and **Sambisari**.

The expansive black-sand **beaches** on the southern coast at **Parangtritis** are only about an hour from the city. Along the way, stop at the scenic hilltop cemetery of Java's rajas at **Imogiri**, and the old silver-making town of **Kota Gede** on Yogya's outskirts.

To escape the heat, simply zip up **Gunung Merapi** to the nearby hill resort of **Kaliurang**. It is possible, in fact, to climb all the way up to the peak of this active volcano for an incredible view over all of Central Java. But this is best done early from Surakarta, on the Boyolali-Blabak road.

Dieng Plateau

The day-long excursion up to the Dieng Plateau (from *di hyang* meaning spirit place), about 100 km (60 mi) and 3 hours to the northwest of Borobudur, is a journey to a 2,000-meter (6,500-ft) mountain shrouded in mist and mysteries. The final climb from Wonosobo to the plateau follows a narrow, twisting course.

The existence of demons, spirits and wrathful giants seems not only plausible but probable here as grey skeins of mist envelop the surrounding ridges. The temples themselves are enigmatic, thought to have been constructed in the 8th century, although the earliest inscription found here is dated AD 809. Eight small stone temples have been partially restored. The foundations of others are nearby, and the remains of several wooden *pendopo* or pavilions may indicate that there was once a palace or monastery here.

The main group of temples is now named after the heroes and heroines of the *Mahabharata,* though these names are certainly later attributions. Arjuna, Puntadewa, Srikandi and Sembadra stand in a row in the center of a flat field, accompanied by their squat, ungainly servant, Semar. The ground around them looks firm enough, but it's mostly marshland. A millennium ago, this marsh was drained by an elaborate series of tunnels cut through the hills, the entrance to which are on the northwest corner of the field.

Perhaps the real reason this area was designated a holy site, despite its remoteness, was the presence of contemplative surroundings and violent volcanic activity. A walk along the wooded pathways encircling **Telaga Warna** (Multicolored Lake) and **Telaga Pengilon** (Mirror Lake) is enchantingly peaceful and beautiful. Nearby knolls and dells, which look like scenes straight from a Chinese brush painting, hide small grottoes. These are still popular as meditation retreats.

Around Prambanan

Sewu and **Plaosan** are two Buddhist candi complexes located nearby. Sewu ("thousand temples"), about 1 km to the north of Prambanan, consists of a tall central monument surrounded by 240 minor shrines. It was probably completed just before Prambanan, or around AD 850, and almost equals the latter in its intricacy. The central temple has an unusual gallery that is reached by passing through enclosed gateways lined with niches. The walls of the smaller shrines have crumbled, revealing a tantalizing array of Buddhist statues.

Plaosan, about 1 km to the east of Sewu, originally consisted of two large, rectangular temples surrounded by a number of little shrines and solid stupas. Both major temples were two-story, three-room buildings with windows (an unusual feature), containing a number of beautiful small Buddhas and bodhisattvas, one of whom wears a large headdress and looks almost Egyptian. This temple complex may date also from the mid 9th century.

The remains of **Candi Ratu Boko** are up on ridge 1.6 km south of Prambanan village, overlooking the entire valley. A steep, stairway leads up to the plateau to the left of the road. Come here at dawn or dusk, when the valley and its temples are bathed in golden light.

Ratu Boko was probably a fortified palace built by the last of the Buddhist Sailendras and later taken over by the Hindu builders of Prambanan.

There are three more temples along the main road back to Yogyakarta. **Candi Sari**, set amongst banana and coconut groves, is similar to the Plaosan temples – a Buddhist temple with two stories, windows, and several internal chambers. Thought to have been a monastery, Sari is distinctive because of its 36 panels of heavenly beings – dancing nymphs, musicians, dragon kings and because of its heavily ornamented roof. Built by the Sailendras, perhaps in the late 8th century.

Candi Kalasan is visible from the road, just to the west of Sari, another Buddhist shrine that may have been begun as early as AD 778. The outstanding feature is a huge, ornate *kala-makara* head above the southern doorway.

Finally, turn north to see **Sambisari**, a small candi that was discovered only in 1966 in the middle of a rice field, and has now been excavated from beneath 5 meters of earth. Many of the temple's reliefs remain curiously unfinished, which has given rise to speculation that it was buried by a volcanic eruption before completion – perhaps the same eruption that buried Borobudur.

Kota Gede

A short distance to the southeast of Yogya, the town of **Kota Gede** is famous for its silver workshops. Kota Gede was founded around 1579 by Senopati, the illustrious founder of the New or Second Mataram dynasty to which all the present-day Central Javanese rulers belong. Kota Gede is thus much older than Yogya itself, and Senopati now lies buried in a small moss-covered graveyard only 500 meters from the town's central market.

In the clearing outside the cemetery is a small white-washed building housing a large, polished black rock the size of a double bed. It is variously described as an executioner's stone or as Senopati's throne, but it has a Dutch inscription. In any case, it is considered to be a magically-powerful *pusaka* or heirloom of the place. Next to it are three large balls of yellow stone, sizes ranging from a softball to a volleyball, and reputedly used for juggling. More likely, these are ancient pre-Islamic "ancestor stones."

Royal Tombs of Imogiri

Another and more splendid link with Yogya's past is at **Imogiri**, 20 km to the south along a narrow road. Imogiri has an ancient, sturdy air about it. A little beyond the village, the road ends in a tiny square containing a single *warung* and an old *pendopo*. Ahead, a broad pathway leads off through an avenue of trees, the starting point for the climb to the royal tombs.

The famous Sultan Agung was the first of his line to be buried there, interned in 1645 on the top of a small rocky outcrop. Since then, almost every prince of the house of Mataram, and of the succeeding royal families of Yogyakarta and Surakarta, has been laid to rest at Imogiri.

A visit to this venerated site takes on the air of a pilgrimage (which indeed it is for many Javanese), for the 345 shallow-tread steps of the wide, formal stairway will exact considerable penance.

The tombs lie within three major courtyards at the top of the stairway. In front are those of Mataram; to the left, those of the Susuhunans of Solo; to the right, those of the Sultans of Yogya. Each great courtyard encloses smaller courts containing the memorials and tombs of the princes. Entry into the smaller courts, and viewing of the tombs, is permitted briefly only on Mondays and Fridays after noontime prayers, and you must wear formal Javanese court costume to visit them. This is less demanding than it may sound, and the necessary garments can be hired on the spot for a low fee.

Parangtritis

The shore at **Parangtritis** is linked with an ancient tradition that may have flourished in pre-Hindu times as a fertility cult, and which was later observed symbolically by Sultan Agung and his successors. Legends claim that Senopati, or perhaps Sultan Agung, was married in fact (not fantasy) to Raden Loro Kidul, the 'Queen of the Southern Ocean' whose domain, also known as the region of death, is beneath the waters of the Indian Ocean. Ritual observances of the marriage are still performed in the Central Javanese courts.

Legend or no, the rips and violent currents, and a heavy surf, make swimming dangerous on most of Java's southern coast. At Parangtritis, this seascape is backed by a forbidding shoreline of jagged cliffs and dunes of shifting, iron-grey sand.

Gunung (Mount) Merapi

On a clear day, Gunung Merapi can be seen in all its glory. Watching it is a full-time job at the Plawangan seismological station, where the volcanologists, armed with binoculars and seismographs, work in month-long shifts before moving on to Gunung Kelud or Ijen, or wherever else Java's crust is growing restless. Merapi is the most volatile of the island's volcanic peaks; the last serious eruption occurred in 1954.

Another observation point is to the west of the mountain. A small side-road, well-marked in English, branches off the main route to Muntilan, 23 km from Yogya, creeping slowly through tunnels of bamboo and tall stands of pine before revealing the ravaged western slope of the volcano, scarred and twisted by a continuing series of lava flows. At night, dull-red globs of molten rock can be seen through the darkness.

To stand on the rim of Merapi, gazing down on the world from a height of 2,900 meters and into the Dantean crater, is probably the most exciting mountain experience in Java. Bromo, in East Java, is usually given more attention, for it is easier to get to. Bromo is a walk. Merapi is a climb.

Surakarta (Solo)

Surakarta, or Solo as it is better known, is an easy hour's drive from Yogyakarta. Although the flat, sprawling city seems less a royal capital than its neighbor, Solo rewards patience.

Partly as a result of the aristocratic emphasis on Javanese traditions and proprieties in this city, Solo is very different from Yogya. It is more sedate, more reserved and more refined, without the young, revolutionary undercurrent. Solo is sleepier and smaller (in area if not in population), with less traffic, and also fewer tourists.

Getting There

The easiest way, from Yogya, is to book a seat on an express mini-bus at one of the travel offices on Jl. Diponegoro, just west of the Tugu monument. They leave all day at half-hour intervals and will drop you anywhere in Solo. You can also flag down a bus or mini-bus heading east on Yogya's Jl. Jend. Sudirman or Jl. Solo, arriving in Surakarta for about half the price, but it takes a lot longer and it is usually very crowded.

The other alternative is to rent your own taxi or mini-bus from Yogya with up to seven other people. Solo also has its own airport, with a few flights operating daily to and from Jakarta and Surabaya. And all trains stopping at Yogya also stop here.

ORIENTATION

Surakarta's main street is Jl. Slamet Riyadi, a broad boulevard running east-west and a continuation of the highway into town from Yogya. At its eastern end stands a Tugu monument, just in front of the northern gates leading into the *alun-alun* (town square) and the Kraton precincts. The General Post Office, government buildings, banks, the telephone office and the central market (*pasar gede*) are all nearby. Most hotels, restaurants and shops are also within walking distance, on or near Jl. Slamet Riyadi. The interesting areas of town to explore on foot are mostly centered around the two palaces – the Kasusuhunan and the Mangkunegaren. Jl. Secoyudan is the main shopping street and runs parallel to Salmet Riyadi. The travel offices are in between these two streets, on Jl. Yos Sudarso, and this is where you book and board an express mini-bus back to Yogya. Most intercity bus companies have offices and representatives along Jl. Veteran in the south of the city, as well as at the bus terminal to the north.

GETTING AROUND

Almost everything is within walking distance. Otherwise take a pedicab (becak). See the Yogykarta section for tips on bargaining for becaks.

ACCOMMODATION

Kusuma Sahid Prince, Jl. Sugiyopranoto 22. Tel: (0271) 46-356, Fax: 44-788.

Cakra Hotel, Jl. Slamet Riyadi 171. Tel: (0271) 45-847, Fax: 48-334.

Riyadi Palace, Jl. Slamet Riyadi 336. Tel: (0271) 33-300, Fax: 51-552.

Solo Inn, Jl. Slamet Riyadi 366. Tel: (0271) 46-075, Fax: 46-076. A bit noisy.

Mangkunegaran Palace, Jl. Puro Mangkunegaran. Tel: (0271) 35-683.

Sahid Solo, Jl. Gajah Mada 104. Tel: (0271) 45-889, Fax: 44-133. One of the older hotels.

EATING OUT

The overall best Javanese restaurant, by general consent, is the **Sari**, on the south side of Jl. Slamet Riyadi (No. 351), but it's about 3 km from the center of town. The specialties here are *nasi liwet* (a Solonese specialty: rice cooked in coconut cream with garnishes), fried chicken and various types of *pepes* (prawns, mushrooms or fish wrapped in a banana leaf with spices and steamed or grilled). Closer to town, the original **Timlo Solo**, Jl. Urip Sumoharjo 106, is also very good. They have excellent daily specials, but also the standard Javanese fried chicken, *pecel* (boiled vegetables with peanut sauce), *nasi gudeg* (local specialty) and *nasi kuning* (rice cooked in turmeric), with *tahu, tempe* and coconut. For the best Javanese-style fried chicken in town, try the **Tojoyo** at Jl. Kepunton Kulon 77. That's all they serve and it goes fast (open only 6 to 9pm). For the best chicken and mutton sate, go over to the **Ramayana** at Jl. Ronggowarsito 2. They also have excellent Chinese dishes such as fried spinach (*kangkong*) and deep-fried pigeon (*burung dara goreng*).

A convenient spot for a light lunch is the **Segar Ayem** restaurant on Jl. Secoyudan, opposite Pasar Klewer (the central batik market), and within walking distance of the Kraton. Excellent iced-fruit drinks here, with some simple Javanese dishes like *gado-gado, pecel* and *nasi rames*.

Another nearby luncheon spot, good for Chinese noodles of many types as well as iced fruit juices and cold beer, is **Bakso Taman Sari** on Jl. Jend. Gatot Subroto (42C), between Secoyudan and Slamet Riyadi. Another good place for Chinese noodles is **Miroso**, Jl. Imam Bonjol 10. The best *nasi padang* place is **Andalas**, on Jl. Ronggowarsito opposite and a bit to the east of the Mankunegaran Palace Hotel entrance.

Finally, you should sample the sweet coconut cream cakes sold at night from little carts all along Jl. Slamet Riyadi, a local specialty called *serabi*.

The best Chinese restaurant is the **Orient**, Jl. Slamet Riyadi 341A. Here you can order a beef hotplate, sweet and sour pork, or fish (a whole gurame), corn and crab (or shark's fin) soup, Chinese broccoli with black beans (*kailan tausi*), and their specialty: boiled chicken with garlic, onion and ginger sauce (*ayam rebus*). **The Centrum** at Jl. Kratonan 151 is much more central and also very good – let the manager order for you. They are famous for their crab rolls (*sosis kepiting*), prawns stir-fried in butter (*udang goreng mentegar*), fish with salted vegetables (*ikan sayur asin*) and fried crab claws (*kepit kepiting*). Other good Chinese restaurants include the **Diamond**, Jl. Brigjen Slamet Riyadi 394, and **Mataram**, Jl. Brigien Slamet Riyadi 262.

SHOPPING

Batik

Solo is known as Batik City and the three largest producers are all based here: **Batik Keris**, **Batik Semar** and **Batik Danar Hadi**. Visit their showrooms. Danar Hadi has many better quality *kain* and batik shirts. Semar aims at the mass-market, with printed batik dresses and shirts. Keris is in between. For the best in Solonese tulis work, visit **Ibu Bei Siswosugiarto** (Sidomulyo is her label) in the south of town. **K.R.T. Hardjonegoro**, one of Java's best-known batik designers, also lives and has his factory here, but generally sells only through outlets in Jakarta. Have a look also at the thousands of pieces for sale in **Pasar Klewer**, and wander the side streets nearby, behind the Grand Mosque, where there are quality producers.

Batik Danar Hadi, Jl. Dr. Rajiman.

Batik Keris, Jl. Yos. Sudarso 37.

Batik Semar (factory showroom), Jl. Pasar Nongko 132. (branch), Jl. R.M. Said 148.

K.R.T. Hardjonegoro, Jl. Kratonan 101.

Sidomulyo (Ibu Bei Siswosugiarto), Jl. Dawung Wetan R.T. 53/54.

Antiques

Visit the **Pasar Triwindu** market on Jl. Diponegoro first, to get an idea what is available: antique brass oil lamps, round marble top tables with matching chairs, and Chinese wedding beds.

Many of the vendors and dealers here also have caches of antique furniture and other valuable items at home, or they can guide you around to some of the refinishing workshops in town. No obligation to buy if you go with them, though you should pay for the *becak*. But then visit the established antique shopfronts on Slamet Riyadi and Urip Sumarharjo, where all sorts of treasures are sitting and gathering dust. They are a bit more reputable and less likely to sell fakes. But still beware and bargain hard.

Eka Hartono, Jl. Dawung Tengah 11/38.
Mertojo "Sing Pellet", Jl. Kepatihan 31.
Mirah Delima, Jl. Kemasan RT XI.
Parto Art, Jl. Slamet Riyadi 103.
Singo Widodo, Jl. Urip Sumoharjo 117.
Trisno Batik & Art Shop, Jl. Bayangkara 2.

Keris

To buy an antique *keris* dagger, visit Pak Suranto Atmosaputro, an English lecturer at the university, at his home just down a narrow alley across from the RRI radio studios (Jl. Kestalan III/21). He is a keris aficionado and member of the Keris-Lover's Association of Solo, and always has pieces of his own for sale, or he can quickly round up a selection to examine. Follow him on a Sunday to observe keris being forged and carved in the village of Komplang, just to the north of Solo (at the home of Ki Lurah Wignyosukadgo).

Wayang puppets

The acknowledged center for wayang kulit production in Java is the village of Manyaran, about 35 km to the south and west of Solo. Here, the village head organizes the village craftsmen and sells their wares at quite reasonable and fixed prices.

You can also go directly to the *dalang* themselves, most of whom make their own puppets in their spare time. **Pak Soetrisno** is descended from a well-known court dalang family and now teaches wayang kulit at ASKI (he also speaks good English and spent some time in the United States). He lives out of town and has no telephone, so get someone to call his office at the university (Tel: 5260) and leave a message that you are interested in buying puppets.

Java's most famous *dalang* is **Pak Anom Suroto**, who lives down a small lane from Jl. Slamet Riyadi. Enter from between the Danar Hadi shop and the Cakra Hotel and ask where he lives. He occasionally has puppets for sale.

Gamelan

To buy a complete gamelan orchestra, a single instrument or just to observe these bronze metallophones being cast and forged as they have been for thousands of years – using hand-operated bellows, teakwood charcoal and simple tools – visit the gamelan assembly of **Pak Tentrem Sarwanto**. His family has been suppliers of instruments to the court for generations. Located in the southeast of town: Jl. Ngepung RT 2/RK I, Semanggi.

Performing Arts

Taman Sriwedari, on Jl. Slamet Riyadi, boasts the most accomplished *wayang orang* troupe in Java.

The **Taman Hiburan Bale Kambang** amusement park complex, located in the northwest of the city, houses two theaters. One, the popular Sri Mulat comedy theater, presents an ordinary fare of slapstick routines such as "Big, Bad Dracula" and "The Commercial Gigolo" nightly. The other offers more serious **ketoprak folk dramas**, enactments of historical tales and legends. There are also several open-air restaurants and billiards hall in the park. Shows begin nightly at 8pm except Sundays (matinee).

Krakatau

Boats may be chartered to the four uninhabited islands of the Krakatau group from Labuan; arrangements can be made through most local hotels, or at the port. The marine club at the Mamruk Quality resort offers a high-speed ride via hovercraft. Tel: (0254) 601-577, Fax: 601-723.

Bring along lunch and refreshments, as it is hot and there is no fresh water. The boat trip can take as long as 5 hours each way, so get an early start.

Most visitors land at the eastern side of Anak Krakatau and then climb up from here to the top of the first ridge for a view into the smoking crater and across to the other three islands: Sertung to the west, Small Krakatau to the east and Big Krakatau to the south. Not recommended during the rainy season, November to March, when the seas are rough.

Most visitors interested in seeing Krakatau will want to visit Ujung Kulon Nature Reserve. The park's guest bungalows are on Pulau Peucang, (7 hours from Labuan), sleeping a total of 16 people with a comfortable lounge area. The island is populated by monitor lizards, wild deer and long-tailed macaques and is worth exploring. The bungalows have resident staff and small motor boats that may usually be hired to cross over the straits and motor upriver, though you may have to supply the gasoline (inquire at the PPA office about this before leaving, and purchase a few 5-liter jerry cans in Labuan if necessary).

Otherwise, charter a boat at the marine club at Mambuk Quality Resort. You can sleep on the boat and they will provide you with food and drinks. They will even get permission to have a shower at the government lodges.

Surabaya

Getting There

Convenient air services connect Surabaya with almost all cities in Indonesia, with regular jet shuttles every other hour to and from Jakarta. Many flights heading for the northern and eastern islands make a stopover here.

A large number of trans-Java express trains and buses terminate or originate in Surabaya, with many immediate onward connections.

Orientation

Jl. Tunjungan/Basuki Rachmat is generally regarded as the main street, running north-south and parallel to the river.

There are three train stations: Pasar Turi, Semut (also known as Kota) and Gubeng. The last is the nearest to the hotel districts. The Joyoboyo Bus Terminal is in the south of the city, just opposite the Surabaya Zoo. Juanda Airport is 15 km (9 mi) farther south, on the road to Malang and Tretes. Intercity bus company offices are around Jl. Basuki Rachmat, and on side-lanes like Embong Sawo.

The Tourist Information Office at Jl. Pemuda 118 has brochures and information, with dates for events like the fortnightly bull races on Madura (August–September) and the Ramayana Ballet performances at Pandaan (June–November).

Tourist Office: Diparda Tk. I Jawa Timur, Jl. Darmokali 35, Surabaya 60241. Tel: (31) 575-488, Fax: 575-449.

GETTING AROUND

There are no metered cabs in this city of more than 3 million. Taxis may be rented by the hour at any hotel and at the airport. City buses and mini-buses (bemos) circulate throughout the city, converging on the Joyoboyo Bus Terminal in front of the zoo.

ACCOMMODATION

Hyatt Regency Surabaya, Jl. Basuki Rachmat 106-128. Tel: (031) 531-1234, Fax: 532-1508.
Garden Palace, Jl. Yos Sudarso 11. Tel: (031) 520-951.
Patra Surabaya Hilton, Jl. Gunungsari, Surabaya 60224. Tel: (031) 582-703, Fax: 574-504. Surabaya's largest pool.
Radisson Plaza, Jl. Pemuda 31-37, Surabaya 60271. Tel: (031) 516-833, Fax: 516-393. Suites for women.
Elmi, Jl. Panglima Sudirman 42-44. Tel: (031) 522-571.
Garden, Jl. Pemuda 21. Tel: (031) 521-001.
Mojopahit, Jl. Tunjungan 65, P.O. Box 199. Tel: (031) 433-515. Built in 1910.
Sahid Surabaya, Jl. Sumatra 1. Tel: (031) 522-711, Fax: 516-292.

EATING OUT

Chinese

Atom Golden Star, Kompleks Pertokoan Pasar Atom Tahap, V 4th floor, Jl. Bunguran 45.
Bima Garden, Jl. Pahlawan 102. Specialists in Hong Kong-style *dim sum.*
Mandarin, Jl. Genteng Kali 93. A well-known banquet house, situated along the river.
Kiet Wan Kie at Jl. Kembang Jepun 51 in Chinatown. Reasonable prices.
There is also a small hole-in-the-wall opposite the New Grand Park Hotel on Jl. Samudra with excellent fish.

Indonesian

Bibi & Baba, Jl. Tunjungan 76.
Taman Sari Indah, Jl. Taman Apsari 5.

SHOPPING

Try the shopping center on **Jl. Tunjungan** or the **Wijaya Shopping Center**. Local items to look out for here include batik from Madura, brass lamps and ornaments, bamboo decorations, stone statues, bronze figurines, basketry, paintings.

There is a whole string of antique and curio shops near the Hyatt on Jl. Basuki Rachmad (**Amongsari** at No. 26-A and **Seruni** at 22-C)). Also on Jl. Tunjungan (**Kendendes** at No. 97 and **Sarinah** at No. 7). Several more are located on Jl. Raya Darmo (**Rochim** at No. 27 and **Bangun** at No. 5).

For batik and hand-woven cotton textiles, the area around the Sunan Ampel mosque in the middle of the Arab quarter is best. There are daily exhibitions of metal and leather handicraft, embroidery and textiles at the **People's Amusement Park (Taman Hiburan Rakyat)**, Surabaya Mall, Jl. Pemuda 31-37.

ENTERTAINMENT

Javanese *wayang orang*, *ludruk* and *ketoprak* folk dramas are performed nightly at two theaters in the **People's Amusement Park** (**THR**), in Surabaya Mall. There is also a hysterically funny Sri Mulat slapstick comedy troupe here featuring a whole gang of transvestites. Shows start at about 8pm. Tickets are cheap.

From June to November, there are fortnightly (first and third Saturdays of each month) *sendratari* classical Javanese dance-drama performances at the huge open-air **Candra Wilwatikta** amphitheater in Pandaan, 45 km (30 mi) south of Surabaya. The Tourist Information Office can arrange an East Javanese *kuda kepang* "hobbyhorse" trance dance performance if notified three days in advance. Regular bull races are now held monthly in the new stadium at **Bangkalan**, just across the straits of Madura. Check with the Tourist Information Office for dates.

Malang

Unlike many Javanese towns which lie dead straight along a dreary, shuttered, down-at-heel main street, Malang sweeps and winds over gentle ridges and gullies along the banks of the Brantas River, with unexpected views and quiet back-streets that beg to be explored. It hasn't experienced the explosive growth of other large Javanese cities, and it remains a small, quiet town.

GETTING THERE

Although there are local third-class trains running along the old tracks from Surabaya to Malang, the express mini-buses taking the highway are quicker, more comfortable, and they deliver you to your doorstep in Malang. Hotels in Surabaya can book a seat. Buses also leave regularly from Surabaya's Joyoboyo bus terminal.

ACCOMMODATION

Kartika Prince, Jl. Jaksa Agung Surpapto 17. Tel: (0341) 61-900.
Malang Regent Park, Jl. Jaksa Agung Suprapto 12-16. Tel: (0341) 63-388.
Pelangi, Jl. Merdeka Selatan 3. Tel: (0341) 65-156.

EATING OUT

There's good Padang food opposite the YMCA at the **Minang Jaya** (Jl. Basuki Rachmat 22). **Oen's** at Jl. Basuki Rachmat 5 is an old colonial place serving Dutch food like *broodjes* and *uitsmijters.* For Chinese food, try the **New Hongkong**, Jl. Arif Rahman Hakim.

SHOPPING

There are many antique and curio stores on **Jl. Basuki Rachmat**. Also try the antique section of the **Pasar Besar** market, on the second floor at the back left-hand corner. This can be a great place to buy old Dutch glasses, trays and silverware.

Bromo

Best approach is by the 20-km road that winds up from the north coast highway at Tongas, just west of Probolinggo, through Sukapura to **Ngadisari**. Lots of mini-buses make this journey, and can be boarded at the Tongas turnoff. From here, a cobblestone road covers the last 3 km up to **Cemara Lawang** on the lip of the caldera, but special permission must be sought from the police in Ngadisari to use this road (if you have your own vehicle). Otherwise, all public transport stops at the Ngadisari parking lot, and you have to walk or rent a pony for the final, steep climb. Try to get up there before sunset. It takes about 5 hours to reach the caldera's rim from Surabaya, a bit less from Tretes.

The Bromo Permai Hotel, Tel: 41-256, at Cemara Lawang sleeps 30 and usually has space available. Call the booking office in Probolinggo (Jl. Panglima Sudirman) for reservations, especially during the peak tourist seasons. The rooms are very basic, many without private bath. The hotel restaurant is quite adequate. Temperatures can drop below freezing at night because of the altitude. The hotel supplies a thin blanket, but bring along extra covers and several layers of warm clothing.

Hire a pony to make the 2-hour trek down into the caldera and across the famous "Sand Sea" to the base of Bromo. From here, a flight of steps leads up to the rim of this volcano-within-a-volcano so that you can peer down into Bromo's steaming, sulphurous pit. The horsemen like to get you up at 3am and ride across to Bromo for the sunrise, so that they get home by 9am while it is still cool, but this is a miserable, cold and windy journey in pitch blackness. The view of the sunrise is better from the caldera's rim anyway, just near the hotel. So watch it from here, have breakfast, and then go down to Bromo.

It is also possible to continue on from Bromo across the Sand Sea in a southerly direction to the village of **Rano Pani** (about 20 km) and then to **Rano Kumbolo** (another 12 km) for the climb up Gunung Semeru, Java's highest mountain (3,700 meters/12,500 ft). Be well prepared for this, though, both physically and with good camping gear. There are three beautiful lakes nestled in this highland massif, amid grassy meadows and pine forests. From Rano Pani, descend to the west via **Ngadas** and **Gubug Klakah**, from where there is a road leading down through Tumpang to Malang.

Bali

To the Balinese, the world is their living-room and its travelers their guests. Do your best to respect their traditions and attitudes:

• Settle all prices beforehand; otherwise, you must pay the price demanded. When shopping, don't ask the price or make an offer unless you intend to buy.

• Dress up rather than down. You are afforded special guest status as a foreigner, so don't abuse it. Old faded or torn clothes, bared thighs and excessively "native" dress are considered bad form.

• Keep all valuables out of sight and preferably locked up. The Balinese have a strong sense of pride and consider temptation an affront, suspicion an insult.

• Wear a temple sash whenever entering a temple, and expect to pay a token entrance fee to the custodian. Behave with reverence and deference.

GETTING THERE

Air: Bali's **Ngurah Rai International Airport**, which straddles the narrow Tuban Isthmus in the south of the island, is served by many daily flights from Jakarta, Yogyakarta, Surabaya and various other cities in Indonesia, as well as a growing number of international flights.

Train: From Jakarta, Bandung or Yogyakarta, travel first to Surabaya's Gubeng Station and change over for the 7-hour trip on the Mutiara Timur, a non-airconditioned train bound for Banyuwangi, at Java's eastern tip. From here, a bus goes across the straits on the ferry and over to Denpasar, an extra 4 hours.

Bus: With improved roads, the bus is now faster than the train. There are air-conditioned buses from Surabaya (a 12-hour trip) to Denpasar, and from Yogya (16 hours) to Denpasar.

GETTING AROUND

Balinese roads are a parade ground, used for escorting village deities to the sea, for funeral cremation processions, for filing to the local temple in Sunday best, or for performances of a trans-island *barong* dance. They are also now increasingly crowded. The volume of traffic has increased dramatically over the past two decades. In the end, the best way to see Bali is on foot. Away from the busy main roads, the island takes on an entirely different complexion.

Taxi: There is a taxi service from the airport, with fixed prices. Taxis and mini-buses are for hire at every hotel, just with a driver, or with an English-speaking driver/guide. Often there is little difference (other than the price) between renting a car and going on a professionally-guided tour, as many drivers speak good English.

Rental cars: The best way to get around the island independently is to rent a self-drive car, available in Kuta, Sanur or Denpasar. You must have a valid International Driving Permit or an ASEAN-country drivers license.

You buy the gas. Buy the extra insurance, too. Book a car through your hotel or directly from any of the companies listed below. Test-drive the car before paying.

Bagus, Jl. Duyung 1, Sanur Beach. Tel: 287-794.
Bali Happy, Jl. Raya Kuta 72X. Tel: 752-756.
CV Bali Jasa Utama Jaya, Jl. Danau Poso 46, Sanur. Tel: 287-370, Fax: 287-373.
CV Wirasana, Jl. Bypass Ngurah Rai 545X, Sanur Kaja. Tel: 286-066.
Norman's, Sanur Beach Street, Sanur. Tel: 288-328, Fax: 288-830.
Toyota Rent A Car, Airport. Tel: 753-744; Jl. Tuban Raya 99X. Tel: 751-356 or Jl. Bypass Ngurah Rai. Tel: 701-774.

Motorcycles: Motorcycles are convenient and inexpensive. But the roads are crowded and traffic is dangerous – the chances of an accident are uncomfortably high. Each year, several tourists are killed in motorbike accidents, and many more are injured. If renting a bike, ride slowly and defensively.

The cost of hiring a motorbike is usually a matter of bargaining, and varies greatly. You provide the gas. Any hotel can arrange a rental for you, and it is a good idea to buy insurance, so that you are not responsible for damages to the bike in case of an accident. Be sure to test-drive it. You must possess an International Driving Permit valid for motorcycles.

Public mini-buses/buses: The local system of pick-ups and mini-buses (collectively known as bemos) and intra-island buses is efficient and inexpensive. In addition, almost every bemo on the road in Bali may be hired by the trip or by the day; you just tell the driver where you want to go and then agree on a price.

These are four bus/bemo terminals

in Denpasar serving points to the south, west, north and east of the city. Rather than taking a taxi from the airport, walk about 1.5 km to the road and catch a local bemo to Kutaor Denpasar. All **intercity buses** leave from Suci Terminal on Jl. Hasannudin, and the bus companies have their offices here.

TOURIST OFFICE

Denpasar: Diparda Tk. I Bali, Jl. S. Parman, Niti Mandala, Denpasar 80235. Tel: (0361) 222-387, 226-313.

Also: Kanwil Depparpostel X Bali, Komplex Niti Mandala, Jl. Raya Puputan, Renon, Denpasar 80235. Tel: (0361) 225-649, Fax: 233-475.

PERFORMING ARTS VENUES

The best way to see Balinese dances, *wayang kulit* and *gamelan* orchestras is to attend a village temple festival. There is one going on somewhere on the island daily. Ask at any hotel.

Public performances are also given at various central locations around the island, but are mainly for tourists. Some of the best dancers and musicians in Bali participate in tourist performances, and for them it's a good source of income.

Kecak Dance
Abian Kapas Art Center
Ayoda Pura, Tanjung Bungkak
Banjar Legian, Kelod
Bona, Gianyar
Padang Tegal
Puri Agung, Peliatan
Pura Dalem, Ubud

Ramayana Ballet
Ayoda Pura, Tanjung Bungkak
Indra Prasta, Kuta
Pura Dalem Puri, Ubud
Ubud Palace

Barong Dance
Banjar Seminiyak, Legian
Saha Dewa, Batubulan
Ubud Palace

Legon Dance
Ayoda Pura, Tanjung Bungkak
Banjar Tegal, Ubud
Puri Agung, Peliatan
Puri Dalem, Tebesaya
Puri Keteran, Peliatan
Ubud Palace

Wayang Kulit
Ubud

Trance Dance/Firewalking
Batubulan
Bona, Gianyar
Pura Dalem, Ubud

SHOPPING

Bali is a great place to shop. Hundreds of boutiques and roadside stalls have set up all over the island, and thousands of artisans, craftsmen, seamstresses, and painters are busy supplying the tourist demand.

Woodcarvings

You are sure to find good woodcarvings in the shops along the main roads in **Mas** (Ida Bagus Tilem's Gallery and Museum is well-known). Also try the villages of **Pujung** (past Tegalalang north of Ubud), **Batuan** and **Jati**. All types of indigenous wood, ranging from the butter-colored jackwood to inexpensive bespeckled coconut, are sculpted here in bold designs that set the standards for carvers elsewhere in the archipelago. Wood imported from other islands – buff hibiscus, Javanese teak and black Sulawesian ebony – are also hewn into delicate forms by Balinese craftsmen. Hunt for antique woodcarvings that once adorned gilded temple pavilions or royal palaces, in shops in **Kuta**, **Sanur** and on the main street of **Klungkung**.

Paintings

The artist's center is **Ubud**, including the villages of **Pengosekan**, **Penestanan**, **Sanggingan**, **Peliatan**, **Mas** and **Batuan**. The famous **Neka Gallery and Museum** and the **Puri Lukisan Museum**, both in Ubud, will give an idea of the range of styles and artistry achieved by the best painters. Then visit some of the other galleries in the area: **Gallery Munut**, **Oka Kartini Art Gallery**, **Gallery Agung** and the gallery of the **Pengosekan Community of Artists**. Examples from every school of painting in Bali are found here, as well as canvasses of young artists portraying festivals and dancers.

For quality works of art, seek out the gallery-homes of well-known artists in Ubud such as **Antonio Blanco**, **Hans Snel**, **Wayan Rendi**, **Arie Smit** and the late, great **I Gusti Nyoman Lempad**. In other villages, seek out **Mokoh** and **I Made Budi** (Batuan).

For traditional astrological calendars and *iderider* – strips of cotton five-meters-long that are suspended from the eaves of shrines during temple ceremonies – paintings in the so-called wayang style, visit **Kamasan**, just south of Klungkung. This style has been around for many centuries and some of the paintings are antique. Examples are found in **Klungkung** and in many antique shops.

Stone Carvings

For traditional sandstone carvings, stop at the workshops in **Batubulan**. And **Wayan Cemul**, an Ubud stone carver with an international following, has a house full of his own creations. Also try **Ida Bagus Tilem Carver**, in Ubud.

Textiles

For batik clothing, try the many boutiques in **Kuta Beach**. Brocades that gleam like gold lame, and also the simpler, handloomed *sarung* cloths, are sold in every village. **Gianyar** is the home of the handloom industry, but the villages of **Blayu**, **Sideman**, **Mengwi**, **Batuan**, **Gelgel**, **Tengganan** and **Ubud** all produce their own style of weavings.

Gold and Silver

The centers for metal working are **Celuk** and **Kamasan**, where all such ornaments are on sale at reasonable prices. **Kuta** is another center for export gold and silver wares. For traditional Balinese jewelry, visit the shops on Jl. Sulawesi and Jl. Kartini in Denpasar.

Handicrafts

Bamboo implements, wayang kulit figures and ornaments made of coconut shell and teakwood are sold at most souvenir shops. Bone-carvings can be had for good prices at **Tampaksiring**, while plaited hats and baskets are the specialty of the women of **Bedulu** and **Bona**. **Sukawati** market and the row of stands opposite **Goa Gajah** are the best places to buy baskets. **Klungkung** market also has some finely worked traditional wares.

The Handicraft Center (**Sanggraha Karya Hasta**) in Tohpati, Denpasar, is a government-run cooperative that has a collection of handicrafts from Bali and the other islands of Indonesia, such as baskets and weavings, at fixed prices. The morning market at **Pasar Badung** in Denpasar is also an eye-opener. Coral-lined alleys lead to a ceremonial knick-knacks section selling baskets of every shape and size.

Antiques

Try the shopping arcades of major hotels for truly outstanding pieces (at outstanding prices). In **Kuta**, Anang's and the East West Artshop have the best collection of antiques and primitive artifacts.

In **Denpasar**, there are several antique shops along Jl. Gajah Mada near the town square. Also on Jl. Arjuna, Jl. Dresna, Jl. Veteran and Jl. Gianyar. In **Sanur**, the shops are along Jl. Tamblingan.

The many antique shops adjacent to the **Kreta Gosa** in **Klungkung** have collections of rare Chinese porcelains, old Kamasan wayang-style paintings, antique jewelry and Balinese weavings. Prices are reasonable. **Singaraja** has some of the best antique shops in Bali, too. They are all on the main roads of this northern city.

Pottery

Some unusual pottery is manufactured in the village of **Pejaten**, in the district of Tabanan about 20 km west of Denpasar. Here, the villagers create striking figurines with twisted limbs and grotesque bodies out of terracotta, as they have done for many generations. Beautiful glazed ceramics in local designs are also produced at **Batu Jimbar**, Sanur.

NIGHTLIFE

Nightlife on the **Sanur** side is relatively tame. There are cocktail lounges with live music at some of the larger hotels. The Grand Bali Beach Hotel's **Bali Hai** supper club offers razzmatazz international entertainers. Also in Sanur, the **Karya Restaurant**, the **Purnama Terrace** (in the Bali Hyatt) and the **Kul Kul Restaurant** (book for the Frog Dance night) are the island's best venues for dinner and a show under the stars. The Grand Hyatt Bali at Nusa Dua has a nightly Pasar Senggol shopping and food-stall market, with cultural entertainment.

For hot, pulsating nightlife with loud, gyrating crowds and ear-shattering music, head over to the **Kuta Beach** side. This formerly somnambulant beach village is now on the go day and night. A number of watering holes along Jl. Legian and Jl. Buni Sari stay open as long as there are people, serving chilled Bintang beer in chilled mugs – a beer drinker's paradise.

Some of the Kuta discos keep going till dawn, after which you can go down to the beach to watch the spectacular sunrise – quite a common pastime in Kuta. A group of bars in a cul de sac in the center of Kuta, anchored by **Peanuts**, is a popular place to bar hop. Or take Peanuts' nightly Pub Crawl by bus, Tuesdays and Saturdays. Then head for the **Rum Jungle** – an open-air dance floor adorned with vines and creepers and packed with gyrating bodies. Farther down, in Seminyak, the happening place for people-watching after 11pm is **Goa 2001**, and on Saturday nights, **Chez Gado-Gado** by the beach.

SPORTS

Aquatic sports: surfing, diving, spearfishing, wind-surfing and deep-sea fishing are all very popular in Bali. **Nusa Lembongan**, the small island directly opposite Sanur, has developed into a haven for surfers and divers alike. Group charters and safari tours are available, together with equipment and instruction if needed.

The best **diving** areas are in Lovina, Tulamben, Padang Bai, Nusa Penida, Menjangan, Tepekong, Lembongan and Cengingan islands.

For the best **surfing/windsurfing**, go down to Uluwatu or Padang Bay on the eastern side of the southern Bukit Peninsula, or else try Medewi Beach in the southwest, and **Terima** and **Lovina** beaches in the northwest.

River kayaking and **whitewater rafting** have become popular in recent years, particularly in the Ayung River Valley.

For water sports of an artificial kind, the new **Waterbom Park** offers fun for the whole family. Popular attractions include the parallel racetrack slides that start 19 meters (50 ft) in the air, and the jungle ride, in which riders twist and turn along a watery banked track through tropical vegetation. Jl. Kartika Plaza, Tuban.

Sailing: The fleet of native outrigger canoes (*jukung*) lining Sanur's beach, with their brightly-colored *bir bintang* sails, are obviously no longer used for fishing, now that the tourists have taken to chartering them for cruises across the water. The fishermen have wisely banded together into a cooperative to standardize their rates.

Mountain biking: The Batur Trail is the best place for a work-out on two wheels. Tour companies can also help plan mountain-trekking expeditions through tropical rain forest.

Adrenalin Sports: Bungy jumping is another new attraction, with several stations in the Kuta and Gianyar areas. Bali Bungy Co., Jl. Pura Puseh, Legian. Tel: 752-658. Bungee in Bali, Banjar Blangsinga, Blahbatuh, Gianyar. Tel: 758-362. A new adrenalin playground, Australian Bungy Jumping Co., near Kuta Square on Jl. Kuta, offers bungie, a climbing wall and a human slingshot.

Sport Tour Companies

Bali Marine Sports, Jl. Bypass Ngurah Rai, Blanjong, Sanur. Tel: 289-308, Fax: 287-872. Diving.

Baruna, Jl. Bypass Ngurah Rai 300B, Denpasar. Tel: 753-820, Fax: 753-809. Diving, cruises, watersports.

Dive & Dives, Jl. Bypass Ngurah Rai 23, Sanur. Tel: 288-052, Fax: 289-309. Diving.

PT Wisata Tirta Agung (Sobek), Jl. Tirta Ening No. 9, Bypass Ngurah Rai, Sanur. Tel: 287-059, Fax: 289-448. Rafting, kayaking, cycling, trekking, bird-watching.

MEDICAL SERVICES

Emergency: Call an **ambulance** by dialing **118**.

Every village in Bali now has a small government clinic called **Puskesmas**, but for major problems, visit one of the hotel clinics or a public hospital in Denpasar.

Pt. Bali Tourist International Assist, 24-hour emergency service. Tel: (0361) 228-996, 231-443.

Pharmacies (*apotik*): Most pharmacies are open daily 8am to 6pm. Pharmacies also stay open late at night, on Sundays and holidays on a rotation system in Denpasar.

Kimia Farma, Jl. Diponegoro 123, Denpasar. Tel: 227-811, 227-812.

Kosala Farma, Jl. Kartini 136, Denpasar. Tel: 222-301.

Ria Farma, Jl. Veteran 35, Denpasar. Tel: 222-635.

Bali Farma, Jl. Melati 9, Denpasar. Tel: 233-231, 233-858.

Dirga Yusa, Jl. Surapati 10, Denpasar. Tel: 222-267.

Sadha Karya, Jl. Gajah Mada 41, Denpasar. Tel: 222-433.

In **Kuta**, there are *apotik* on Jl. Legian and the main road to the airport. In **Sanur**, try **Farmasari**, Jl. Segara Ayu. Tel: 288-062, 288-061.

AIRLINE OFFICES

Air France, Grand Bali Beach, Sanur. Tel: 288-511.

Air New Zealand, Wisti Sabha Building, Airport. Tel: 756-170.

Ansett Australia, Grand Bali Beach, Sanur. Tel: 289-636.

Bouraq, Jl. Sudirman 7A. Tel: 237-420.

Cathay Pacific, Grand Bali Beach, Sanur. Tel: 753-942.

Continental Air Micronesia, Grand Bali Beach, Sanur. Tel: 287-065, 287-774.

EVA Air, Wisti Sabha Building, Airport. Tel: 298-935.

Garuda, Jl. Melati 61, Denpasar. Tel: 225-245; Sanur Beach Hotel, Kuta. Tel: 287-915; Nusa Dua Beach Hotel, Nusa Dua. Tel: 771-444; Grand Bali Beach. Tel: 288-243.

Japan, Grand Bali Beach, Sanur. Tel: 287-576, 287-577.

KLM, Wisti Sabha Building, Airport. Tel: 756-127.

Korean, Wisti Sabha Building, Airport. Tel: 754-856, 757-298.

Lufthansa, Grand Bali Beach, Sanur. Tel: 287-069.

Malaysia, Grand Bali Beach, Sanur. Tel: 288-716, 288-511.

Merpati, Jl. Melati 51, Denpasar. Tel: 235-358.

Qantas, Grand Bali Beach, Sanur. Tel: 288-331.

Sempati, Grand Bali Beach, Sanur. Tel: 288-824; Jl. Dipenogoro, Komplek Dipenogoro Megah, Blok B/27. Tel: 237-343.

Singapore, Grand Bali Beach, Sanur. Tel: 287-940.

Thai, Grand Bali Beach, Sanur. Tel: 285-071/3.

FOREIGN CONSULATES IN BALI

Australia, Jl. Prof. Moch. Yamin 51, Renon, Denpasar. Tel: 235-092, 235-093, Fax: 225-146. (Also represents citizens of Canada, New Zealand, United Kingdom and Papua New Guinea.)

France, Jl. Tambaksari 5, Sanur. Tel/Fax: 287-383.

Germany (Honorary), Jl. Pantai Karang 17, Sanur. Tel/Fax: 299-826.

Italy (Honorary), Jl. Cemara, Semawang, Sanur. Tel: 288-896, Fax: 287-642.

Japan, Jl. Raya Puputan 1, Denpasar. Tel: 234-808, Fax: 231-308.

Netherlands, Jl. Raya Kuta 99, Kuta. Tel: 751-517, Fax: 752-777.

Norway/Denmark, Jl. Jayagiri VIII/10, Denpasar. Tel: 235-098. Fax: 234-834.

Sweden/Finland, Segara Village Hotel, Jl. Segar Ayu, Sanur. Tel: 288-407, Fax: 287-242.

Switzerland/Austria (Honorary), Swiss Restaurant, Jl. Pura Bagus.

United States, Jl. Segara Ayu 5, Sanur. Tel: 288-478, Fax: 287-760.

Sanur

Sanur is for gracious living, peace and quiet – more international but far less cosmopolitan than frantic Kuta. Foreigners have been staying in Sanur since the 1920s. Seek out the lovely Sanur temples, particularly when they are having their commemoration ceremonies (*odalan*) every seven months.

ACCOMMODATION

There are so many excellent first-class hotels in Sanur that one can scarcely go wrong. The main choice is between the convenience and luxury of a big hotel or the quiet of a private bungalow by the sea. Reservations are advisable during the peak seasons: July to September, and December to January. But if you are the adventurous type or are visiting off-season, arrive with a reservation only for the first night, and then the next day, just wander along the beach and choose where you want to stay for the rest of your holiday. Odds are, you'll end up in a magical place, paying much less than if booked from abroad. Try bargaining for rates at the smaller hotels.

Deluxe

Bali Hyatt, P.O. Box 392, Sanur. Tel: (0361) 288-271, Fax: 287-693. Ten minutes from Denpasar. Restaurants offering Indonesian, Italian, Chinese, Western and seafood cuisine. Bars and lounges, two pools, tennis and volleyball courts, water sports, pitch and putt course, disco, gardens.

Grand Bali Beach, Jl. Hang Tuah, Sanur, P.O. Box 3275, Denpasar 80032. Tel: (0361) 288-511, Fax: 287-917. Constructed by the Japanese in the early 1960s, fully renovated after 1993 fire. Bali's only high-rise hotel looks more like a traditional Miami Beach luxury hotel.

Sanur Beach, Sanur, P.O. Box 3279, Denpasar 80032. Tel: (0361) 288-011, Fax: 287-566. Asian, Thai, seafood restaurants and pizzaria. Lounge, two pools, tennis, badminton and volleyball courts, miniature golf, water sports, fitness center, shops, conference facilities.

Respati Beach Bungalows, Jl. Danau Tamblingan 33, Sanur, P.O. Box 223, Denpasar. Tel: (0361) 286-834, Fax: 288-046. Cottages grouped around a small garden with a private beach.

Segara Village, Jl. Segara Ayu, Sanur, P.O. Box 91, Denpasar. Tel: (0361) 288-407, Fax: 287-242. On the beach. The best rooms are the cottages overlooking the new swimming pool.

Tanjung Sari, Jl. Danau Tanblingan, Sanur P.O. Box 25, Denpasar 80228. Tel: (0361) 288-441, Fax: 287-930. Serene, stylish and exclusive, with private bungalows by the sea, and lovely gardens.

EATING OUT

The **Tanjung Sari Hotel Restaurant** has a formidable reputation for Indonesian *rijsttafel* and a sublime atmosphere. A bamboo *tingklink* orchestra provides the ideal accompaniment to dinner in a cozy, antique-filled dining area by the beach. The restaurant's menu has a creative nouveau-Balinese slant, and the famous bar, designed by Australian artist Donald Friend, is an elevated pavilion overlooking the sea.

Si Pino's Home of Fine Food, opposite the front gate to the Grand Bali Beach, is another Sanur institution. Mr. Pino is not only Bali's best boxing coach, but also one of its most imaginative chefs.

The **Kul Kul** Restaurant, Jl. Danau

Tamblingan 166, has an elegant bar and serves good western, Indonesian and Chinese cuisine in its garden pavilion. Book for the dinner-dance night (Batuan's famous Frog Dance Troupe).

The nearby **Swastika Gardens**, Jl. Danau Tamblingan, is also a great favorite with those who are tired of paying hotel prices. The food is fair and the menu varied enough to satisfy most tastes – try the Balinese specialty, curried duck (*bebek tutu*).

Telaga Naga, opposite the Bali Hyatt, is a stylish Szechuan restaurant in a lake, designed by Hyatt architect Kerry Hill. The food is good and the prices are non-hotel. Try the chicken with dried chili pepper, the king prawn, and the duck dishes.

Good Italian food is available at **Trattoria Da Marco**, where Reno and Diddit da Marco have guarded their reputation and clientele for nearly two decades. Try the grilled fish, spaghetti carbonara, bean salad and steaks.

La Taverna, Jl. Danau Tamblingan, is part of a Hong Kong-based chain of Italian restaurants in Asia. The Sanur branch is a charming bar and open dining area on the beach, with a menu that features imported cheese, French pepper steak, seafood and pizza from a real pizza oven.

Japanese fare can be found at **Kita**, Jl. Danau Tamblingan 104. Also offered are Korean specialties plus some Indonesian, Chinese and European thrown into the bargain at **New Seoul Korean**, Jl. Danau Tamblingan 79.

For more local flavors, try the inexpensive **Sanur Beach Market**, Jl. Segara (right at the beach), a little outdoor restaurant run by Sanur's mayor. Great for lunch (*sate, nasi goreng* and fresh fried fish) or dinner (grilled lobster), with delicious Balinese desserts, all at unbeatable prices.

The original **Swastika I** (opposite the La Taverna) also has a domestic section, with reliable *nasi campur*, good fruit juices and a variety of Balinese dishes at local prices.

The last *warung* (Mak Beng's) on the left on Jl. Danau Tamblingan (just north of the Grand Bali Beach) has fantastic grilled fish.

For Javanese cuisine, seek out **Warung Betawi** at the Renon roundabout (on the road to Denpasar) – a bit out of the way, but worth the trip.

Jimbaran, Tuban, Kuta and Legian Beaches

Kuta is like a malignant seaside Carnaby Street of the 1960s. Chaotic, noisy, lots of hype, but a great playground. What first attracted visitors to Kuta was the wide beach and the surf, and it still has one of the best oceanfronts on the island, though it is now clustered with hundreds of hotels, restaurants, bars, boutiques, travel agencies, antique shops, car and motorbike rentals, banks, and countless numbers of tourists. There are now many first-class hotels, but the 5-km strip still caters best for the economy traveller who likes to be in the thick of things. If you don't like the idea of staying in a frenetic, holiday-camp type atmosphere, stay away from the Kuta strip and consider Jimbaran, Tuban or Legian instead.

ACCOMMODATION

This area has so many bungalows, beach hotels and homestays (*losmen*) that no list could ever be complete, nor is a list really needed. Drop in and shop around. The difference between this area and Sanur is that the visitor has far more choices in the lower price range here. Reservations are wise for the larger hotels during July to September, and December to January.

Bali Intercontinental, Jl. Uluwatu 45, Jimbaran 80361. Tel: (0361) 701-888, Fax: 701-777. Asian, seafood, Japanese and Italian cuisine. Lounges, pubs and bars. Three pools, tennis and squash courts, beach volleyball, fitness center, children' mini resort.

Bali Oberoi, Jl. Kayu Aya, Legian Beach, P.O. Box 3351, Denpasar 80033. Tel: (0361) 730-361, Fax: 730-791. Away from it all at the far end of the beach. Tasteful air-conditioned beachside bungalows in an attractive garden.

Four Seasons, Jimbaran, Denpasar 80361. Tel: (0361) 701-010, Fax: 701-020. Luxurious villas are situated in village squares, each administered by a "village chief". Each villa has a private plunge pool, and wonderful, classic bathtubs inside.

Bali Padma, Jl. Padma 1, Legian. Tel: (0361) 752-111, Fax: 752-140. Indonesian, Japanese, Asian, Italian and Western dishes available in four restaurants. Bars and pubs, two pools, tennis and squash courts, snooker, fitness center.

Bintang Bali, Jl. Kartika Plaza, Tuban. Tel: (0361) 753-292, Fax: 753-288. Set among six acres of Balinese-style gardens, which extend down to a private beach. Karaoke supper club, pizzeria, cafe, pool-side theater.

Ritz-Carlton Bali, Jimbaran, Denpasar 80361. Tel: (0361) 771-631, Fax: 772-192. Four-story, 56-hectare resort perched on bluff overlooking beach and ocean. 15 minutes from airport.

Bali Dynasty, Jl. Kartika Plaza, P.O. Box 2047, Tuban 80361. Tel: (0361) 752-403, Fax: 752-402. A Shangri-La managed hotel. Chinese and international restaurants, pub, disco, pool, tennis courts, billiards, games room, water sports, children's center and conference facilities.

Intan Bali Village Spa and Club, Jl. Petitenget, Batubelig Beach, Kerobokan, P.O. Box 3493, Denpasar 80034. Tel: (0361) 730-777, Fax: 730-778. Located on 11 hectares of beachfront land. Seafood restaurant, pizzeria and coffee shop. Lounge, bars, disco. Fitness center, pools, squash and tennis courts.

Budget: There are some 300 *losmen* or homestays in the Kuta–Legian area. Often you'll be approached at the airport or at the bus terminal on arrival in Bali. But the best way to find a room is just to walk around in any area that you fancy – whether near Kuta or Legian, near the beach, or far back in the coconut groves, away from the crowds. Some have luxurious garden bathrooms and second-story sleeping lofts with bamboo staircases.

EATING OUT

New restaurants seem to open daily in this area, from small salad-and-yoghurt stands by the beach to large Chinese, French or seafood establishments. The quality of the food changes as cooks come and go, so we list here only a few old standbys. Ask around for tips on the latest "in" restaurant.

Made's Warung on Jl. Pantai hasn't missed a beat in its metamorphosis from one of only two foodstalls on the main street of a sleepy fishing village, into a hip cafe. It has great food: spare ribs, Thai salad, escargots, turtle steaks, home-made ice cream, chocolate mousse, capuccino, fresh squeezed orange and carrot juices, breakfast specials.

Poppies, Poppie's Gang, Br. Pengabetan, Kuta. Down a narrow lane, this outdoor restaurant is another Kuta fixture. Avocado seafood salads, pate, tacos, grilled lobster, steaks, shishkebab and tall mixed drinks pack this garden idyll to capacity during the peak tourist seasons. Get there early to get a table.

The **Blue Ocean Hotel's beach-side cafe** in Legian is a popular gathering point for breakfast and lunch.

La Marmite (also known as Chez Gado-Gado) in Seminak serves Balinese "nouvelle cuisine" in a secluded open-air location by the beach. The after-dinner disco on Saturday nights is the happening place.

Nusa Dua

Nusa Dua was at a bit of disadvantage when it was first developed, as it is rather isolated from the rest of Bali. However, the hotels in this planned resort area have made up for this by providing a "total" resort environment – everything you could possibly ask for is available on the premises. The convention center helps to fill up a number of rooms year-round. There is also a whole village of restaurants and souvenir shops on the outskirts, and an upmarket shopping complex in the heart of the resort. There are no budget hotels inside the resort, nor the pesky street hawkers found nearly everywhere else.

ACCOMMODATION

Amanusa, P.O. Box 33, Nusa Dua. Tel: (0361) 772-333, Fax: 771-267. This elegant hotel – with villas only – has a magnificent pool and lobby area, but lacks big hotel trappings. Each luscious villa has a private courtyard, and eight have private swimming pools. Guests can choose between a golf course, Nusa Dua peninsula or Indian Ocean views.

Bali Hilton, P.O. Box 46, Nusa Dua 80361. Tel: (0361) 771-102, Fax: 771-616. Indonesian, Japanese and Continental restaurants. Lounges, bars, pubs and disco. Pools, tennis and squash courts, water sports.

Grand Hyatt Bali, P.O. Box 53, Nusa Dua. Tel: (0361) 771-234, Fax: 772-038. On a 40-acre beachfront site, guest rooms are decentralized into four village-like clusters. Indonesian, French, Japanese, Cantonese and seafood restaurants. Six pools, tennis and squash courts.

Melia Bali, Nusa Dua, P.O. Box 1048, Tuban. Tel: (0361) 771-510, Fax 771-360. One of this area's original properties, refurbished in 1996, this hotel is especially proud of its gardens. French, Japanese, Chinese, Asian seafood restaurants, pizzeria.

Nusa Dua Beach, P.O. Box 1028, Denpasar. Tel: (0361) 771-210, Fax: 771-229. Nusa Dua's first deluxe property, many heads of state have stayed here. Indonesian, Italian, grill and international restaurants.

Sheraton Laguna, P.O. Box 2044, Kuta 80363. Tel: (0361) 771-327/8, Fax: 771-326. Set among 17 acres of landscaped grounds and swimmable lagoons. Indonesian, Western and seafood grill restaurants. Lounges and bars, pools, tennis courts, water sports, fitness center.

Sheraton Nusa Indah, P.O. Box 36, Denpasar 80363. Tel: (0361) 771-906, Fax: 771-908. Situated adjacent to the convention center. Balinese seafood, Italian, Japanese and French restaurants. Pool, tennis courts, water sports, fitness center.

Bali Tropic Palace, Jl. Pratama 34, P.O. Box 41, Tanjung Benoa, Nusa Dua 80361. Tel: (0361) 772-130, Fax: 772-131. Private terraced rooms with sea-view. Seaside pool with sunken bar.

Grand Mirage, Jl. Pratama 74, Tanjung Benoa, P.O. Box 43, Nusa Dua 80361. Tel: (0361) 771-888, Fax: 772-148. French thalassotherapy spa is part of the hotel.

Bali Clarion Suites, Jl. Dalem Tarukan 7, P.O. Box 133, Taman Mumbul, Nusa Dua 80363. Tel: (0361) 773-808, Fax: 773-737. Situated on a hillside overlooking Nusa Dua, it's a self-contained complex for family holidays, with a living and dining area, and kitchenette.

Bali Royal, Jl. Pratama, Tanjung Benoa, Nusa Dua 80361. Tel: (0361) 771-039, Fax: 771-885. Beachfront gardens with pool and restaurant. Some bungalows with open-air baths. Suites with ocean-view and private gardens.

Club Bali Mirage, Jl. Pratama 72, Tanjung Benoa, P.O. Box 43, Nusa Dua 80361. Tel: (0361), Fax: 772-156. All inclusive club with meals, beverages, entertainment and non-motorized sports packaged in accommodation price. Balinese atmosphere with beachfront pool and gardens. No children under age 16.

Club Med, P.O. Box 7, Lot 6, Nusa Dua 80361. Tel: (0361) 771-521/3, Fax: 771-853. All the recreational facilities expected of a Club Med hotel, including, tennis, squash and badminton, archery, golf, water sports, children's facilities and circus activities.

Candidasa/Klungkung

ACCOMMODATION

Amankila, P.O. Box 133, Klungkung. Tel: (0363) 41-333, Fax: 41-555. The third spectacular Aman resort in Bali, this hotel is situated between two headlands on the island's east coast and commands ocean views across the Lombok and Bandung Straits. Free-standing villas, three-level swimming pool, and a spectacular beach.

Candi Beach Cottage, Desasengkidu, Kecamatan, Manggis. Tel: (0363) 41-234, Fax: 41-111. Hotel and cottage rooms with satellite TV, mini-bar, verandah, pool, diving school, fitness center and tennis court.

Serai, Desa Buitan, Manggis, P.O. Box 13, Karangasem 80871. Tel: (0363) 41-011/2, Fax: 41-015. Secluded beachfront hotel with swimming pool, fine restaurant. Privacy and luxury are the hallmarks.

Denpasar

ACCOMMODATION

Natour's Bali, Jl. Veteran 3, P.O. Box 3, Denpasar 80111. Tel: (0361) 225-681, Fax: 235-347. Historic hotel. Centrally located in Denpasar, just a block from the main intersection and town square. Good restaurant and bar.

Denpasar, Jl. Diponegoro 103, P.O. Box 111, Denpasar. Tel: 26-336, 26-363. Half of the rooms have air-conditioning and hot water. A favorite of large Indonesian tour groups from Java.

Pemecutan Palace, Jl. M.H. Thamrin 2, P.O. Box 489, Denpasar. Tel: (0361) 423-491. This hotel takes up one side of the extensive Badung palace.

Eating Out

Denpasar has the best Chinese and Indonesian restaurants on Bali, so if passing through or have errands to run here, be sure to stop in for a meal.

A popular little streetside restaurant located off Jl. Gajah Mada near the banks, on Jl. Sumatra, is **Depot 88**. It serves excellent Chinese food, such as asparagus and crab soup, frog's legs and sweet-sour pork. Other Chinese restaurants to try on this street include the **Atoom Baru** and the **Hongkong.**

Most fun in Denpensar is the **night market**, just off Jl. Gajah Mada, where portable kitchens on wheels provide sate, fried rice, noodle soup and hot drinks. For local fare, the expatriate's favorite is **Rumah Makan Betty** on Jl. Sumatra, which has a not-so-spicy menu of Javanese and Chinese dishes. Try the *tahu goreng kentang* (beancurd and potato curry), *bubur ayam* (rice porridge with chicken) and *nasi campur.*

The Balinese favorite, however, is the **Rumah Makan Gema Rempah** at Jl. Supratman 11, a modest dinner serving *babi guling* roasted pork.

For a full range of Indonesian chicken dishes – soups, fried chicken legs, liver *sate*, curries – visit the ever-popular **Kartini Restaurant**, diagonally opposite the Indra Cinema near the petrol pump.

Ubud

Accommodation

Amandari, P.O. Box 33, Ubud. Tel: (0361) 975-333, Fax: 975-335. This stunning property was the first of the Aman resorts to be built in Bali. Designed to provide privacy and supreme luxury. Half of the villas overlook rice paddies and natural vegetation, the others a spectacular river gorge. Each suite has its own walled garden and outdoor marble tub; six have private swimming pools. European and Indonesian restaurant, bar, tennis courts, adventure sports.

Kupu-Kupu Barong, P.O. Box 7, Desa Kedewata, Ubud 80571. Tel: (0361) 975-478, Fax: 975-079. Perched on Sayan Valley edge overlooking Ayung River, has dramatic views. Pool and restaurant are popular spots. Not suitable for children.

Eating Out

Like much of Bali, restaurants spring up virtually overnight in Ubud and disappear just as quickly. The best thing to do is just walk around until you see something that strikes your fancy and ask to see the menu – or ask around to see what are the popular restaurants of the day. As a rule, though, the cuisine here is Balinese and unpretentious, with meals often served on an open pavilion in a garden.

At the foot of the Tjampuhan bridge stands **Murni's Warung**, the sign outside proclaiming "the best hamburgers this side of the black stump" and so they are! Also fruit salads and yoghurt. Murni serves all kinds of excellent Western and Chinese food at reasonable prices. The **Cafe Lotus**, at Puri Saraswati in the center of Ubud, serves delicious Western and Balinese cuisine, including pasta dishes, salads, omelettes and cups of frothy capuccino. Excellent cakes. **Ary's Warung** is an old-time favorite haunt for consistent fare, creative menu, extensive beverage list and good information from its resident owner, Odek.

Lombok

If the "tourist scene" on Bali turns tedious, then Lombok is an excellent escape. Those with only a few days on Bali should probably leave Lombok for the next trip. But if you have more than a week on Bali and would like to see more of Indonesia without traveling great distances, Lombok is perfect. And for the jaded expatriate Bali or Jakarta resident, Lombok is a must.

For any traveller, a two- to three-day excursion is a complete enough sampler of Lombok's attractions – all of its sights are located within an hour's drive of the old capital, Cakranegara. A week or more is needed if diving at Gili Air or climbing to the summit of Gunung Rinjani.

Getting There

Choose between a quick 20-minute flight from Bali to Lombok's **Selaparang Airport**; a leisurely cruise on the ferry that shuttles between Padang Bali on Bali's eastern coast, and the port of Lembar on Lombok's west coast; or speedy and comfortable two-hour jet-catamaran service out of south Bali's Benoa Harbor. The **Mabua Intan Express** (Tel: (0361) 772-521 in Bali, (0364) 37-224 in Lombok) catamaran departs Benoa Harbor daily at 8am and 2.30pm and departs Lombok's Lembar Harbor at 11.30am and 5.30pm. Three classes of reasonable fares include snacks. The 6-hour ferry passage, with the majestic volcanic peaks of Bali and Lombok in the distance, is well worth the inconvenience of traveling all the way out to Padand Bai and from the ports.

From Sanur or Kuta, it takes more than 2 hours to get to Padang Bali by private car, 3 hours or more by public transport, so start early. Better yet, go to East Bali the day before and spend the night in a beach bungalow at Candidasa, just 20 minutes from Padang Bali.

There is a snack bar on board the ferry serving *nasi rawon*, soft drinks, beer, coffee and tea. Or, buy food packets from vendors at the port before departing.

Orientation

The port of Lembar, where the ferry and jet catamaran arrive from Bali, is located about 20 km (12 mi) to the south of Mataram. Lombok's Selaparang Airport is right in Mataram and no more than 3 km from any hotel in the city area. A daily motorboat ferry departs for Alas on Sumbawa from the port of Labuhan Lombok, on Lombok's eastern shore. A highway cuts right across the island, from Ampenan to Labuhan Lombok, a distance of only 75 km (50 mi).

The strip of Ampenan, Mataram and Cakranegara is the island's main business, administrative and shopping district. Call at the West Nusa Tenggara **Regional Tourist Office** (DIRARDA) – Jl. Langko 70, Ampenan 83114. Tel: 31-730, 37-828, 21-866 or Jl. R. Suprapto 36, Ampenan. Tel: 21-658 – for brochures and maps of the island. They haven't much information on cultural activities, however.

Women should be aware that naked thighs and plunging necklines are severely frowned upon, particularly by Lombok's Muslim majority; this applies particularly to towns on the eastern and southern parts of the island. Cases of harassment have been reported and women are advised not to travel alone outside of the urban areas, if undiscreetly covered.

Getting Around

Once in Lombok, transport is easy, though it is time consuming to rely upon public transport. Taxis and mini-buses (bemos) are readily available for charter. Bring a motorcycle from Bali on the ferry (rental cars are not supposed to leave Bali). It is possible to rent motorcycles in Ampenan and Mataram. Ask at the hotel, or at any motorcycle shop. (You must have an international or Indonesian license.)

Major hotels will pick up guests at the airport without charge. Arrange a taxi at the airport or at your hotel for a day-trip around the island. Try to get a Lombok Balinese driver who speaks English.

Bemo and buses service all towns on the island. Buy a bemo ticket at the snack bar on the ferry for the ride into Mataram from the port of Lembar. The central bemo and bus terminal is at the crossroads at Sweta, just to the east of Cakranegara; there is a signboard displaying the official fares to all points on the island.

You can charter a bemo for the day and they will take you anywhere on the island. Bemos are slow and uncomfortable, so you are better off paying a bit more for a taxi (perhaps with an English-speaking driver).

Accommodation

Sheraton Senggigi, Jl. Raya Senggigi, km 8, Senggigi, P.O. Box 1154, Mataram 83015. Tel: (0364) 93-333, Fax: 93-140. The focal point of this resort is the terraced, beachfront pool area with a giant water-slide sculpture forming a traditional Sasak legend. Indonesian and international buffet, seafood and grill.

Senggigi Beach, Jl. Senggigi Ray, Batu Layar, P.O. Box 1001, Mataram. Tel: (0364) 93-210, Fax: 93-200. On 30 acres of beachfront, accommodation includes thatched-roof beachfront bungalows or rooms in several "longhouses". Seafood, Italian and buffet restaurants.

Eating Out

The Balinese roast suckling pig, *babi guling*, as prepared by the Lombok Balinese, beats anything on Bali. Arrange a feast (through your hotel or driver) and ask if it can be served in one of the spacious courtyards of a Lombok Balinese home. Ask for *tuak* (palm toddy) to go with the pig, and a folk dance (also easily arranged).

The old Chinese restaurants on Jl. Yos Sudarso in Ampenan (the **Tjirebon** and the **Pabean** – No. 146) are central and favorite hang-outs of budget travelers. The Tjirebon has cold beer and steak with chips (don't eat the salad).

The Muslim restaurants of Mataram in some cases serve both Yemeni and Lombok dishes. The **Taliwang II** on Jl. Pejanggik, in the shopping center, specializes in *ayam pelicing* – the searing hot curried chicken that is Lombok's specialty. The **Garden House Restaurant** nearby, on Jl. Pusat Pertokoan, serves Indonesian and Chinese food.

In Cakranegara, there are many restaurants along Jl. Selaparang. The **Asia** and the **Harum** serve Chinese food, so does the **Friendship** on Jl. Panca Usaha. The **Minang** has *nasi padang,* and other Indonesian dishes can be had at **Siti Nurmaya** at Jl. Palapa 34 and **Indonesia** at Jl. Selaparang 62.

Shopping

Traditional textiles are the best buy on Lombok. Visit the villages where the threads are dyed and woven by hand: **Sukarare** (for *tenun Lombok*), **Pujung** (for *kain lambung*), **Purbasari** (for *kain Purbasari*) and **Balimurti** (for the sacred *beberut* cloths). **Labuhan Lombok**, on the east coast, also produces fine blankets.

The best weaving factories for contemporary textiles are found in Cakranegara. Many of Bali's resident Italian couturiers buy fabrics from Pak Abdullah of **C.V. Rinjani Handwoven**, next door to the Hotel Selaparang (on Jl. Selaparang). His stockroom often has leftovers from bolts of top-designer fabrics. His silk *sarung* and matching *selendang* scarves are highly regarded. The **Selamat Ryadi** weaving factory in the Arab quarter on Jl. Ukir Kawi is another excellent source of material. The **Balimurti** factory nearby produces weavings in the traditional *purbasari* style.

Lombok's bamboo baskets are extremely fine and sturdy. Many are produced in the eastern Lombok villages of **Kotaraja** and **Loyok**. Ceramic pots and earthenware are also beautifully crafted and elegantly shaped here. Shop for them also at the main market by the bus and bemo terminal in Sweta, or in the **Cakranegara Market** to the west of the Pura Meru temple.

There is an antique shop known as **Sudirman's**, a few hundred meters down a side lane from Jl. Pabean in Ampenan. (Enter across from the bemo station, and ask for directions.) Enterprising antique merchants may call on you in your hotel. They have old Chinese ceramics, antique carvings and ceremonial weavings. Bargain hard and nonchalantly, never appear eager or rushed.

There are a few factories in Lombok doing a trade in primitive bottletops, wooden spoons and carved canisters – in some cases these are excellent reproductions of traditional pieces. Most of what's available is new and made to look old.

The 6-km main street running through the center of Ampenan, Mataram and Cakranegara (Jl. Langko/Pejanggik/Selaparang) is one long shopping mall.

Climbing Gunung Rinjani

Lombok's central highlands, circling the upper reaches of Gunung Rinjani (Indonesia's second-highest peak outside Irian Jaya at 3,726 meters/ 12,220 ft), are sparsely populated due to the vagaries of climate and the rough terrain. Up to about 2,000 meters (6,500 ft), the mountain is covered in dense jungle and forest. But above this level, scattered stands of pine and low scrub take over. The volcano's windswept rim is quite barren, and from here there are spectacular morning views across Lombok to Bali and Sumbawa on either side. The only time to attempt the climb is during the dry season (June to October), and even then, plan to reach the top in the early morning hours, as swirling mist envelops the peak after mid morning.

Inside the vast crater is a large lake, Segara Anak (Child of the Sea). The steep descent from the rim down into the crater is precarious, and only possible from a single point at the northern side. Not for the timid.

It is important to have warm clothing (temperatures can drop below freezing near the summit at night), a tent, boots or sturdy shoes, sleeping bag, water bottle, cooking utensils and enough food for up to four days, including for the guide. Camping equipment can be rented in Ampenan at the Wisma Triguna Hotel, on Jl. Koperasi. Another trekking guide is Mr. Juvent of Bidy Tour, Jl. Ragigenep 17, Ampenan. Cooking utensils may be borrowed or rented, along with guides and porters, at villages along the way.

There are two principle ways of approaching the crater's rim. Many people begin from the eastern hill town of **Sapit**, which can be reached by bemo from the main highway at **Pringgabaya** (about 3 hours altogether from the central Sweta terminal). From Sapit, it is about a 5-hour hike along a well-worn trail up to the villages of **Sembulan Bumbung** and **Sembulan Lawang**. Arrangements can be made through the village chief of Sembulan Lawang for a guide (and porters) to the summit; spend the night here. The next day, hike up to a base camp just below the rim and spend the night, so as to make the final one-hour ascent in the early morning, when it is clear. Return via Sembulan Lawang and Sapit, or continue on to the north coast at Bayan.

A shorter and easier route begins from the northern village of **Bayan**, reached via the northwestern coastal road by bus (a 3-hour journey from Sweta). From Bayan, where the bus stops, you may be able to get a lift on a truck farther on to the end of the road at **Batu Kok**. If arriving early enough in the day (before noon), it may be possible to begin the ascent immediately. From Batu Kok, it is about 6-hour hike past the traditional Sasak village of **Senaro** to a base camp just below the crater's rim. Camp overnight here, and climb up to the summit early in the morning. From this point, you may want to turn back, or else descend into the crater and spend the night comfortably by the crater lake (after soaking away sore muscles in the adjacent hot springs). The return journey to Batu Kok from within the crater takes a full 12 hours.

Nusa Tenggara

Travel to Sumbawa and the islands to the east requires a rudimentary knowledge of Indonesian and a spirit of adventure – not to mention a willingness to endure discomforts. Over the last few years, communications and roads have improved remarkably, and island-hopping has been made easier.

Hotels and losmen are found only in the district capitals. After leaving the main population centers, you will need to rely on local hospitality.

Conservative and modest dress is very important in Nusa Tenggara. Women should be cautious and conscious of Muslim sensitivities in this respect, keeping shoulders and thighs covered.

It is best to carry all the cash you will need once you leave Bali or Lombok. Everything shuts at around 11am on Fridays, the Muslim sabbath.

Getting There

Air: Most of the *kabupaten* (district capitals) are served by flights – from one per week to several each day.

Sea: There are large PELNI passenger ships on scheduled runs.

Road: The road network within the islands also links together the *kabupaten*. There have been improvements of roads over the last few years, but sometimes the conditions still leave much to be desired. Flores has perhaps the worst roads. Public transport is cramped though cheap.

Tourist Offices

Ampanan: Diparda Tk. I Nusa Tenggara Barat, Jl. Langko 70, Ampanan 83114. Tel: (364) 21-730.

Kupang: Diparda Tk. I Nusa Tenggara Timur, Jl. Jend. Basuki Rachmat 1, Kupang 85117. Tel: 21-540.

Sumbawa

Getting There

Sea and Road: A number of travelers reach Sumbawa by taking one of the several daily, 3-hour ferry trips from Labuhanlombok (Lombok) to Alas (western Sumbawa). Bemos meet the ferries at Alas to take passengers to either Sumbawa Besar (another 3 hours) or all the way to Bima (9 hours).

Air: Merpati runs a flight from Denpasar to Sumbawa Besar via Ampenan (Lombok), and from Denpasar to Bima, continuing on to Labuhanbajo and Ruteng (Flores). Bouraq and Garuda also fly from Denpasar to Sumbawa Besar several times a week.

Ask for information and details at Bali's airport or at the offices of the respective airlines in Denpasar. When you check flight times, remember the time difference: Lombok and points east are one hour ahead of Bali.

Accommodation

Amanwana, P.O. Box 33, Sumbawa Besar 83401. Tel: (0371) 22-233, Fax: 22-288. Yet another deluxe retreat from Amanresorts. This secluded hideaway is on Pulau Moyo, about 15 km off the coast of Sumbaya. Lush and almost entirely undeveloped, the island is protected as a wildlife refuge. The resort comprises 20 luxury tents, and a dining, bar and lounge area. Reached by boat.

Eating Out

You should try the **Aneka Rasa** for Chinese or local food. Bintang, Anker and San Miguel beer is served. There are a number of other local coffee shops and restaurants.

Pulau Komodo

Getting There

Sea and land: There are a number of choices in arranging a trip to Komodo. Travel agencies in Jakarta, Bali and even Lombok can set up a tour for one or for a group. Indonesian tourist offices can supply names of travel agents who deal specifically with Komodo. Prices of trips depend upon the duration of the visit and the size of the group. Whatever the arrangements, tours such as these are inevitably expensive.

An overland trip from Bali on your own is much easier now than before, although plenty of time is needed. Travel first from Bali by ferry and bus across Lombok and Sumbawa to Sape, a port on the eastern side of Sumbawa.

From Sape, take a third ferry to complete the journey to Labuhanbajo, on the western tip of Flores. If you don't want to stay too long in Flores, check the schedule carefully, as the ferry only continues on to Komodo a few times a week. The duration of the crossing varies according to sea conditions, but the Sape–Komodo trip usually takes 8 hours, while the Komodo–Labuhanbajo trip takes about 3 hours. Once the ferry anchors off from

Komodo, local boats will land you on the island for a small fee. For groups of 15 or more, the ferry will stop at Komodo on any of its regular runs in either direction for an extra fee per person. When you board the ferry, get final confirmation from the captain that the ferry will call at Komodo.

Boat charter is another way, one that solves the headaches of scheduled services. Both Sape and Labuhanbajo provide charter services. As the landing point for Komodo is on the eastern side, it is much closer to Labuhanbajo (about 50 km) than to Sape (120 km). In addition, the sea tends to be much rougher between Sape and Komodo than to the east. Currents are strong in these seas, although boatmen don't take unnecessary risks. Do be punctual once you have arranged departure times, as they depend upon tides and currents.

When arriving in either Sape or Labuhanbajo, you must report to the local PPA office (Directorate of National Conservation). They will call the PPA camp in Komodo to advise them of your visit, and to make certain that beds and food are available.

Accommodation

At the PPA site in Loho Liang, there are several large and comfortable local-style cabins with a total capacity of 80 beds. Each cabin has two bathrooms. Cheap meals of rice and fish are available. On arriving in Komodo, register and pay a fee at the PPA office in Loho Liang. Any time you leave the PPA compound, you must be accompanied by a guide (one for every three visitors) who charges a nominal daily fee.

Sumba

Getting There

Air: There are several flights a week between Bali and Waingapu on Merpati and Bouraq airlines, in addition to flights from Java and Jakarta.

Sea: West Sumba has a small harbor on the north coast at Waikelo, about 50 km (30 mi) from Waikabubak. East Sumba has a better and busier harbor at Waingapu. Unscheduled, freight-carrying motor boats call at these two ports and will take on deck passengers. Larger ships call twice a month at these ports on their way to and from Surabaya, and four times a month from Kupang (Timor). Passengers sleep on deck. These ships call at several other harbors of neighboring islands; if time permits, and one lacks a yacht, this is an excellent way to island hop.

Road: The two district capitals, Waikabubak and Waingapu, are linked by a 140-km (80-mi) road. Two buses cover the 5-hour trip daily. Smaller roads, mainly unpaved, provide public transport (bemos) to small towns and villages.

Accommodation

Waikabubak

Rakuta, Jl. Veteran. Run by Heroe Nugroho, it is by far the best in town. Bathroom and toilet shared between two rooms.

Losmen Pelita, 14 rooms with two or four beds. No interior toilet or bath.

Wisma Pemuda, five rooms, two with clean, modern bathroom, toilets. The other three share a bath and toilet. Meals are available.

Waingapu

Elim, Jl. A. Yani 35. Tel: 32 or 162. Eighteen rooms each with private bath and toilet. Meals available.

Lima Saudara, Jl. Wanggametti 2. Tel: 83. Twelve rooms, some with toilet and bath. Meals available.

Surabaya, Jl. Eltari 2. Tel: 125. Seventeen rooms.

Sandalwood, Jl. Matawai. Tel: 117. The best in town. All 13 rooms have attached bath and toilet.

Attractions

Many traditional activities that involve paying homage to spirits take place between July and October. These include the building of *adat* houses, and burials in which sometimes hundreds of pigs, horses, water buffalo and dogs are sacrificed.

Other ceremonies include the *pajura* (traditional boxing matches), festivals for the New Year in October and November, and horseraces and ritual dances on August 17th – National Day. Contact the head of the Waikabubak cultural office (Kepala Seksi Kebudayaan) for advice on cultural events, or for the hire of a guide.

Shopping

Textiles: Traditional Sumbanese textiles will be the top purchase for most visitors. Shop carefully, as much inferior work is sold. For a good piece of work, the lines should curve smoothly, with intricate patterns. Check to see if the colors are clean or if the dyes have run into each other. (If there are white patches in the design, they must be sharp and clean.) Bargain hard, as the final price could well be one-third the first asking price. Most *hinggi* come in pairs, one as a body-wrap and another as a shawl. **Prailiu** and **Mangili** (outside Waingapu) are the centers of the weaving industry. **Melolo** (on the southeast coast) is also a good source of old Sumban handwoven fabrics.

Flores

Getting There

Air: Air links between the centers are increasing. Labuhanbajo, Ruteng, Banjawa, Ende, Maumere and Larantuka all have airstrips.

Sea: Larantuka's port is the place to hitch or buy a ride on a boat to points east of Flores. Plenty of unscheduled sea traffic to all points will enable some decent island hopping.

Road: Of all the major islands in Nusa Tenggara, Flores has the worst road network because of its rugged terrain. Mountains and 14 active volcanoes make for beautiful scenery, but also for an engineering headache. Travel the length of Flores by public transport, but don't be fooled by the fact that there is a 670-km (400-mi) road running the length of the island. It will take at least four to five days to finish, as transport seldom runs at night. During the rainy season (November–May), roads between the principle towns could be cut for days.

Accommodation

All accommodation is in losmen, of which none particularly stand out above the others. Look around and chose the one that fit your needs.

West Timor

Accommodation

Astiti, Jl. Jend Sudirman 146, Kupang. Tel: (0391) 21-810.

Cendana, Jl. Raya El Tari 15, Kupang. Tel: (0391) 21-541.
Sasando International, Jl. Kartini 1, Kupang. Tel: (0391) 22-224.
Laguna Inn, Jl. G Kelimuto 25, Kupang. Tel: (0391) 21-559.
Orchid Garden, Jl. G Fatuleu, Kupang. Tel: (0391) 32-004.

EATING OUT

Istana Garden, Jl. Timtim, Oesapa, Kupang. Indonesian, Chinese, European.
Lima Jaya Raya, Jl. Sukarno 15A, Kuang. Indonesian, Chinese, European.
Pantai Laut, Jl. Ikan Duyung 3, Kupang. Indonesian, Chinese, European.
Susi, Jl. Sumatera, Kupang.

Kalimantan

GETTING THERE

Air: The major gateway for flights to and within Kalimantan is **Balikpapan**. Garuda, Bouraq, Merpati and Sempati offer flights from Jakarta, Palangkaraya, Surabaya, and Ujung Pandang. These airlines also serve the other main areas in Kalimantan from Jakarta, Yogyakarta, Unjung Pandan, Menado, Surabaya, Singapore and Brunei. As the airline schedules change quite frequently, it's best to contact them directly for the most up-to-date information. For flights to the more remote parts of Kalimantan, there are often delays and cancellations, and, at times, too many passengers for the available space. Try to catch a ride on a MAF (Missionary Aviation Fellowship) flight in small Cessnas heading to really inaccessible places. There are no fixed schedules with MAF, and it is strictly on a seat-available basis. The MAF office is on Jl. Rahayu, Balikpapan. Tel: (0542) 23-628.

Sea and river: The national shipping company's inter-Indonesian island route stops in Balikpapan. Because the itinerary takes in Surabaya and Ujung Pandang before Balikpapan, traveling by sea makes more sense if planning to visit more than just Kalimantan.

Inland by river from Banjarmasin, travelers can follow the Barito River north to near its headwaters. With a couple of weeks to spare, the whole river could be explored. Boats can be chartered upriver as far as Mauratewe. From here, it's by canoes to approach the headwaters. A long trek northeast (with the possibility of shortening some of the journey by road) leads across swamps to Intu and finally to Long Iram, on the Mahakam River. Long Iram is a relatively short 36-hour journey upriver from Samarinda. The other, more adventurous, alternative on arrival in Long Iram is to boat it up the Mahakam to the Dayak villages of Longbangun, then through the rapids to Long Pahangai, Tiong Ohang and further.

Speedboats depart Samarinda daily and arrive in Bontang about five hours later. Water taxis take about twice as long to cover the same distance. Enquire at one of the offices of P.T. Kayu Mas for more information.

Road: The **Trans-Kalimantan Highway** extends from Batakan, south of Banjarmasin, through Balikpapan and on to Samarinda. It will eventually connect to Bontang and Tarakan. Buses run on a regular schedule from Banjarmasin to Balikpapan and Samarinda.

There is a reasonable road running north from Pontianak and which forks at the village of Seipenyu. Continuing north, the road approaches the Sarawak border and passes through an area well-known for its excellent handwoven cloth. The border cannot be crossed without a visa. The right fork heads due east to Sintang on the Kapuas River.

Meanwhile, logging roads provide a crude path for sturdy vehicles in some areas. Bridges are often made of rotting logs; erosion and mud-slides create common obstacles. On dry days, it may be possible to use a jeep on these roads.

TOURIST OFFICES

Banjarmasin: Diparda Tk I Kalimantan Selatan, Jl. Mayjend. D.I. Panjaitan 23, Banjarmasin 70114. Tel: (0511) 2982.
Palangkaraya: Diparda Tk. I Kalimantan Tengah, Jl. Mayjen S. Parman 21, Palangkaraya 73111. Tel: (0514) 21-416.
Pontianak: Diparda Tk. I Kalimantan Barat, Jl. Achmad Sood 25, Pontianak 78121. Tel: (0561) 36-712.
Samarinda: Diparda Tk I Kalimantan Timur, Jl. Ade Irma Nasution 1, Samarinda 75117. Tel: (0541) 21-669, Fax: 22-111.

Pontianak

ACCOMMODATION

Mahkota Kapuas, Jl. Sidas 8, Pontiank. Tel: (0561) 36-022.
Kupuas Palace, Jl. Imam Bonjol, Pontianak. Tel: (0561) 36-122.
Kartika, Jl. Rahadi Usman, Pontianak. Tel: (0561) 34-401.

Banjarmasin

ACCOMMODATION

Kalimantan, Jl. Lambung Mangkurat, P.O. Box 32, Banarmasin 70111. Tel: (0511) 66-818, Fax: 67-345.
Barito Palace, Jl. Haryono MT 16-20, Banjarmasin 70111. Tel: (0511) 67-300, Fax: 52-240.
Banjarmasin, Jl. A. Yani Km 3.5, Banjarmasin 70111. Tel: (0511) 67-007.
Maramin, Jl. Pangeran Lambung Mangkurat 32, Banjarmasin 70111. Tel: (0511) 68-944, Fax: 53-350.
New River City, Jl. R.E. Martadinata 6, Banjarmasin 70112. Tel: (0511) 52-983, Fax: 52-312.
Sampaga, Jl. Mayjen Soetoyo 128, Banjarmasin 70117. Tel: (0511) 52-753, Fax: 52-480.

Balikpapan

ACCOMMODATION

Benakutai, Jl. Jendr. A. Yani, P.O. 299, Balikpapan 76101. Tel: (0542) 31-896, Fax: 31-823. Operated by Novotel Hotels, has all the comfort and facilities of a top-rated hotel.
Dusit Inn, Jl. Jendr. Sudirman, Balikpapan 76114. Tel: (0542) 20-155, Fax: 20-150. Cantonese restaurant and international cafe, lounge and bar, adult and children's pools.
Bahtera Jaya Abadi, Jl. A. Yani 2, Balikpapan. Tel: (0542) 22-563.
Blue Sky, Jl. Letjen. Suprapto, Balikpapan. Tel: (0542) 22-267.

EATING OUT

Benua Patra, Jl. Yos Sudarso. Truly an international cuisine with European, Korean, Japanese and Chinese food.

Bondi's, Jl. Mayjend. Sutoyo 7 (near the Benakutai). The front is an ice-cream and pastry parlor, but at the back is an open-air restaurant, which specialists in grilled fish. Local and imported steaks are also available.

Hapkoen, Jl. D.I. Panjaitan XX/55. Chinese cooking with the usual dishes, and shark-fin and bird-nest soup.

Ikan Bakar Dalle, Jl. K.S. Tubun. Specialists in grilled fish.

Shangrila, Jl. Mayjend. Sutoyo IV/102. About 15 mins walk from Benakutai, claimed to be the best Chinese restaurant. The basic Chinese cooking with the "masakan special" of hot plate – with vegetables with pigeon eggs and a choice of chicken, shrimp, beef and squid.

Salero Minang, Jl. Gajah Mada. Typical Padang-style, lots of dishes on your table but you pay only for what's eaten.

Samarinda

ACCOMMODATION

Mesra International, Jl. Pahlawan 1, Samarinda. Tel: (0541) 32-772, Fax: 41-017.

Sewarga Indah, Jl. Jend. Sudirman 43, Samarinda. Tel: (0541) 22-066.

Kota Tepian, Jl. Pahlawan 4, Samarinda. Tel (0541) 32-510.

Kutai National Park

Apart from the obvious rewards once you arrive in the wildlife reserve at Kutai, the act of arriving there can often be a mini-adventure in itself.

Sea and river: Access to the east of the reserve is by boat from Samarinda. Regular water taxis run to Bontang and Sengatta, taking 18 hours. Speed boats are faster. The Santan and Sengatta rivers are navigable, the latter as far as Mentoko. Beyond here, rapids make progress difficult, particularly at low water. The best boats are powered canoes called *ketinting*. Progress is slow but steady, and underwater obstacles are easily avoided. They also have the advantage of employing an engine that is less sophisticated then the two-stroke outboard. In the west, reach Sedulang in one day from Samarinda by speed boat, or by water taxi in double the time. From Sedulang to Klampa is about 4 hours if the water is high; at other times, it takes much longer.

Air: Balikpapan has connecting services to Samarinda. If room is available, fare-paying passengers can travel by P.N. Pertamina aircraft from Balikpapan to one of three airstrips owned by oil companies. There are airstrips at Tanjung Santan, Bontang and Sengatta, and the oil companies are prepared to allow for charter flight landings if previous arrangements are made.

Road: A number of roads exit both close to and within the reserve. A highway links Balikpapan and Samarinda and goes as far as Bontang, the site of the LNG plant. Logging roads exit in the south of the reserve and extend at least 50 km (30 mi). Another road joins the other road and continues in a westerly direction. In the Sengatta area, Pertamina has a network of roads extending about 16 km (10 mi) to the south and then eastwards to the coast. There are numerous abandoned roads that are navigable by jeep. **Teluk Kaba** is accessible this way from Sengatta on dry days.

Dayak Country

ARTS AND CRAFTS

The center of attention in Kalimantan's arts and crafts is the culture of the Dayak people. Their work displays an extraordinary and vibrant sense of design; the characteristic flowing geometrical patterns used in portraying scenes of jungle life have Chinese and Vietnamese Dong Son influences.

Weaving has just about died out. At the village of Tanjung Isuy, in East Kalimantan, it has been revived for the tourist trade. There, the *ikat* is the common technique in weaving; it originally used bark fibers, natural plant dyes and earth dyes. Now, commercial yarn and dyes are used more often. Dayak cloth is as good if not better than the famous Sumban ikat.

More than any other ethnic group in Indonesia, the Dayak are famed for their beadwork. Thousands of tiny glass beads are used to decorate purses, tobacco pouches, scabbards, baby carriages, basket lids, hems, caps and headbands.

Yet another craft is basketry, and a wide variety of work in characteristic two-tone patterns can be obtained.

Sex roles differentiate most of the Dayak crafts. Men are more at home carving wood and working metal, while the women tend more to plaiting, weaving and beadwork.

Sulawesi

GETTING THERE

Air: Garuda has several flights a day making the two-hour trip from Jakarta to Ujung Pandang. Merpati flies a few times weekly via Surabaya and costs about 15 percent less.

Many of the outlying towns in Sulawesi are also served. Garuda flies to Kendari, Manado and Palu, while Merpati flies to Gorontalo and Manado. Bouraq makes the connection between Ujung Pandang and Manado, flying via Palu and Gorontalo.

The Manado airport, located at Mapanget, is a good half-hour's drive from the city itself. Buses ply the route through coconut groves and past a winding river, but they are not on a fixed schedule. A bemo or shared taxi can also be hired.

Sea: The national shipping company PELNI runs a passenger service throughout the archipelago. The last portion of its itinerary offers access into Sulawesi and, incidentally, Kalimantan. Surabaya is the embarkation point for a passenger ship that sails to Ujung Pandang, Balikpapan (Kalimantan), and Bitung (northeastern Sulawesi), and then back again on the same route. Cabins are cheap.

In Jakarta, visit the national shipping company's head office: PT PELNI, Jl. Angkasa 18. Tel: 471-569 or 415-428.

TOURIST OFFICES

Manada: Diparda Tk. I Sulawesi Utara, Komplek Perkantoran, Jl. 17 Agustus, Manada 95117. Tel: (0341) 64-299.

Ujung Pandang: Diparda Tk. I Sulawesi Selatan, Jl. Sultan Alaudin 105 B, Ujung Pandang 90223. Tel: (0411) 83-897.

Kendari: Diparda Tk I. Sulawesi Tenggara, Jl. Lakidende 9, Kendari 93111. Tel: (0401) 21-764.

Palu: Diparda Tk. I Sulawesi Tengah, Jl. Raya Moili 103, Palu 94111. Tel: (0451) 21-795.

Eating Out

Sulawesi has a well-developed cuisine; prices are reasonable. Minahassans, in particular, are gourmets and gourmands. The local staple is *tinutuan*; a rice porridge cooked with sundry vegetables, pieces of pumpkin and shredded maize, and eaten with salted fish and very hot chili sauce.

Bakpiah, a big dumpling filled with meat, eggs, and vegetables, is a popular treat. A fresh salad called *dabu-dabu*, made of fresh but sour tomato, cucumber, onions, chilies and lemon juice, accompanies any meal. Breakfast consists of cooked banana, *bolu* cakes and coffee. A favorite treat is *es kacang* – cooked red beans topped with shaved ice, a splash of chocolate syrup and another splash of condensed milk. It is cooling and invigorating on a hot day.

For the daring, Minahassan cuisine features a number of unusual dishes: fruitbats on the spit, field mice and snake. The greatest local delicacy is dog meat, stewed in hot spices and peppers. The dish is called RW, a code meaning "the pig with short hair." When in doubt, the diner can always ask to look at the carcasses in the kitchen; the cook will not be offended.

Ujung Pandang

Getting There

Though Merpati flies daily to Rantepau in Torajaland, most locals agree that the 9-hour bus journey is still worth taking. **Liman Express**, leaving from Jl. Laiya downtown, with a scheduled stop in front of the Ramayana Hotel, has morning and evening buses.

For other areas of South Sulawesi, shared taxis are the best bet. **CV Taxis**, Jl. Durian 2, and **MPS**, Jl. Martadinata 142, have frequent taxis to towns on the South Coast and Watampone, the ferry terminal for southeast Sulawesi.

C.V. Omega, Jl. Hati Murni.

Liman Express, Jl. Laiya 25.

Transport Offices

Garuda, Jl. Slamet Riyadi 6. Tel: 317-704, 315-405.

Merpati, Jl. G. Bawakaraeng 109. Tel: 4114 or 4118.

Bouraq, Jl. Keteran Selatan Nol. Tel: 83-039.

Mandala, Jl. Iriam 2F. Tel: 21-289.

PELNI, Jl. Martadinata. Tel: 6967.

Accommodation

Unlike other large towns in eastern Indonesia, Ujung Pandang is a nice place to spend a day or two. Stay in one of the hotels near the waterfront, within walking distance of most places of interest and the best restaurants.

Marannu City, Jl. Sultan Hasanuddin 3-5, Ujung Pandang. Tel: (0411) 315-087, Fax: 321-821.

Makassar Golden, Jl. Pasar Ian 52, Ujung Pandang. Tel: (0411) 31-408, Fax: 317-999. Excellent location.

Makassar City, Jl. Khairil Anwar 28, Ujung Pandang. Tel: (0411) 317-055, Fax: 311-818.

Victoria, Jl. Jend. Sudirman 24, Ujung Pandang. Tel: (0411) 311-553, Fax: 312-468.

Losari Beach, Jl. Penghibur 3, Ujung Pandang. Tel: (0411) 323-609, Fax: 313-976.

Pessanggrahan Beach, Jl. Somba Opu 279. Tel: (0411) 324-217. A 50-year-old white-washed structure. The rooms are small, with narrow, rickety folding beds, but all rooms face the sea and include a balcony, where you can enjoy the huge breakfast included in the room rate.

Ramayana, Jl. Gunung Bawakaraeng 121, Ujung Pandang. Tel: (0411) 322-165, Fax: 322-165. Opposite the Liman Express office. The Ramayana Travel agency, located in the hotel, specialists in arranging tours through Torajaland, including trekking to Mamasa.

Eating Out

The sea-going Makassarese are famous seafood cooks, using simple but delicious recipes. Their most famous dish is *ikan bakar*, red snapper or sea bass grilled over an open flame, served with rice and spicy sambal. It is best eaten while sitting on the wooden benches of a waterfront *warung* in the company of Bugis sailors, but you may also sample it in the more gentile environment of restaurants in town.

If seafood is not to your liking, another specialty is *soto makassar*, a thick and nutritious soup made from various parts of the water buffalo. Best eaten in the afternoon, it is served at **Soto Daeng**, near the Istana cinema, or at roadside warung in town.

Arts & Crafts

Artshop, Jl. Somba Opu 20. Indonesian statues, carving, batik, sarung, basket-work and leather.

Asdar Art, Jl. Somba Opu 199. Paintings, carving, silk sarung, basket-work.

Kanebo Art, Jl. Pattimura 27. Paintings, statues, sea shells, animal hides, traditional dress of South Sulawesi.

Mutiara Art, Jl. Somba Opu 117A. Statues, carvings, sarung, sea shells and animal hides.

Paleori Art, Jl. Somba Opu 108. Paintings, Toraja weaving and bamboo.

Silver Handicraft Center, Jl. Dangko.

Rantepao & Makale

Getting Around

Most of the attractions are in the immediate vicinity of Rantepao, and can be reached by local transportation and much walking. Old motorcycles and jeeps are available for hire. During the months of August to October, the funeral season, someone will always be organizing some sort of shared transportation to the event. Ask around.

For extended excursions through the outlying villages, you will need standard mountain gear and a guide. The guide will also carry your pack – helpful if you are not used to high altitudes. Although the people of Rantepao will tell you to pay with barter goods, this is no longer the case. Villagers these days want cash. In each village, ask the *kepala desa* (village headman) to arrange for you to sleep in someone's house. If you have a guide, he will arrange it.

The treks from Rantepao involve making a loop through several villages, ending where you began. The longest and most interesting walk, however, will take you 60 km (40 mi) to pristine (at least with regards to tourists) Mamasa.

The walk to Mamasa begins in Bituang, with a 4-hour bemo ride from Makale. The path is a major trading route between Toraja and Mamasa. The trek takes up to four days. In Mamasa, check in at the **Losmen Mini** for a few days before braving the horrendous 90-km (60-mile) ride to Polewali on the coast.

ACCOMMODATION

Misiliana, Jl. Ray Makale, Rantepao. Tel: (0423) 21-212.
Toraja Cottage, Jl. Paku Balasara, Rantepao. Tel: (0423) 21-268, Fax: 21-369.
Barana Hill, Jl. Pontiku, Makale. Tel: (0423) 22-510, Fax: 22-515.
Indra II, Jl. Ratulangi 26, Rantepao. Tel: (0423) 21-583.

Kendari

GETTING THERE

Air: Garuda flies daily to Kendari from Ujung Pandang, while Merpati has flights several times a week to Kendari and Bau-Bau, though schedules on the latter are likely to be changed without notice.

Sea: A ferry leaves Bone (Wantampone) daily, arriving in Kolaka early next morning. No cabins are available, only deck class; renting an army cot is the best alternative. There is a direct taxi connection to Kendari from the terminal. From dock to terminal is about 1 km; bargain hard with the becak driver.

Another possibility is a PELNI boat stopping once a week in Bau-Bau en route to Ambon from Ujung Pandang, or vice versa. A ferry leaves Kendari every afternoon for Raha and Bau-Bau, four berths to a cabin, arriving in Raha late at night and Bau-Bau in the very early morning; passengers are allowed to stay on board until a civilized hour.

ACCOMMODATION

It's impossible to get lost in this town, as it has only one main road, though its name has been changed several times. The best hotel is the Kendari Beach. Other hotels are farther along the main street toward the wharves. Try Arnin's Hotel, Jl. A. Yani or the Wisma Andika.
Arnis, Jl. Diponegoro 75. Tel: (0401) 21-751.
Kendari Beach, Jl. Sultan Hasanudin 44. Tel: (0413) 21-988.

Maluku

GETTING THERE

Air: Garuda, Sempati, Merpati and Mandala fly regularly to Ambon and Ternate from Jakarta, Surabaya, Denpasar, Ujung Pandang, Ambon and Manado.
Garuda, Jl. A. Yani, Ambon. Tel: (0911) 52-481.
Mandala, Jl. A Patty, Ambon. Tel: (0911) 42-551, Fax: 42-377.
Merpati, Jl. A. Yani, Ambon. Tel: (0911) 52-481.
Sempati, Jl. Wim Reamaru SK.1, 14, Ambon. Tel: (0911) 51-612, Fax: 56-600.

Sea: Sea travel is the traditional means of transportation. Sailing vessels occasionally carry agricultural and commercial products over long distances. The deep-water harbor at Ambon is the principal port of Maluku.

On the east coast of Ambon, speedboats and other motorized vessels dock at Tulehu and connect with the towns of Seram and Banda.

Once every two weeks, PELNI lines' huge passenger ship calls on Ternate on its way to Manado and Sorong (and again on its way back) as part of its run from Jakarta to Jayapura. In Ternate's harbor there are motorboats connections with the surrounding islands as far as Morotai, Tonelo and Patani on Halmahera's east coast, and to Gebe and Bachan.

Road: Bemos travel the few exciting roads throughout the Maluku archipelago. In Ambon city and Ternate, the main terminals are in the center of town next to shopping centers. In some of the more remote areas, there is nothing to stop you walking if you think you have discovered something to visit. Village hopping on the coast is easy with numerous prahu sailing vessels willing to take a passenger or two.

Tourist office: Diparda Tk I. Maluku (Moluccas), c/o Kantor Gubernur KDH Tk.I Maluku, Jl. Pattimura, P.O. Box 113, Ambon 97124. Tel: (0911) 52-471.

EATING OUT

The lifestyle in Maluku is reflected in what is a rather basic cuisine. Sago is the staple food in the south, supplemented by sweet potatoes and cassava. Fish is the main source of protein, with meat and fowl reserved for feasts. Kanari, a nut similar to the almond, is made into a sauce of *gado-gado* style salads. In the north, the yellow rice eaten with curries or sate is very popular.

Mixed Arab and Chinese families have more varied dishes and eat more meat. Dining out is not a widespread habit, though coffee houses serve lunches. To cater for the many immigrant workers, a number of food stalls and restaurants are beginning to appear. Ambon and Ternate have plenty of restaurants. Elsewhere, meals are usually served at your lodgings.

Ambon

ACCOMMODATION

Ambon Manise, Jl. Pantai Mardika, Ambon. Tel: (0911) 44-000.
Manise, Jl. W.R. Supratman, Ambon. Tel: (0911) 41-445. Business facilities.
Mutiara, Jl. Pattimura, Ambon. Tel: (0911) 53-075.
Abdulalie, Jl. Sultan Babullah, Ambon. Tel: (0911) 52-796.
Amboina, Jl. Kapten Ulupaha 5A, Ambon. Tel: (0911) 41-725.
Eleonoor, Jl. Anthoni Rhebok 30, Ambon. Tel: (0911) 52-834.

Ternate

ACCOMMODATION

Neraca, Jl. Pahlawan Revolusi 30, Ternate. Tel: (0921) 21-668.
Nirwana, Jl. Pahlawan Revolusi 58, Ternate. Tel: (0921) 21-787.

Banda

ACCOMMODATION

Maulana, Jl. Pelabuhan, Bandanaira. Tel: (0910) 21-022, Fax: 21-024.
Naira, Jl. Pantai, Banda.

Seram

Losman Maharani, Jl. Kesturi, Masohi, Ceram.

If venturing farther afield, enquire about accommodation before heading off. You might seek the hospitality of a Christian mission, in which case a "donation" would be a fair way of showing gratitude.

Irian Jaya

All visitors to Irian Jaya **must** obtain a letter of recommendation and *surat jalan* from the police in Jayapura before traveling to the interior. Unauthorized visitors to sensitive areas are sent back to Jayapura at their own expense. It is not always possible to know in advance which parts of the island are considered "sensitive." For the most up-to-date information and details on Irian Jaya, contact:

Tourist Development Board of Irian Jaya, Bapparda, Governor's Office of Irian Jaya, P.O. Box 499, Jayapura. Tel: (0967) 2138, ext: 263;

Irian Jaya Promotion Board, Jl. Suwirojo 43, Jakarta. Tel: (021) 345-3579.

Travel agents experienced in operating tours to Irian Jaya are **Tunas Indonesia** and **Pacto**.

GETTING THERE

Air: Garuda has at least one flight daily from Jakarta to Jayapura, with transfers in Ujung Pandang or Biak and Sorong. Merpati also flies from Jakarta to Biak via Surabaya and Ujung Pandang (no transfers), with connections to Jayapura daily. From Jayapura and Biak, Merpati has flights to Sorong, Manokwari, Serui and Nabire on the north coast; Fakfak, Kaimena, Kokenau, Timika and Merauke on the south coast; and Enarotali and Wamena in the highlands.

In addition, missionary aircraft travel to isolated settlements throughout the highlands and coastal regions. Two missionary groups have bases at Jayapura's Sentani Airport (34 km from Jayapura): the Missionary Aviation Fellowship (MAF) for the Protestants and one for the Roman Catholics. MAF is by far the largest, with 27 planes and two helicopters. Other missionary groups in Irian Jaya are the Australian Baptist Mission (ABMS), Asian Pacific Christian Mission (APCM), Regions Beyond Missionary Alliance (RBMU), The Evangelical Alliance Mission (TEAM), and the Unevangelised Fields Mission (UFM) and the Roman Catholics. Rather than fix travel plans before arriving, it would be far better to investigate some of these organizations, ask around and find out just what you might be able to do. The possibility for getting to some of the remotest corners of the province is there with some initiative, a spirit of adventure, and a valid surat jalan.

Sea: It is definitely worth trying to hitch free rides on some of the coastal steamers. The oil industry here is served by considerable sea-going traffic. On the south coast, Merauke is the major port. Other vessels carry passengers, but a fare is charged. If thinking of using the state shipping company PELNI, then enquire in Jakarta concerning routes, schedules and fares. Planning a sea itinerary means traveling via Maluku. If your sole intended destination is Irian Jaya, stick to air travel. But if you have time, take the Pelni ship *Umsini*, which takes one week from Jakarta to Jayapura.

Tourist Office: Diparda Tk. I Irian Jaya, Jl. Soa Siu Dok II, P.O. Box 499, Jayapura 99115. Tel: (0967) 2138, ext: 263.

SHOPPING

The demand for Asmat carvings has increased over the years. Simple colors – red, black and white – are an Asmat trademark. The UN project that has been protecting the craft has restored the prestige of the master-carvers by giving them a recognized place as teachers in the education system.

Contact the **Asmat Handicraft Project** at Dinas Perindustriaan, Kotakpos 294, Jayapura, if you want to buy Asmat carvings. There is an official warehouse on Jl. Batu Karang outside Jayapura. The **Cama** shop and the souvenir counter at Sentani airport sells carvings.

ACTIVITIES

Though the government has succeeded in "settling" a number of tribes, there are still a few isolated ethnic groups in remote areas. Tours can be arranged. In Jayapura, guides can be hired from the Cenderawasih University anthropology department of Jl. Sentani Abepura (20 km from the city). Less expensive guides can also be hired in Wamena.

Jayapura

ACCOMMODATION

Matoa International, Jl. Jend. A. Yani 14, Jayapura 99111. Tel: (0967) 31-633.

Dafonsoro, Jl. Percetakan 20-24. Tel: (0967) 31-695.

Natour's Hotel Numbai, Jl. Trikora Dok. V Atas, P.O. Box 22. Tel: 34-185.

Triton, Jl. Jend. A. Yani 52. Tel: (0967) 21-218.

A cheaper alternative to staying in Jayapura is to sleep in Sentani, 32 km (20 mi) inland.

EATING OUT

Jayapura has a large Bugis population, so *ikan bakar* is the meal of choice. The alley behind the Import-Export Bank near the bemo terminal is lined with warungs serving *ikan bakar* and sate.

Dafonsoro, Jl. Percetakan 20-24. Indonesian, Chinese.

Hawaii, Jl. Irian 2. Tel: 22-706. Indonesian, Chinese.

Jaya Grill, Jl. Kota 5. Tel: 23-436. Indonesian, European.

Wamena

ACCOMMODATION

Baliem Cottages, Jl. Tharin, P.O. Box 32, Wamena 99511.

Jayawijaya Hotelama, P.O. Box 57, Wamena.

Nayak, Jl. Gatot Subroto, Wamena 99511. Across the road from the airport terminal. The best value in town, and the best food.

For accommodation outside Wamena, any village chief will let you sleep in a communal *honnay* for a small charge and perhaps a gift of cigarettes. The missionaries will sometimes put you up, and many Indonesians working in the villages would be honored to have you as a house guest.

Timika

ACCOMMODATION

Sheraton Inn Timika, P.O. Box 3, Timika 98663. Tel: (0979) 549-4949, Fax: 549-4950. Located at the foot of the Puncak Jaya Mountain near the Lorentz Nature Preserve, this hotel is ideal for nature lovers who wish comfortable accommodation. Full facilities.

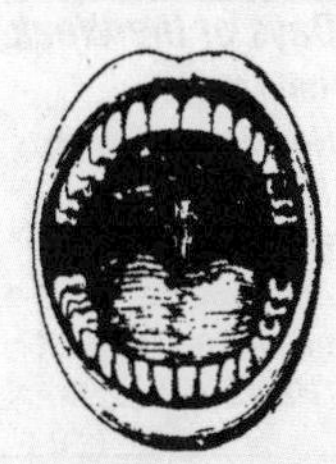

Language

General

Indonesia's motto, *Bhinneka Tunggal Ika* (unity in diversity) is seen in its most driving, potent form in the work of language. Although there are over 350 languages and dialects spoken in the archipelago, the one national tongue, *Bahasa Indonesia,* will take you from the northernmost tip of Sumatra through Java and across the string of islands to Irian Jaya. Bahasa Indonesia is both an old and new language. It is based on Malay, which has been the lingua franca throughout much of Southeast Asia for centuries, but it has changed rapidly in the past few decades to meet the needs of a modern nation.

Although Bahasa Indonesia is a complex language demanding serious study, the construction of basic Indonesian sentences is relatively easy. Indonesian is written in the Roman alphabet and, unlike some Asian languages, is not tonal.

Indonesians always use their language to show respect when addressing others, especially when a younger person speaks to elders. The custom is to address an elder man as *bapak* or *pak* (father) and an elder woman as *ibu* (mother), and even in the case of slightly younger people who are obviously VIPs, this form of address is suitable and correct. *Bung* (in West Java) and *mas* (in Central and East Java) roughly translate as "brother" and are used with equals, people your own age whom you don't know all that well, and with hotel clerks, taxi drivers, tour guides and waiters (it's friendly, and a few notches above "buddy" or "mate").

a short as in 'father'
(*apa* = what, *ada* = there is)

ai rather like the 'i' in 'mine'
(*kain* = material, *sampai* = to arrive)

k hard at the beginning of a word as in 'king', hardly audible at the end of a word.
(*kamus* = dictionary, *cantik* = beautiful)

kh (*ch*) slightly aspirated as in 'khan' or the Scottish 'ch' in 'loch'
(*khusus* = special, *khabar* = news)

ng as in 'singer', never as in 'danger' or 'Ringo'
(*bunga* = flower, *penginapan* = cheap hotel)

ngg like the 'ng' in 'Ringo'
(*minggu* = week, *tinggi* = high)

r always rolled
(*rokok* = cigarette, *pertama* = first)

u (*oe*) as in 'full', never as in 'bucket'
(*umum* = public, *belum* = not yet)

y (*j*) as in 'you'
(*saya* = I or me, *kaya* = rich)

c (*tj*) like the 'ch' in 'church'
(*candi* = temple, *kacang* = nut)

e 1. often unstressed as the barely sounded 'e' in 'open'
(*berapa,* sounded like *b'rapa* = how much?)
2. sometimes stressed, sounding somewhere between the 'e' in 'bed' and 'a' in 'bad'
(*boleh* = may, *lebar* = wide)

g hard as in 'golf', never as in 'ginger'
(*guntur* = thunder, *bagus* = very good)

h generally lightly aspirated
(*hitam* = black, *lihat* = to see)

i either short as in 'pin' or a longer sound like 'ee' in 'meet'
(*minta* = to ask for, *ibu* = mother)

j (*dj*) as in 'John'
(*jalan* = road or street, *jahit* = to sew)

Two minor points about spelling. Despite the new rules you will find many instances where people's names continue to be spelled with the old 'oe' rather than the current 'u', some may change, but most stick to their birthright, including the President whose name is Soeharto and only rarely used by the press as Suharto. Less important are the subtle distinctions in Central Java between two forms of 'o' and the liquid sounds of 'l' or 'r'; the niceties are of interest only to experts in phonetics, but in practical terms it means that the city of Solo may also appear as Sala, and that the Siva temple at Prambanan may be written (in its popular form) as Lara Janggrang, Loro Jonggrong or Roro Jonggrang…and they are all correct.

Greetings & Civilities

thank you (very much)/*terima kasih (banyak)*
please/*silahkan*
good morning/*selamat pagi*
good day (roughly 11am–3pm)/ *selamat siang*
good afternoon, evening/*selamat sore, malam*
goodbye (to person going)/*selamat jalan*
goodbye (to person staying)/*selamat tinggal*
I'm sorry/*ma'af*
welcome/*selamat datang*
please come in/*silahkan masuk*
Please sit down/*silahkan duduk*
what is your name?/*siapa nama saudara?*
my name is…/*nama saya…*
where do you come from?/*saudara datang dari mana?* or *dari mana?*
I come from…/*saya datang dari…*

Pronouns & Forms of Address

you (singular)/*kamu* (to children), *saudara, anda*
he, she/*dia*
we/*kami* (not including the listener)
we/*kita* (including the listener)
you (plural)/*saudara-saudara, anda*
they/*mereka*
Mr/*Tuan/'Pak/Mas/'Bung*
Mrs/*Nyonya/Ibu*
Miss/*Nona*
I/*saya*

Directions & Transport

left/*kiri*
right/*kanan*
straight/*terus*
near/*dekat*
far/*jauh*
from/*dari*
to/*ke*
inside/*didalam*
outside of/*diluar*
between/*antara*
under/*dibawah*

here/*disini*
there/*disana*
in front of/*didepan, dimuka*
at the back/*dibelakang*
next to/*disebelah*
to ascend/*naik*
to descend/*turun*
pedicab/*becak*
car/*mobil*
bus/*bis*
train/*kereta-api*
aeroplane/*kapal terbang*
ship/*kapal laut*
bicycle/*sepeda*
motor cycle/*sepeda motor*
where do you want to go?/*mau kemana?*
I want to go.../*saya mahu ke...*
stop here/*berhenti disini, stop disini*
I'll be back in five minutes/*aya akan kembali lima menit*
turn right/*belok kekanan*
how many kilometres?/*berapa kilometer jauhnya?*
slowly, slow down/*pelan-pelan/ perlahan-perlahan*

Important Places

hotel/*hotel, penginapan, losmen*
shop/*toko*
train station/*stasium kereta-api*
airport/*lapangan terbang*
cinema/*bioskop*
bookshop/*toko buku*
petrol station/*pompa bensin*
bank/*bank*
post office/*kantor pos*
swimming pool/*tempat pemandian, kolam renang*
Immigration Dept./*Departemen Immigrasi*
tourist office/*kantor parawisata*
embassy/*kedutaan besar*

Shopping

shop/*toko*
money/*uang*
change (of money)/*uang kembali*
to buy/*beli*
price/*harga*
expensive/*mahal*
cheap/*murah*
fixed price/*harga pas*
How much is it?/*Berapa?/Berapa harganya?*
It is too expensive./*Itu terlalu mahal.*
Do you have a cheaper one?/*Adakah yang lebih murah?*
Can you reduce the price?/*Bisa saudara kurangkan harganya?*
What is this?/*Apa ini?*
I'll take it./*Saya akan ambil ini.*
I don't want it./*Saya tidak mau.*
I'll come back later./*Saya akan kembali nanti.*

Time

day/*hari*
night/*malam*
today/*hari ini*
morning (to about 10.30am)/*pagi*
noon (broadly 10.30am–3pm)/*siang*
evening (3–8pm)/*sore*
now/*sekarang*
just now/*baru saja*
soon, presently/*nanti*
always/*selalu*
before/*dahulu, dulu*
when (= the time that)/*waktu*
when? (interrogative)/*kapan?*
tomorrow/*besok*
yesterday/*kemarin*
minute/*menit*
hour/*jam*
week/*minggu*
month/*bulan*
year/*tahun*
past (the hour)/*liwat*
to (before the hour)/*kurang*
What is the time?/*Jam berapa sekarang?*
It is ten past eight./*Jam delapan liwat sepuluh.*

Numbers

one/*satu*
two/*dua*
three/*tiga*
four/*empat*
five/*lima*
six/*enam*
seven/*tujuh*
eight/*delapan*
nine/*sembilan*
ten/*sepuluh*
eleven/*sebelas*
twelve/*duabelas*
thirteen/*tigabelas*
fourteen/*empatbelas*
fifteen/*limabelas*
sixteen/*enambelas*
seventeen/*tujuhbelas*
eighteen/*delapanbelas*
nineteen/*sembilanbelas*
twenty/*duapuluh*
twenty-one/*duapuluh satu*
thirty/*tigapuluh*
forty/*empatpuluh*
fifty-eight/*limapuluh delapan*
one hundred/*seratus*
two hundred and sixty-three/*duaratus enampuluh tiga*

Days of the Week

Sunday/*Hari Minggu*
Monday/*Hari Senin/Senen*
Tuesday/*Hari Selasa*
Wednesday/*Hari Rabu*
Thursday/*Hari Kamis*
Friday/*Hari Jum'at/Juma'at*
Saturday/*Hari Sabtu*

Interrogatives

who/*siapa*
what/*apa*
when/*kapan*
where (location)/*dimana*
where (direction)/*kemana*
why/*kenapa, mengapa*
how/*bagaimana*
how much, how many/*berapa*
which, which one/*yang mana*
A few more nouns:
cigarette/clove cigarette/*rokok/kretek*
matches/*korek api*
train (railway)/*kereta-api*
house/*rumah*
paper/*kertas*
newspaper/*surat khabar, koran*
hair/*rambut*
map/*peta*
place/*tempat*
stamp (postage)/*prangko, perangko*
electricity/*listrik*
foreigner/*orang asing*
tourist/*turis, wisatawan*

Useful Adjectives

big/*besar*
small/*kecil*
young/*muda*
old (person)/*tua*
old (thing)/*lama*
new/*baru*
beautiful/*cantik*
good/*baik*
no good/*tidak baik*
hot/*panas*
cold/*dingin*
delicious/*enak*
clean/*bersih*
dirty/*kotor*
red/*merah*
white/*putih*
blue/*biru*
black/*hitam*
green/*hijau*
yellow/*kuning*
gold/*mas*
silver/*perak*

Understanding Signs

Many Indonesian words have been borrowed from other languages, and quickly reveal their meanings: *sekolah, universitas, mobil, bis, akademi, sektor, proklamas* and *polisi*. Other important signs leave you guessing; the following short list may help you.

open/*buka, dibuka*
closed/*tutup, ditutup*
entrance/*masuk*
exit/*keluar*
don't touch/*jangan pegang*
no smoking/*dilarang merokok*
push/*tolak*
pull/*tarik*
gate/*pintu*
ticket window/*loket*
information/*keterangan*
public/*umum*
hospital/*rumah sakit*
pharmacy/*apotik*
ticket/*karcis*
house (institutional sense)/*wisma*
central/*pusat*
city/*kota*
district/*daerah*
zoo/*kebun binatang*
market/*pasar*
church/*gereja*
golf course/*lapangan golf*
customs/*bea dan cukai*

Filling in Forms

Forms are an unavoidable part of travel. Within Indonesia few forms carry translations into other languages, so here with a few key words and phrases to help you out.

name/*nama*
address/*alamat*
full address/*alamat lengkap*
male, female/*laki-laki, perempuan*
age/*umur*
date/*tanggal* (*tgl.*)
time/*jam*
departure/*berangkat*
marital status/*kawin*
religion/*agama*
nationality/*kebangsaan*
profession/*pekerjaan*
identification (passport, etc.)/*surat keterangan*
issued by/*pembesar yang memberikan*
purpose of visit/*maksud kunjungan*
signature/*tanda tangan*

Further Reading

History

Day, Clive. ***The Policy and Administration of the Dutch in Java***. Oxford: Kuala Lumpur, 1966.
Hall, D.G.E. ***A History of Southeast Asia***. MacMillan: London, 1977.
Hanna, Willard A. ***Bali Profile: People, Events, Circumstances 1901–1976***.
Pigeaud, T.G. Th. and De Graaf, H.J. ***Islamic States in Java 1500–1700***. Martinus Nijhoff: the Hague, 1976.
Ried, Anthony. ***Indonesian National Revolution 1945–1950***. Longman: Hawthorn, 1974.
Ricklefs, M.C. ***Jogjakarta Under Sultan Mangkubumi 1749–1792, A History of the Division of Java***. Oxford: London, 1974. ***A History of Modern Indonesia***. MacMillan: London, 1981.
Schnitger, F.M. ***Forgotten Kingdoms in Sumatra***. E.J. Brill: Leiden, 1939.
Van Heekeren, H.R. ***The Stone Age of Indonesia***. Martinus Nijhoff: The Hague, 1972.

Geography & Natural History

Fisher, C.A. ***Southeast Asia: A Social, Economic and Political Geography***. Methuen: London, 1964.
Wallace, Alfred Russel. ***The Malay Archipelago: The Land of the Orang-utan and the Bird of Paradise***. Reprint, Graham Brash: Singapore 1983.

Society & Religion

Belo, Jane. ***Trance in Bali***. Columbia University Press: New York, 1960.
Covarrubias, Miguel. ***Island of Bali***. Alfred A. Knopf: New York, 1937. Oxford: Kuala Lumpur, reprint 1984.
Fox, J.J. ***Indonesia: the Making of a Culture***. Australian National University: Canberra, 1980.
Geertz, Clifford, ***Negara, the Theatre State in Nineteenth-Century Bali***. Princeton University Press: Princeton, 1980. ***The Religion of Java***. Free Press: Glencoe, 1960.
Kennedy, Raymond. ***Bibliography of Indonesian Peoples and Cultures***. HRAF: New Haven, 1974 (2nd revised ed.).
McVey, Ruth (ed). ***Indonesia: Its People, Its Society, Its Culture***. HRAF Press: New Haven, 1963.
Mulder, Niels. ***Mysticism & Everyday Life in Contemporary Java***. Singapore University Press: Singapore, 1978.

The Arts

Becker, Judith. ***Traditional Music in Modern Java, Gamelan in a Changing Society***. University Press of Hawaii: Honolulu, 1980.
Brandon, James. ***On Thrones of Gold: Three Javanese Shadow Plays***. Harvard University Press: Cambridge, 1967.
Elliot, Inger McCabe. ***Batik, Fabled Cloth of Java***. Clarkson N. Potter: New York, 1984.
Fischer, Joseph (ed). ***Threads of Tradition, Textiles of Indonesia and Sarawak***. University of California: Berkeley, 1979.
Gittinger, Mattiebelle. ***Splendid Symbols: Textiles and Tradition in Indonesia***. The Textile Museum: Washington D.C., 1979.
Holt, Claire. ***Art in Indonesia: Continuities and Change***. Cornell University Press: New York, 1967.
Kempers, A.J. Bernett. ***Ageless Borobudur***. Servire/Wassenaar, 1976. ***Ancient Indonesian Art***. Harvard University Press: Cambridge, 1959. ***Monumental Bali: Introduction to Balinese Archaeology and Guide to the Monuments***. Van Goor Zonen: The Hague, 1977.
Kunst, Jaap. ***Music in Java***. Martinus Nijhoff: The Hague, (3rd ed). 1973, 2 volumes.
Soedarsono. ***Dances in Indonesia***. Gunung Agung: Jakarta, 1974.
Tirtaamidjaja N. ***Batik: Pattern and Motif***. Djambatan: Jakarta, 1966.
Zoete, Beryl de and Spies, Walter. ***Dance and Drama in Bali***. Faber and Faber: London, 1938.

Art/Photo Credits

Amsterdam Institute 89, 90, 91, 102, 111, 112, 145
Apa Archives 25, 28, 32/33, 34, 35, 37, 43, 227, 256, 314
Archives of the Royal Tropical 52, 144, 206
Bruechman, Peter 2, 22/23, 63, 117, 158, 165, 249L, 250, 261L/R, 266, 269, 281, 289, 291, 292, 296, 298, 299, 300, 301, 303, 307, 309, 310
Carvalho, Christiana 320, 323
Castle, Frank 36, 38, 51, 66, 274
Compost, Alain 60/61, 65, 67L/R, 164
Galli, Cesare 83
Gary Gartenberg Collection 107
Gocher, Jill 186
Hillhouse, Tony 324
Höfer, Hans 18, 21, 39, 40/41, 59, 64, 70, 71, 72L/R, 75, 76/77, 78, 84R, 96/97, 120/121, 122/123, 138, 163, 168/169, 174, 180, 182/183, 191, 193, 194, 201, 205, 208, 215, 216, 219, 226, 232, 235R, 237, 238, 239, 240L/R, 241, 242, 245, 252/253, 270/271, 276, 277, 279, 280, 282, 284
Indonesian Department of Information 48/49, 50, 53L/R, 54, 55, 56
Invernizzi Tettoni, Luca 14/15, 24, 29, 30L/R, 42, 45, 46L/R, 57, 62, 68/69, 86/87, 88, 92, 93, 104/105, 124/125, 172, 173, 176, 181, 184, 187, 189, 190, 192, 196, 197, 198/199, 200, 202, 203R, 207R, 209, 211R, 212, 213, 217, 218, 220, 225, 326
Iwan Tirta 110
Jakarta History Museum 47
Jezierski, Ingo 195, 234, 235L
Lawrence, Max 136/137, 210, 290
Lawson, Lyle 1, 12/13, 118/119, 177
Lloyd, Ian 233
Lontcho, Frederic 159R
Müller, Kal 73R, 74L, 84L, 85, 106, 109, 142L/R, 146R, 147, 151, 178, 188, 221, 230, 236R, 243, 246, 247, 248, 249R, 251, 257, 260, 262, 264, 265L/R, 267, 305
Oey, Eric M. 10/11, 26, 27, 31, 73L, 82, 94, 98, 99, 101, 108L/R, 113, 179, 207L, 222, 223, 224R
Photobank 16/17, 58, 62, 78, 80, 81, 114, 115, 116, 136/137, 140, 143, 154, 157, 158L, 162, 167, 172, 254, 255, 258, 259, 263, 268, 273, 275, 278, 283, 285, 286/287, 293, 294, 295, 297, 304, 306, 308, 311, 312, 313, 315, 316/317, 318, 319, 321, 322, 325
Pierres, Susan 74R
Reichelt, G.P. 211L, 236L
Rutherford, Scott 9, 141, 146L, 148, 149, 150, 156, 160, 161
Van Riel, Paul 175
Verhengt, Wim 185
Vilhar, Goradz 103, 203L, 214
Wassman, Bill 95
Wee, Christopher 224L
Yogerst, Joseph 272

Maps Berndtson & Berndtson

Visual Consultant V. Barl

Index

R

S

T

U

V

W

Y, Z